THE GOLDEN AGE

SUPERMAN

VOLUME FOUR

JERRY SIEGEL
WRITER

JOE SHUSTER
LEO NOWAK
JOHN SIKELA
PAUL CASSIDY
ED DOBROTKA
ARTISTS

EVAN "DOC" SHANER
COLLECTION COVER ARTIST

THE GOLDEN AGE

SUPERMAN

VOLUME FOUR

WHITNEY ELLSWORTH Editor – Original Series
JEB WOODARD Group Editor – Collected Editions **TYLER-MARIE EVANS** Editor – Collected Edition
STEVE COOK Design Director – Books **MEGEN BELLERSEN** Publication Design

BOB HARRAS Senior VP – Editor-in-Chief, DC Comics
PAT McCALLUM Executive Editor, DC Comics

President **DIANE NELSON**
Publisher **DAN DiDIO**
Publisher **JIM LEE**
President & Chief Creative Officer **GEOFF JOHNS**
Executive VP – Business & Marketing Strategy, Direct to Consumer & Global Franchise Management **AMIT DESAI**
Senior VP & General Manager, Digital Services **SAM ADES**
VP & Executive Editor, Young Reader & Talent Development **BOBBIE CHASE**
Senior VP – Art, Design & Collected Editions **MARK CHIARELLO**
Senior VP – Sales & Trade Marketing **JOHN CUNNINGHAM**
Senior VP – Business Strategy, Finance & Administration **ANNE DePIES**
VP – Manufacturing Operations **DON FALLETTI**

LAWRENCE GANEM VP – Editorial Administration & Talent Relations
ALISON GILL Senior VP – Manufacturing & Operations
HANK KANALZ Senior VP – Editorial Strategy & Administration
JAY KOGAN VP – Legal Affairs
JACK MAHAN VP – Business Affairs
NICK J. NAPOLITANO VP – Manufacturing Administration
EDDIE SCANNELL VP – Consumer Marketing
COURTNEY SIMMONS Senior VP – Publicity & Communications
JIM (SKI) SOKOLOWSKI VP – Comic Book Specialty Sales & Trade Marketing
NANCY SPEARS VP – Mass, Book, Digital Sales & Trade Marketing
MICHELE R. WELLS VP – Content Strategy

SUPERMAN: THE GOLDEN AGE VOLUME FOUR

DC Comics, 2900 West Alameda Ave., Burbank, CA 91505
Printed by LSC Communications, Owensville, MO, USA. 4/20/18. First Printing.
ISBN: 978-1-4012-7867-0

Library of Congress Cataloging-in-Publication Data is available.

MIX
Paper from
responsible sources
FSC® C132124

FSC
www.fsc.org

All stories by **JERRY SIEGEL.**

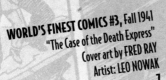

*These stories were originally untitled and are titled here for reader convenience.

In the preparation of this collection, we have used our best efforts to review any surviving
Until the 1970s, it was not common practice in the comic book industry to credit all stories.
records and consult any available databases and knowledgeable parties. We regret the innate limitations of this process and any missing or misassigned attributions that may occur.

The comics in this volume were produced in a time when racism played a larger role in society and popular culture both consciously and unconsciously. They are unaltered in this collection,
with the understanding that they are presented as historical documents.

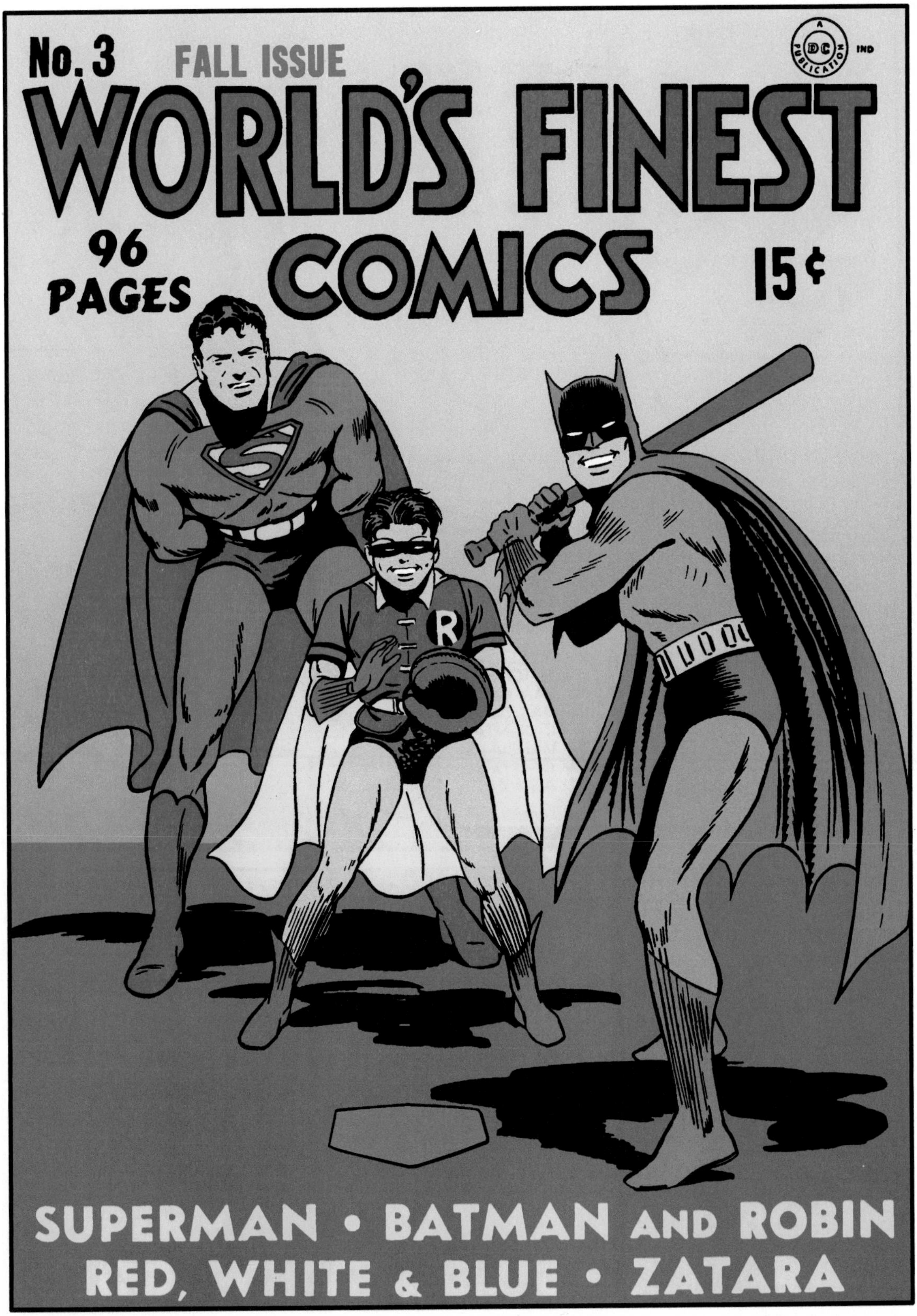
No. 3
FALL ISSUE
A DC PUBLICATION
IND
WORLD'S FINEST COMICS
96 PAGES
15¢
R
SUPERMAN • BATMAN AND ROBIN
RED, WHITE & BLUE • ZATARA

SUPERMAN

by JERRY SIEGEL *and* JOE SHUSTER

MOST FOUL OF ALL CRIMES IS DELIBERATE MASS MURDER. WHEN IT COMES TO THE ATTENTION OF THE AMAZING *MAN OF TOMORROW* THAT A SERIES OF RAILROAD ACCIDENTS ARE FAR FROM ACCIDENTAL, HE DETERMINES TO BRING THE VANDALS TO JUSTICE! ONCE AGAIN *MAN OF STEEL* AND THE FORCES OF EVIL CLASH IN STIRRING COMBAT!

THE *BENTON EXPRESS* AND A FREIGHT TRAIN COLLIDE HEAD-ON IN A DISASTROUS CRASH...!

NEWS FLASH! AN EXPRESS TRAIN AND A FREIGHT TRAIN HAVE COLLIDED ON THE OUTSKIRTS OF METROPOLIS!

COVER THAT!

AT ONCE!

BUT NO SOONER DOES CLARK LEAVE THE NEWSPAPER OFFICE THAN HE STEPS INTO AN ALLEY AND SWIFTLY STRIPS OFF HIS OUTER GARMENTS....

THIS CALLS FOR SPEED --AND THAT MEANS **SUPERMAN!**

A MOMENT LATER, THE *MAN OF TOMORROW* IS STREAKING PAST AUTOS ON THE ROAD AT A PACE THAT MAKES THEM APPEAR TO STAND STILL....

PERHAPS I'LL BE ABLE TO BE OF HELP!

THIS IS THE WORST WRECK I'VE SEEN IN YEARS!

THERE ARE DOZENS OF PEOPLE TRAPPED IN THE WRECK, WE'LL NEVER GET THEM OUT ALIVE!

HUH? WH-WHERE DID **YOU** COME FROM?

NEVER MIND ABOUT THAT. QUICK! IN WHICH CAR ARE THE WRECK VICTIMS TRAPPED?

IN THERE! BUT--!

THAT'S ALL I WANT TO KNOW!

EASILY, **SUPERMAN** FLIPS ASIDE THE CARS THAT PIN DOWN THE ONE WHICH CONTAINS THE TRAPPED PASSENGERS....

J-JUST **LOOK** AT HIM!

I--, **AM**--AND I **STILL** DON'T BELIEVE MY EYES!

SUPERMAN SWINGS THE PASSENGER CAR COMPLETELY FREE FROM THE OTHERS....

THERE!

YOUR STRENGTH IS BEYOND ALL BELIEF! BUT THE EXITS ARE CRUMPLED AND THE PASSENGERS ARE STILL TRAPPED IN THERE!

CAN YOU DO ANYTHING ABOUT *THAT*?

JUST WATCH ME!

SEIZING THE SIDE OF THE CAR, **SUPERMAN** RIPS THE SOLID STEEL APART WITH HIS BARE HANDS....

IT'S NOT AS DIFFICULT AS IT LOOKS!

G-GOSH!

WAIT! YOU'RE ENTITLED TO SOME REWARD FOR THIS!

I'M NOT INTERESTED IN GLORY. I'VE DONE MY PART. NOW YOU DO YOURS. TAKE CARE OF THOSE INJURED PEOPLE.

A SHORT DISTANCE AWAY, THE MAN OF TOMORROW CHANGES BACK TO HIS IDENTITY AS CLARK KENT....

NOW TO GET SOME FACTS FOR MY ARTICLE!

SHORTLY AFTER....

HM-MM! IT LOOKS AS THO SEVERAL SECTIONS OF TRACK WERE DELIBERATELY REMOVED!

WHAT ARE YOU UP TO?

ER-- I'M FROM THE *DAILY PLANET*.

A REPORTER, EH?

THROW HIM OUT!

AND STAY OUT!

YOU CAN'T DO THIS TO THE PRESS!

BUT WE *ARE*! YOU'LL PRINT ONLY WHAT THE COMPANY WANTS YOU TO!

LATER...AT THE *DAILY PLANET*...

MANHANDLE ME, WILL THEY? I'LL WRITE AN ARTICLE THAT'LL BURN THEIR EARS OFF!

AN INTERESTING ARTICLE, CLARK--BUT I'M AFRAID I CAN'T PRINT IT. RAILROAD ACCIDENTS ARE REGRETTABLE, BUT SOMETIMES THEY CAN'T BE HELPED.

IN THIS CASE THE ACCIDENT MIGHT HAVE BEEN AVERTED HAD THE RAIL-WAY MANAGE-MENT NOT BEEN SO SLACK!

WHAT'S *THAT*? ANOTHER *GARTH & COWLES* TRAIN ACCIDENT!

I'M CALLING FROM A TELEPHONE BOOTH NEAR THE SCENE OF THE WRECK. I'VE NEVER SEEN SUCH UTTER DESTRUCTION!

I'VE CHANGED MY MIND! THAT ARTICLE WILL APPEAR IN PRINT AFTER ALL!

NO SOONER IS THE ARTICLE SET UP IN TYPE THAN THE GIANT PRESSES START ROLLING....

AND MINUTES LATER, EXTRAS ARE ON SALE....

A MR. GRANT DOUGLAS TO SEE YOU, CHIEF!

DOUGLAS --HE'S THE ATTORNEY FOR THE *GARTH & COWLES* RAILROAD!

THIS OUGHT TO PROVE INTERESTING!

I DEMAND A RETRACTION! AND IF YOU PRINT ANY MORE SUCH ARTICLES, THERE WILL BE SERIOUS CONSEQUENCES.

I'LL PRINT WHAT-EVER I WISH!

DO YOU REALIZE THE RESULT OF THAT DAMAGING ARTICLE? *GARTH & COWLES* STOCK IS FALLING RAPIDLY IN VALUE! AND IT'S YOUR FAULT!

YOU FORGET, MR. DOUGLAS THAT IF THE RAILWAY MANAGEMENT WERE TO TAKE MORE SAFETY PRECAUTIONS, THERE WOULD BE NO NEED FOR SUCH ARTICLES!

AFTER DOUGLAS DEPARTS....

WELL, WHITE-- WHAT ARE YOUR INSTRUCTIONS NOW?

DISREGARD THAT LAWYER'S THREATS. THE MORE ARTICLES YOU PRODUCE ON THE SUBJECT-- AND THE JUICIER THEY ARE-- THE BETTER!

MINUTES LATER, CLARK CHANGES TO **SUPERMAN** ATOP THE *PLANET* BUILDING . . . .

I'D LIKE SOME MORE INFORMATION CONCERNING THIS CASE-- AND GRANT DOUGLAS MAY BE ABLE TO SUPPLY IT!

THRU THE SKY HURTLES THE FIGURE OF THE *MAN OF STEEL*, KEEPING IN SIGHT THE ATTORNEY'S CAR FAR BELOW...

HE'S ENTERING THE RAILWAY COMPANY'S OFFICES!

⑤

NOW FOR AN EARFUL!

WITHIN THE OFFICE, A MEETING OF THE RAILROAD'S BOARD OF DIRECTORS IS IN SESSION....

THESE WRECKS WILL RUIN US!

BUT THE PUBLICITY IS EVEN WORSE!

ANY LUCK, DOUGLAS?

NOT MUCH!

PRESIDENT ATKINSON MAKES AN ANNOUNCEMENT....

GENTLEMEN, INVESTIGATION HAS REVEALED THAT THOSE WRECKS WERE ANYTHING BUT ACCIDENTAL! THEY WERE ACCOMPLISHED BY DELIBERATE SABOTAGE!

WHAT --!?!

NOTIFY THE POLICE!

MEET "SPARKY" WATERS, A VERY CAPABLE PRIVATE DETECTIVE WHOM I'VE HIRED TO TRACK DOWN THE CULPRITS!

HI' YA, GENTS!

I'M HOT ON THE TRAIL ALREADY, SEE? JUST SIT BACK AND STOP WORRYIN'--I'LL HAVE THOSE CROOKS NABBED IN NO TIME!

SOUNDS ADMIRABLE!

--IF HE KEEPS HIS WORD!

LATER, AS "SPARKY" WATERS DRIVES, A GREAT LEAP LAUNCHES **SUPERMAN** DOWN TOWARD HIS AUTO...

I'D ENJOY A CHAT WITH "SPARKY"!

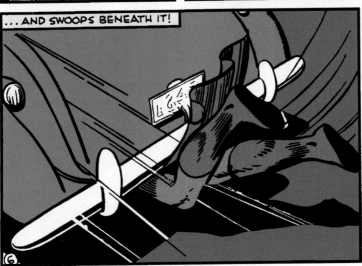

...AND SWOOPS BENEATH IT!

NEXT MOMENT HE SPRINGS SKYWARD, THE AUTO HELD OVERHEAD...!

HOPE WATERS ISN'T TOO FRIGHTENED!

HEY! WHAT GOES ON?

SUPERMAN! --WHAT'S THE IDEA?

I THOUGHT THIS WOULD BE A GOOD SPOT FOR US TO TALK IN PRIVACY!

I'D LIKE TO VOLUNTEER MY ASSISTANCE. HAVE YOU UNCOVERED ANY CLUES?

WHAT I'VE LEARNED MAKES ME BELIEVE THAT THE BUTCH FLETCHER MOB IS BEHIND THESE WRECKS!

THANKS! I'LL PAY BUTCH A VISIT!

HEY! HOW AM I GONNA GET MY CAR DOWN OFFA HERE?

MINUTES LATER--THE MAN OF STEEL ALIGHTS OUTSIDE THE FLETCHER MOB HIDEOUT....

A LITTLE X-RAY VISION AND SUPER-SENSITIVE HEARING WOULDN'T BE AMISS AT THIS MOMENT!

WHAT THE MAN OF TOMORROW WITNESSES....

A FEW MORE MINUTES AND THERE'LL BE ANOTHER WRECK!

AT THE RATE WE'RE GOIN' IT WON'T BE LONG BEFORE GARTH & COWLES WON'T BE WORTH A CENT!

I'VE HEARD ENOUGH!

IT'S--

SUPERMAN!

QUICKLY RACING FROM THE ROOM, THE THUGS SLAM THE DOOR SHUT BEHIND THEM...

CAN'T ESCAPE ME *THAT* EASILY!

NEXT MOMENT-- A DEADLY GAS POURS INTO THE ROOM...

GAS!

EVERY-THING-- GOING BLANK!

AFTER THE ROOM IS CLEARED OF GAS, THE GANGSTERS ENTER AGAIN....

HE'S OUT!

JUST AS WE PLANNED!

WHA--??

YOU--YOU'RE WIDE AWAKE!

EVER HEAR OF SOME-ONE PLAYING POSSUM?

A SECOND LATER THE CRIMINALS CATAPULT HITHER AND YON AS THO STRUCK BY A HUMAN TORNADO!

MERCY!

EEE-EEE!

YOU HAD NO MERCY FOR THE TRAIN CRASH VICTIMS!

HOW DID YOU KNOW I WAS COMING?

YOU'LL LEARN NOTHING FROM ME!

I'D BETTER-- OR THIS GAS GOES ON--AND YOU GO OUT!

DON'T DO IT! I'LL TALK!

"SPARKY" WATERS TELEPHONED US THE WARNING! WE GET OUR ORDERS FROM HIM. HE'S THE ONLY ONE WHO KNOWS WHO THE BIG BOSS IS!

WHAT'S THE NEXT SCHEDULED ACT OF DESTRUC-TION?

THE GRAND-SPAN BRIDGE--! IT'S BEEN FIXED SO THAT WHEN THE LIMITED CROSSES, IT'LL COLLAPSE!

LEAVING THE THUGS HELPLESSLY TIED, SUPERMAN LEAPS OFF AND AWAY....

GOT TO REACH THE BRIDGE BEFORE THE LIMITED GETS THERE!

AND WELL HE SHOULD! FOR THE FOUNDATIONS OF THE BRIDGE HAVE BEEN SERIOUSLY DAMAGED...!

9

WITHIN THE SPEEDING TRAIN, PASSENGERS ARE TOTALLY UNAWARE OF THE DOOM THAT LIES AHEAD....

ON RACES THE LIMITED, NOW ONLY A SHORT DISTANCE FROM THE GRAND-SPAN...!

DOWN PLUMMETS SUPERMAN BESIDE THE FOOT OF THE BRIDGE....

THE LIMITED --ABOUT TO CROSS THE BRIDGE!

WHIRLING, THE MAN OF STEEL PITS HIS TREMENDOUS STRENGTH AGAINST THE GRAND-SPAN'S TOTTERING FOUNDATIONS...

KEEPING THIS STRUCTURE FROM FALLING IS GOING TO BE NO CINCH!

AS THE LIMITED CHUGS ALONG THE BRIDGE, THE GREAT STRUCTURE SWAYS DANGEROUSLY....

SUDDENLY, THE MIGHTY BRIDGE COLLAPSES UPON SUPERMAN!

I'VE LOST!

THE MAN OF STEEL BURROWS HIMSELF FREE FROM THE DEBRIS....

UP THERE!

THE LIMITED HAD REACHED THE OTHER SIDE OF THE BRIDGE JUST IN TIME TO ESCAPE DESTRUCTION!

JUST THINK HOW NARROWLY WE ESCAPED DEATH!

I'LL SEND ON A MESSAGE AT ONCE TO STOP ALL TRAINS HEADED TOWARD THE BRIDGE!

AND NOW TO SQUARE ACCOUNTS WITH A CERTAIN DOUBLE-CROSSING WORM NAMED "SPARKY" WATERS!

SHORTLY AFTER--SUPERMAN STREAKS IN THRU THE WINDOW OF "SPARKY'"S OFFICE,....

THIS IS GOING TO BE A PLEASURE!

THE OFFICE IS EMPTY--BUT-- WHAT'S THIS?

A MEMORANDUM TO MEET THORNTON BIGSBY AT ABOUT THIS TIME.

BIGSBY IS ONE OF THE MOST POWERFUL INDUSTRIALISTS IN THE NATION! WHAT CONNECTION COULD HE HAVE WITH WATERS?

MEANWHILE--IN THE SUMPTUOUS MANSION OF THORNTON BIGSBY.

SUPERMAN BECAME INTERESTED IN YOUR --ER--ACTIVITIES, BUT I ARRANGED TO HAVE HIM TAKEN CARE OF.

YOU HAVE DONE VERY WELL, WATERS!

NEAT SCHEME YOU HAVE! FIRST YOU RUIN THE REPUTATION OF GARTH & COWLES SO THAT ITS STOCK DROPS TO A LOW LEVEL, THEN YOU BUY CONTROL OF THE COMPANY FOR A SONG!

WITHOUT YOU TO SUPERVISE THE STRONG-ARM TACTICS I'D NEVER HAVE BEEN SUCCESSFUL!

BUT NOW THAT YOUR USEFULNESS IS DONE--AND BECAUSE YOU ARE THE ONLY MAN LIVING WHO CAN CONNECT ME WITH THE RAILWAY SABOTAGE-- YOU MUST DIE!

NO, BOSS! I'LL NEVER SQUEAL ON YOU! DON'T SHOOT!

AND THAT FINISHES YOU! I'LL DISPOSE OF YOUR BODY PERMANENTLY, LATER!

"SPARKY" --THROWN OUT THE WINDOW --!!

PLUMMETING DOWN AFTER THE FALLING FIGURE, SUPERMAN CATCHES IT....

SO THE PARTNERS IN CRIME HAVE FALLEN OUT, EH?

ONE MINUTE LATER....

SUPERMAN! BUT I THOUGHT...

YOU THOUGHT WRONG! I'M ALIVE --AND VERY MUCH CAPABLE OF WRINGING YOUR CRAVEN NECK!

I'VE KILLED ONE MAN TODAY-- I CAN KILL ANOTHER!

PERHAPS!

UNANIMOUSLY THE DEADLY PELLETS PING OFF **SUPER-MAN'S** SUPER-TOUGH SKIN....

WHY NOT TRY A PEA-SHOOTER? IT MIGHT BE MORE EFFECTIVE!

AND NOW YOU'RE GOING TO GET THE FATE YOU DESERVE-- BUT LEGALLY --IN A COURT OF LAW!

I'LL NEVER BE CONVICTED! "SPARKY" WAS THE ONLY ONE WHO COULD HAVE SUPPLIED DAMAGING TESTIMONY AGAINST ME, AND HE'S DEAD!

THAT IS OPEN TO CONJECTURE!

I HEARD EVERYTHING HE SAID!

YOU SEE--"SPARKY" IS SEVERELY WOUNDED...BUT STILL ALIVE!

DON'T TESTIFY AGAINST ME! I'LL PAY YOU ANYTHING!

THIS TIME I CAN'T BE BOUGHT OFF. IT'LL GIVE ME THE GREATEST PLEASURE TO SEE YOU CONVICTED!

THE INDUSTRIALIST RAISES A PILL TO HIS MOUTH...

YOU'LL NEVER GET ME ALIVE!

THAT'S WHAT YOU THINK! YOU'RE GOING TO PAY THE FULL PENALTY FOR YOUR CRIME!

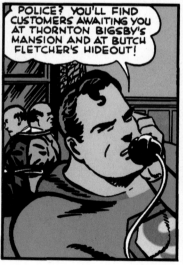

POLICE? YOU'LL FIND CUSTOMERS AWAITING YOU AT THORNTON BIGSBY'S MANSION AND AT BUTCH FLETCHER'S HIDEOUT!

LATER--AT THE *DAILY PLANET*...

NICE JOB--EVEN THE RAILROAD PEOPLE ARE PLEASED AT YOUR COMPLETE EXPOSÉ OF BIGSBY'S PLOT!

MORE IMPORTANT TO ME IS THAT THOSE COLD-BLOODED MASS MURDERERS GOT WHAT WAS COMING TO THEM!

THE END

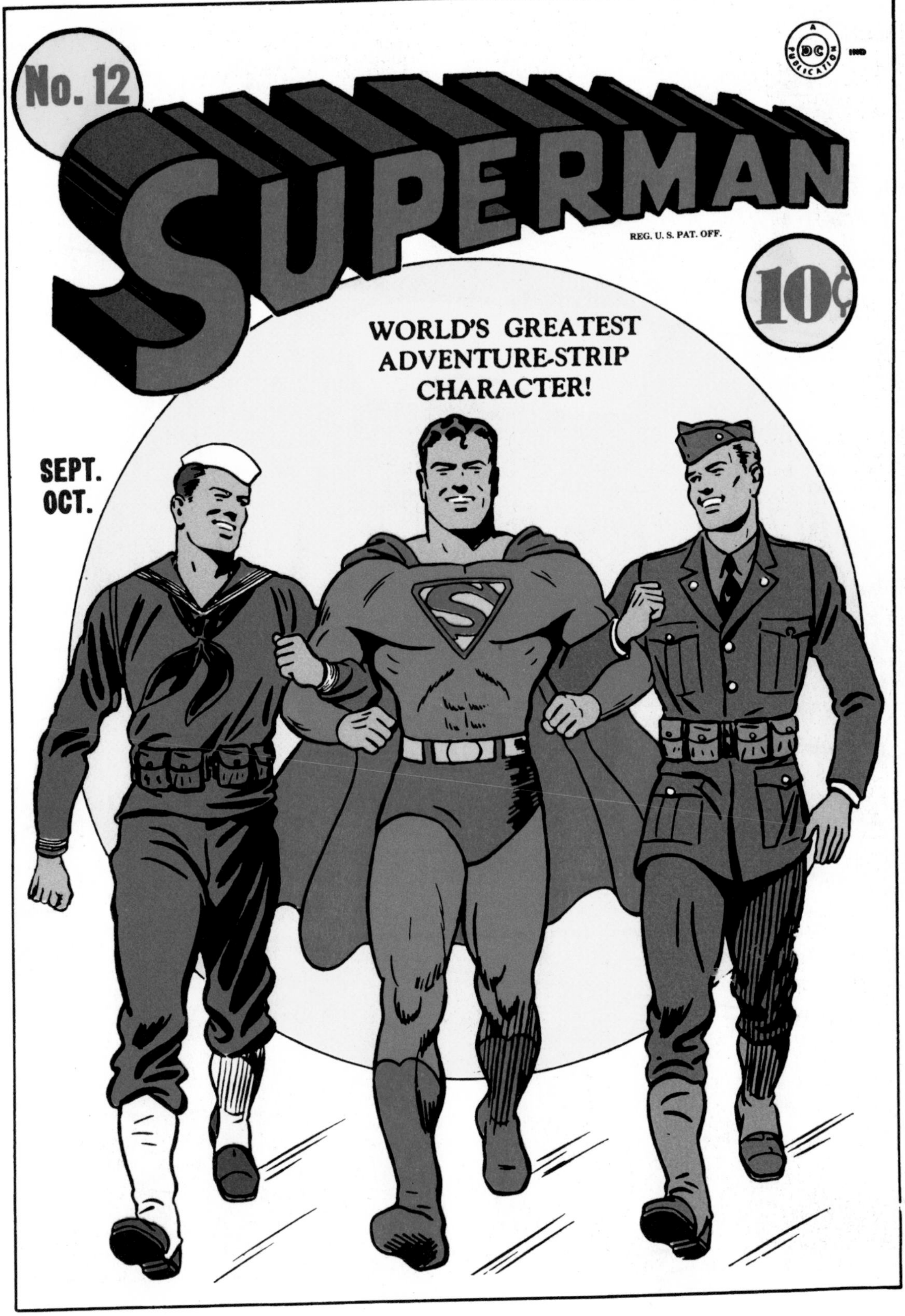
No. 12
A DC PUBLICATION
SUPERMAN
REG. U. S. PAT. OFF.
10¢
WORLD'S GREATEST
ADVENTURE-STRIP
CHARACTER!
SEPT.
OCT.

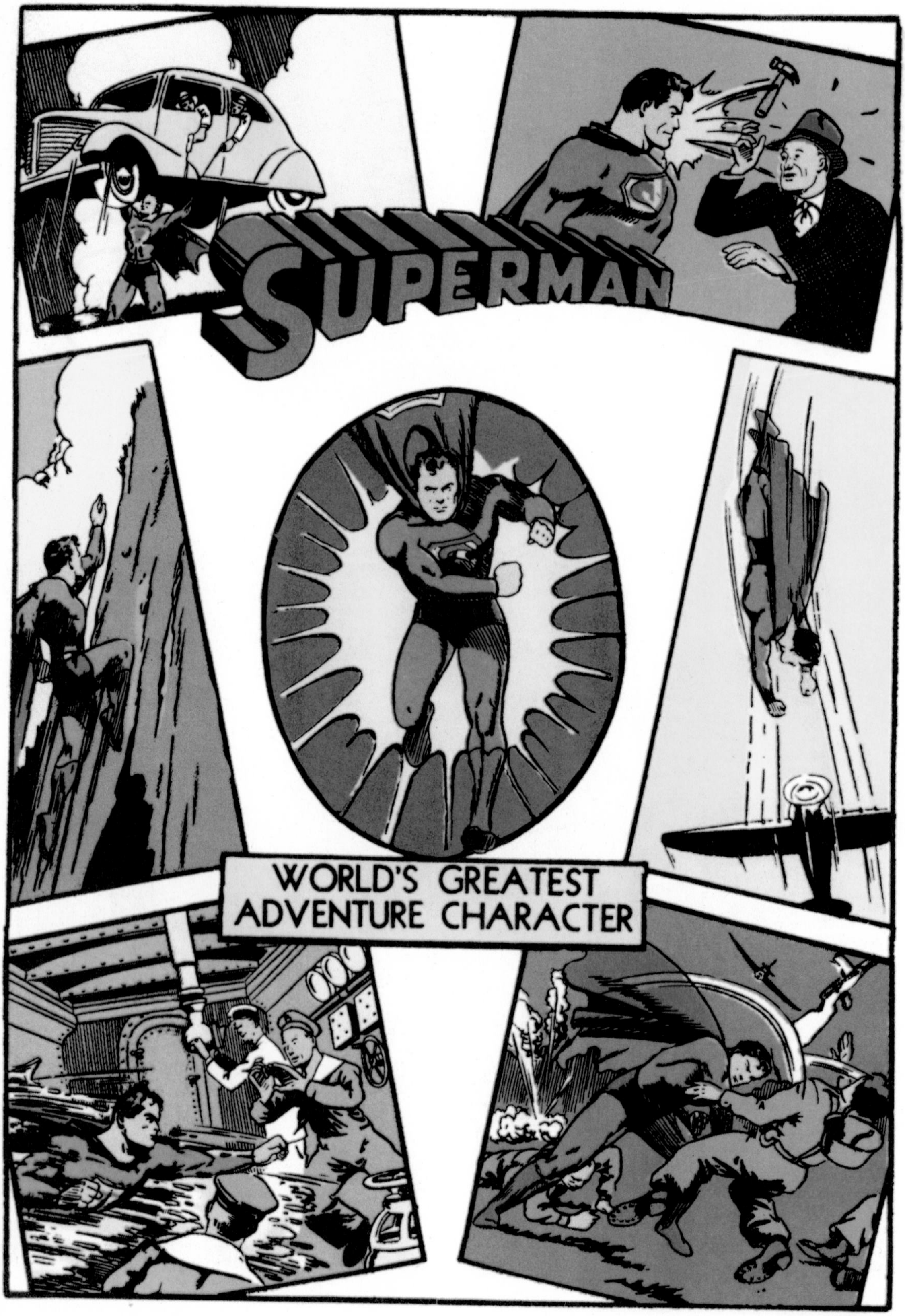
SUPERMAN
WORLD'S GREATEST
ADVENTURE CHARACTER

SUPERMAN

by

JERRY SIEGEL *and* JOE SHUSTER

WHEN LOIS LANE AND CLARK KENT SET OUT UPON A VACATION, IT APPEARS THAT THE CUSTOMARY EXCITEMENT AND ADVENTURE WHICH PERSIST IN INTRUDING UPON A REPORTER'S LIFE ARE LEFT BEHIND. BUT BEFORE THEY REALIZE IT, THEY ARE IN THE MIDST OF ANOTHER THRILL-PACKED EXPERIENCE MADE ALL THE MORE DRAMATIC BY THE TIMELY APPEARANCE OF THE AMAZING *MAN OF STEEL:* **SUPERMAN!**

YOU TWO HAVE BEEN PLUGGING AWAY STEADILY FOR MONTHS AND DOING A SWELL JOB, SO HERE-- AS A TOKEN OF THE NEWSPAPER'S APPRECIATION--ARE TWO TICKETS FOR A VACATION CRUISE ON THE *GRENODIER!*

A--A VACATION!

THAT'S **GRAND** OF YOU!

SEVERAL EVENINGS LATER, LOIS AND CLARK HAVE SET OUT TO SEA. ALONE AT THE RAIL, CLARK IS STARTLED TO SEE....

A GIRL-- FALLING INTO THE SEA!

INSTANTLY, CLARK DIVES AFTER HER.

THE *GRENODIER* -- QUITE A DISTANCE OFF!

SWIMMING AT TERRIFIC SPEED, CLARK SWIFTLY CLOSES THE DISTANCE BETWEEN THE BOAT AND HIMSELF....

WE'LL OVERTAKE IT IN A MOMENT!

AS THEY NEAR THE VESSEL, THE GIRL REVIVES....

WH-WHERE ARE WE?

OVERBOARD! SHOUT FOR HELP--AND **LOUD**!

THEIR CRIES ARE HEARD....
MAN OVERBOARD!

HEAVE THEM A LIFE PRESERVER!

THE TWO BEDRAGGLED FIGURES ARE HOISTED ABOARD...

TAKE THE GIRL TO HER STATEROOM.

YOU'RE LUCKY WE HEARD YOUR SHOUTS.

JUST THINK, CLARK--YOU'RE A HERO!

DON'T TELL ANY ONE, BUT I FELL IN ACCIDENTLY AFTER HER!

NEXT MORNING...

THIS IS MY FIRST OP-PORTUNITY TO THANK YOU FOR SAVING MY LIFE. MEET NILES GRANT, MY FIANCE. I'M NAN WILSON.

HOW DO YOU DO? MEET LOIS LANE.

IF IT HADN'T BEEN FOR YOU, KENT, NAN WOULD HAVE PERISHED AFTER FALLING FROM THE UPPER DECK.

HOW DID YOU HAPPEN TO FALL INTO THE WATER?

THERE CAME A SWIFT BLOW FROM BEHIND---THE NEXT THING I KNEW WAS WHEN I REVIVED IN THE WATER WITH YOU.

DURING THE ENSUING DAYS, CLARK, LOIS AND NAN AND NILES BECOME GREAT FRIENDS

YOU SAY YOU'RE STOPPING OFF AT AN ISLAND YOU'VE INHERITED?

YES. POGO ISLAND. I INHERITED IT YEARS AGO, BUT THIS WILL BE MY FIRST VISIT TO IT

I TRIED TO TALK NAN OUT OF THIS VISIT-- BUT SHE HAS HER MIND SET ON IT!

I'VE JUST LEARNED THAT IT WOULD BE POSSIBLE FOR YOU TO STAY ON THE ISLAND WITH US WHILE THE GRENODIER DIS-CHARGES HER CARGO AT A NEARBY PORT. WOULD YOU CARE TO?

WE'D LOVE IT!

NEXT DAY, AS THE SMALL PARTY GETS OFF AT POGO ISLAND....

MEET CARL BOGART, FORE-MAN OF MY PLANTATION.

GLAD TO SEE YOU I HOPE YOU ENJOY YOUR STAY HERE!

③

AS THE NATIVE CARRIERS SIGHT NAN, THEY DROP THEIR BURDENS AND FLEE IN TERROR....

INGA! INGA!

WHAT'S COME OVER THEM?

IT'S HARD TO GUESS WHAT THOSE SUPERSTITIOUS NATIVES ARE UP TO!

INGA! INGA!

AS THE SMALL PARTY MAKES ITS WAY TOWARD THE PLANTATION HOUSE...

HOW ARE THE PLANTATION'S BUSINESS AFFAIRS?

NOT VERY GOOD I'M AFRAID. IT SEEMS TO BE A LOSING PROPOSITION.

THAT'S WHAT I TRIED TO TELL NAN -- BUT SHE WOULDN'T BELIEVE ME.

WHAT'S *THAT*?

LOOKS LIKE SOME SORT OF NATIVE TOKEN. PERHAPS IT'S A GIFT FOR YOU!

HOW THOUGHTFUL OF THEM! I'LL KEEP IT AS A SOUVENIR!

BUT CLARK'S SUPER-SENSORY POWERS INFORM HIM...

("-THAT DOLL--COATED WITH A DEADLY POISON! IF NAN TOUCHES IT, SHE'LL DIE!-")

ACTING SO SWIFTLY THAT THE EYE CANNOT FOLLOW, CLARK STREAKS FORWARD....

("GOT TO ACCOMPLISH THIS IN A FRACTION OF A SECOND!-")

SWIFTLY HE RIPS THE FIGURE FROM THE DOOR, HURLS IT AWAY, THEN RETURNS TO HIS FORMER POSITION!

④

THAT'S ODD! --THAT FIGURE-- GONE!

BUT IT WAS THERE A MOMENT AGO!-- PERHAPS IT'S SOME SORT OF NATIVE MAGIC!

("-WHEW! THAT WAS A CLOSE CALL FOR NAN!)

WHERE ARE THE SERVANTS?

BLAST THOSE IGNORANT SAVAGES! COME WITH ME. I'M GOING TO THEIR VILLAGE AND THRASH THIS MATTER OUT!

LATER-- WHEN THEY REACH THE VILLAGE....

--THE NATIVES-- CHANTING!

WHAT DOES IT MEAN?

THEY'RE PRAYING FOR PROTECTION FROM EVIL SPIRITS!

THE ANGRY PLANTATION FOREMAN INTERRUPTS THE CEREMONY.

STOP THIS NONSENSE AND GET BACK TO WORK!

INGA! INGA!

INGA!

WHAT IN THE WORLD DOES "INGA" MEAN, AND WHY DO THEY ACT SO FRIGHTENED OF ME?

"INGA" MEANS "WITCH" THEY SAY THEIR WITCHDOCTOR HAS INFORMED THEM YOU ARE AN EVIL OCCULT CREATURE!

AT THAT MOMENT...A TERRIFIED YOUNGSTER ACCIDENTALLY FALLS INTO THE FIRE...!

LEAPING IN, NAN SNATCHES THE BADLY BURNED BOY FROM THE FLAMES....

COME BACK WITH THAT CHILD! THE NATIVES SAY YOU WANT TO PERFORM BLACK MAGIC ON IT!

THIS BOY NEEDS FIRST AID TREATMENT, AND I'M GOING TO SEE TO IT THAT HE GETS IT!

RACING AHEAD OF THE RUNNING PARTY, NATIVES SURREPTITIOUSLY PLANT DYNAMITE ALONGSIDE THE JUNGLE PATH AT THE FOOT OF A TREE.

CLARK'S TELESCOPIC EYESIGHT INFORMS HIM OF THIS DEVELOPMENT. SLIPPING AWAY FROM THE OTHERS, HE QUICKLY REMOVES HIS OUTER GARMENTS, AND....

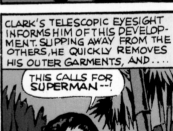

THIS CALLS FOR SUPERMAN --!

LOOK OUT!

THAT GIANT TREE -- FALLING!

LEAPING IN, THE MAN OF STEEL CATCHES, THEN LOWERS THE TREE TO THE GROUND BEFORE IT CAN HARM THE INTENDED VICTIMS...

SUPERMAN! --HOW DID YOU GET ON THIS ISLAND?

JUST BE GLAD I AM HERE!

I'VE HEARD OF YOU--AND OF YOUR INCREDIBLE STRENGTH!

BUT I ALWAYS THOUGHT YOU WERE A LEGENDARY CHARACTER!

YOU'D BETTER HURRY BACK TO THE PLANTATION!

HE'S RIGHT-- RUN!

AS THE OTHERS HURRY ON, AMAZED NATIVES STEP FROM CONCEALMENT AND BOMBARD THE PARTY WITH POISONED DARTS!

STILL DETERMINED TO GET THEM, EH?

RAPIDLY, SUPERMAN SNATCHES THE DARTS FROM THE AIR AS FAST AS THE NATIVES SEND THEM.

THESE OUGHT TO MAKE INTEREST-ING ADDITIONS TO MY COLLECTION!

WHEN THE FUGITIVES REACH THE PLANTATION HOUSE....

WHAT'S HAPPENED TO CLARK?

HE'S GONE!

I'LL GO AFTER HIM! HE HASN'T A CHANCE FACING THOSE NATIVES ALONE!

ATOP A HILL ABOVE THE PLANTATION HOUSE..!

6

BEWILDERED AT **SUPERMAN'S** APPARENT IMMUNITY TO THEIR POISONED DARTS, THE NATIVES ATTACK HIM EN MASSE....

WANT TO FIGHT, EH?

GLAD TO OBLIGE!

TURNING, **SUPERMAN** SIGHTS....

THAT BOULDER!

...I'VE GOT TO **STOP** IT!

AS **SUPERMAN** RACES TOWARD THE BOULDER, THE NATIVES ATOP THE HILL DISLODGE ANOTHER!

MAN OF **STEEL** AND HUGE BOULDER MEET IN A HEAD-ON COLLISION! THE BOULDER GRINDS TO A STOP!!

WHOA!

UP WITH YOU!

--AND THAT ATTENDS TO **BOTH** OF YOU!

TERRIFIED BY THEIR ENCOUNTER WITH THIS BEING OF TREMENDOUS PHYSICAL POWERS, THE NATIVES RETREAT IN A BODY....

BUT LEAPING OVERHEAD, **SUPERMAN** KEEPS THEM IN SIGHT....

NEVER CAN TELL WHAT THEY'LL BE UP TO NEXT!

BACK IN THEIR VILLAGE, THE NATIVES CHATTER EXCITEDLY...

SPIRIT POWERFUL BAD MEDICINE!

BETTER LEAVE WHITE ONES ALONE!

WE ARE HELPLESS AGAINST THEIR MAGIC--!

AS LONG AS THEY STICK TO THAT ATTITUDE WE'RE SAFE.

BUT ABRUPTLY A WITCH-DOCTOR IN WEIRD HEADDRESS SPRINGS BEFORE THE OTHER NATIVES, BERATES THEM....

FIGHT THE EVIL ONES! WITCH-DOCTOR'S MEDICINE MORE POWERFUL THAN THEIRS!

BUT THEY HAVE A TERRIBLE DEMON AIDING THEM! IF WE ATTACK, IT WILL SLAY US!

WEAR THESE CHARMS--THEY WILL PROTECT YOU FROM HARM! FIGHT THE FOREIGN ONES. WIPE THEM OUT!

MINUTES LATER....

THE NATIVES --!!

CHARGING AGAIN!

WITH FIENDISH THOROUGHNESS, THE ATTACKERS START A SERIES OF FIRES ABOUT THE PLANTATION HOUSE...!

A POWERFUL BREEZE FANS THE FLAMES SO THAT THEY SWEEP HUNGRILY TOWARD THE STRUCTURE...!

MUST ACT QUICKLY-- BEFORE THE FLAMES REACH THE HOUSE!

SUPERMAN RACES ABOUT THE PLANTATION AT A GREAT SPEED, USING THE GREAT TREE AS A PLOW, FURROWING A DITCH...

THE FLAMES --COMING CLOSER!

HIS TASK COMPLETED, THE MAN OF TOMORROW SURVEYS HIS HANDIWORK WITH SATISFACTION.

THAT DID IT! THE FLAMES CAN'T CROSS THE DITCH!

BUT NATIVES CRASH IN THRU THE REAR OF THE HOUSE AND QUICKLY OVERCOME ITS OCCUPANTS...

EEE-EEEE--!

LET GO-- UHH-HHH!

THE HELPLESS CAPTIVES ARE HURRIED THRU THE THICK JUNGLE TOWARD THE NATIVE VILLAGE....

TRY NOT TO THINK ABOUT IT!

WH-WHAT ARE THEY GOING TO DO TO US?

NILES-- --I'M AFRAID!

FINDING THE PLANTATION HOUSE EMPTY, SUPERMAN SPEEDS TO THE VILLAGE IN TIME TO SEE....

LOIS--AND THE OTHERS --TIED TO STAKES!

9

AMIDST THE BEATING OF DRUMS, THE WITCHDOCTOR SPRINGS IN-TO VIEW....

DEATH TO THE EVIL ONES! DEATH AT THE STAKE! *DEATH!*

THEY NOT HURT MY CHILD. LOOK --THEY DRESS HIS WOUNDS!

SINCE THEY NOT HARM CHILD, MAYBE THEY ARE NOT EVIL SPIRITS!

PERHAPS WE SHOULD FREE THEM!

DISREGARDING THE OTHERS, THE WITCH-DOCTOR SETS AFLAME THE BRANDS AT THE CAPTIVES' FEET...

NO MERCY! EVIL SPIRITS MUST DIE!!

AND THAT'S MY CUE TO ENTER!

THE POWERFUL ONE!!

SWIFTLY, **SUPERMAN** EXTINGUISHES THE FLAMES WITH HIS BARE HANDS....

LEAVE IT TO ME TO SHOW UP WHEN THINGS GET HOT FOR YOU!

HOT IS PUTTING IT MILDLY!

COWARDS! DON'T FLEE! ATTACK HIM!

THERE! --THAT FREES ALL OF YOU!

THE WITCH-DOCTOR SEEMS TO BE HAVING SOME TROUBLE WITH HIS FOLLOWERS.

ABRUPTLY, UNIFORMED SOLDIERS CHARGE ONTO THE SCENE....

I DON'T KNOW WHERE THESE SOLDIERS ARE FROM--BUT THEIR PRESENCE MAKES IT UNNECESS-ARY FOR ME TO REMAIN.

DON'T MOVE-- ANYONE!

HOW FORTUNATE THAT YOU CAME WHEN YOU DID!

WE'RE VERY GRATEFUL TO YOU!

SAVE YOUR THANKS!-- YOU'RE UNDER ARREST, ALL OF YOU!

UNDER ARREST? BUT--WHAT DOES THIS MEAN?

WE ARE NOT REQUIRED TO OFFER AN EXPLANATION. COME WITH US!

YOU COME ALONG, TOO.

THE SMALL GROUP MARCHES INTO A CAVE AT THE OCEAN'S EDGE...

SOLDIERS ON THIS ISLAND! --DO YOU KNOW THE EXPLANATION?

MY ISLAND--YET I KNOW NO MORE ABOUT IT THAN YOU DO!

A PUZZLED **SUPERMAN** FOLLOWS SWIFTLY IN PURSUIT....

I CAN'T UNDERSTAND THIS STRANGE DEVELOPMENT, BUT PERHAPS I'LL SOON KNOW THE ANSWER.

DEEP WITHIN THE CAVE...

A SUBMARINE! --HERE-- BENEATH THE CAVE...

CAN YOU BEAT IT!

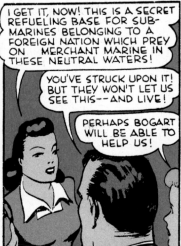

I GET IT, NOW! THIS IS A SECRET REFUELING BASE FOR SUB-MARINES BELONGING TO A FOREIGN NATION WHICH PREY ON MERCHANT MARINE IN THESE NEUTRAL WATERS!

YOU'VE STRUCK UPON IT! BUT THEY WON'T LET US SEE THIS--AND LIVE!

PERHAPS BOGART WILL BE ABLE TO HELP US!

YOU CAN FORGET THAT HOPE!

WHAT HAVE YOU DONE-- KILLED HIM?

BECAUSE / AM BOGART.--I OFTEN FOUND ASSUMING THE IDENTITY OF NATIVE WITCH-DOCTOR TO BE HELPFUL-- AND EFFECTIVE!

YOU! BUT WHY--?

AS YOU HAVE ASSUMED, THIS IS A SECRET REFUELING BASE FOR A COUNTRY AT WAR. I AM IN THAT COUNTRY'S PAY. IT WAS MY JOB TO KEEP PEOPLE OFF THIS ISLAND--AND I HAD THE SOLDIERS STEP IN ONLY WHEN THE INTER-FERENCE OF **SUPERMAN** MADE IT NECESSARY!

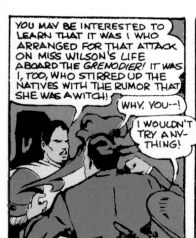

YOU MAY BE INTERESTED TO LEARN THAT IT WAS I WHO ARRANGED FOR THAT ATTACK ON MISS WILSON'S LIFE ABOARD THE GRENODIER! IT WAS I, TOO, WHO STIRRED UP THE NATIVES WITH THE RUMOR THAT SHE WAS A WITCH!

WHY, YOU--!

I WOULDN'T TRY ANYTHING!

MY X-RAY VISION HAS DISCLOSED **ENOUGH!** NOW TO **ACT!**

IT'S-- **SUPER-MAN!**

SHOOT HIM DOWN!

THE BULLETS DON'T AFFECT HIM!

UH-HH!

YOU'RE SO EAGER FOR COMBAT-- HERE'S A TASTE OF IT!

SUPERMAN --FORCING HIS WAY INTO THE CAVE!

WE'VE GOT TO GET OUT OF HERE!

INTO THE SUBMARINE -- QUICK!

THE SUB-- GONE!

HA! WE'VE ELUDED HIM!

I CAN TELL THAT YOU DON'T KNOW **SUPERMAN!**

GUESS I'LL HAVE TO GO FISHING!

RAPIDLY, THE *MAN OF TOMORROW* OVERTAKES THE SUBMARINE....

INSTRUMENTS INDICATE *SOMETHING APPROACH-ING!*

IT MUST BE SUPERMAN! FIRE!

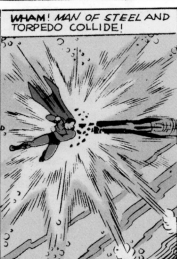

WHAM! *MAN OF STEEL* AND *TORPEDO* COLLIDE!

BUT **SUPERMAN** IS UNHARMED! MINUTES LATER, HE MARCHES UP ON LAND HOLDING THE SUB OVERHEAD!

IF THEY KEEP THAT UP, I'LL BEGIN TO BELIEVE THEY DON'T LIKE ME!

CRASHING THRU THE SIDE OF THE SUB, **SUPERMAN** OVER-POWERS THE FOREIGN SOLD-IERS SINGLE-HANDED ..!

BE CAREFUL! THERE ARE A DOZEN OF THEM!

ONLY A DOZEN? TCH! TCH!

⑬

SUPERMAN SPRINGS AWAY -- LEAVING HIS FOES HELPLESSLY TIED. LATER, HE RETURNS AS CLARK KENT...

IS-- IS IT SAFE FOR ME TO COME OUT OF HIDING N-NOW??

PERFECTLY SAFE...NOW THAT THE EXCITEMENT'S OVER.

WE'LL HAVE TO RADIO THE AUTH-ORITIES!

A DAY LATER-- AS CLARK AND LOIS ONCE AGAIN BOARD THE *GRENODIER*...

THANKS A LOT FOR YOUR HOS-PITALITY. WE HAD A THRILLING TIME!--AND GOT A SWELL STORY!

WE PROMISE NOT TO HAVE ANY INTERNAT-IONAL PLOTTERS DISTURB YOUR REST NEXT TIME!

PLEASE COME AGAIN NEXT TIME!

THE END

SUPERMAN

by JERRY SIEGEL and JOE SHUSTER

SUPERMAN MEETS A FOE WORTHY OF HIS METTLE WHEN HE MATCHES WITS WITH A SUPER-CRIMINAL WHO WILL GO TO ANY LENGTHS TO COMMIT HIS EVIL DEEDS

THOMAS CORDAY TRIPS AT THE HEAD OF A GREAT STAIRWAY AND FALLS TO HIS DEATH...

DANIEL STEELE FALLS ASLEEP AT THE WHEEL OF HIS AUTO AND IS FATALLY INJURED IN A RESULTING CRASH WITH A STREET CAR...

...THE *DAILY PLANET* COMES OUT WITH A STARTLING REFUTATION BY-LINED BY CLARK KENT, ITS FOREMOST REPORTER....

ROBERT STARBUCK IS FOUND WITH A BULLET THRU HIS BRAIN.....SO DIE THESE THREE PROMINENT MEN, AND THEIR PASSING IS MOURNED AS UNFORTUNATE WHIMS OF FATE UNTIL--

"ACCIDENTAL" DEATHS IN REALITY COLD-BLOODED MURDER
By CLARK KENT

WHITE WANTS TO SEE YOU, MR. KENT.

HE PROBABLY WANTS TO BAWL YOU OUT FOR THAT "BRILLIANT" BRAINSTORM OF YOURS.

I TOLD HIM IT WOULD BE THE MOST SENSATIONAL STORY OF THE YEAR!

CLARK, THAT STORY OF YOURS IS GETTING US IN A MESS. ARE YOU SURE YOU KNOW WHAT YOU'RE TALKING ABOUT?

I EXAMINED THE SCENE OF EVERY ONE OF THOSE TRAGEDIES, AND I'M CONVINCED THOSE DEATHS WEREN'T ACCIDENTAL-- BUT MURDER!

BUT THE EVIDENCE IN EACH CASE PLAINLY SHOWED NO REASON TO BELIEVE IT ANYTHING BUT ACCIDENTAL.

THAT WAS JUST THE TROUBLE. IT WAS TOO CUT AND DRIED. I ASCERTAINED THAT EACH DEATH COULD HAVE BEEN CUNNINGLY CONCEALED MURDER.

THEN YOU BELIEVE--?

--THAT ALL THESE DEATHS WERE CAUSED BY THE SAME PERSON. SOMEWHERE, WHITE, THERE LURKS A CROOK OF UNUSUAL CRIMINAL INTELLIGENCE.

WELL, I CERTAINLY HOPE YOU'RE RIGHT. -- OR THE DAILY PLANET IS PUT IN A VERY BAD LIGHT. CALL SERGEANT CASEY AT HEADQUARTERS. HE WANTS TO SPEAK TO YOU.

OKAY. MAY I USE YOUR PHONE?

CASEY? THIS IS KENT. YOU WANTED TO SPEAK TO ME?

THAT I DID, YOU CRAZY LOON! WHAT'S THE IDEA OF PRINTING THAT ARTICLE?

BUT EVERY WORD OF IT IS THE TRUTH! I'LL SOON BE ABLE TO PROVE IT IS!

OH, SO YOU'RE GOING TO PROVE IT? WELL, LET ME TELL YOU THIS: EITHER RETRACT THAT STORY OR I'LL MAKE IT PLENTY HOT FOR YOU!

②

WELL? WHAT DID HE HAVE TO SAY?

ENOUGH TO MAKE ME REALIZE THAT UNLESS I CAN DIG UP PROMPT CONFIRMATION FOR MY CLAIMS, YOU'LL HAVE TO FORWARD MY FAN MAIL TO ME CARE OF THE CITY JAIL!

PERHAPS I'VE TAKEN TOO MUCH FOR GRANTED, BUT I WAS *POSITIVE* THAT THERE WAS ONE SINISTER CRIMINAL MIND BEHIND THOSE DEATHS. INASMUCH AS ALL THE MEN WHO DIED WERE WEALTHY--

A EUGENE STARBUCK TO SEE YOU, MR KENT.

STARBUCK... STARBUCK... THE NAME SEEMS FAMILIAR.

IT OUGHT TO BE! I'M THE BROTHER OF ROBERT STARBUCK, WHO YOU CLAIM DID NOT COMMIT SUICIDE, BUT WAS MURDERED, **WHERE ARE YOUR FACTS?**

IF ROBERT WAS SLAIN, NATURALLY I WANT TO SEE HIS KILLER TRACKED DOWN AND MADE TO PAY THE FULL PENALTY. WILL YOU PLEASE COME TO LUNCH WITH ME SO WE CAN DISCUSS THIS MATTER TOGETHER?

YES--WHY DON'T YOU?

BUT--ER-- THERE'S A LOT OF WORK I HAVE TO GET OUT, AND...

THAT WORK CAN WAIT.-- YOU'RE COMING WITH ME! I WANT THAT INFORMATION!

IT LOOKS LIKE CLARK HAS GOTTEN HIMSELF INTO A FINE MESS.

I'M NOT SURPRISED. IT'S A WONDER CLARK HASN'T BEEN TRIPPED UP LONG BEFORE THIS.

("-WHAT A SPOT TO BE IN. AS YET I HAVE NO DEFINITE PROOF TO SUPPORT MY CONTENTIONS.-")

HEAVY TRAFFIC, ISN'T IT?

ABRUPTLY, TWO HANDS SHOVE UNEXPECTEDLY AT CLARK---- HE TUMBLES INTO THE STREET..!

HEY! WHAT--?

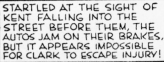

STARTLED AT THE SIGHT OF KENT FALLING INTO THE STREET BEFORE THEM, THE AUTOS JAM ON THEIR BRAKES, BUT IT APPEARS IMPOSSIBLE FOR CLARK TO ESCAPE INJURY!

-- CLARK GOES THRU A SERIES OF REMARKABLE GYRATIONS. APPARENTLY, HE IS TWISTING IN TERROR ON THE STREET, ACCIDENTLY MISSING EACH OF THE SKIDDING CARS IN TURN...BUT ACTUALLY HE IS DODGING THEM THRU SUPER-SPEED...!

A SHEER MIRACLE YOU DIDN'T DIE! NEXT TIME BE CAREFUL WHERE YOU TRIP AND FALL.

WHO SAID I TRIPPED?

("-NO SIGN OF EUGENE STARBUCK ANYWHERE!-")

EUGENE DELIBERATELY SHOVED ME BEFORE THAT CAR SO THAT I'D BE KILLED AND UNABLE TO OFFER FURTHER EVIDENCE. THIS ONLY SERVES TO INCREASE MY CONTENTION THAT THESE DEATHS WERE NOT ACCIDENTAL!

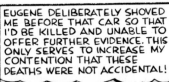

HOW DID YOUR LITTLE TETE-A-TETE TURN OUT?

LET ME GET AT THE TELEPHONE BOOTH!

SWIFTLY, CLARK TELEPHONES THE STARBUCK RESIDENCE....

WHEN EUGENE COMES IN, WILL YOU PLEASE TELL HIM THAT CLARK KENT CALLED?

EUGENE, DID YOU SAY? I'M SORRY BUT THERE IS NO ONE NAMED EUGENE STARBUCK. NO-- MY HUSBAND NEVER HAD A BROTHER!

THEN-- THIS FELLOW WHO CLAIMED HE WAS STARBUCK'S BROTHER WAS A PHONY! HE'S EITHER THE KILLER OR ASSOC- IATED WITH THE MURDERER! AND TO THINK I FELL FOR HIS LINE!

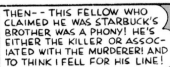

BURTON STEELE IS HERE TO SEE YOU. SAYS HE'S A COUSIN OF DANIEL STEELE.

HUH??-- LEAD ME TO HIM!

SO YOU'RE BURTON STEELE, DANIEL'S COUSIN, EH?

THAT'S RIGHT. AND. I'VE COME HERE TO DEMAND WHATEVER INFORMATION YOU MAY POSSESS REGARDING THE MURDER OF MY COUSIN!

CLARK'S SUPER-VISION INFORMS HIM . . . .

("-A FALSE BEARD! THAT SO-CALLED MASTERMIND ISN'T AS CLEVER AS I GAVE HIM CREDIT FOR... TRYING TO PULL THE SAME TRICK TWICE!-")

GOT YOU! YOU WON'T ESCAPE THIS TIME!

LET GO! HELP!!

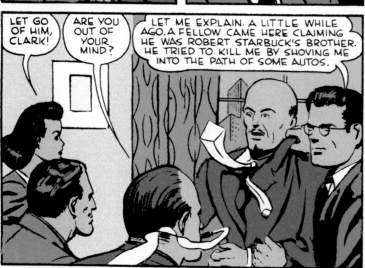

LET GO OF HIM, CLARK!

ARE YOU OUT OF YOUR MIND?

LET ME EXPLAIN. A LITTLE WHILE AGO, A FELLOW CAME HERE CLAIMING HE WAS ROBERT STARBUCK'S BROTHER. HE TRIED TO KILL ME BY SHOVING ME INTO THE PATH OF SOME AUTOS.

I CONTEND THAT THE MAN WHO PASSED HIMSELF OFF AS EUGENE STARBUCK IS A CLEVER CRIMINAL, RESPONSIBLE FOR THE DEATH OF MANY INNOCENT MEN. I FURTHER BELIEVE THAT HE IS A MASTER OF DISGUISE. FURTHER, THAT EUGENE STARBUCK AND THIS FELLOW ARE ONE AND THE SAME!

BUT WHATEVER GAVE YOU THIS IDEA?

THIS FALSE BEARD, FOR ONE THING!

YOU STUPID FOOL! I AM BURTON STEELE!

A LIKELY STORY! THEN WHY DID YOU COME HERE DISGUISED?

BECAUSE I'M AN ACTOR, THAT'S WHY! I'M APPEARING AT THE ACME THEATRE, AND SLIPPED OVER HERE BETWEEN PERFORMANCES.

THEATRE

THAT'S RIGHT. I SAW HIS SHOW THE OTHER DAY.

ACCEPT MY APOLOGIES!

YOU'LL BE FORTUNATE IF I DON'T SUE YOU FOR ASSAULT AND BATTERY!

ARE YOU SATISFIED, NOW THAT YOU'VE MADE A SAP OUT OF YOURSELF?

BUT ANYONE COULD HAVE MADE THE SAME MISTAKE.

YOU'D BETTER STICK TO ROUTINE STUFF, CLARK, AND KEEP AWAY FROM ANYTHING THAT REQUIRES MORE THAN COMMON SENSE.

("--I'VE CERTAINLY MUFFED EVERYTHING THUS FAR. WHEREEVER THE CRIMINAL MASTER MIND IS, IF HE COULD KNOW OF MY BLUNDERS, HE'D BE ENJOYING A GOOD LAUGH AT MY EXPENSE RIGHT NOW!--")

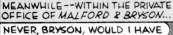

MEANWHILE--WITHIN THE PRIVATE OFFICE OF MALFORD & BRYSON...

NEVER, BRYSON, WOULD I HAVE SUSPECTED THAT MY OWN PARTNER WAS A CROOK. I GAVE YOU YOUR FIRST BREAK, COMPLETELY TRUSTED YOU, AND HOW DO YOU REPAY ME? BY MISAPPROPRIATING $25,000 OF THE FIRM'S MONEY!

I'M SORRY...MY GAMBLING DEBTS WERE DRIVING ME MAD. I WAS GOING TO REPLACE THE MONEY.

YOU CERTAINLY WILL REPLACE IT!--BY TOMORROW MORNING!

BY TOMORROW? BUT THAT DOESN'T GIVE ME ENOUGH TIME! HOW COULD I EVER HOPE TO RAISE THAT MUCH MONEY SO SOON?

THAT'S YOUR CONCERN! YOU GOT YOURSELF INTO THIS MESS, NOW GET YOURSELF OUT OF IT! UNDERSTAND? $25,000 BY TOMORROW MORNING OR YOU GO TO PRISON!

$25,000 --- BY TOMORROW MORNING! IMPOSSIBLE! I'M RUINED!

THAT'S HIM!

GET GOIN'!

WH-WHAT--?

YOU HEARD WHAT I SAID!

GET INTO THAT CAR--AND DON'T LET OUT A PEEP!

WHAT ARE YOU GOING TO DO WITH ME? IS THIS ROBBERY? HAS MALFORD HIRED YOU TO KILL ME IN VENGEANCE? WHAT...?

QUIET! YOU'LL LEARN IN TIME!

SOMETIME LATER....

--IN *THERE*? BUT WHAT--?

STOP BLUBBER-ING!

GET MOVIN'!

HERE HE IS, BOSS--BRYSON.

IF YOU'RE THINKING OF HOLDING ME FOR RANSOM--

YOU'LL SOON LEARN WHAT I'M THINKING. MEANWHILE--SIT DOWN!

YOU HEARD THE BOSS --SIT DOWN!

NOW, AS I UNDERSTAND YOUR SITUATION, UNLESS YOU CAN DIG UP $25,000 BY MORNING, YOUR NAME WILL BE DISGRACED. AND YOU'LL BE SENT TO JAIL--A PROSPECT YOU CERTAINLY DON'T RELISH!

HOW--HOW DID *YOU* KNOW?

THERE ARE A LOT OF THINGS I KNOW, BRYSON-- THINGS I MAKE IT MY BUSINESS TO FIND OUT. FOR YOU SEE, I'M GOING TO HELP YOU.

IT SEEMS TO ME THAT YOUR PROBLEM WOULD BE SOLVED IF YOUR PARTNER, MALFORD... WERE TO BE--ER--LIQUIDATED, YOU WOULD THEN BE THE SOLE OWNER OF A THRIVING BUSINESS AND THE THREAT OF JAIL WOULD BE A THING OF THE PAST.

BUT-- THAT WOULD BE MURDER!

AND SO IT WOULD. BUT A PROFITABLE MURDER FOR BOTH OF US. MY PROPOSITION IS AS FOLLOWS, BRYSON. I REMOVE MALFORD SO THAT NO SUSPICION OF MURDER APPEARS. AND AT THE EARLIEST OPPORTUNITY YOU PAY ME $10,000.

I--I DON'T KNOW WHAT TO SAY!

THEN I'LL MAKE UP YOUR MIND FOR YOU, BRYSON. MALFORD DIES! THEN-- ONCE THE BUSINESS IS IN YOUR CONTROL-- YOU PAY ME MY FEE. AGREED?

I'VE NO ALTER-NATIVE! IT'S-- IT'S AGREED!

NOW YOU'RE SHOWING SOME SENSE. CHEER UP, BRYSON! MALFORD WILL BE REMOVED SWIFTLY-- EXPERTLY--AND WITH HIS PASSING, YOUR TROUBLES WILL DISAPPEAR!

⑦

WITHIN HIS APARTMENT, CLARK KENT SHEDS HIS CIVILIAN GARMENTS, STANDING EXPOSED IN THE COLORFUL **SUPERMAN** COSTUME....

ONLY ONE WAY TO SHOW THAT THERE REALLY IS A COLD-BLOODED KILLER BEHIND THESE SEEMINGLY ACCIDENTAL DEATHS--

-- THAT'S TO VENTURE FORTH AND **PROVE IT!**

MEANWHILE...

HURRY-- BEFORE MALFORD EMERGES FROM HIS OFFICE.

I'LL HAVE THE BRAKE ROD DISCONNECTED IN A JIFFY!

MINUTES LATER... MALFORD ENTERS HIS CAR AND DRIVES OFF, UNAWARE THAT IT HAS BEEN TAMPERED WITH...!

BUT AS MALFORD DRIVES DOWN A STEEP INCLINE, HE DISCOVERS TO HIS HORROR....

THE BRAKES... THEY **DON'T WORK!**

AS A LARGE TRUCK COMES AROUND A CURVE ON THE INCLINE, MALFORD JABS FRANTICALLY AT THE BRAKE-PEDAL, BUT IN VAIN. A CRASH APPEARS CERTAIN!

⑧

IN THE SKY ABOVE, A KEEN-EYED STREAKING FIGURE SIGHTS THE TENSE SCENE BELOW...

A CAR-- OUT OF CONTROL!

DOWN PLUMMETS THE *MAN OF TOMORROW* AT BREAKNECK SPEED!

SPLIT-SECONDS TO GO..!

ALIGHTING BESIDE MALFORD'S CAR, **SUPERMAN** JERKS IT ASIDE SO THAT IT NARROWLY MISSES THE ONRUSHING TRUCK!

THAT WAS REALLY CLOSE!

BEYOND CONTROL, THE AUTO FLIES OFF THE ROAD....

BUT SEIZING THE REAR BUMPER, **SUPERMAN** YANKS IT BACK TO SAFETY....

WHOA! THAT'S THE WRONG DIRECTION!

SWIFTLY, THE *MAN OF STEEL* SLIPS UNDER THE CAR....

I THINK I KNOW WHAT'S TO BLAME!

A SINGLE GLANCE ACQUAINTS HIM WITH THE CAUSE OF THE TROUBLE. IT TAKES BUT A MOMENT FOR HIM TO REPAIR THE DISCONNECTED BRAKE-ROD!

THERE! THAT DOES IT!

⑨

A TERRIFIED MALFORD SUCCEEDS IN HALTING THE CAR....

THE BRAKES SEEM ALL RIGHT NOW! *WHEW!* THE ONLY THING THAT SAVED ME FROM DEATH WAS SHEER LUCK!

SHEER LUCK? THAT'S DEBATABLE! AND SO IS THE MANNER IN WHICH THAT BRAKE-ROD WAS DISCONNECTED!

NEXT MORNING...

("—HE'S STILL ALIVE!—")

N-NO-- I FAILED TO RAISE THE MONEY.

THEN ARREST THAT MAN!

I SEE WHERE MALFORD NARROWLY ESCAPED DEATH.... AND THAT BRYSON WAS ARRESTED THIS MORNING. CHIPS, WHEN I TOLD YOU I WANTED THAT BRAKE-ROD DISCONNECTED, I MEANT IT!

BUT I DID! I SWEAR IT!

DON'T LIE!

YAA-AA-AAA!

YOU KILLED CHIPS JUST BECAUSE HE MADE A LITTLE MISTAKE-- WHY?

BECAUSE I CAN'T AFFORD TO SLIP UP ON IMPORTANT JOBS IT'S BAD FOR MY REPUTATION -- AND MY POCKETBOOK. I FEAR I MUST FORGET ABOUT BRYSON AND LOOK FOR A NEW CLIENT.

BUT WHERE WILL YOU FIND THIS CLIENT?

RIGHT HERE IN THIS NEWSPAPER. HM-MM! FORMER MULTI-MILLIONAIRE MAX BINDER IS GOING BANKRUPT!

HOME OF MAX BINDER...AS THE FORMER CAPITALIST IS ABOUT TO FIRE A BULLET INTO HIS HEAD. THE GUN IS SHOT OUT OF HIS HAND...!

10

WH-WHO ARE YOU?

THAT IS UNIMPORTANT. WHAT DOES COUNT IS THAT YOU POSSESS A LARGE INSURANCE POLICY --IF YOU WERE TO DIE AN ACCIDENTAL DEATH, RATHER THAN PERISH THRU SUICIDE, YOUR FAMILY WOULD RECEIVE ENOUGH TO GIVE THEM SECURITY.

YOU PROPOSE TO KILL ME -- AND MAKE IT LOOK LIKE AN ACCIDENT?

THAT'S RIGHT. NO DOUBT YOU'VE A FEW THOUSAND LEFT. TURN THEM OVER TO ME AND YOU'LL SUFFER AN UNFORTUNATE "ACCIDENT" ENABLING YOUR FAMILY TO SECURE THE BENEFITS OF THAT POLICY!

45

Panel 1:

CALL ON MAX BINDER, CLARK, AND DIG UP SOME POINTERS ON HOW IT FEELS TO LOSE A FEW MILLIONS.

I'M SURE THE *DAILY PLANET* READERS WILL FIND THE INFORMATION VERY APPLICABLE TO THEIR DAILY LIVES.

Panel 2:

INTERVIEWING THE FORMER CAPITALIST, CLARK FINDS HIM BEHAVING IN PECULIAR MANNER....

WHAT DID I THINK OF MY LIFE? NOT MUCH. I WOULD HAVE BEEN HAPPIER HAD I NEVER BEEN BORN.

("--ODD!-- HE SPEAKS OF HIS LIFE IN THE PAST TENSE. AND THERE'S A DISTURBING AIR ABOUT HIM.--")

Panel 3:

OUTSIDE THE MANSION, CLARK SWIFTLY CHANGES TO HIS **SUPERMAN** COSTUME....

I'VE A HUNCH I'D BETTER KEEP BINDER UNDER SURVEILLANCE ... FOR HIS OWN GOOD!

Panel 4:

AS **SUPERMAN** WATCHES, BINDER WALKS OUT UPON A BALCONY... IT BEGINS TO GIVE WAY...

THE BALCONY'S SUPPORTS... CRUMBLING --!!

Panel 5:

SUPERMAN CATCHES THE FALLING EX-CAPITALIST IN MID-AIR...

Panel 6:

--THEN ALIGHTS GENTLY WITH HIM!

IN THE MOMENT THAT THE BALCONY CRUMPLED, I SAW THAT THE SUPPORTS HAD BEEN DELIBERATELY AND CUNNINGLY SABATOGED. WHAT EXPLANATION HAVE YOU?

SUPERMAN! NO SENSE IN WITHHOLDING INFORMATION FROM YOU!--SOMEONE OFFERED TO SLAY ME AND MAKE IT LOOK ACCIDENTAL SO THAT MY FAMILY WOULD BENEFIT FROM MY INSURANCE POLICY!

Panel 7:

I'M SURPRISED THAT A MAN OF YOUR CALIBRE WOULD EVEN CONSIDER SUCH A PLAN. YOU'VE MADE AND LOST FORTUNES BEFORE. I'M SURE YOU CAN MAKE ANOTHER COMEBACK.

SOMEHOW, YOU FILL ME WITH NEW CONFIDENCE. I PROMISE NOT TO TAKE THE EASY WAY OUT!

Panel 8:

BUT--LATER THAT EVENING...

I MANAGED TO EVADE THE TRAP FOR MY LIFE, I'M GLAD TO SAY. I'VE CHANGED MY MIND. I WANT TO LIVE.

THAT'S JUST TOO BAD FOR YOU. THE BOSS WANTS MORE DOUGH OR HE'LL CARRY OUT THE ORIGINAL AGREEMENT!

AS THE THUG DEPARTS FROM THE BINDER MANSION, A STRONG ARM ABRUPTLY SEIZES HIS COLLAR AND WHIRLS HIM ALOFT...

HEY--!

LET'S YOU AND I HAVE A TALK!

ULP!-- SUPERMAN!

YOU RECOGNIZE ME?-- THEN YOU'D BETTER TALK FAST! WHO'S YOUR BOSS? WHAT'S HIS RACKET? WHERE CAN I FIND HIM?

HE'S THE GUY WHO KILLED STARBUCK, CORDAY, AND THE OTHERS AND MADE IT LOOK ACCIDENTAL. TONIGHT HE'S GONE CALLING ON SENATOR McPHAIL. A SUBVERSIVE GROUP HAS PAID HIM PLENTY TO FINISH OFF THE SENATOR AND MAKE IT LOOK ACCIDENTAL.

THANKS FOR THE INFORMATION!

HEY! DON'T LEAVE ME HERE!

MEANWHILE, ENTERING McPHAIL'S HOME, THE MASTER CRIMINAL SPECULATIVELY REGARDS THE DOZING SENATOR....

ONE WELL-PLACED SHOT-- THEN I PLACE THE GUN IN HIS HAND--AND IT LOOKS LIKE SUICIDE!

AS HIS TELESCOPIC X-RAY VISION BRINGS TO HIM THE SCENE BELOW, SUPERMAN STREAKS DOWN...

HERE GOES!

AS THE MASTER-CRIMINAL FIRES, SUPERMAN CRASHES IN THRU THE WINDOW AND CATCHES THE BULLET IN HIS BARE HAND!

I'LL TAKE THAT IF YOU DON'T MIND!

WH-WHA--??

SUPERMAN!

I'M NO MATCH FOR THE MAN OF TOMORROW! MY ONLY HOPE-- FLIGHT!

⑫

HE'S PURSUING ME-- LIKE A HURTLING ARROW! -- I'VE GOT TO DO SOMETHING QUICK -- OR I'M DONE FOR! THAT BICYCLE!

DELIBERATELY, THE FLEEING CRIMINAL CRASHES INTO A BOY ON HIS BICYCLE...!

THAT SHOULD DO IT! WHILE HE'S ATTENDING TO THE BOY, I'LL HAVE A CHANCE TO DUCK UP AN ALLEY AND LOSE HIM FOR GOOD! THE OLD BRAIN IS STILL CLICKING!

SUPERMAN PAUSES TO CATCH THE BOY....

NO SERIOUS INJURY TO YOU -- FOR WHICH LET'S BE THANKFUL!

BUT FOR ONCE THE MASTERMIND HAS MISCALCULATED EASILY, THE MAN OF TOMORROW OVERTAKES HIS AUTO AND RIPS THE TOP CLEAR OFF...!

AWK!-- SUPERMAN! BUT I THOUGHT

THAT YOU'D EVADE JUSTICE? ANYONE CAN TELL YOU THAT CRIME DOESN'T PAY!

DON'T HURT ME! I'LL CONFESS! --I'LL CONFESS EVERYTHING!

LATER --AT HEADQUARTERS...

A PRISONER FOR YOU-- FREE OF CHARGE!

I MURDERED CORDAY, STEELE AND STARBUCK-- THEN MADE THE DEATHS LOOK ACCIDENTAL!

WELL--!

13

WAIT! YOU DESERVE A MEDAL OR SOMETHING FOR THIS!

I HEREBY BEQUEATH IT TO YOU!

REMARKABLE, CLARK! UNCANNY HOW YOU WERE ABLE TO SENSE THAT THOSE ACCIDENTAL DEATHS WERE REALLY MURDER!

YOU'RE NOT FORGETTING THAT SUPERMAN DESERVES MOST OF THE CREDIT. I HOPE.

THE END

SUPERMAN

REG. U.S. PAT. OFF.

by JERRY SIEGEL and JOE SHUSTER

DUE TO TURBULENT CONDITIONS OVERSEAS, IT IS NECESSARY FOR THE UNITED STATES TO REARM RAPIDLY. SINISTER FORCES, HOWEVER, SEEK TO IMPEDE AMERICA'S EFFORT TO ARM ITSELF SO THAT IT WILL BE SAFE FROM ANY ATTACK. BUT PATRIOT NUMBER ONE, **SUPERMAN**, TAKES UPON HIMSELF THE TASK OF BATTLING THE SECRET FOES OF OUR NATION--AND THE RESULTING CLASH IS ONE LONG TO BE REMEMBERED!

THE CLAYTON CHEMICAL CORPORATION'S GREAT FACTORY BUILDINGS ARE SWEPT BY A DEVASTATING FIRE....

A NUMBER OF STEEL FACTORIES ARE SCENES OF TERRIFIC EXPLOSIONS....

THESE ACCIDENTS ARE TOO FREQUENT TO BE MERE CO-INCIDENCE!

RIGHT, CHIEF!

IT'S TIME WE STOPPED TALKING --AND *DID* SOMETHING!

WHERE TO??

THE CITY JAIL!

JAIL, YOU SAID?--BUT WHAT--?

A SUSPICIOUS CHARACTER WAS FOUND NEAR ONE OF THE DISASTERS.--HE REFUSES TO TALK--BUT MAYBE WE CAN GET SOMETHING OUT OF HIM!

AT THE CITY JAIL....

SO YOU'RE GOING TO WALTZ INTO THIS GUY'S CELL AND ACCOMPLISH WHAT THE BEST MEN ON THE FORCE HAVE FAILED TO DO--MAKE HIM TALK!

AW BE A SPORT, CASEY'!

OKAY. I'LL ARRANGE FOR YOU TO ENTER HIS CELL. BUT BE CAREFUL. HE'S A HARD CUSTOMER.

I'VE NOTHING TO FEAR. CLARK WILL BE THERE TO PROTECT ME.

ER--LOIS--ISN'T IT POSSIBLE THAT WE'RE WASTING OUR TIME? THIS FELLOW MAY BE REALLY INNOCENT.

NOW DON'T GO TIMID ON ME. REMEMBER--USE TACT, BUT IF HE TRIES TO ACT TOUGH, LET HIM HAVE IT. GOT IT?

S-SURE...

GET UP! YOU'VE GOT VISITORS!

WHAT DO YOU WANT?

WE'RE FROM THE DAILY PLANET. WE'D LIKE A STATEMENT. NOW SUPPOSE WE START WITH WHAT YOU WERE DOING IN THE VICINITY OF THAT PLANT.

②

YOU DO HAVE AN EXPLANATION, DON'T YOU?

REPORTERS, EH?--I DON'T LIKE REPORTERS!

AS THE PRISONER ADVANCES ON LOIS, CLARK HESITANTLY STEPS FORWARD....

SEE HERE --CAN'T YOU ANSWER A CIVIL QUESTION?

YOU WANT TROUBLE, EH?

I'LL GIVE YOU PLENTY OF IT!

("--HERE'S AN OPPORTUNITY TO CONVINCE LOIS I'M YELLOW CLEAR THRU!--")

AS CLARK DUCKS, THE FIST WHIZZES BY HIS EAR....

MISSED--!

GET HIM, CLARK!

BUT I'LL GET YOU NEXT TIME!

THE PRISONER STRIKES AT CLARK REPEATEDLY, BUT CLARK DEXTEROUSLY EVADES THE BLOWS.

WHY DON'T YOU DO SOMETHING BESIDES JUST DODGE?

I CAN'T HIT HIM!

SO YOU WERE GOING TO MAKE THE POLICE FORCE LOOK SILLY, EH?

I'M GETTING OUT OF HERE!

BUT LOIS--!

THERE SHE GOES! THAT LEAVES ME ALL ALONE...

STEPPING INTO AN ALLEY, CLARK CHANGES TO HIS SUPERMAN COSTUME....

A PERFECT OPPORTUNITY TO SWITCH TO SUPERMAN!

③

LEAPING ATOP A NEAR-BY BUILDING, CLARK AVAILS HIMSELF OF HIS TELESCOPIC VISION...

THAT PRISONER IS VERY UNCOMMUNICATIVE, BUT PERHAPS I CAN FIND WAYS TO MAKE HIM TALK. MEAN-WHILE, I'LL TAKE A LOOK AND SEE WHAT'S GOING ON.

THE *MAN OF TOMORROW'S* EYES NARROW AT THE UNEXPECTEDNESS OF WHAT HE SEES....

WHAT'S THIS?!?

SEVERAL THUGS HAVE INVADED THE JAIL, AND CATCHING THE POLICE OFF-GUARD, HAVE THEM AT THEIR MERCY....

THAT'S RIGHT-- --OPEN IT UP!

YOU'LL NEVER GET AWAY WITH THIS!

YOU CAME FOR ME! GOOD!

YOU WON'T GET A BLOCK AWAY FROM THE JAIL BEFORE EVERY POLICE CAR IN THE CITY WILL BE ON YOUR TRAIL!

WE THOUGHT OF THAT. THAT'S WHY YOU'RE COMING *WITH* US! ---- REMEMBER-- IF WE'RE FOLLOWED, IT'LL BE THE END OF SERGEANT CASEY!

NEVER MIND ME -- GET THEM!

A TENSE COSTUMED FIGURE SEES CASEY FORCED INTO A WAITING CAR....

NO DOUBT OF IT NOW! THAT PRISONER HOLDS IMPORTANT KNOWLEDGE!

AS THE AUTO SPEEDS OFF, A LONE FIGURE TRAILS IT HIGH IN THE SKY!

④

FIFTEEN MINUTES LATER....

-- IT WORKED!

THOUGHT YOU'D HOLD ME, EH?

WE DODGED THE COPS! WHAT DO WE DO WITH **HIM** NOW?

WE GET RID OF HIM!

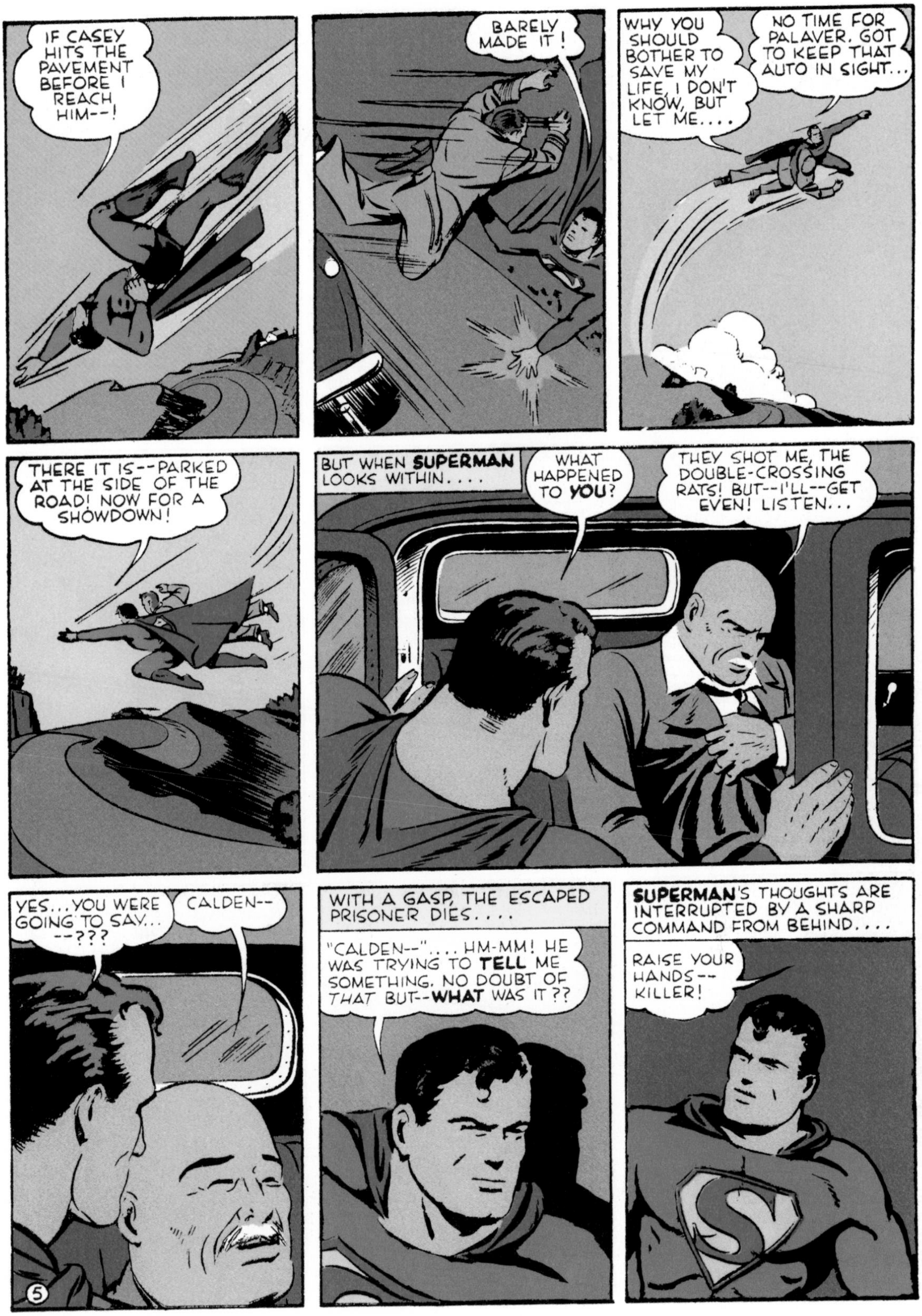
IF CASEY HITS THE PAVEMENT BEFORE I REACH HIM--!
BARELY MADE IT!
WHY YOU SHOULD BOTHER TO SAVE MY LIFE, I DON'T KNOW, BUT LET ME....
NO TIME FOR PALAVER. GOT TO KEEP THAT AUTO IN SIGHT...
THERE IT IS--PARKED AT THE SIDE OF THE ROAD! NOW FOR A SHOWDOWN!
BUT WHEN SUPERMAN LOOKS WITHIN....
WHAT HAPPENED TO YOU?
THEY SHOT ME, THE DOUBLE-CROSSING RATS! BUT--I'LL--GET EVEN! LISTEN...
YES...YOU WERE GOING TO SAY... --???
CALDEN--
5
WITH A GASP, THE ESCAPED PRISONER DIES....
"CALDEN--"....HM-MM! HE WAS TRYING TO TELL ME SOMETHING. NO DOUBT OF THAT BUT--WHAT WAS IT??
SUPERMAN'S THOUGHTS ARE INTERRUPTED BY A SHARP COMMAND FROM BEHIND....
RAISE YOUR HANDS--KILLER!

STATE TROOPERS!

THAT'S RIGHT! AND IT LOOKS AS THO WE'VE GOT YOU RED-HANDED!

BUT I DIDN'T KILL HIM. HE WAS SPIRITED OUT OF JAIL BY HIS SO-CALLED COMRADES, WHO IN REALITY DID IT SO THAT *THEY* COULD KILL *HIM!* THEY WERE PROBABLY AFRAID HE'D TALK!

SAVE YOUR LIES. YOU'RE WASTING YOUR BREATH.

PUT OUT YOUR WRISTS!

YOU'RE MAKING A MISTAKE!

TAKE ANOTHER STEP--AND-- WE'LL *SHOOT!*

AS THE *MAN OF TOMORROW* WHIRLS AND DASHES OFF AT METEORIC PACE, HE IS FOLLOWED BY A FUSILADE OF SHOTS...

WOULD YOU CALL THIS A FAIR RACE?

BUT HE EASILY OUTDISTANCES THE DEADLY METAL PELLETS...!

WELL--I GOT OUT OF THAT! OR AM I IN A WORSE PREDICAMENT? NOW THEY THINK I KILLED THAT FELLOW!

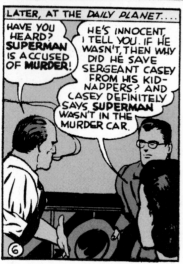

LATER, AT THE *DAILY PLANET*....

HAVE YOU HEARD? *SUPERMAN* IS ACCUSED OF *MURDER!*

HE'S INNOCENT, I TELL YOU. IF HE WASN'T, THEN WHY DID HE SAVE SERGEANT CASEY FROM HIS KID-NAPPERS? AND CASEY DEFINITELY SAYS *SUPERMAN* WASN'T IN THE MURDER CAR.

("-IT'S MIGHTY NICE TO KNOW THAT AT LEAST LOIS IS STICK-ING UP FOR ME. SHE'S A GREAT GIRL. WHAT A TEMPTATION IT IS TO INFORM HER WHO I REALLY AM!-")

GET GOING, YOU TWO. A NARROWLY AVERTED EXPLOSION AT THE *PELHAM PLANT.* LOOKS LIKE ANOTHER ATTEMPT TO SABOTAGE AMERICA'S NATIONAL DEFENSE EFFORT.

YOU NEEDN'T BOTHER TO COME IF YOU'RE AFRAID.

THIS IS NO TIME TO ARGUE. LET'S GET GOING!

WHEN THEY REACH THE GUARD-ED *PELHAM PLANT*....

WHAT'S YOUR BUSINESS HERE?

WE'RE FROM THE *DAILY PLANET*. WE'VE COME TO LEARN ABOUT THE NEAR-EXPLOSION.

OKAY FOR THEM TO ENTER--AFTER WE'VE SEEN THEIR REPORTERS' CARDS.

IN THE OFFICE OF STANLEY PELHAM, OWNER OF THE PLANT...

IT WAS A TIME-BOMB. ONE OF OUR WORKERS FOUND IT A FEW MINUTES BEFORE IT WAS TO GO OFF. THAT WAS A CLOSE CALL!

IT CERTAINLY WAS!

COULD YOU SHOW US JUST WHERE THE BOMB WAS CON-CEALED?

THIS ATTEMPT, LIKE THOSE IN OTHER PLANTS, MUST BE CAUSED BY PEOPLE WHO WISH TO BLOCK OUR COUNTRY'S REARMAMENT.

I'LL INTRODUCE YOU TO SAM SPENCER, FORE-MAN OF THE SECTION IN WHICH THE BOMB WAS FOUND.

SAM, I'D LIKE YOU TO MEET LOIS LANE AND CLARK KENT OF THE *PLANET*. SHOW THEM WHERE THAT BOMB WAS FOUND.

SURE...I'LL SHOW THEM.

RIGHT HERE!--AND IF I HADN'T SEEN THAT QUEER LITTLE BOX WITH MY OWN EYES, WE'D ALL HAVE BEEN BLOWN TO KINGDOM COME!

I GUESS THIS IS ALL THE INFORMATION WE'LL REQUIRE. THANKS AGAIN!

THO APPARENTLY WORKING BUSILY AT HIS TASK, ONE OF THE WORK-MEN ON A NEARBY MACHINE KEEPS THE VISITORS UNDER FURTIVE SURVEILLANCE....

⑦

I'VE A HUNCH THAT WHOEVER FAILED TO DESTROY THAT PLANT MAY TRY AGAIN. WHAT SAY WE BREAK INTO THE FACTORY TONIGHT AND WAIT FOR DEVELOPMENTS?

YOU CAN COUNT ME OUT.

THAT EVENING--LOIS LEAVES HER HOME TO START ON HER BREATH-TAKING ADVENTURE...

SO CLARK REFUSES TO ACCOMPANY ME, EH? WELL, I'M NOT THE LEAST BIT SURPRISED!

BUT LOIS WOULD HAVE REVISED HER LOW OPINION OF CLARK COULD SHE HAVE WITNESSED THE SCENE AT THAT MOMENT IN THE REPORTER'S APARTMENT....

SO LOIS IS GOING TO STICK HER NECK OUT AGAIN, EH?

THAT MEANS THAT ONCE AGAIN I'VE GOT TO KEEP WATCH OVER THAT VENTURESOME MISS!

I'D BETTER LEAVE MY CAR HERE.--AND NOW TO GET INTO THE FACTORY WITHOUT BEING SIGHTED BY THE NIGHT WATCHMAN!

HIDDEN IN SHADOW, LOIS SLIPS PAST THE WATCHMAN AND INTO THE DEEPER SHADOWS OF THE FACTORY BUILDING....

("-MADE IT!-")

THAT WATCHMAN MUST BE BLIND AS A BAT-- NOT TO HAVE APPREHENDED LOIS.

BUT THE ANSWER BECOMES CLEAR A MOMENT LATER WHEN ANOTHER FIGURE SWIFTLY APPROACHES THE WATCHMAN....

OKAY?

OKAY--BUT BE CAREFUL. THAT NOSEY GIRL REPORTER JUST SLIPPED PAST ME AND INTO THE FACTORY. I PRETENDED NOT TO SEE HER.

THAT'S FINE. WE'LL DESTROY HER AND THE FACTORY AT THE SAME TIME. IF THEY FIND HER REMAINS, THEY'LL THINK HER RESPONSIBLE.

PERFECT!

WITHIN THE FACTORY, LOIS HIDES....

THIS MAY BE A WASTE OF TIME--BUT I'M WILLING TO TAKE THAT CHANCE.

AS THE WATCHMAN AND THE WORKMAN WHO HAD SO CLOSELY SPIED UPON CLARK AND LOIS, PREPARE TO ENTER THE FACTORY.

I'LL TEACH THOSE MURDER-OUS RASCALS A LESSON!

BUT IN MID-FLIGHT, SUPERMAN CHANGES HIS MIND AND ARCHES BACK....

WAIT--!

ON SECOND THOUGHT, I'LL BIDE MY TIME--GIVE THEM PLENTY OF OPPORTUNITY TO INCRIMINATE THEMSELVES!

LOIS IS UNAWARE OF TWO FIGURES STEALING UP ON HER FROM BEHIND, UNTIL....

NOTHING HAPPENS. PERHAPS THIS IS A WASTE OF TIME.

SWIFTLY, THEY BIND AND GAG THE GIRL REPORTER.—THEN, SETTING A LARGE CHARGE OF DYNAMITE BESIDE HER, THEY LIGHT THE FUSE....

HURRY--WE'VE GOT TO GET OUT OF HERE BEFORE IT GOES OFF!

YOU GOT A LITTLE MORE THAN YOU BARGAINED FOR, SISTER!

9

ALONE IN THE FACTORY, LEFT TO A HORRIBLE FATE, LOIS HELP-LESSLY WATCHES THE FUSE BURN CLOSER TO THE DYNAMITE....

DOWN STREAKS **SUPERMAN**...!

I'VE WAITED LONG ENOUGH!

STREAKING INTO THE FACTORY, HE EXTINGUISHES THE FUSE JUST IN TIME!

ONE SECOND LATER AND IT WOULD HAVE BEEN ANOTHER STORY!

ONCE AGAIN I OWE MY LIFE TO YOU. YOU MUST THINK ME A TERRIBLE NUISANCE!

MUST I ANSWER THAT?

OUTSIDE THE FACTORY, THE TWO CONSPIRATORS ARE CONFUSED....

THAT BOMB SHOULD HAVE GONE OFF BY NOW.

YET--IT HASN'T!

NEXT INSTANT, THEY LEARN THE ANSWER...

SUPERMAN!

L-LET'S BEAT IT!

OFF SPEEDS THE AUTO. BUT IT IS A SIMPLE MATTER FOR THE MIGHTY *MAN OF TOMORROW* TO OVERTAKE IT!

IF THEY THINK THEY CAN OUT-DISTANCE ME THEY'RE WAST-ING GASOLINE!

⑩

UP, HE WHIRLS THE CAR...!

GET OFF THE ROAD!

THEN UP INTO THE AIR HE LEAPS WITH HIS MASSIVE BURDEN...!

WE'RE OFF!!

THRU THE SKY HURTLES THE FANTASTIC, CLOAKED FIGURE...

RAILROAD TRACKS-- BELOW!

NOW TO CONFAB!

WHO PUT YOU UP TO DESTROYING THAT FACTORY?

YOU WON'T LEARN ANY-THING FROM US!

WE WON'T TALK!

NO? HEAR THAT TRAIN WHISTLE? IT'S STREAK-ING RIGHT TOWARD THIS AUTO, UNLESS YOU SPEAK UP, YOU'LL BE SMASHED TO SMITHEREENS!

HE'S BLUFF-ING!

HE WOULDN'T DARE!

TOWARD THE AUTOMOBILE RACES THE TRAIN...!

IT'S GOING TO HIT US!!

WILL YOU TALK?

YES! YES

⑪

SUPERMAN LIFTS THE MEN INTO THE AIR A MOMENT BEFORE THE TRAIN ROARS PAST...!

WE'RE MEMBERS OF THE GROTAK BUND! LIKE OTHER MEMBERS, WE HAVE ORDERS TO DESTROY CERTAIN FACTORIES-

--SO THAT AMERICA'S DEFENSE OPERATIONS WILL BE SLOW-ED DOWN AND DESTROYED!

YOU'RE GOING TO GUIDE ME TO THE GROTAK BUND'S MEETING PLACE!

LATER--

--IN THERE!

YOU'RE TO GO IN THERE--AND INFORM YOUR LEADER THAT YOU FAILED.

AWED BY THE *MAN OF STEEL*, THE TWO OBEY....

HOW DID THINGS WORK OUT?

N-NOT SO GOOD.

IN FACT --WE FAILED!

YOU KNOW THE PENALTY!

DEATH!

NO-- PLEASE!

THERE'LL BE NO MURDER DONE!

STOP HIM!

THE *GROTAK BUND* MEMBERS FLING THEMSELVES UPON THE *MAN OF STEEL* EN MASSE--BUT SOMERSAULT BACK AS HE CRASHES THRU THEM...!

OUT OF MY WAY!

THE LEADER HAS FLED INTO A SECRET TUNNEL....

ESCAPE --I'VE GOT TO ESCAPE!

BUT **SUPERMAN** FOLLOWS CLOSE BEHIND...!

IT'LL TAKE BUT A MOMENT FOR ME TO OVERTAKE HIM!

12

SUDDENLY, THE *MAN OF STEEL* IS ENGULFED IN A TERRIFIC EXPLOSION...!

I SEE HE PLANNED IN ADVANCE FOR THIS FLIGHT!

RETURNING TO THE MEETING HALL, **SUPERMAN** BINDS THE UNCONSCIOUS MEMBERS, THEN TELEPHONES THE AUTHORITIES...

COME TO THIS ADDRESS AND YOU'LL FIND A NEST OF TRAITORS TO OUR GOVERNMENT.--ALSO RECORDS PROVING THEIR GUILT.

LATER, AS CLARK KENT, HE ENTERS WITH THE FEDERAL RAIDERS....

WHO IS YOUR LEADER?

WE DON'T KNOW. HE REMAINED MASKED!

("-NO SENSE IN REMAINING HERE. I'LL RETURN TO THE DAILY PLANET!-")

WHEN KENT REACHES THE NEWSPAPER OFFICE....

WHERE'S LOIS?

SHE'S GONE TO INTERVIEW CALVIN DENBY, THE PROMINENT PATRIOT, FOR HIS OPINION ON THE OUTBREAK OF SABATOGE.

("-CALVIN DENBY--'CALDEN'--! NOW I'VE GOT IT! THE SLAIN MAN SOMEHOW KNEW WHO THE HEAD OF THE GROTAK BUND WAS AND TRIED TO NAME THE MAN WHO HAD ORDERED HIS SLAYING!--IF THAT'S TRUE, LOIS NEEDS ME!-")

YES, MR. DENBY--I HAVE A PRETTY GOOD SUSPICION WHO IS RESPONSIBLE FOR ALL THE SABATOGE.

YOU DO, EH?

("-SOMEHOW SHE MUST HAVE LEARNED THAT I'M THE HEAD OF THE GROTAK BUND. THEREFORE-- SHE MUST DIE!-")

WHEN LOIS GLANCES AWAY, DENBY SWIFTLY PRODUCES A WEAPON, TAKES A SWIFT AIM --AND FIRES...!

THAT'LL KEEP HER MOUTH SHUT!

IN THRU THE WALL CRASHES SUPERMAN. AS HE STREAKS BETWEEN THE TWO, THE BULLET DEFLECTS BACK, STRIKING DENBY....

IT ALMOST WORKED!

Y///-///!

HE--HE TRIED TO KILL ME! IS HE DEAD?

NO, ONLY STUNNED. KEEP HIM COVERED UNTIL THE POLICE GET HERE--IT WON'T TAKE MUCH PRESSURE TO MAKE HIM CONFESS HE'S THE HEAD OF THE GROTAK BUND.

⑬

LATER...

I KNOW YOU GOT THIS SPY STORY INTO THE NEWSPAPER BEFORE I HAD A CHANCE TO, BUT--HOW DID YOU DO IT?

THAT'S STRICTLY A BUSINESS SECRET!

THE END

SUPERMAN

by JERRY SIEGEL and JOE SHUSTER

FANTASTIC RUMORS EMERGE FROM A FAR-OFF ISLAND--RUMORS OF INCREDIBLE SCIENTIFIC FEATS AND UNBELIEVABLE MONSTROSITIES. WHEN CLARK KENT AND LOIS LANE TAKE ON THE TASK OF CHECKING UP ON THESE RUMORS, THEY LITTLE REALIZE THE MAZE OF STARTLING ADVENTURE THEY ARE ENTERING--OR THAT **SUPERMAN**, AMAZING *MAN OF STEEL*, IS TO MAKE HIS APPEARANCE AND FIGHT SCIENTIFIC HORROR IN HIS INIMITABLE DYNAMIC MANNER!

EDITORIAL OFFICE OF THE *DAILY PLANET*....

PLEASE BELIEVE ME! I'M DUDLEY BARNES--I'VE COME THOUSANDS OF MILES FROM *BARACODA ISLAND* TO WARN YOU OF A TERRIBLE MENACE THAT THREATENS HUMANITY!

OFF WITH YOU! YOU'RE JUST A TRAMP LOOKING FOR A HAND-OUT, AND I'VE NO TIME TO WASTE ON YOU!

SHALL WE--?

--WHY NOT!!

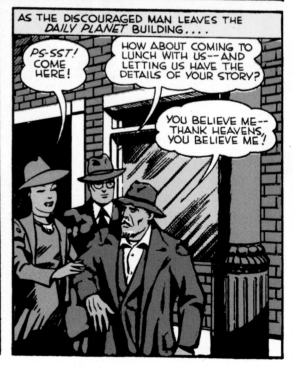

AS THE DISCOURAGED MAN LEAVES THE *DAILY PLANET* BUILDING....

PS-SST! COME HERE!

HOW ABOUT COMING TO LUNCH WITH US--AND LETTING US HAVE THE DETAILS OF YOUR STORY?

YOU BELIEVE ME-- THANK HEAVENS, YOU BELIEVE ME!

IT HAPPENED A YEAR AGO. ONE DAY AS I WAS WORKING IN MY LABORATORY, I SUDDENLY FELT A GUN PRESSED AGAINST MY RIBS...!

EVEN IF IT ISN'T TRUE, THIS SHOULD MAKE EXCITING LISTENING!

DON'T MIND CLARK!-- GO ON WITH YOUR STORY!

"--AGAINST MY WILL, I WAS TAKEN ON A LONG SEA VOYAGE-- "

BUT-- PLEASE TELL ME WHERE YOU'RE TAKING ME!

I'LL TELL YOU-- NOTHING!

"--AT LENGTH, WE DROPPED ANCHOR AT *BARACODA ISLAND*, ONE OF THE MANY ISLANDS IN THE *CODA GROUP*. THERE I WAS MET BY...!-- "

STEPHEN CARDINE-- THE FAMOUS BIOLOGIST! PERHAPS YOU CAN TELL ME WHAT THIS MEANS!

WE REGRET THE FORCEFUL MEANS TAKEN TO SPIRIT YOU HERE, BUT ONCE YOU LEARN WHAT THE WORK IS HERE, I'M SURE YOU'LL BE GLAD TO REMAIN.

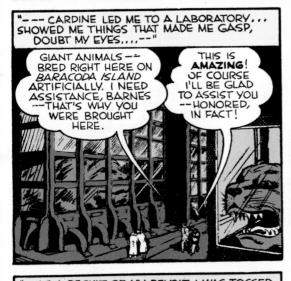

"--- CARDINE LED ME TO A LABORATORY... SHOWED ME THINGS THAT MADE ME GASP, DOUBT MY EYES....--"

GIANT ANIMALS-- BRED RIGHT HERE ON *BARACODA ISLAND* ARTIFICIALLY. I NEED ASSISTANCE, BARNES --THAT'S WHY YOU WERE BROUGHT HERE.

THIS IS **AMAZING**! OF COURSE I'LL BE GLAD TO ASSIST YOU --HONORED, IN FACT!

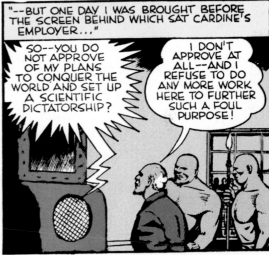

"--BUT ONE DAY I WAS BROUGHT BEFORE THE SCREEN BEHIND WHICH SAT CARDINE'S EMPLOYER..."

SO-- YOU DO NOT APPROVE OF MY PLANS TO CONQUER THE WORLD AND SET UP A SCIENTIFIC DICTATORSHIP?

I DON'T APPROVE AT ALL--AND I REFUSE TO DO ANY MORE WORK HERE TO FURTHER SUCH A FOUL PURPOSE!

"--AS A RESULT OF MY REVOLT, I WAS TOSSED INTO A JUNGLE FILLED WITH MONSTROUS HORRORS. --- I MANAGED TO ESCAPE AND RETURN TO *METROPOLIS*--"

②

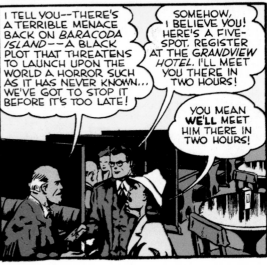

I TELL YOU--THERE'S A TERRIBLE MENACE BACK ON *BARACODA ISLAND*--A BLACK PLOT THAT THREATENS TO LAUNCH UPON THE WORLD A HORROR SUCH AS IT HAS NEVER KNOWN... WE'VE GOT TO STOP IT BEFORE IT'S TOO LATE!

SOMEHOW, I BELIEVE YOU! HERE'S A FIVE-SPOT. REGISTER AT THE *GRANDVIEW HOTEL*. I'LL MEET YOU THERE IN TWO HOURS!

YOU MEAN **WE'LL** MEET HIM THERE IN TWO HOURS!

WHERE HAVE YOU TWO WANDERING CHILDREN BEEN? I'VE BEEN LOOKING ALL OVER FOR YOU!

WE'RE CHECKING UP ON A BIG STORY YOU'RE DETERMINED TO MUFF!

THE STORY OF HOW GIGANTIC ANIMALS ARE BEING BRED ON BARACODA ISLAND.

KINDLY STOP WASTING YOUR TIME AND THE PAPER'S TIME ON THAT NONSENSE. I WANT YOU TO DASH DOWN TO THE RESIDENCE OF ALLEN MASTERS, MULTI-MILLIONAIRE HUNTER AND EXPLORER JUST ARRIVED IN TOWN, AND GET AN INTERVIEW.

OKAY!

--BUT WE STILL THINK YOU'RE PASSING UP A REALLY IMPORTANT STORY!

LATER-- AT THE MASTERS' MANSION....

YES--I'VE BAGGED MUCH BIG GAME IN MY TIME.

BIG GAME, DID YOU SAY? THAT'S A MATTER OF OPINION!

YOU WOULDN'T THINK IT SO BIG IF YOU KNEW WHAT WE KNOW!

YOU INTRIGUE ME. WHAT IS THIS BIG SECRET OF YOURS?

WE'VE HEARD THERE ARE GIGANTIC ANIMALS ON BARACODA ISLAND. THEY ARE BEING BRED THERE DELIBERATELY TO ATTACK THE WORLD.

AND WE'RE WRACKING OUR BRAINS TO THINK OF SOME WAY TO COMBAT THE MENACE

YOU INTEREST ME. I POSSESS A SUBMARINE. SUPPOSE WE WERE TO FORM A PARTY AND GO TO THIS BARACODA ISLAND AND SEE WHAT THERE IS TO SEE.

THAT WOULD BE TERRIFIC!

THEN IT'S SETTLED. WE'LL STOP BACK LATER, THEN WE'LL ALL GO TOGETHER TO THE GRANDVIEW HOTEL AND MEET BARNES.

LATER--AFTER TURNING IN THEIR STORY, THEY RETURN TO MASTERS' RESIDENCE AND ACCOMPANY THE FAMOUS EXPLORER TO THE GRANDVIEW HOTEL....

I HOPE THIS IS NOT A HOAX.

DON'T YOU WORRY ABOUT THAT.

WE'VE A LOT OF INTUITIVE CONFIDENCE IN BARNES.

BUT SHORTLY AFTER...

THAT'S ODD-- HE DOESN'T ANSWER!

BUT I'M SURE HE MUST BE IN.

BETTER CALL THE HOTEL MANAGER.

THE MANAGER ADMITS THEM INTO THE SUITE WITH A PASS-KEY....

LOOK! THERE ON THE FLOOR...

BARNES --!!

DEAD!!!

A DOCTOR IS SUMMONED. AFTER A BRIEF EXAMINATION...

YOU LOOK PUZZLED, DOCTOR!

AND WHY NOT? THIS MAN WAS POISONED!

THIS MAN DIED OF POISON ANTS SECRETING IN MINUTE QUANTITIES----YET HE RECEIVED A DOSE SO POWERFUL THAT IT WOULD HAVE TAKEN THOUSANDS OF ANTS TO ADMINISTER IT!!

THAT SEEMS TO INDICATE--A GIANT ANT -- THUS SUBSTANTIATING BARNES' STORY!

I'M GETTING A SUDDEN LACK OF INTEREST IN THIS CASE!

OH, NO, CLARK-- YOU'RE NOT GOING TO BACK OUT NOW! YOU AGREED AND YOU'RE GOING TO SEE THIS THING THRU!

A RELUCTANT BUT PUZZLED WHITE GIVES IN TO THEIR IMPORTUNITIES....

VERY WELL, YOU CAN GO OFF ON THIS WILD-GOOSE CHASE SINCE IT WON'T COST THE PLANET A CENT.

BUT IT'S NOT A WILD-GOOSE CHASE! WE'LL BRING BACK A STORY, PERRY, THAT WILL MAKE HISTORY!

--IF WE GET BACK!

D-DID YOU SAY --ER-- IF???

NEXT DAY....
IT'S TIME TO LEAVE -- AND STILL NO SIGN OF CLARK KENT. HAS YOUR FRIEND LOST HIS COURAGE AGAIN?

A CAB-- SPEEDING ONTO THE DOCK! PERHAPS CLARK'S IN IT!

IT'S CLARK ALL RIGHT--AND HE REQUIRES ASSISTANCE GETTING A LARGE TRUNK INTO THE SUB...

WHAT IN THE WORLD ARE YOU TAKING THAT ALONG FOR?

FOR CHANGE OF CLOTHES, NATURALLY! CLOTHES FOR ANY OCCASION!

YOU'D THINK HE WAS GOING ON A PLEASURE JAUNT!

THE SUBMARINE SETS OFF TO SEA AND SOON ENCOUNTERS HEAVY WEATHER....

OH- HH --MY HEAD! M-MIND IF I GO TO MY STATEROOM?

I'M AFRAID CLARK HAS A TOUCH OF SEA-SICKNESS!

HE WOULD!

ONCE IN HIS STATEROOM, CLARK DROPS HIS POSE OF SICKLINESS AND MAKES USE OF HIS X-RAY VISION....

SURE 'NOUGH--! WE'RE HEADED FOR TROUBLE!

A MOMENT LATER...THE SUB BECOMES WEDGED IN SOME ROCKS!

I HAD A HUNCH I MIGHT HAVE TO MAKE USE OF MY IDENTITY AS SUPERMAN-- THAT'S WHY I LEFT THE OTHERS.

OPENING THE LARGE TRUNK, SUPERMAN REVEALS A STRANGE MECHANISM OF HIS OWN INVENTION.... A MECHANISM WHICH ENABLES HIM TO ENTER OR LEAVE THE SUBMARINE THRU A LOCK ARRANGEMENT....!

I THOUGHT THIS MIGHT COME IN HANDY!

A MOMENT LATER. THE MAN OF TOMORROW IS THRU THE ENTRANCE AND OUT INTO THE WATER....

SEIZING THE SUB, SUPERMAN HEAVES--AND FREES IT FROM ITS HELPLESS POSITION....!

THERE! THAT DID IT!

RETURNING TO HIS STATEROOM, HE AGAIN DONS THE IDENTITY OF THE CRAVEN REPORTER...

CONCEALING THE OUTER ENTRANCE OF THE LOCK SO IT'S NOT VISIBLE IS A TICKLISH JOB-- BUT I'VE SUCCEEDED IN DOING IT!

⑤

REACHING SABRACODA, CENTER OF THE CODA ISLAND GROUP, THEY SEEK AUDIENCE WITH BILL GRIMES, TOUGH FORMER SAILOR WHO HAS SEIZED CONTROL OF THE ISLANDS....

BUT ALL WE WANT IS PERMISSION TO VISIT BARACODA ISLAND.

EXCLUSIVE RIGHTS TO APPROACH BARACODA HAVE ALREADY BEEN LEASED TO SOMEONE. -- YOU'VE ENTERED OUR WATERS UNINVITED -- SO WE HAVE THE RIGHT TO CONFISCATE YOUR SUBMARINE!

YOU CAN'T DO THAT TO US!

YOU HEARD VON HARBITZ! NOT ONLY THAT, BUT I ORDER ALL OF YOU IMPRISONED UNTIL YOU CAN BE DEPORTED BACK TO THE UNITED STATES!

DESPITE THEIR PROTESTS, MASTER S' PARTY AND HIS SAILORS ARE THROWN INTO CELLS...!

YOU'LL PAY FOR THIS OUTRAGE!

OUCH!

UNSEEN BY THE OTHERS, CLARK CHANGES TO SUPERMAN AND TWISTS THE BARS OF HIS CELL APART....

I HATE TO STAY LONG ON ONE SPOT!

TWISTING THE BARS BACK INTO SHAPE, HE ATTENDS TO THE GUARDS...!

ROCKABYE--!

UHH-HH!

SWIFTLY, HE FREES THE OTHERS FROM THEIR CELLS...

SUPERMAN!

WHERE'S CLARK?

I'VE ALREADY ATTENDED TO HIM. FOLLOW ME TO THE SUB... BUT TRY TO BE QUIET ABOUT IT!

LEAD ON!

BUT AS THE OTHERS STEAL ABOARD THE VESSEL, SUPERMAN'S X-RAY VISION REVEALS TO HIM...

WELL, WELL-- --A FAMILY CONFERENCE!

WHAT SUPERMAN SIGHTS--! WITHIN THE SUB, GRIMES AND VON HARBITZ PLOT....

THAT OUGHT TO KEEP THEM AWAY FROM THE ISLAND.

NOT ONLY THAT, BUT WE'VE GAINED A VALUABLE ADDITION TO OUR NAVY!

ALL IN ALL, GENTLEMEN, YOU'VE PUT OVER A PRETTY SLICK DEAL, EH?

WHAT--!

WHERE DID HE COME FROM?

WHAT'S MORE IMPORTANT IS WHERE YOU'RE GOING!

HELP!

6

SWIFTLY, SO FAST THAT THE OTHERS DO NOT SIGHT HIM, **SUPERMAN** STREAKS TO HIS CABIN, CHANGES TO CLARK KENT, THEN CONFRONTS THE OTHERS...

SO HE SAVED YOU, TOO!

WHEN **SUPERMAN** DOES A JOB, IT'S THOROUGH!

NO TIME FOR REUNION TALK NOW, CAPTAIN-- SHOVE OFF--AND I'D ADVISE **SPEED**!

BUT THE ANGERED MASTERS OF THE CODA ISLAND GROUP SEND ARMORED VESSELS IN SEARCH OF THE SUB WITH INSTRUCTIONS TO DESTROY IT...

I WANT THAT SUB BLASTED OUT OF THE WATER!

WE SHOULD QUICKLY OVERTAKE IT!

DESTROYERS IN PURSUIT--THAT CALLS FOR ANOTHER QUICK CHANGE TO **SUPERMAN**!

EMERGING FROM THE SUB, THE MAN OF STEEL SOARS UP...

THEY'RE PREPARING TO RELEASE DEPTH BOMBS!

THE BATTLE COMMENCES...!

LET 'ER GO!

SEIZING THE DEPTH BOMB, **SUPERMAN** SWIMS OFF WITH IT UNDERWATER AT GREAT SPEED...

NOW TO MAKE TRACKS!

...SO THAT IT EXPLODES A GREAT DISTANCE AWAY...!

SA-AAY! WHAT GOES ON HERE?

I--I CAN'T UNDER- STAND IT. IT COULD NOT HAVE DRIFTED SO FAR IN SO SHORT A SPACE OF TIME!

UNNOTICED, THE MAN OF TOMORROW SWARMS UP THE SIDE OF THE VESSEL....

IF MY PLAN WORKS --!!

FINDING A LARGE OIL CONTAINER ON BOARD THE VESSEL, **SUPERMAN** SPRINGS OVERBOARD WITH IT, ...

ONCE UNDERWATER, I'LL PUNCTURE IT!

LOOK! OIL-- ON THE WATER'S SURFACE!

WE'VE DESTROYED THE SUBMARINE! THAT WILL TEACH THEM IT DOESN'T PAY TO MEDDLE WITH BILL GRIMES!

BUT **SUPERMAN'S** TASK ISN'T COMPLETED. AS THE SUB NEARS *BARACODA* ISLAND, HE GUIDES IT THRU INTRICATE MINE FIELDS

SOMEONE CERTAINLY IS DETERMINED TO KEEP STRANGERS AWAY FROM THIS ISLAND AND FOR A GOOD REASON NO DOUBT!

UNEXPECTEDLY, A MONSTER OCTOPUS SEIZES THE UNDERSEA VESSEL IN ITS GREAT TENTACLES . . . !

SUPERMAN STREAKS TO THE ATTACK!

GOT TO GET IT OFF THE SUB BEFORE IT CRUSHES IT TO BITS!

A GIANT OCTOPUS--!

NOW DO YOU BELIEVE THAT STORY ABOUT GIANT ANIMALS?

THE OCTOPUS, MIGHTY THO ITS BULK, IS NO MATCH FOR THE MAN OF *STEEL'S* POWERFUL MUSCLES . . . .

NOW TO GET BACK INTO THE SUB AS CLARK KENT BEFORE THEY MISS ME!

8

AS THE SUBMARINE DOCKS, IT IS GREETED BY NONE OTHER THAN . . . .

WELCOME TO BARACODA ISLAND!

STEPHEN CARDINE!

("-AND WHAT A WELCOME! MINE FIELDS! A GIGANTIC OCTOPUS--!-")

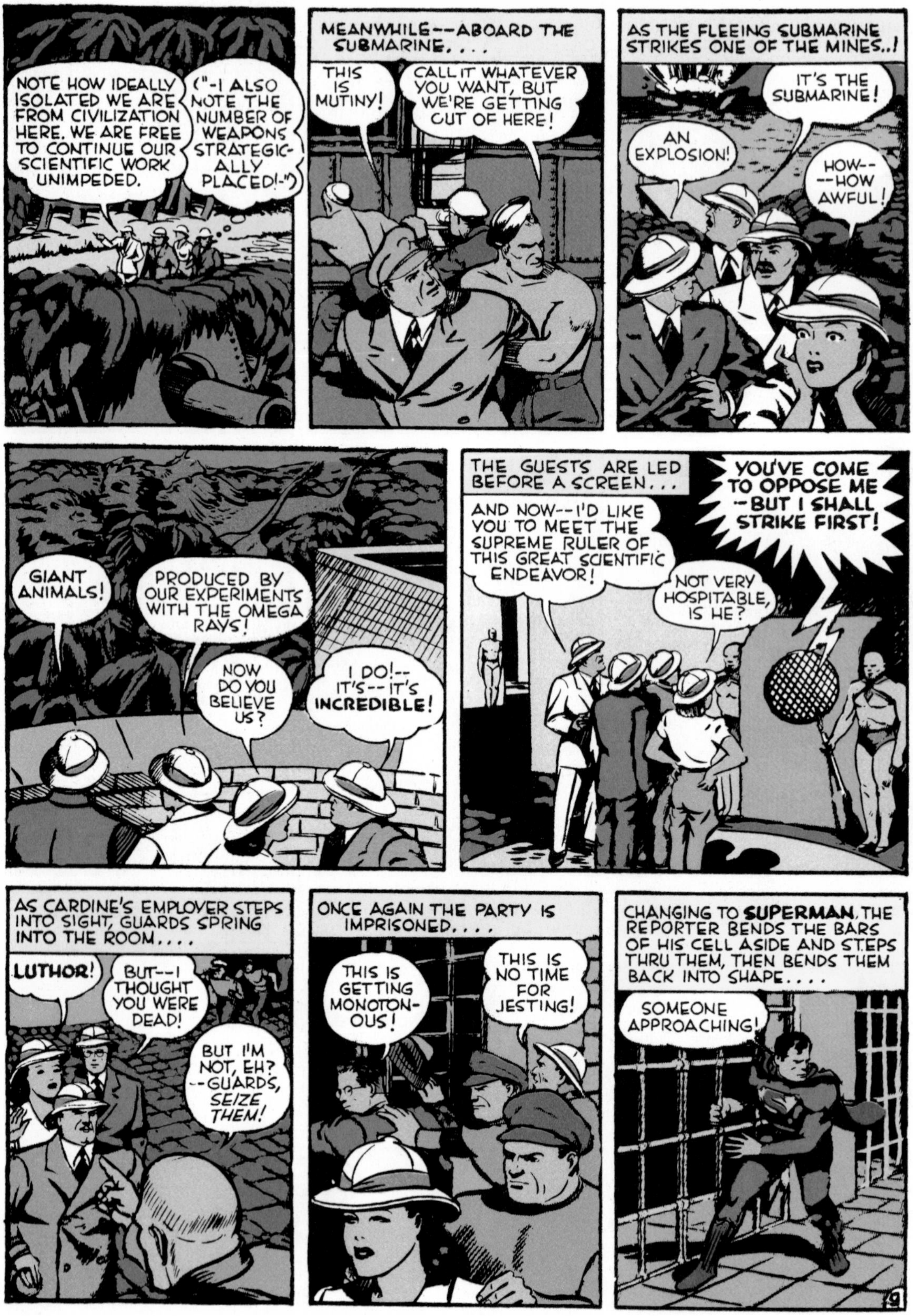
NOTE HOW IDEALLY ISOLATED WE ARE FROM CIVILIZATION HERE. WE ARE FREE TO CONTINUE OUR SCIENTIFIC WORK UNIMPEDED.
("-I ALSO NOTE THE NUMBER OF WEAPONS STRATEGIC-ALLY PLACED!-")
MEANWHILE--ABOARD THE SUBMARINE. . . .
THIS IS MUTINY!
CALL IT WHATEVER YOU WANT, BUT WE'RE GETTING OUT OF HERE!
AS THE FLEEING SUBMARINE STRIKES ONE OF THE MINES..!
AN EXPLOSION!
IT'S THE SUBMARINE!
HOW-- --HOW AWFUL!
GIANT ANIMALS!
PRODUCED BY OUR EXPERIMENTS WITH THE OMEGA RAYS!
NOW DO YOU BELIEVE US?
I DO!-- IT'S--IT'S INCREDIBLE!
THE GUESTS ARE LED BEFORE A SCREEN. . .
AND NOW--I'D LIKE YOU TO MEET THE SUPREME RULER OF THIS GREAT SCIENTIFIC ENDEAVOR!
YOU'VE COME TO OPPOSE ME --BUT I SHALL STRIKE FIRST!
NOT VERY HOSPITABLE, IS HE?
AS CARDINE'S EMPLOYER STEPS INTO SIGHT, GUARDS SPRING INTO THE ROOM. . . .
LUTHOR!
BUT--I THOUGHT YOU WERE DEAD!
BUT I'M NOT, EH? --GUARDS, SEIZE THEM!
ONCE AGAIN THE PARTY IS IMPRISONED. . . .
THIS IS GETTING MONOTON-OUS!
THIS IS NO TIME FOR JESTING!
CHANGING TO SUPERMAN, THE REPORTER BENDS THE BARS OF HIS CELL ASIDE AND STEPS THRU THEM, THEN BENDS THEM BACK INTO SHAPE. . . .
SOMEONE APPROACHING!
9

CARDINE FEELS A SUDDEN GUST OF WIND.

WHAT WAS THAT?

NEXT INSTANT....

QUIET--AND YOU WON'T BE HARMED!

TELL ME, CARDINE-- HOW CAN YOU WORK FOR A MAN OF LUTHOR'S EVIL CHARACTER?

SUPERMAN!--B-BUT IS HE EVIL? HE PICKED ME UP WHEN I WAS PENNILESS--GAVE ME THIS WONDERFUL OPPORTUNITY TO WORK UNDISTURBED--AND HAS PROMISED ME RULE OF THE SCIENTIFIC CIVILIZATION TO BE LAUNCHED.

IF LUTHOR IS AS INNOCENT AS YOU PAINT HIM, I SUPPOSE HE HAD NOTHING TO DO WITH BARNES' MURDER WITH THE POISON FROM A GIANT ANT?

LUTHOR TELLS ME HE RETURNED BARNES BACK SAFELY TO CIVILIZATION. I WON'T BELIEVE THAT LUTHOR IS THE VILLAIN YOU MAKE HIM OUT UNTIL I HAVE PROOF!

SNATCHING UP CARDINE, SUPERMAN WHISKS THE SCIENTIST OFF TO HIS LABORATORY, THEN....

WAIT HERE! I'LL GET THAT PROOF FOR YOU!

A MOMENT LATER, AS HE STREAKS ALONG THE CORRIDOR, SUPERMAN COMES FACE TO FACE WITH--

GRIMES AND VON HARBITZ!

SUPERMAN!

WHAT ARE YOU DOING HERE?

LUTHOR HAS PROMISED ME I CAN RULE THE CIVILIZATION-TO-COME!

HE CAN'T DO THAT!

THE CHISELER!

WITHIN CARDINE'S LABORATORY....

HE PROMISED THAT I WOULD BE THE RULER OF THE NEW WORLD!

YOU MEAN, HE PROMISED ME!

THERE'S YOUR PROOF, CARDINE!

THEN--LUTHOR LIED!

FOR SUPPOSEDLY INTELLIGENT MEN YOU CERTAINLY ARE GULLIBLE. CAN'T YOU SEE THAT LUTHOR WAS USING YOU AS PAWNS--PROMISING EACH OF YOU EVERYTHING--AND INTENDING TO GIVE YOU NOTHING? WILL YOU HELP ME SETTLE HIS HASH?

THE RAT!

YOU CAN COUNT ME IN!

WHAT A FOOL I'VE BEEN!

10

SUPERMAN FREES HIS FRIENDS FROM THEIR CELLS....

HOW CAN WE THANK YOU?

WHERE'S CLARK?

NO TIME TO ANSWER QUESTIONS. WE'VE GOT TO BREAK INTO LUTHOR'S LABORATORY.

AND I THOUGHT THE CREATION OF GIANT ANIMALS AN AMAZING FEAT!

YOU HAVEN'T SEEN ANYTHING REALLY STARTLING UNTIL YOU'VE SEEN SUPERMAN IN ACTION!

THERE! THAT ATTENDS TO THE DOOR!

QUICK! WHAT IS THE VITAL PART OF THIS APPARATUS?

THOSE GLOBES! SMASH THEM-- AND WITHOUT THE RAYS THEY EMANATE, THE GIANT ANIMALS WILL BE DEAD IN A FEW HOURS.

NO YOU DON'T!

ONE MOVE TOWARD ME AND I FIRE! GET AWAY FROM THOSE GLOBES!

PUT DOWN THAT GUN! ARE YOU MAD?

HE'S MERELY DROPPING HIS MASK!

I'VE A GREAT STAKE IN LUTHOR. I FINANCED HIM. IT WAS I WHO KILLED BARNES--AND WHEN IT APPEARED YOU WERE GROWING TOO CURIOUS FOR YOUR OWN GOOD, I BROUGHT YOU HERE SO THAT YOU WOULDN'T LIVE TO PLAGUE US.

GOOD WORK, MASTERS. SUPERMAN, EH?-- SEIZE HIM, MEN!

GIVING AN ORDER IS ONE THING-- HAVING IT CARRIED OUT IS ANOTHER.

THIS PARALYSIS GUN WILL STOP YOU!

LOOK OUT!

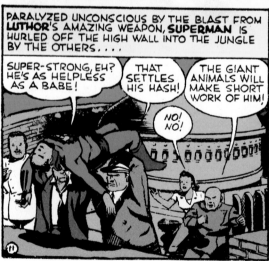

PARALYZED UNCONSCIOUS BY THE BLAST FROM LUTHOR'S AMAZING WEAPON, SUPERMAN IS HURLED OFF THE HIGH WALL INTO THE JUNGLE BY THE OTHERS....

SUPER-STRONG, EH? HE'S AS HELPLESS AS A BABE!

THAT SETTLES HIS HASH!

THE GIANT ANIMALS WILL MAKE SHORT WORK OF HIM!

NO! NO!

AS LUTHOR PRESSES A PROJECTING LEDGE, THE OTHERS FALL THRU A TRAP DOOR DOWN INTO THE JUNGLE AFTER SUPERMAN!

YAA-AAA!

AND THAT ATTENDS TO THEM! NOW-- ONLY YOU AND I REMAIN TO RULE THE NEW WORLD --TOGETHER!

YOU-- KILLER--!

LUTHOR'S FORMER ALLIES ARE RUTHLESSLY DESTROYED BY THE VORACIOUS MONSTERS....

FORCING LOIS INTO HIS LABORATORY, LUTHOR SURVEYS THE DESTRUCTION OF HIS VICTIMS THRU A TELEVISION SCREEN, BUT SUDDENLY THE RUTHLESS SCIENTIST GIVES A HOARSE CRY...

SUPERMAN-- REVIVING--!

I KNEW YOU WOULDN'T BE ABLE TO DISPOSE OF HIM!

DON'T BE TOO CERTAIN OF THAT! --OBSERVE THE MAN OF TOMORROW'S DESTRUCTION..!

A PORTION OF THE GREAT WALL COLLAPSES UPON SUPERMAN, HIDING HIS FIGURE FROM VIEW...

BUT INSTANTS LATER, THE MAN OF STEEL BURROWS HIS WAY FREE, UNHARMED....

SO HE'S STILL DETERMINED TO GET ME! WELL, THAT GOES BOTH WAYS!

IN CRASHES SUPERMAN THRU THE LABORATORY WALL, NEATLY DODGING THE RAY....

THAT WON'T WORK THIS TIME!

I'LL DESTROY US ALL!

SNATCHING UP LOIS, SUPERMAN LEAPS HIGH UP INTO THE SKY AS THE ENTIRE ISLAND BLOWS INTO SMITHEREENS....

THE END OF LUTHOR!

CLARK-- DESTROYED WITH THE OTHERS!

YOU NEEDN'T WORRY ABOUT YOUR WEAK-KNEED BOY-FRIEND. I'VE ALREADY TAKEN HIM TO A SAFE SPOT!

LOOK-- BELOW!

⑫

IT HAS TAKEN THE MAN OF TOMORROW ONLY MINUTES TO RETURN TO METROPOLIS. BELOW THEY SIGHT A BLOOD-FREEZING SIGHT. A GIANT MONSTER LURCHING OUT OF THE OCEAN AND ONTO SHORE...!

LUTHOR MUST HAVE DISPATCHED THIS MONSTER TOWARD *METROPOLIS* BEFORE THE OTHERS WERE DESTROYED. REMAIN HERE.

PLEASE BE CAREFUL!

THE GIANT CREATURE MOVES INEXORABLY TOWARD THE TERRIFIED CITY....

BUT STREAKING IN, SUPERMAN BRINGS THE HUGE MONSTROSITY DOWN IN A TACKLE...!

THIS IS THE END OF THE LINE FOR YOU!

MONSTER AND SUPERMAN LOCK IN DEADLY COMBAT

ABRUPTLY THE THING GOES LIMP AS ITS SPINE CRACKS BENEATH THE IRRESISTABLE STRENGTH OF *SUPERMAN'S* STEELY MUSCLES...!

THAT ATTENDS TO YOU!

A GIGANTIC TOSS--AND THE MONSTER FLIES INTO SPACE, TO PLUMMET DOWN INTO THE OCEAN A MILE AWAY AND SINK FROM VIEW...!

13

SUPERMAN LEAPS OFF LATER-- AS LOIS DASHES INTO THE *DAILY PLANET* EDITORIAL ROOM..

GIVE ME ROOM! WOW!--WHAT A STORY I'VE GOT!

YOU'RE NOT REFERRING TO THIS WRITE-UP BY ANY CHANCE?

SCOOPED AGAIN! I--I ALMOST WISH *SUPERMAN* HAD LEFT YOU BACK THERE ON *BARACODA ISLAND!*

THE END

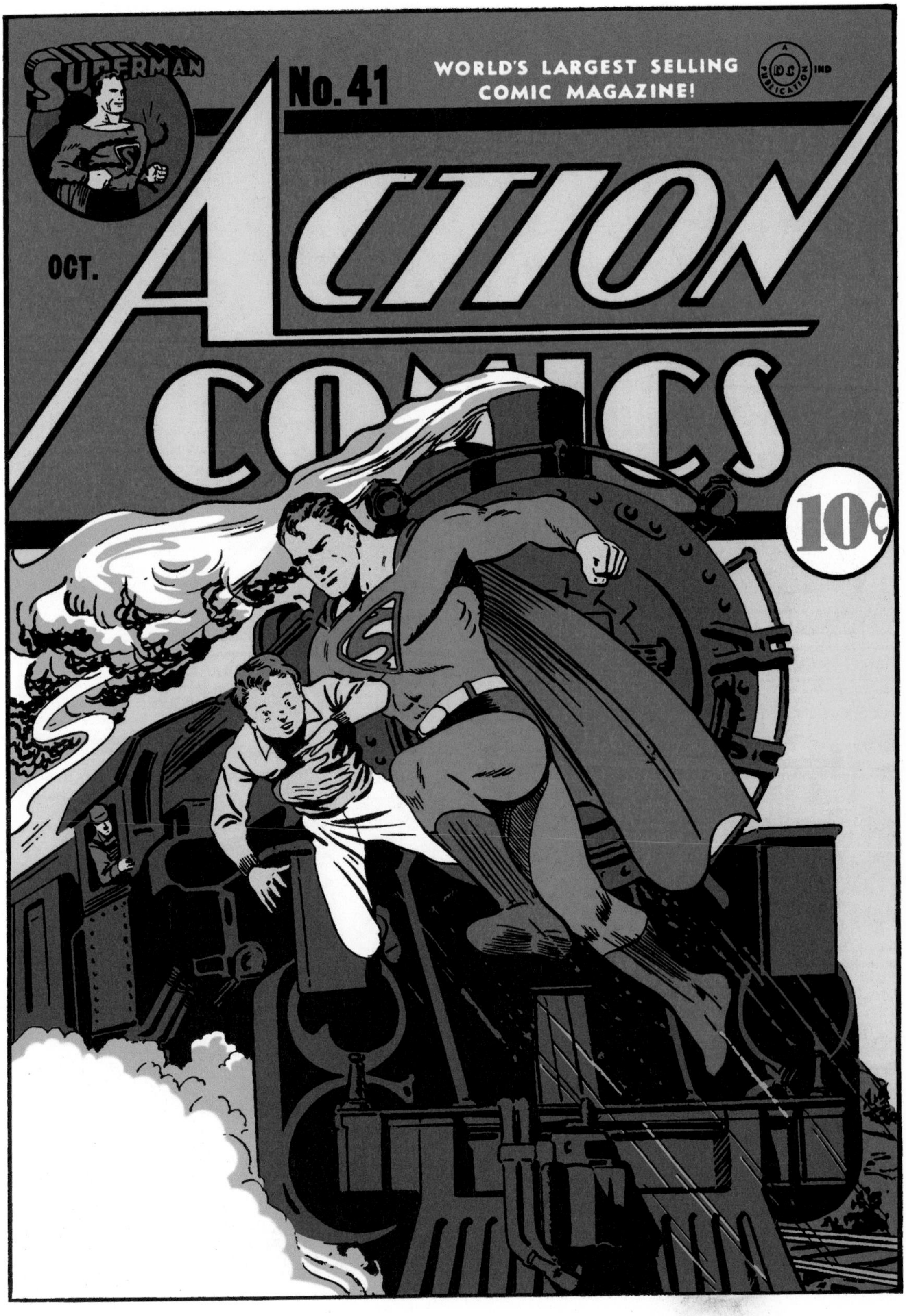
SUPERMAN
No. 41
WORLD'S LARGEST SELLING
COMIC MAGAZINE!
A DC PUBLICATION INC
OCT.
ACTION COMICS
10¢

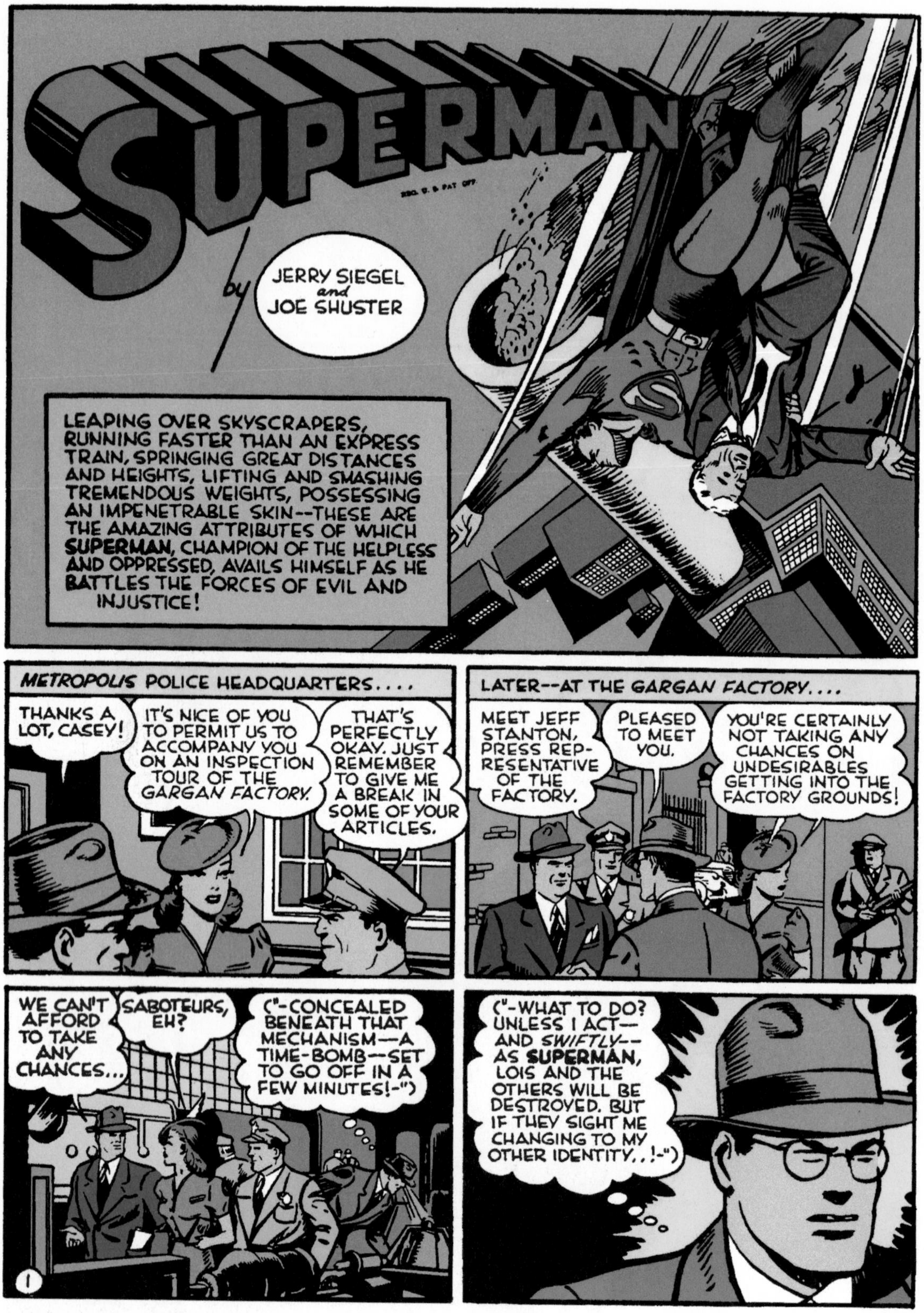
SUPERMAN
REG. U. S. PAT. OFF.
by JERRY SIEGEL and JOE SHUSTER
LEAPING OVER SKYSCRAPERS, RUNNING FASTER THAN AN EXPRESS TRAIN, SPRINGING GREAT DISTANCES AND HEIGHTS, LIFTING AND SMASHING TREMENDOUS WEIGHTS, POSSESSING AN IMPENETRABLE SKIN--THESE ARE THE AMAZING ATTRIBUTES OF WHICH SUPERMAN, CHAMPION OF THE HELPLESS AND OPPRESSED, AVAILS HIMSELF AS HE BATTLES THE FORCES OF EVIL AND INJUSTICE!
METROPOLIS POLICE HEADQUARTERS....
THANKS A LOT, CASEY!
IT'S NICE OF YOU TO PERMIT US TO ACCOMPANY YOU ON AN INSPECTION TOUR OF THE GARGAN FACTORY.
THAT'S PERFECTLY OKAY. JUST REMEMBER TO GIVE ME A BREAK IN SOME OF YOUR ARTICLES.
LATER--AT THE GARGAN FACTORY....
MEET JEFF STANTON, PRESS REPRESENTATIVE OF THE FACTORY.
PLEASED TO MEET YOU.
YOU'RE CERTAINLY NOT TAKING ANY CHANCES ON UNDESIRABLES GETTING INTO THE FACTORY GROUNDS!
WE CAN'T AFFORD TO TAKE ANY CHANCES...
SABOTEURS, EH?
("-CONCEALED BENEATH THAT MECHANISM--A TIME-BOMB--SET TO GO OFF IN A FEW MINUTES!-")
1
("-WHAT TO DO? UNLESS I ACT--AND SWIFTLY--AS SUPERMAN, LOIS AND THE OTHERS WILL BE DESTROYED. BUT IF THEY SIGHT ME CHANGING TO MY OTHER IDENTITY..!-")

NOISELESSLY, CLARK DROPS BACK OUT OF THE VIEW OF THE OTHERS....

THIS CALLS FOR QUICK ACTION...

RAPIDLY, THE *DAILY PLANET* REPORTER REMOVES HIS OUTER GARMENTS, REVEALING THE COLORFUL COSTUME BENEATH....

IT'S MORE THAN A CO-INCIDENCE THAT CLARK KENT IS NEVER AROUND WHEN **SUPERMAN** MAKES HIS APPEARANCE. ONE OF THESE DAYS, LOIS IS GOING TO PUT TWO AND TWO TOGETHER...

WHERE'S CLARK?

LOST AS USUAL, NO DOUBT.

KEEP WALKING. HE'LL SOON CATCH UP.

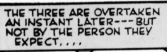

THE THREE ARE OVERTAKEN AN INSTANT LATER--- BUT NOT BY THE PERSON THEY EXPECT....

SUPERMAN! WHAT ARE YOU DOING HERE?

YOU'LL SEE IN A MOMENT!

WHAT I CAN'T UNDERSTAND IS HOW HE GOT IN!

LEAPING AT THE MECHANISM, **SUPERMAN** COMMENCES TO TEAR UP PART OF THE FLOOR...

HE'LL WRECK THE PLANT!

GUARDS! GUARDS!

IN RESPONSE TO STANTON'S SHOUTS, COMPANY GUARDS DASH ONTO THE SCENE AND ATTEMPT TO DIVERT **SUPERMAN** FROM HIS TASK....

WE CAN'T BUDGE HIM!

LET HIM ALONE-- I'M SURE HE KNOWS WHAT HE'S DOING!

YOU SEE--? A BOMB-- SET TO GO OFF IN A FEW SECONDS...

A BOMB!

GET RID OF IT!

②

OUT THRU A WINDOW AND UP INTO THE AIR HURTLES THE *MAN OF STEEL*....

GOT TO COVER TERRITORY!

NEXT MOMENT...

NO SIGN OF **SUPERMAN!**

HE MUST HAVE BLOWN TO BITS!

NOT *HIM!*

BUT AN INSTANT BEFORE THE FORCE OF THE EXPLOSION COULD STRIKE HIM, **SUPERMAN** HAD PLUMMETED DOWNWARD...

CONVENIENT TO BE ABLE TO STREAK SO FAST--IT PROTECTS ME FROM PRYING EYES...

BACK TO CLARK KENT ONCE MORE!

I--I HEARD THE EXPLOSION --**WHAT HAPPENED** --???

YOU MEAN-- WHAT **DIDN'T** HAPPEN...

SUPERMAN DISCOVERED A BOMB IN TIME TO PREVENT ALL OF US FROM BEING BLOWN TO BITS!

THAT BOMB WAS PLANTED DELIBERATELY! BUT HOW ANYONE COULD HAVE GOT PAST THE GUARDS IS BEYOND ME!

UNLESS, OF COURSE, IT WAS AN INSIDE JOB. MAY I FIND OUT WHAT WORKMEN WERE ABSENT FROM WORK TODAY?

I THINK THE SERGEANT'S GOT SOMETHING THERE!

MISSING TODAY WERE BILL BOWSWORTH, HYMAN CHANDLER, AND STEVE GRANT.

THANKS. NOW MAY I HAVE THEIR ADDRESSES, PLEASE?

LOOKS LIKE WE'VE STUMBLED ONTO A REAL STORY!

NICE FELLOW! YOU DRIVE US HERE--THEN DROP US LIKE HOT-CAKES...

SORRY--CAN'T LET YOU COME WITH ME NOW -- OFFICIAL BUSINESS...

SO LONG, LOIS. YOU CAN TURN IN THE STORY WHILE I GET SOME IMPORTANT SHOPPING DONE.

POLICE

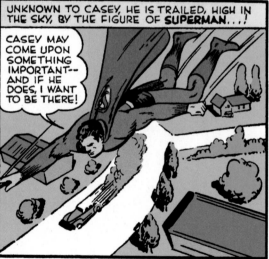

UNKNOWN TO CASEY, HE IS TRAILED, HIGH IN THE SKY, BY THE FIGURE OF **SUPERMAN...!**

CASEY MAY COME UPON SOMETHING IMPORTANT-- AND IF HE DOES, I WANT TO BE THERE!

③

LATER....

AS YOU CAN SEE, BILL BOWSWORTH IS SERIOUSLY ILL. I CAN VOUCH FOR IT THAT HE HASN'T LEFT HIS BED FOR DAYS.

I'LL TAKE YOUR WORD FOR IT, DOC!

THAT RULES OUT BOWSWORTH!

HYMAN CHANDLER? IF YOU WANT TO FIND HIM, YOU'LL HAVE TO TAKE A TRAIN FOR NIAGARA FALLS. THAT'S WHERE HE'S HEADED FOR. YOU SEE, HE WAS MARRIED THIS MORNING!

I WON'T BOTHER HIM. IF HE JUST GOT MARRIED, HE'LL HAVE ENOUGH TROUBLES AS IT IS.

STEVE GRANT--THE FINAL SUSPECT... IT BEGINS TO LOOK AS THO THE SERGEANT AND I HAVE EMBARKED ON A WILD-GOOSE CHASE!

AT GRANT'S HOME, THE DOOR CAUTIOUSLY OPENS AS CASEY KNOCKS VIGOROUSLY....

I SAID, OPEN UP, GRANT!

AS GRANT ATTEMPTS TO SLAM THE DOOR, CASEY ACTS....

NO YOU DON'T!

THIS MAY PROVE INTERESTING!

④

SO WHAT IF I DIDN'T SHOW UP TO WORK TODAY? I FELT LIKE TAKING THE DAY OFF, DO ME SOMETHING!

IF YOU'RE AS INNOCENT AS YOU PRETEND, YOU WON'T MIND MY SEARCHING THE PLACE.

AS CASEY SYSTEMATICALLY SEARCHES THE PREMISES...

KEEP AWAY FROM THAT CLOSET!

ONE SIDE!

WELL--! SO YOU JUST WANTED TO TAKE THE DAY OFF, EH?

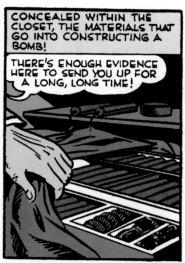

CONCEALED WITHIN THE CLOSET, THE MATERIALS THAT GO INTO CONSTRUCTING A BOMB!

THERE'S ENOUGH EVIDENCE HERE TO SEND YOU UP FOR A LONG, LONG TIME!

YOU'LL NEVER GET ME!

THE COP FOUND THE BOMB-MAKING MATERIALS--WHAT'LL I DO WITH HIM?

DISPOSE OF HIM, NATURALLY, THEN-- GO TO THE "USUAL PLACE"!

SEND ME TO THE PENITENTIARY, EH? THAT'S WHAT YOU THINK, COPPER!

AND THAT FINISHES YOU!

NOW TO PUT PLENTY OF DISTANCE BETWEEN ME AND THAT DEAD COP!

5

SIGHTING THE SERGEANT'S BODY FALLING OUT THE WINDOW, **SUPERMAN** INSTANTLY HAD SPRUNG INTO ACTION....

GOOD THING FOR YOU, CASEY, I TAGGED ALONG!

CAUGHT YOU!

GOT TO LEAVE YOU NOW--!

GRANT'S CAR--AHEAD!

SUDDENLY AN AUTO SWERVES OUT OF A SIDE STREET TOWARD STEVE GRANT'S MACHINE-- A DISASTROUS COLLISION IS **CERTAIN...!**

RACING IN SO SWIFTLY THAT THE HUMAN EYE CANNOT FOLLOW, **SUPERMAN** SEIZES THE SIDE OF GRANT'S CAR AND QUICKLY TURNS IT SO THAT IT FACES THE OPPOSITE DIRECTION...

YOU'RE TOO VALUABLE TO ME TO BE PERMITTED TO DIE!

GRANT'S CAR TURNS SAFELY ASIDE, THE COLLISION NARROW-LY AVERTED....

WHAT AMAZING LUCK! IF I HADN'T SKIDDED COMPLETELY ABOUT WHEN I DID... I....I'D HAVE **CRASHED**

LATER...

THERE HE GOES --INTO THE APPOINTED PLACE... NOW TO KEEP HIM UNDER CLOSE SURVEILLANCE!

WHAT **SUPERMAN'S** AMAZING X-RAY VISION DISCLOSES....

I WISH SOMETHING WOULD *HAPPEN*-- THERE GOES THE TELEPHONE BELL..!

YOU'VE OUT-LIVED YOUR USEFULNESS, GRANT--THOSE WHO FUMBLE MISERABLY-- DIE!

NO-- NO-- SPARE ME...!

WHA-- --???

WE'VE GOT TO GET OUT OF HERE!

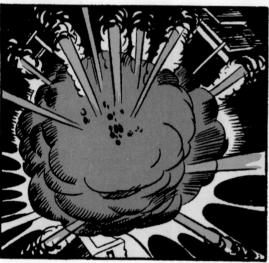

WE BARELY MADE IT IN TIME!

G-G-GULP..!!

YOU PLANTED THAT BOMB IN THE GARGAN FACTORY! WHY?

I--I'M AFRAID TO TELL YOU. THE BOSS IS TOUGH ON SQUEALERS!

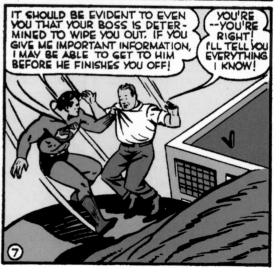

IT SHOULD BE EVIDENT TO EVEN YOU THAT YOUR BOSS IS DETER-MINED TO WIPE YOU OUT. IF YOU GIVE ME IMPORTANT INFORMATION, I MAY BE ABLE TO GET TO HIM BEFORE HE FINISHES YOU OFF!

YOU'RE --YOU'RE RIGHT! I'LL TELL YOU EVERYTHING I KNOW!

⑦

I WAS HIRED TO DESTROY PRODUCTION IN THAT PLANT.

THAT'S OBVIOUS. CAN YOU TELL ME **WHO** YOUR BOSS IS-- AND *WHY* HE WANTED THAT FACTORY CRIPPLED...?

ALL I KNOW IS THAT HE IS DOING EVERYTHING HE CAN TO HALT THIS COUNTRY'S NATIONAL DEFENSE EFFORT. WHO HE IS--I DON'T KNOW. WE ONLY KNOW HIS VOICE-- AS HEARD OVER THE TELEPHONE.

THAT'S NOT MUCH HELP. I'D BETTER SEE THAT YOU GO WHERE YOU'LL BE SAFE FROM YOUR BOSS' VENGEANCE.

MEANWHILE...

OH--HHH, MY HEAD!-- SA-AAY! HOW'D I EVER GET **HERE?**

HERE'S YOUR PRISONER, CASEY!

STEVE GRANT! I SEE! HE TRIED TO ESCAPE FROM ME, AND YOU BROUGHT HIM BACK.-- THANKS!

YOU'RE LUCKY, COPPER! THAT FALL SHOULD HAVE KILLED YOU!

SUPERMAN SPRINGS OFF-- LATER THAT DAY--NEWSPAPER HEADLINES PROCLAIM GRANT'S CAPTURE....

DAILY PLAN

BRAVE POLICE SERGEANT CAPTURES SABOTEUR

STEVE GRANT   SERGEANT CASEY

EDITORIAL OFFICE OF THE *DAILY PLANET*....

I WANT YOU AND LOIS TO GO DOWN TO THE JAIL AT ONCE AND TRY TO INTERVIEW GRANT.

ER--DO YOU THINK IT'S NECESSARY?

NO TIME FOR ONE OF YOUR DISPLAYS OF NERVOUS-NESS, CLARK! LET'S GO!

LATER--AT THE JAIL...

ER--YOU'RE *SURE* YOU HAVEN'T ANYTHING TO QUOTE FOR THE PRESS?

POSITIVE! NOW LET ME ALONE!

CLARK'S X-RAY VISION TREATS HIM TO A STARTLING SIGHT...

("--A GUN-- HIDDEN UP HIS SLEEVE!--")

AS THE NEARBY MAN SWIFTLY DRAWS HIS GUN, CLARK STUMBLES AGAINST HIM, APPARENTLY ACCIDENTALLY...

UH-HH! P-PARDON ME--!

...SO THAT THE BULLET, AIMED AT GRANT, NARROWLY MISSES ITS TARGET...!

GRAB HIM!

WATCH OUT! HE'S GOT A GUN!

DISARM HIM!

WHY DID YOU WANT TO KILL GRANT?

IT'S OBVIOUS. HE'S A MEMBER OF THE SAME GANG AS GRANT-- THEY'RE DETERMINED TO RUB HIM OUT!

I'LL TELL YOU NOTHING!

WHERE TO, LOIS?

A TELEPHONE-- WE'VE GOT TO RUSH IN THIS STORY!

THAT EVENING..., IN A TREE NEAR THE CITY JAIL....

I'VE A HUNCH THEY MAY TRY TO GET GRANT AGAIN, AND IF THEY DO, I'LL BE WAITING!

LATER--AN ARMORED CAR WHIZZES AROUND A CORNER AND HEADS STRAIGHT FOR GRANT'S CELL....

IN THRU THE WALL IT CRASHES...!

9

GET IN THERE!

NO!-- DON'T DO THIS TO ME --DON'T!

HURRY!

A MOMENT LATER--OFF SPEEDS THE ARMORED CAR WITH THE POLICE CARS HOT IN PURSUIT...

SUPERMAN LEAPS THRU THE SKY, KEEPING THE ESCAPING AUTO IN SIGHT....

THE ARMORED CAR SKIDS TO A STOP. ONE OF THE THUGS JUMPS OUT, TOSSES A DETOUR SIGN INTO SOME BUSHES. THEN THE CAR DRIVES ON, INTO A ROAD THAT BRANCHES OFF...

THAT'LL FIX 'EM!

THE POLICE-CARS STREAK STRAIGHT ONTO THE ROAD THAT HAD BEEN BLOCKED OFF....

...UNAWARE OF THE DANGER AHEAD....

DOWN BEFORE THE FOREMOST POLICE-CAR DROPS THE *MAN OF TOMORROW*...

THEY'VE GOT TO STOP **RIGHT HERE!**

PITTING HIS STRENGTH AGAINST THE AUTO, **SUPERMAN** FORCES IT TO A STOP....

WHAT'S THE IDEA?

A SHORT DISTANCE AHEAD-- THE ROAD-- WASHED OUT...!

NO SIGN OF THE ARMORED CAR! IT--IT'S VANISHED!

THE *MAN OF STEEL'S* SUPER-SENSITIVE EARS PICK UP A RADIO NEWS FLASH....

THE STATE HAS BEEN STUNNED BY AN INCREASING WAVE OF SABOTAGE WITHIN THE LAST HOUR!

THEY'RE STRIKING EVEN MORE BOLDLY! THIS HAS GOT TO *STOP!*

BEHIND THAT HUGE ROCK-- THE FAINT SOUND OF VOICES...!

SUPERMAN AVAILS HIMSELF AGAIN OF HIS X-RAY VISION...

WHAT THE *MAN OF TOMORROW* SEES....

DON'T SHOOT ME-- PLEASE!

BEGGING WON'T DO YOU ANY GOOD!

WE'RE ONLY FOLLOWING THE BOSS' ORDERS--HE WON'T STAND FOR BUNGLING!

IT'S--!

SUPER-MAN! SAVE ME!

IN A MOMENT!

HUH?

THE *MAN OF STEEL* OVER-COMES HIS OPPONENTS INSTANTLY....

THIS IS *TOO* EASY!

SPEAK UP! --WHAT DEVILTRY DOES YOUR BOSS PLAN NEXT?

THE *DAILY PLANET!* HE'S GONNA BLOW IT UP BECAUSE IT'S BEEN TOO OUTSPOKEN AGAINST THE WAVE OF SABOTAGE!

SHORTLY AFTER--**SUPERMAN** DUMPS THE SABOTEURS BEFORE THE POLICE STATION....

SOME MORE PRISONERS FOR YOU, CASEY!

GOSH! WHAT WE WOULDN'T GIVE TO HAVE YOU ON THE POLICE FORCE!

ON TO THE *DAILY PLANET!*

AT THE NEWSPAPER OFFICE...

I'VE COME TO REPAIR THE TELEPHONE. WHERE IS IT?

IN THE NEXT ROOM. ("–ODD! I'M POSITIVE THERE'S NOTHING WRONG WITH THE TELEPHONE!–")

SUSPICIOUS, LOIS TRAILS THE ELECTRICIAN....

HE'S PLANTING ...A BOMB!

SNOOPING, EH?-- YOU'LL BE SORRY!

LET GO OF ME!

LOIS IS LEFT BOUND AND GAGGED TO WATCH THE SPUTTERING FUSE IN HELPLESS TERROR....

ANOTHER SECOND OR TWO, AND...

IN THRU THE WINDOW STREAKS SUPERMAN....

NOT A MOMENT TO SPARE! THERE--THAT MAKES IT HARMLESS!

WHAT HAPPENED?

SOMEONE-- POSING AS AN ELECTRICIAN-- PLACED THE BOMB HERE. IF YOU HURRY, WE MAY OVERTAKE HIM!

THERE HE GOES-- INTO THAT BUILDING!

GOOD GIRL!

ENTERING AN OFFICE, THE "ELECTRICIAN" REMOVES HIS GRIMY GARMENTS AND SUBSTITUTES THEM FOR IMMACULATE CLOTHES....

NO ONE WOULD EVER SUSPECT THE ULTRA-RESPECTABLE RALPH COWAN OF ENGAGING IN SABOTAGE FOR CASH! I'LL LOSE NO TIME IN SIGNALING MY HENCHMEN TO LAUNCH THE SWEEPING DESTRUCTION WE'VE PLANNED!

12

SURE ABOUT THAT?

SUPERMAN!

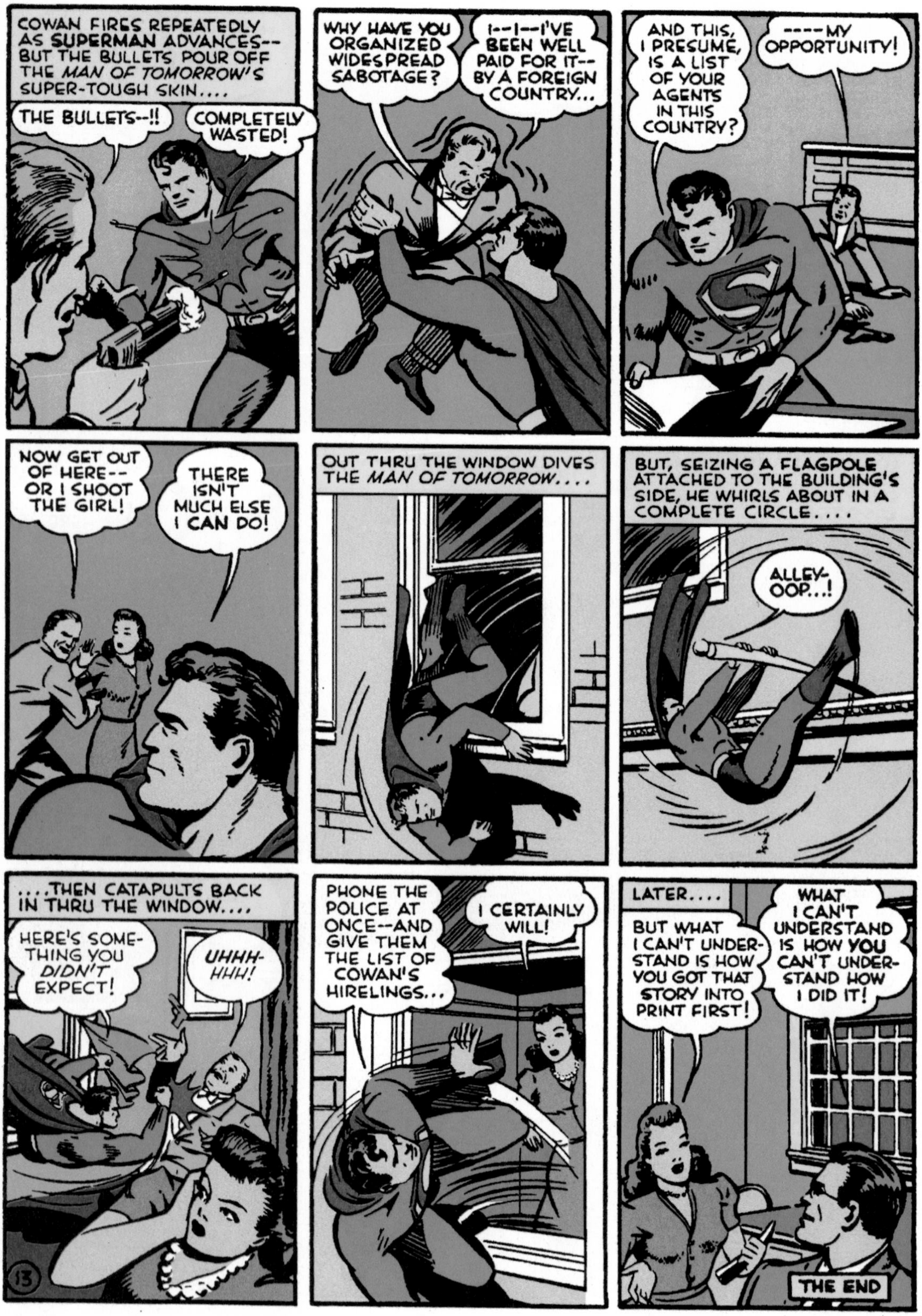
COWAN FIRES REPEATEDLY AS SUPERMAN ADVANCES--BUT THE BULLETS POUR OFF THE MAN OF TOMORROW'S SUPER-TOUGH SKIN....
THE BULLETS--!!
COMPLETELY WASTED!
WHY HAVE YOU ORGANIZED WIDESPREAD SABOTAGE?
I--I--I'VE BEEN WELL PAID FOR IT--BY A FOREIGN COUNTRY...
AND THIS, I PRESUME, IS A LIST OF YOUR AGENTS IN THIS COUNTRY?
----MY OPPORTUNITY!
NOW GET OUT OF HERE--OR I SHOOT THE GIRL!
THERE ISN'T MUCH ELSE I CAN DO!
OUT THRU THE WINDOW DIVES THE MAN OF TOMORROW....
BUT, SEIZING A FLAGPOLE ATTACHED TO THE BUILDING'S SIDE, HE WHIRLS ABOUT IN A COMPLETE CIRCLE....
ALLEY-OOP...!
....THEN CATAPULTS BACK IN THRU THE WINDOW....
HERE'S SOMETHING YOU DIDN'T EXPECT!
UHHH-HHH!
13
PHONE THE POLICE AT ONCE--AND GIVE THEM THE LIST OF COWAN'S HIRELINGS...
I CERTAINLY WILL!
LATER....
BUT WHAT I CAN'T UNDERSTAND IS HOW YOU GOT THAT STORY INTO PRINT FIRST!
WHAT I CAN'T UNDERSTAND IS HOW YOU CAN'T UNDERSTAND HOW I DID IT!
THE END

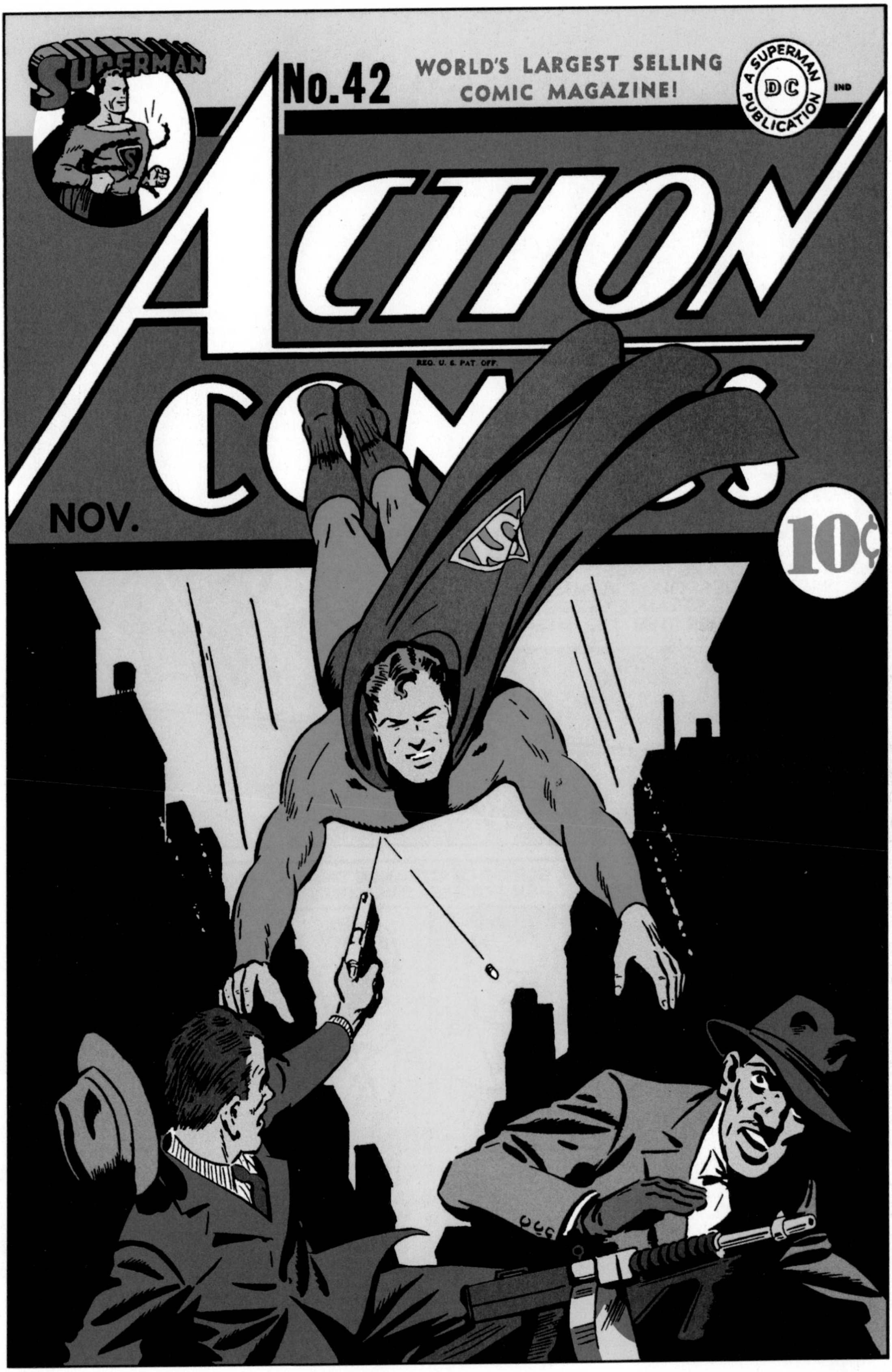
SUPERMAN
No.42
WORLD'S LARGEST SELLING
COMIC MAGAZINE!
A SUPERMAN
DC
PUBLICATION
ACTION
REG. U. S. PAT. OFF.
COMICS
NOV.
10¢

SUPERMAN

by JERRY SIEGEL and JOE SHUSTER

ALWAYS ON THE ALERT TO HELP SOMEONE IN NEED IS **SUPERMAN**, AMAZING *MAN OF STEEL*. WHEN A NUMBER OF THE WORLD'S MOST POWERFUL INTELLECTUALS SUDDENLY VANISH FROM SIGHT, HE HAS EVIDENCE TO BELIEVE THAT THEY ARE IN NEED OF HIS AID, AND WHEN HE RESPONDS HE HAS ABSOLUTELY NO IDEA OF THE STRANGE SERIES OF STARTLING ADVENTURES THAT LIE AHEAD!

A SERIES OF STRANGE DISAPPEARANCES OF PROMINENT MEN PUZZLES THE CITIZENS OF *METROPOLIS*....

CARL BRANSOM, LECTURER, SCIENTIST, DOESN'T SHOW UP AT A MEETING...

NICK FLAHERTY'S CAR IS FOUND SMASHED, BUT THERE IS NO SIGN OF THE FAMOUS WRITER...

POLITICAL BOSS JOHN STANDING DOESN'T RETURN HOME...

CAPITALIST FREEMAN CHASE FAILS TO APPEAR AT A BOARD MEETING...

①

EDITORIAL OFFICE OF THE *DAILY PLANET*...

CLARK, THIS ARTICLE YOU WROTE INTERESTS ME!

IT'S MY CONTENTION, CHIEF, THAT THESE MEN AREN'T THE VICTIMS OF AN ORDINARY KIDNAPPING BECAUSE THO THEY'VE BEEN MISSING FOR WEEKS, NO RANSOM NOTES HAVE BEEN RECEIVED.

YOU MAY HAVE SOMETHING THERE, CLARK, AND IF YOU CAN GET AT THE TRUTH, WE'D HAVE A REALLY IMPORTANT STORY!

A NEWS FLASH ON THE TELETYPE!

CARL BRANSOM'S FAMILY HAVE RECEIVED A RANSOM DEMAND FOR $50,000!

THAT KIND OF KNOCKS MY THEORY INTO A COCKED HAT... BUT I'LL COVER THIS LEAD!

BUT WHEN CLARK REACHES THE BRANSOM RESIDENCE...

SORRY... NO REPORTERS ARE BEING ADMITTED!

HE DIDN'T BELIEVE US!

CASEY'S IN THERE! IF WE ONLY KNEW WHAT WAS BEING SAID!

("-BUT *I* CAN HEAR WHAT'S GOING ON INSIDE THE HOUSE! MY SUPER-SENSITIVE HEARING HAS COME IN HANDY MORE THAN ONCE!-")

WHAT KENT OVERHEARS...

I INSIST THAT I BE PERMITTED TO PLACE THAT $50,000 UNDER THE CAREY BRIDGE! MY HUSBAND'S SAFETY COMES FIRST!

WHATEVER YOU SAY, MRS. BRANSOM, BUT THOSE KIDNAPPERS WON'T KEEP THAT MONEY LONG IF I CAN HELP IT!

LATER... THE MEEK REPORTER REMOVES HIS CIVILIAN GARMENTS, TRANSFORMING HIMSELF TO DYNAMIC SUPERMAN!

MEETING THAT KIDNAPPER IS GOING TO BE A PLEASURE— BUT I DOUBT IF THE FEELING WILL BE MUTUAL!

IN A GREAT LEAP THAT CARRIES THE *MAN OF STEEL* HIGH INTO THE CLOUDS, **SUPERMAN** IS ON HIS WAY TO THE RENDEZVOUS....

CAREY BRIDGE, EH? I SEEM TO RECALL A CERTAIN LARGE TREE NEAR IT THAT OUGHT TO PROVE A PERFECT HIDING-PLACE!

ALIGHTING ON A HIGH LIMB, **SUPERMAN** MAKES HIMSELF COMFORTABLE....

NOW TO WAIT!

UNDER THE *MAN OF STEEL'S* SURVEILLANCE, MRS. BRANSOM PLACES A SMALL SATCHEL BENEATH THE BRIDGE, THEN JUST AS SWIFTLY HURRIES OFF.

SHORTLY AFTER, A HARD-FACED INDIVIDUAL DRIVES UP AND ANNEXES THE SUITCASE....

GOOD... I KNEW SHE WOULDN'T DARE REFUSE!

BUT AS THE MAN DRIVES OFF WITH THE LOOT, **SUPERMAN** LEAPS DOWN AFTER HIS CAR...

HERE'S WHERE WE GET ACQUAINTED!

SEIZING THE AUTO'S REAR BUMPER, **SUPERMAN** DRAGS IT TO A STOP....

THIS IS MORE FUN THAN BULLDOGGING A STEER!

EASILY, HE KICKS THE REAR TIRES CLEAR OFF...

JUST TO MAKE SURE HE'LL STICK AROUND!

WHAT'S TH' IDEA OF.... OH-MY-GOSH! IT'S-- S-SUPERMAN!!

*THAT'S RIGHT! AND NOW, I'D LIKE TO KNOW WHO **YOU** ARE!*

M-ME? I-- I'M JAKE MOBRAY.

HI' YA, JAKE!

NOW LOOK, JAKE! YOU SEEM TO BE IN PRETTY GOOD PHYSICAL CONDITION. IT WOULD BE A PITY IF I HAD TO PULVERIZE YOU TO GET THE INFORMATION I'M AFTER.

D-DON'T HIT ME! I-I'M A SICK MAN. I'LL TELL YOU EVERYTHING!

THAT'S BETTER. NOW-- HOW DID YOU HAPPEN TO PICK UP THAT RANSOM, AND-- WHERE'S BRANSOM?

I-I'M A MEMBER OF THE DIRK CHADWICK MOB. THE BOSS TOLD ME WHERE TO GO FOR THE DOUGH, BUT WHERE BRANSOM IS, I -- I DON'T KNOW!

DO YOU EXPECT ME TO BELIEVE THAT?

I...! I...!

AT THAT MOMENT A GREAT RAY SIZZLES DOWN FROM ABOVE...!

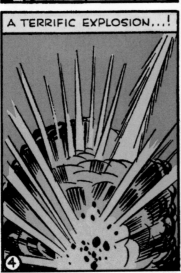

A TERRIFIC EXPLOSION...!

AND **SUPERMAN** ALONE SURVIVES...!

NO SIGN OF JAKE! HE WAS BLOWN **CLEAR TO BITS!** -- WHERE DID THAT RAY COME FROM?

NOTHING OVERHEAD! BUT THAT INCREDIBLY DESTRUCTIVE RAY COULDN'T HAVE MATERIALIZED OUT OF EMPTY SPACE-- **OR COULD IT?!!**

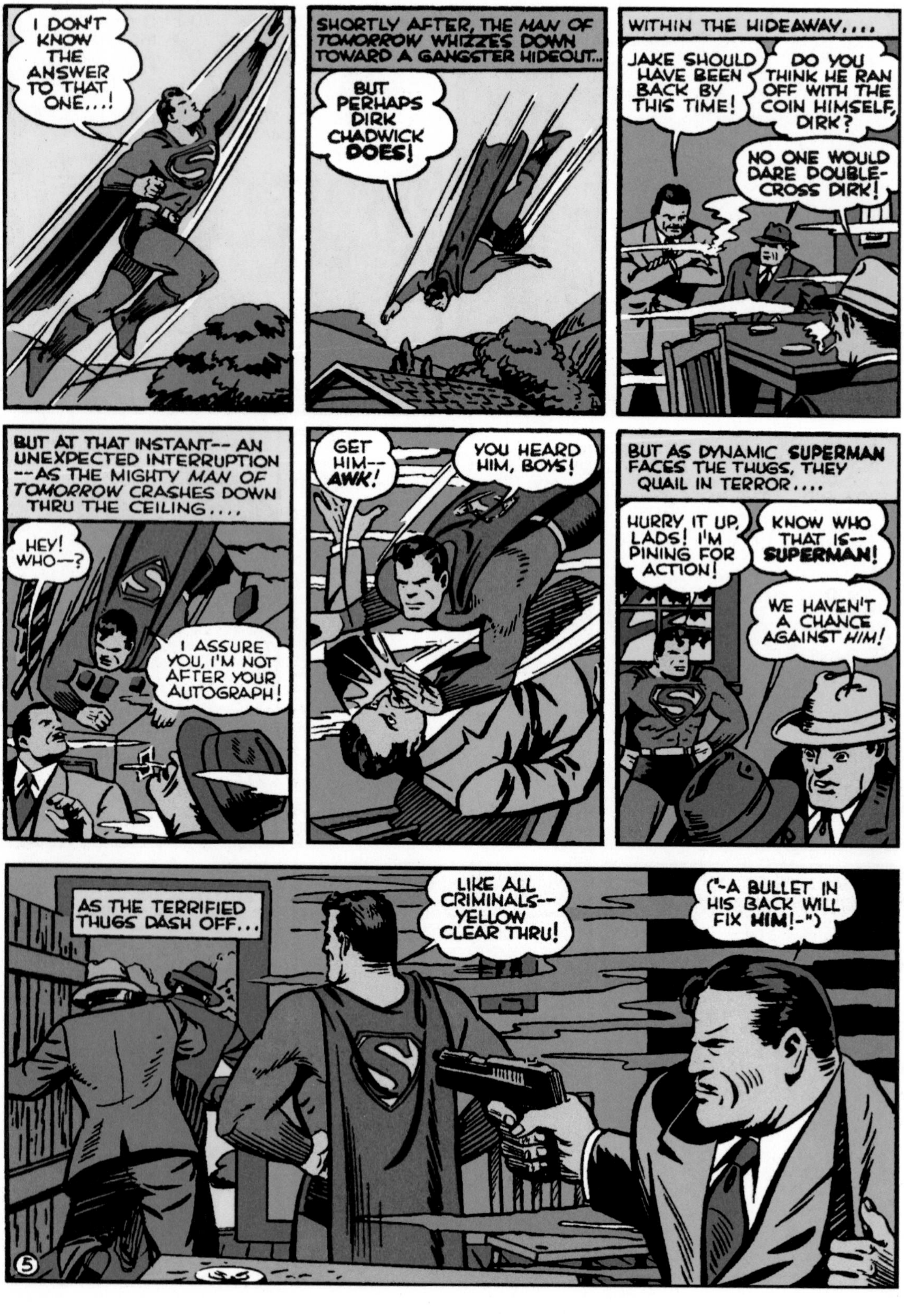
I DON'T KNOW THE ANSWER TO THAT ONE...!
SHORTLY AFTER, THE MAN OF TOMORROW WHIZZES DOWN TOWARD A GANGSTER HIDEOUT...
BUT PERHAPS DIRK CHADWICK DOES!
WITHIN THE HIDEAWAY....
JAKE SHOULD HAVE BEEN BACK BY THIS TIME!
DO YOU THINK HE RAN OFF WITH THE COIN HIMSELF, DIRK?
NO ONE WOULD DARE DOUBLE-CROSS DIRK!
BUT AT THAT INSTANT-- AN UNEXPECTED INTERRUPTION --AS THE MIGHTY MAN OF TOMORROW CRASHES DOWN THRU THE CEILING....
HEY! WHO--?
I ASSURE YOU, I'M NOT AFTER YOUR AUTOGRAPH!
GET HIM-- AWK!
YOU HEARD HIM, BOYS!
BUT AS DYNAMIC SUPERMAN FACES THE THUGS, THEY QUAIL IN TERROR....
HURRY IT UP, LADS! I'M PINING FOR ACTION!
KNOW WHO THAT IS-- SUPERMAN!
WE HAVEN'T A CHANCE AGAINST HIM!
AS THE TERRIFIED THUGS DASH OFF...
LIKE ALL CRIMINALS-- YELLOW CLEAR THRU!
("-A BULLET IN HIS BACK WILL FIX HIM!-")
5

LAUGHING TRIUMPHANTLY, DIRK FIRES....

DIE, SAP!

BUT CHADWICK'S LAUGHTER CHANGES TO A GURGLE OF BEWILDERMENT AS **SUPERMAN** SWIFTLY TURNS, UNHARMED...!

STILL LOOKING FOR TROUBLE, EH?

BUT HOW --??

THIS IS TO CONVINCE YOU THAT I'M IN EARNEST!

UHHH-HHHH!

WANT SOME MORE?

NO!--DON'T HIT ME AGAIN-- YOUR FISTS ARE LIKE SLEDGE- HAMMERS!

THEN TELL ME-- WHERE ARE BRANSOM AND THE OTHER VANISHED MEN?

I DON'T KNOW!

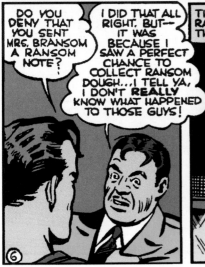

DO YOU DENY THAT YOU SENT MRS. BRANSOM A RANSOM NOTE?

I DID THAT ALL RIGHT, BUT-- IT WAS BECAUSE I SAW A PERFECT CHANCE TO COLLECT RANSOM DOUGH...I TELL YA, I DON'T **REALLY** KNOW WHAT HAPPENED TO THOSE GUYS!

THAT MOMENT--A STRANGE RAY PENETRATES THE ROOM THRU THE HOLE IN THE ROOF.

WHAT'S **THAT**?

YOUR DOOM, I'M AFRAID!

⑥

THE FORCE OF THE EXPLOSION FLINGS **SUPERMAN** QUITE A DISTANCE FROM THE SPOT WHERE THE DESTROYED HIDEOUT HAD BEEN LOCATED.

THAT FINISHES DIRK!

THEN IF DIRK DIDN'T KIDNAP THOSE MEN-- **WHO DID?** OBVIOUSLY HE RESENTS DIRK'S EFFORTS TO CUT IN... AND HAS ACTED ACCORDINGLY.

STREAKING BACK TO HIS APARTMENT....

IF ONLY I COULD LEARN THE SOURCE OF THAT FANTASTIC RAY!

...HE CHANGES BACK TO HIS IDENTITY AS THE *DAILY PLANET* STAR REPORTER!

I GIVE UP...TEMPORARILY! I'LL MAKE ANOTHER TRY AT SOLVING THE ENIGMA -- TOMORROW!

BUT THAT EVENING.... AS CLARK SLEEPS, SEVERAL STEALTHY FIGURES CREEP INTO HIS BEDROOM....

THERE IS A BRIEF STRUGGLE...

WHA—??

QUICK-- THE CHLOROFORM!

CLARK'S APPARENTLY UNCONSCIOUS BODY IS CARRIED ABOARD AN AUTOGIRO....

⑦

SKYWARD SOARS THE AUTOGIRO FROM THE APARTMENT ROOF, CARRYING THE *DAILY PLANET* SCRIBE TO WHAT WEIRD DESTINATION???

UP--UP RISES THE MYSTER-IOUS AUTOGIRO HIGH INTO THE STRATOSPHERE....

HOW--HOW DID I GET--

QUIET, YOU!

WHERE ARE YOU TAKING ME?

I TOLD YOU TO SHUT UP!

IT MAKES NO DIFFERENCE NOW. LET HIM LOOK OUT THE WINDOW!

AS THE REPORTER GLANCES OUT THE WINDOW, HE GLIMPSES A STARTLING SIGHT--A STRANGE, FANTASTIC CITY, FLOATING IN THE STRATOSPHERE....

A CITY--HANGING IN EMPTY AIR--! WHAT MANNER OF MIRACLE IS THIS?

LOOK HOW AMAZED HE IS!

THIS IS ONLY ONE OF THE MANY SURPRISES IN STORE FOR YOU!

SECONDS LATER, THE AUTO-GIRO ALIGHTS WITHIN THE WEIRD CITY....

WH-WHERE NOW??

JUST KEEP WALKING!

BUT AS THEY WALK ALONG, CLARK SUDDENLY GASPS WITH AMAZEMENT....

CARL BRANSOM--JOHN STANDING! WHY--THEY'RE SOME OF THE VANISHED MEN! THEY'RE BEING HELD CAPTIVE HERE!

IF YOU THINK THEY'RE HERE AGAINST THEIR WILL, ASK THEM!

YOU MEAN, BRANSOM, THAT YOU WANT TO STAY HERE--HAVE NO DESIRE TO LEAVE?

EXACTLY. AND YOU'LL HAVE THE SAME ATTITUDE SOON YOURSELF, KENT... I'M SURE OF IT!

AS CLARK IS LED INTO WHAT OBVIOUSLY IS THE CITY'S GOVERNING BUILDING....

("-THIS IS ASTON-ISHING! THESE MEN SEEM TO WANT TO STAY! BUT-- WHY....?? MAYBE I'LL SOON KNOW!-")

THIS IS-- ZYTAL-- THE BOSS!

WELCOME TO THE "EMPIRE CITY IN THE SKY," CLARK KENT.

WHY HAVE I-- AND THOSE OTHER MEN-- BEEN BROUGHT HERE?

TO ANSWER THAT, I MUST GO BACK IN MY EXPLANATION TO AN OCCURRENCE OF CENTURIES AGO. I AM FROM ANOTHER UNIVERSE, KENT. I HAVE ALWAYS POSSESSED A TREMENDOUS THIRST FOR KNOWLEDGE.

HUNDREDS--NAY, THOUSANDS OF YEARS AGO, I FELT THAT I HAD ACCUMULATED ALL THE KNOWLEDGE I COULD FIND UPON MY OLD WORLD, SO I CONSTRUCTED THIS FLYING CITY AND SET FORTH TO EXPLORE THE UNIVERSE WITH IT.

AN INTER-PLANETARY VOYAGER!

IN EACH OF THE WORLDS I EXPLORED, I SELECTED A GROUP OF THE WORLD'S MOST SUPERIOR MEN TO JOIN ME IN MY QUEST FOR KNOWLEDGE. YOU SHOULD FEEL VERY HONORED TO BE AMONG THE CHOSEN.

I--I DON'T KNOW WHAT TO THINK!

THAT'S WHY THOSE MEN ARE CONTENT TO REMAIN HERE. THEY ARE ANXIOUS TO JOIN ZYTAL IN HIS EXPLORATION OF INFINITY ITSELF!

CLARK IS LED TO A MAGNIFICENTLY FURNISHED APARTMENT....

THIS IS TO BE YOUR HOME. GET ACQUAINTED WITH IT.

YOU'LL BE HERE A LONG TIME!

BUT LATER--AS THE OTHERS SLEEP, CLARK SITS ERECT....

I'M NOT COMPLETELY SATISFIED WITH THAT EXPLANATION!

⑨

AND HERE'S WHERE I DO SOME CHECKING UP ON MY OWN!

MINUTES LATER--AVAILING HIMSELF OF HIS ASTOUNDING X-RAY VISION, SUPERMAN PEERS THRU THE WALLS OF ZYTAL'S SUITE--TO MAKE AN ASTONISHING DISCOVERY!

WHAT--!!

THE *MAN OF STEEL* OBSERVES *ZYTAL* REMOVE A FALSE FACE....

NOW THAT I'M ALONE I CAN DISPENSE WITH THE PRETENSE!

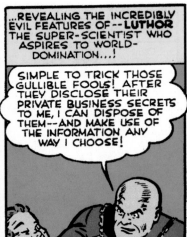

...REVEALING THE INCREDIBLY EVIL FEATURES OF--**LUTHOR** THE SUPER-SCIENTIST WHO ASPIRES TO WORLD-DOMINATION...!

SIMPLE TO TRICK THOSE GULLIBLE FOOLS! AFTER THEY DISCLOSE THEIR PRIVATE BUSINESS SECRETS TO ME, I CAN DISPOSE OF THEM--AND MAKE USE OF THE INFORMATION ANY WAY I CHOOSE!

BUT YOU RECKONED WITHOUT **ME**!

SUPERMAN! HOW--??

IT WILL BE A DISTINCT HONOR TO END YOUR CRIMINAL CAREER!

YOU HAVEN'T GOT ME **YET**!

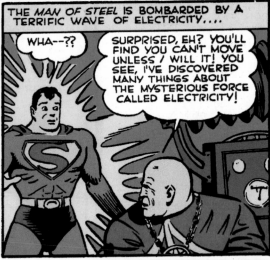

THE *MAN OF STEEL* IS BOMBARDED BY A TERRIFIC WAVE OF ELECTRICITY....

WHA--??

SURPRISED, EH? YOU'LL FIND YOU CAN'T MOVE UNLESS I WILL IT! YOU SEE, I'VE DISCOVERED MANY THINGS ABOUT THE MYSTERIOUS FORCE CALLED ELECTRICITY!

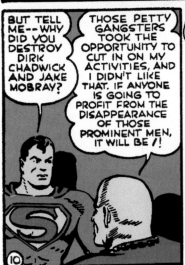

BUT TELL ME--WHY DID YOU DESTROY DIRK CHADWICK AND JAKE MOBRAY?

THOSE PETTY GANGSTERS TOOK THE OPPORTUNITY TO CUT IN ON MY ACTIVITIES, AND I DIDN'T LIKE THAT. IF ANYONE IS GOING TO PROFIT FROM THE DISAPPEARANCE OF THOSE PROMINENT MEN, IT WILL BE I!

10

AND **NOW**?

YOU'VE ACCIDENTALLY PLAYED INTO MY HANDS...A VERY FORTUNATE CIRCUMSTANCE FOR ME! YOU SHALL DO AS I ORDER--AND MY ORDER IS: RETURN TO EARTH AND DIVERT THE PRESS'S ATTENTION FROM MY ACTIVITIES BY CAUSING HAVOC!

EARTHWARD PLUMMETS THE *MAN OF TOMORROW* ON HIS DISTRESSING ERRAND....

IF ONLY I COULD THROW OFF HIS MENTAL COMPULSION...! BUT I DON'T SEEM ABLE TO!

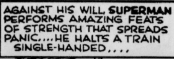
AGAINST HIS WILL, **SUPERMAN** PERFORMS AMAZING FEATS OF STRENGTH THAT SPREADS PANIC.....HE HALTS A TRAIN SINGLE-HANDED....

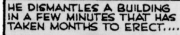
HE DISMANTLES A BUILDING IN A FEW MINUTES THAT HAS TAKEN MONTHS TO ERECT....

L-LOOK...! AND THE BUILDING WAS ALMOST **FINISHED!**

NOW IT'S ONLY A SKELETON OF ITSELF!

HE RACES THRU HEAVY CITY TRAFFIC...DELIBER-ATELY DISORGANIZING IT...

THESE FANTASTIC REPORTS ABOUT **SUPERMAN** RUNNING AMUCK... I STILL CAN'T BELIEVE THEM! I'D BETTER CONSULT CLARK.

THERE GOES LOIS LANE INTO CLARK KENT'S APARTMENT BUILDING!

WE'VE GOT ORDERS TO GET HER!

MEANWHILE-- THE *MAN OF TOMORROW* STREAKS BACK TO HIS APARTMENT....

PERHAPS IF I LIE DOWN FOR A WHILE--MARSHAL MY WILL-POWER, I CAN BREAK FREE OF **LUTHOR**'S COMPULSION!

BEFORE CLARK'S APARTMENT DOOR, LOIS IS SEIZED BY THE WICKED SCIENTIST'S HIRELINGS....

LET GO!

YOU'RE COMING WITH US!

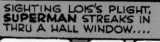
SIGHTING LOIS'S PLIGHT, **SUPERMAN** STREAKS IN THRU A HALL WINDOW....

TAKE YOUR HANDS OFF THAT GIRL!

AWK!

BUT WE THOUGHT --!!

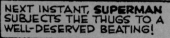
NEXT INSTANT, **SUPERMAN** SUBJECTS THE THUGS TO A WELL-DESERVED BEATING!

GOOD FOR YOU, **SUPERMAN!**

A PLEASURE!

BUT NEXT INSTANT, AS **LUTHOR**'S COMPULSION SWEEPS OVER **SUPERMAN** ONCE AGAIN, HE SEIZES LOIS ROUGHLY....

YOU'RE COMING WITH ME!

YOUR EYES! YOU LOOK SO-- **STRANGE!**

AS THEY STREAK SKYWARD...

WHERE ARE YOU TAKING ME?

TO MY MASTER-- LUTHOR!

AND LATER--WHEN THEY REACH LUTHOR'S PRESENCE

SO YOU'VE BROUGHT LOIS LANE TO ME, EH? GOOD WORK! AND NOW, REMAIN HERE WHILE I CONFRONT HER WITH CLARK KENT!

CLARK HERE-- ALSO A CAPTIVE?

NO SOONER DOES LUTHOR DEPART THAN SUPERMAN CONCENTRATES MIGHTILY...

GOT TO GET BACK AND CHANGE TO CLARK KENT BEFORE IT'S --TOO LATE...

GAINING SOME CONTROL OF HIMSELF, SUPERMAN RACES PAST LUTHOR AND LOIS SO QUICKLY HE CANNOT BE SEEN....

AND AFTER YOU MEET KENT, I'M GOING TO DESTROY THE BOTH OF YOU!

YOU'RE STILL AS COLD-BLOODED AS EVER!

SWIFTLY, SUPERMAN DONS HIS OTHER GARMENTS...

THEY'RE ALMOST OUTSIDE THE DOOR...

LUTHOR-- AND LOIS! WHAT--?

I'VE BEEN CAPTURED BY HIM, TOO. --BROUGHT HERE BY AN ENSLAVED SUPERMAN.

AND NOW, DIE-- BOTH OF YOU!

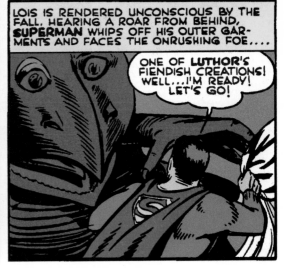

LOIS IS RENDERED UNCONSCIOUS BY THE FALL. HEARING A ROAR FROM BEHIND, SUPERMAN WHIPS OFF HIS OUTER GARMENTS AND FACES THE ONRUSHING FOE....

ONE OF LUTHOR'S FIENDISH CREATIONS! WELL...I'M READY! LET'S GO!

SUPERMAN DESTROYS HIS MASSIVE OPPONENT WITH ONE TREMENDOUS BLOW...

WHAT A PUSH-OVER!

SPRINGING FROM THE DUNGEON, HE FINDS--

LUTHOR--GONE! I'LL LEAVE LOIS HERE--AND ATTEND TO HIM!

SUPERMAN! --BACK! I COMMAND YOU-- KEEP BACK!

SORRY, LUTHOR, THAT ELECTRICAL HYPNOSIS-- TREATMENT HAS HAD SUFFICIENT TIME TO WEAR OFF. I'M AT LAST FREE!

THEN THE EMPIRE IN THE SKY-- AND ALL ON IT-- DIE!

DON'T!

YOU WON'T GET ME ALIVE!

SUPERMAN LEAPS DOWN TOWARD EARTH AHEAD OF THE FALLING SKY CITY IN A DESPERATE RACE AGAINST TIME....

LUTHOR'S FATE ISN'T AS IMPORTANT AS THE FACT THAT THE LIVES OF LOIS AND THOSE MEN MUST BE SAVED!

CATCHING THE GREAT MECHANISM, SUPERMAN LOWERS THE CITY TO SAFETY...

THERE YOU ARE!

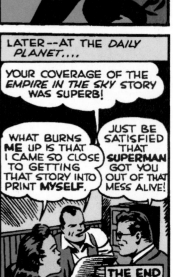

LATER--AT THE DAILY PLANET....

YOUR COVERAGE OF THE EMPIRE IN THE SKY STORY WAS SUPERB!

WHAT BURNS ME UP IS THAT I CAME SO CLOSE TO GETTING THAT STORY INTO PRINT MYSELF.

JUST BE SATISFIED THAT SUPERMAN GOT YOU OUT OF THAT MESS ALIVE!

THE END

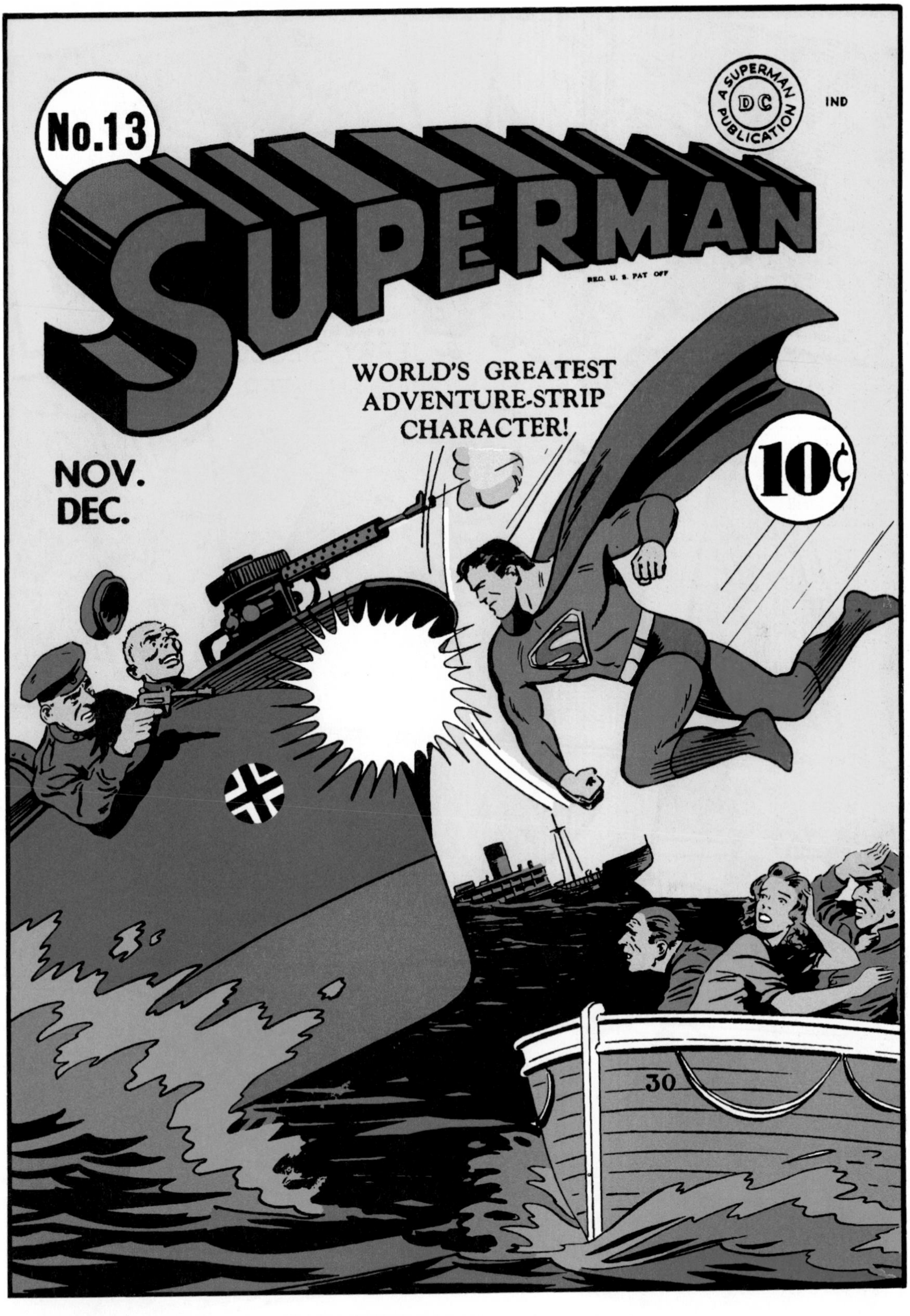
No.13
A SUPERMAN DC PUBLICATION
IND
SUPERMAN
REG. U. S. PAT OFF
WORLD'S GREATEST ADVENTURE-STRIP CHARACTER!
10¢
NOV. DEC.
30

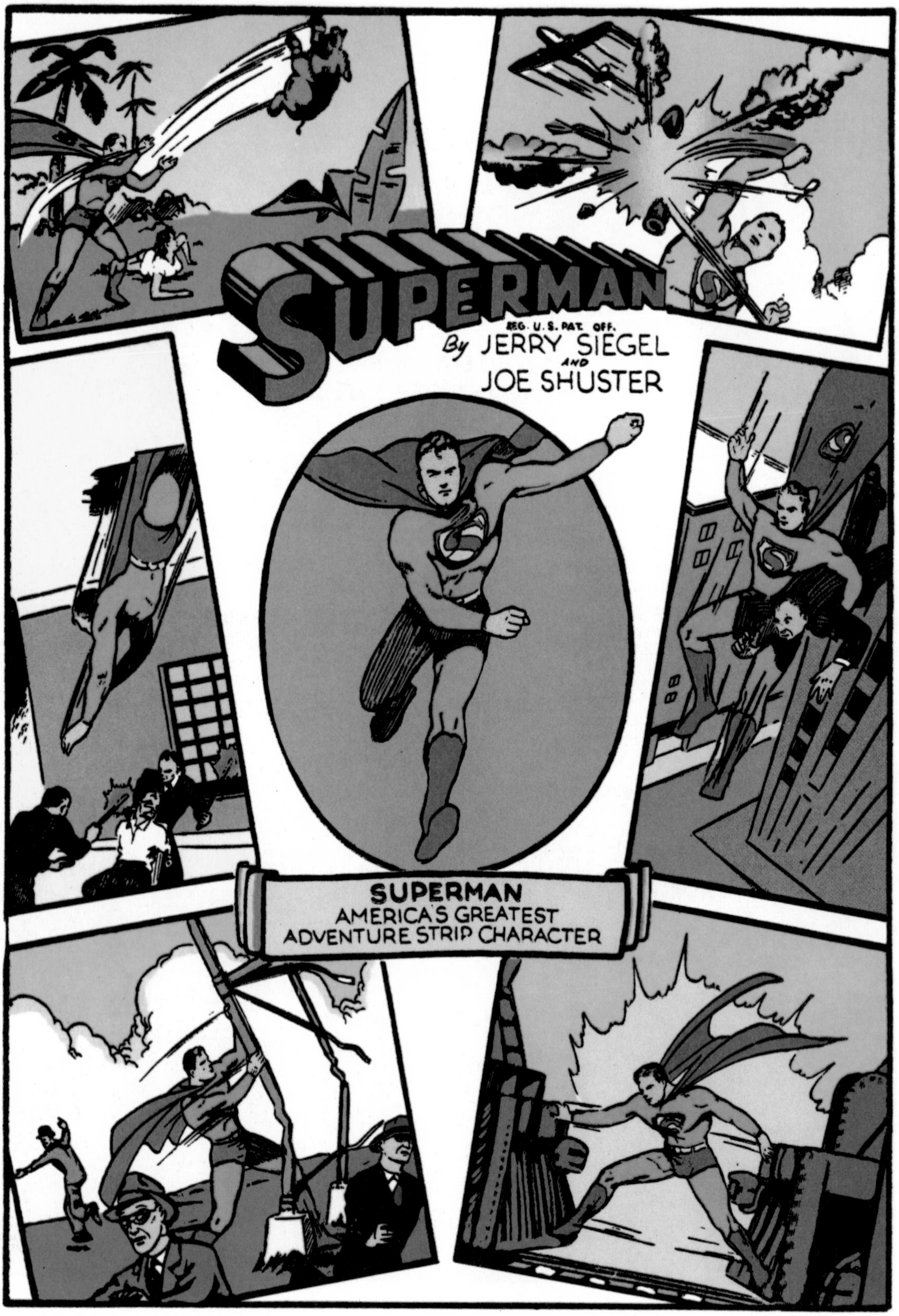
SUPERMAN
REG. U.S. PAT. OFF.
By JERRY SIEGEL AND JOE SHUSTER
SUPERMAN
AMERICA'S GREATEST
ADVENTURE STRIP CHARACTER

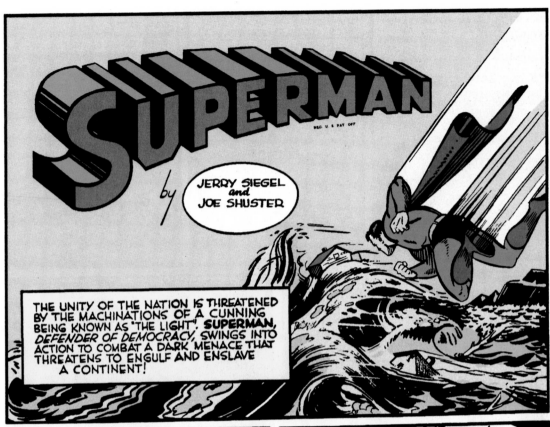

SUPERMAN

REG. U.S PAT OFF

by JERRY SIEGEL and JOE SHUSTER

THE UNITY OF THE NATION IS THREATENED BY THE MACHINATIONS OF A CUNNING BEING KNOWN AS "THE LIGHT". SUPERMAN, *DEFENDER OF DEMOCRACY*, SWINGS INTO ACTION TO COMBAT A DARK MENACE THAT THREATENS TO ENGULF AND ENSLAVE A CONTINENT!

EDITORIAL OFFICE OF THE *DAILY PLANET*....

SENATOR BILLINGSLEY IS TO SPEAK AT *NATIONAL HALL*. I WANT BOTH OF YOU TO COVER THE EVENT.

A POLITICAL SPEECH!

WHY NOT ASSIGN US SOMETHING MORE INTERESTING?

I'VE BEEN INFORMED ON THE QUIET THAT SOMEONE NAMED "THE LIGHT" HAS ISSUED A WARNING THAT BILLINGSLEY WILL NEVER SPEAK AT THAT MEETING. ANYTHING MAY HAPPEN!

THAT'S *DIFFERENT!*

COME ON, CLARK!

LATER...

HE'S ALREADY LATE-- DO YOU THINK...?

I DON'T KNOW **WHAT** TO THINK! EXCUSE ME, LOIS. I'D LIKE TO MAKE A TELEPHONE CALL.

①

BUT INSTEAD OF APPROACHING THE TELEPHONE BOOTH, CLARK STEPS INTO AN EMPTY OFFICE AND REMOVES HIS OUTER GARMENTS...

"THE LIGHT" MAY NOT BE A CRANK AFTER ALL-- I'D BETTER LOOK INTO THIS-- AS **SUPERMAN**,...!

MOMENTS LATER--THE COLORFUL COSTUMED FIGURE OF THE MIGHTY *MAN OF TOMORROW* STREAKS THRU THE FLEECY CLOUDS AT BREATHTAKING SPEED....

THE SENATOR'S CAR SHOULD BE COMING ALONG THE *CARROLL HIGHWAY.* IT'S ENTIRELY POSSIBLE THAT I'M BEING UNDULY APPREHENSIVE, BUT...

THAT INSTANT--WITHIN SENATOR TOM BILLINGSLEY'S AUTO....

"THE LIGHT" MAY BE A JOKE TO YOU, SENATOR-- BUT WE'RE NOT TAKING ANY CHANCES!

NONSENSE! "THE LIGHT" IS A HARMLESS POISON PEN WRITER.

TOWARD THE SENATOR'S CAR DRIVES A SEDAN.--UNUSUAL? DEFINITELY *NOT!* THAT IS, *UNTIL...*

THE HEADLIGHTS OF THE NEARING CAR UNEXPECTEDLY FLASH ON! FROM THEM EMERGES A BRILLIANCE OF SUCH STARK, BLINDING QUALITIES THAT THE HUMAN EYE INSTANTLY CAN DETECT NOTHING MORE THAN A WHITE HAZE!

THOSE HEADLIGHTS--! I--I CAN'T SEE!

WHAT --!!

NEITHER CAN I!

BLINDED, THE DRIVER OF THE SENATOR'S AUTO INSTINCTIVELY JAMS ON HIS BRAKES! THERE IS THE SOUND OF APPROACHING FOOTSTEPS--THEN SILENCE, EXCEPT FOR THE SHOUTS OF THE CONFUSED BODYGUARDS...

ABRUPTLY--THE GLARE IS GONE! IT TAKES SOME TIME FOR THEM TO ACCUSTOM THEIR EYES AGAIN TO NORMAL LIGHT, BUT WHEN THEY DO, THE GUARDS DISCOVER....

HE'S GONE--! THE SENATOR IS **GONE!**

KIDNAPPED!

AT THAT MOMENT, THE *MAN OF STEEL* ALIGHTS BESIDE THE SENATOR'S CAR....

WHAT HAPPENED?

IT'S SUPERMAN!

HE MUST BE TO BLAME! GET HIM!

AS THE DAZED GUARDS ARE ABOUT TO SEIZE HIM, SUPER-MAN SUDDENLY GALVANIZES INTO ACTION. . . .

WE'LL MAKE YOU TALK!

WHERE HAVE YOU TAKEN SENATOR BILLINGSLEY?

THE *MAN OF TOMORROW*, MOVING AT SUPER-SPEED, IS NO LONGER BEFORE THEM. . . .

HUH? WHERE IS HE?

YOU MIGHT TURN AROUND, YOU KNOW!

I'VE NOTHING TO DO WITH THE SENATOR'S KIDNAPPING, I ASSURE YOU. --JUST WHAT DID HAPPEN?

YOU KNOW VERY WELL.--YOUR MEN TURNED ON THAT BLINDING LIGHT IN THEIR HEAD-LIGHTS--AND YOU SNATCHED THE SENATOR.

HE'S TRYING TO ESCAPE!

WHAT DO YOU MEAN "TRYING"? HE IS ESCAPING!

SAVE YOUR BULLETS, BOYS! THEY'RE AS HARM-LESS AS PEAS!

AN AUTO--ARMED WITH A BLINDING LIGHT THAT RENDERS THOSE WHO SIGHT IT HELPLESS! FANTASTIC! AND YET-- THERE'S NO DOUBT THAT THE SENATOR *HAS* DISAPPEARED!

A SPEED-ING AUTO BELOW-- MIGHT BE A JOY-RIDER --BUT I'LL GLANCE WITH-IN IT WITH MY X-RAY VISION.

③

WHAT SUPERMAN'S MARVELOUS SUPER-SIGHT REVEALS TO HIM!

THAT'S THE SENATOR. --NO DOUBT ABOUT IT! HERE I GO!!

DOWN IN THE VERY PATH OF THE ONRUSHING AUTO PLUMMETS **SUPERMAN**...!

WHOA, THERE!

THE CAR *INCREASES* SPEED! ON FLASH THE HEADLIGHTS, BOMBARDING THE *MAN OF STEEL* WITH BLINDING BEAMS...

WANT TO FIGHT, EH?

FULL INTO THE FIGURE OF **SUPERMAN** CRASHES THE MYSTERY-AUTO! UP INTO THE AIR HIS BODY IS WHIRLED...!

BUT--SOMERSAULTING--THE *MAN OF TOMORROW* ALIGHTS UPON THE AUTOMOBILE'S REAR BUMPER...!

CAN'T GET RID OF ME *THAT* EASILY!

ONE SWIFT MOVEMENT AND **SUPERMAN** RIPS OPEN THE BACK OF THE CAR....

I'VE BEEN MIGHTY PATIENT UP TO NOW, BUT DON'T GET ME SORE!

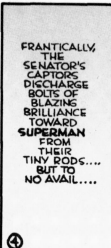

FRANTICALLY, THE SENATOR'S CAPTORS DISCHARGE BOLTS OF BLAZING BRILLIANCE TOWARD **SUPERMAN** FROM THEIR TINY RODS.... BUT TO NO AVAIL....

④

HERE'S SOME OF THE PUNISHMENT YOU'VE BEEN BEGGING FOR!

OUT OF CONTROL, THE AUTO PLUNGES TOWARD A RAVINE. BUT SEIZING THE LIMB OF A PROJECTING TREE, **SUPERMAN** HALTS THE MACHINE AT THE VERY EDGE OF THE SHARP INCLINE....

THAT'S FAR ENOUGH!

MOMENTS LATER--DOWN OUT OF THE SKY PLUMMETS THE AMAZING *MAN OF STEEL.* DEPOSITING THE CAR BEFORE THE ASTOUNDED GUARDS, HE SPRINGS OFF....

YOU'LL FIND THE SENATOR AND THE MEN WHO CAPTURED HIM IN THERE--CONFISCATE THEIR LIGHT-RODS!

FIRST YOU KIDNAP THE SENATOR, THEN RETURN HIM! I DON'T GET IT!

RETURNING TO *NATIONAL HALL,* **SUPERMAN** DONS HIS OUTER GARMENTS, ONCE AGAIN ASSUMING HIS IDENTITY OF THE MEEK *DAILY PLANET* REPORTER....

BETTER HURRY BACK TO LOIS BEFORE SHE BEGINS TO WONDER WHETHER I'M DICTATING A NOVEL OVER THE TELEPHONE!

IT CERTAINLY TOOK YOU LONG ENOUGH!

I MIGHT SAY THE SAME FOR THE SENATOR.

SHORTLY AFTER, SENATOR BILLINGSLEY ENTERS THE AUDITORIUM--HE LOSES NO TIME IN MAKING A SPECIAL ANNOUNCEMENT....

A FANATIC NAMED *"THE LIGHT"* PROPHESIED I WOULD NOT SPEAK TO YOU TODAY. HE TRIED TO MAKE THAT THREAT COME TRUE.-- FORTUNATELY, HE FAILED!

LATER--AS THE SENATOR MAKES THE ANNOUNCED ADDRESS, CLARK, KEEPING KEEN WATCH, OBSERVES A SUSPICIOUS INDIVIDUAL ENTER...

("-HE DELIBERATELY DROPPED A SMALL PILL BEHIND THAT VASE!-")

MOMENTS LATER--THERE IS A SUDDEN BLINDING FLASH--AN EYE-SCORCHING BLAZE OF LIGHT. THEN....

WHAT --!!

SHIELD YOUR EYES!

A MESSAGE IS TO BE SEEN ON THE WALL, WRITTEN IN LETTERS OF BLAZING *LIGHT!*

YOU MAY HAVE ESCAPED THIS TIME, SENATOR, BUT THERE WILL BE OTHER ATTEMPTS, AND THEY MAY NOT FAIL

--*"THE LIGHT"*

IN THE CONFUSION THAT FOLLOWS, CLARK ATTEMPTS TO FOLLOW THE SUSPICIOUS CHARACTER HE HAD OBSERVED, BUT LOIS BLOCKS HIS PATH....

LET GO, LOIS!

FORGET YOUR PANIC! GO TO THE PHONE AND CALL THE NEWSPAPER OFFICE!

THAT YOU, CLARK? GET BACK TO THE OFFICE AT ONCE! PROMINENT MEN ARE VANISHING BY THE DOZEN--KIDNAPPED BY *"THE LIGHT"*!

I'LL BE RIGHT THERE, WHITE!

AND TO THINK WE BELIEVED *"THE LIGHT"* MIGHT BE A HARMLESS CRANK!

THAT'S ALL CHANGED NOW!

("-I'D LIKE TO HAVE TRAILED THAT SUSPICIOUS CHAP, BUT THAT PLEASURE WILL HAVE TO BE INDEFINITELY POSTPONED.-")

UNKNOWN TO CLARK AND LOIS, THEY ARE PURSUED BY A SLEEK SEDAN....

WITHIN THE TRAILING CAR....

BUT WHY WASTE OUR TIME ON THESE TWO REPORTERS?

"THE LIGHT" CONSIDERS THEM DANGEROUS, AND THAT'S ENOUGH FOR ME.

DRAWING ABREAST OF THE REPORTERS' CAR, THE GOGGLED THUGS UNEXPECTEDLY FLASH THEIR ROD-WEAPONS AT CLARK....

("-I'LL PRETEND TO BE BLINDED.-")

I--I--CAN'T SEE!

MY--EYES--!

CLARK SLAMS ON THE BRAKES. HE AND LOIS, BOTH APPARENTLY DAZED, ARE DRAGGED INTO THE INTERIOR OF THE SEDAN....

WH-WHAT--??

NOT A PEEP OUTA EITHER OF YA-- GET IN THERE!

MINUTES LATER....

I SEE THE EFFECTS OF *"THE LIGHT"* HAVE WORN OFF!

I SEE, NOW! YOU'RE AGENTS OF *"THE LIGHT"*!

BRIGHT GIRL!

SHORTLY AFTER... .THE TWO REPORTERS ARE FORCED INTO AN OUT-OF-THE-WAY BUILDING...

IN THERE!

WHAT-- WHAT ARE YOU GOING TO DO TO US?

THAT'S WHAT WE'D LIKE TO KNOW.

6

THE BOSS SAYS TO RUB 'EM OUT!

THERE'S YOUR ANSWER, LADY!

NO!

("-WHAT A PREDICAMENT!--I CAN'T PERMIT THESE THUGS TO GET AWAY WITH MURDER, YET--IF I ACT AS *SUPERMAN* I'LL BE FORCED TO REVEAL MY TRUE IDENTITY!-")

NOW?

SURE, WHY NOT?

LET'S GET IT OVER WITH!

THE THUGS WHIRL AT THE SOUND OF AN UNEXPECTED VOICE BEHIND THEM....

DROP THOSE GUNS!

WHA----!!

I DON'T SEE ANYONE!

BUT I HEARD A VOICE!

SO DID I!

ACTING AT TERRIFIC SPEED, SUPERMAN REMOVES HIS OUTER GARMENTS....

HOPE THIS LITTLE BIT OF VENTRILOQUISM DOES THE TRICK...!

OUT THRU THE DOOR HE SPEEDS FASTER THAN A GUST OF WIND...

...AROUND THE SIDE OF THE BUILDING....

THIS CALLS FOR SPEED... AND I MEAN SPEED PLUS!!

CRASHING IN THRU A WINDOW, SUPERMAN BANGS THE THUGS TOGETHER....

SURPRISE!

HEY! OUCH!

UH-HHH!

HUH!

...THEN, BACK AROUND THE HOUSE SPEEDS SUPERMAN, RETRACING HIS STEPS....

ALL I HOPE IS THAT LOIS HASN'T YET HAD TIME TO GLANCE BACK TOWARD ME!

⑦

...SWIFTLY SUPERMAN DIVES INTO HIS OUTER GARMENTS AS LOIS COMMENCES TO TURN....

("-SECONDS... TO MAKE IT...!-")

CLARK-- DID YOU SEE THAT? SUPERMAN!

GOOD THING FOR US HE SHOWED UP!

("-AND A GOOD THING FOR ME LOIS DIDN'T TURN A SECOND SOONER!-")

CASEY? HURRY DOWN TO THE FOLLOWING ADDRESS--WE'VE GOT SOME OF *"THE LIGHT"'S* THUGS HERE--AND I'M NOT KIDDING!

WE'D BETTER GET THEM TIED BEFORE THEY REVIVE!

LATER....

SO YOU WEREN'T FOOLING, AFTER ALL! HOW DID YOU EVER CAPTURE ALL THOSE MEN SINGLE-HANDED, CLARK?

THE TRUTH IS THAT CLARK WAS STANDING BESIDE ME, WHILE SUPERMAN CLEANED UP THOSE CRIMINALS.

WHO IS *"THE LIGHT"?*

YOU'LL LEARN NOTHIN' FROM US, COPPER!

PERHAPS YOU'LL HAVE BETTER LUCK WITH THEM AT HEAD-QUARTERS, SERGEANT!

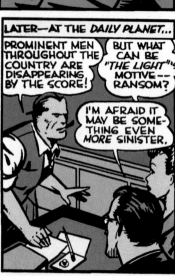

LATER--AT THE *DAILY PLANET*...

PROMINENT MEN THROUGHOUT THE COUNTRY ARE DISAPPEARING BY THE SCORE!

BUT WHAT CAN BE *"THE LIGHT"'S* MOTIVE-- RANSOM?

I'M AFRAID IT MAY BE SOME-THING EVEN MORE SINISTER.

NEWS FLASH! GOVERNOR BENSON HAS JUST RECEIVED A *THREAT* FROM THE NOTO-RIOUS CRIMINAL KNOWN AS *"THE LIGHT"!*

COVER THAT STORY!

BUT AS LOIS AND CLARK EMERGE FROM THE *PLANET* BUILDING,....

WHERE'S CLARK?-- WELL, I CAN'T WASTE ANY TIME WAITING FOR THAT SLOW-POKE!

LOIS WOULD HAVE BEEN VERY SURPRISED TO KNOW THAT THE "SLOWPOKE" HAS NEARLY REACHED THE GOVERNOR'S RESIDENCE BY THIS TIME....

I'LL KEEP AN EYE ON THE GOVERNOR'S MANSION.

NO SOONER DOES THE MIGHTY *MAN OF STEEL* ALIGHT UPON A TREE LIMB HIGH ABOVE THE GOVERNOR'S ESTATE WHEN,....

SO WE MEET AGAIN...

SUPERMAN'S TELESCOPIC VISION HAS REVEALED TO HIM THAT ONE OF THE GUARDS PATROLLING THE ESTATE IS THE SUSPICIOUS CHARACTER HE HAD SEEN AT *NATIONAL HALL*....

AS THE GUARD WALKS UNDER THE TREE, A HAND SUDDENLY JERKS HIM UP INTO THE FOLIAGE

ULP—!

THEN—TWO FIGURES HURTLE HIGH UP INTO THE SKY LIKE AN UNLEASHED BOLT....

LET GO! WHAT'S THE IDEA—?

DON'T PLAY INNOCENT! I KNOW YOU WERE PLANTED THERE BY *"THE LIGHT"*! WHAT ARE HIS PLANS?

PLANS? I DON'T KNOW WHAT YOU'RE TALKING ABOUT!

WOULDN'T IT BE A PITY IF I WERE TO LOSE MY GRIP?

A MOMENT LATER—AS THE *MAN OF STEEL* RELEASES HIS HOLD, DOWN PLUNGES THE SCREAMING GUARD....

YEEE-EEEE!

AS HE DROPS, A VOICE BOOMS OUT OF THE CLOUDS NEAR HIM...

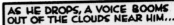

WHERE ARE YOU?

HERE I AM! CATCH ME! CATCH ME!

STRANGE—BUT UNLESS YOU'RE WILLING TO TALK, I'M AFRAID I WON'T BE *ABLE* TO FIND YOU!

I'LL TALK! I'LL TALK!

⑨

THAT'S BETTER!

I'LL TELL YOU ANYTHING YOU WANT TO KNOW—ANYTHING!

I'M WAITING!

THEY'RE GOING TO OVERCOME THE GOVERNOR'S GUARD--*"THE LIGHT"'S* MEN ARE PLANTED AMONG THEM--AND TAKE HIM OFF TO THE HIDEOUT.

AND WHERE IS *THAT* LOCATED?

BENEATH *BARROWS' RIDGE!*

STREAKING BACK TO THE GOVERNOR'S ESTATE, **SUPERMAN** DISCOVERS--CONFUSION!

TOO LATE!

HELP! THE GOVERNOR'S --GONE!

NEXT STOP--*BARROWS' RIDGE*--IT'S TIME *"THE LIGHT"* AND I CAME FACE TO FACE!

MEANWHILE--BENEATH THE RIDGE IN AN UNDERGROUND CHAMBER....

I THINK IT'S HIGH TIME YOU GENTLEMEN LEARNED WHY I'VE KIDNAPPED YOU.--I INTEND TO SEIZE CONTROL OF THIS NATION--AND **YOU** ARE GOING TO HELP ME!

NEVER!

WE'LL DIE FIRST!

INTO THE CHAIR WITH HIM!

COME ON, YOU!

NO! NO!

INTO THE STEEL SEAT THE VICTIM IS FORCED. SOON HE IS STRAPPED DOWN HELPLESSLY....

NOW WATCH!

NO! DON'T DO IT!

DOWN INTO THE FACE OF THE TERRIFIED CAPTIVE OF *"THE LIGHT"* STREAMS A BLAZE OF BLINDING BRILLIANCE....

GRADUALLY, THE BEAM CHANGES COLORS,—BLUE, RED, ORANGE, GREEN, YELLOW, PURPLE—"THE LIGHT" WHISPERS HYPNOTICALLY TO HIS CAPTIVE....

THOSE LIGHTS—BEATING INTO YOUR BRAIN—ROBBING YOU OF ALL INITIATIVE.

THE LIGHTS—THE PRETTY COLORED LIGHTS...

NOW—FREE HIM!

MOMENTS LATER, THE CAPTIVE RISES AT "THE LIGHT"'S COMMAND..

NOW WILL YOU OBEY ME?

YOU ARE MY MASTER, I SHALL DO AS YOU DIRECT...

YOU SEE HOW HE IS NOW AN INSTRUMENT OF MY WILL? SO SHALL IT BE WITH ALL OF YOU! YOU ARE ALL PROMINENT MEN IN YOUR LINES—WITH YOUR HELP, VICTORY IS ASSURED!

SOMEONE IS COMING!

SUPERMAN! I MIGHT HAVE EXPECTED HIS APPEARANCE—AND SO I AM PREPARED!

PLUNGING STRAIGHT AT BARROWS' RIDGE, SUPERMAN CLEARS A WAY FOR HIMSELF THRU THE SOLID ROCK....

HERE'S WHERE I PUT OUT "THE LIGHT"!

INTO THE VILLAINOUS SCIENTIST'S LABORATORY CRASHES THE MAN OF TOMORROW....

WE MEET AT LAST!

A MOMENT I HAVE LONG AWAITED!

THE MECHANISM BLASTING FORTH VARI-COLORED BEAMS OF LIGHT STRIKES AT THE MAN OF STEEL...

CAN'T—MOVE!

HE'S HELPLESS! AND NOW—I HAVE PLANS FOR SUPERMAN!

MY INSTRUCTIONS ARE AS FOLLOWS—COMPLETELY DESTROY ANY MILITARY MATERIALS THAT MAY BE USED AGAINST ME! GO!

I—OBEY!

SHORTLY AFTER...THE *MAN OF STEEL* PLUNGES DOWN OUT OF THE SKY BEFORE A GOVERN-MENT ARMORY....

CRUSH-- DESTROY --!!

DRIVING BY, LOIS HALTS HER AUTO AS SHE SIGHTS THE *MAN OF TOMORROW*....

IT'S-- SUPERMAN!

WHAT'S HAPPENED TO YOU-- YOUR EYES...

"THE LIGHT" HAS COMMANDED ME TO CAUSE WHOLE-SALE DESTRUC-TION--AND I MUST OBEY!

BUT YOU MUSTN'T- YOU CAN'T--YOU'VE ALWAYS FOUGHT EVIL... NEVER CHAMPIONED IT!

FOUGHT EVIL... FOUGHT IT...!

AIDED BY LOIS' APPEAL, SUPER-MAN'S MIND CLEARS OF *"THE LIGHT"'*S INFLUENCE....

I--I'M ALL RIGHT NOW. YOU'LL NEVER KNOW HOW CLOSE I CAME TO...

I KNOW. BUT HADN'T YOU BETTER HURRY AND STOP *"THE LIGHT"* BEFORE IT'S TOO LATE?

MEANWHILE...

NOW TO MAKE ALL OF YOU MY SLAVES!

ABRUPTLY--IN THRU THE WALL CRASHES...

SUPERMAN! BUT I THOUGHT--

THAT I'D BE BUSY SPREADING DESTRUCTION? GUESS AGAIN!

⑫

AND AS FOR YOUR HYP-NOTIZING THESE MEN TO DO YOUR WILL... THAT'S *OUT!*

YOU'VE DESTROYED THE CONTROL-BOARD...BUT I'VE AN ACE UP MY SLEEVE!

MY FOOT RESTS ON A PLUNGER... ONE MOVE TOWARD ME AND I BLOW US ALL TO KINGDOM COME!

YOU THINK OF EVERYTHING, DON'T YOU?

HERE'S ANOTHER SURPRISE FOR YOU, MAN OF STEEL!

LUTHOR!

SUPERMAN TAKES A GREAT LEAP FORWARD....

I THREATENED TO BLOW US UP --AND I WILL!

YOU MEAN YOU'LL TRY TO!

THE MAN OF STEEL SUCCEEDS IN WEDGING HIS POWERFUL FINGERS BETWEEN THE SMALL PLUNGER AND THE FLOOR...

LUTHOR ATTEMPTS FLIGHT...

NO YOU DON'T!

GET HIM!

AS LUTHOR'S HIRELINGS CLOSE IN, SUPERMAN SENDS THEM FLYING IN ALL DIRECTIONS....

WANT TO FIGHT, EH?

BUT WHEN HE TURNS BACK TO SEIZE HIS CAPTIVE....

GONE! HE MADE GOOD HIS ESCAPE WHILE MY BACK WAS TURNED!

LATER, AT THE DAILY PLANET, AFTER SUPERMAN HAS RETURNED THE PROMINENT MEN TO SAFETY....

SO LUTHOR WAS AT THE BOTTOM OF THIS MESS! WE MIGHT HAVE SUSPECTED IT!

WHEN I THINK HOW CLOSE SUPERMAN CAME TO BECOMING A DESTRUCTIVE FORCE, I SHUDDER. IT'S A LUCKY THING HE'S ON THE SIDE OF LAW AND ORDER!

THE END

SUPERMAN

by JERRY SIEGEL and JOE SHUSTER

SUPERMAN MEETS A STRANGE FOE IN THE MYSTERIOUS BEING KNOWN ONLY AS *"THE ARCHER."* VICTIMS ARE GIVEN THE CHOICE OF PAYING A HEAVY FEE OR PERISHING BEFORE THE UNIQUE CRIMINAL'S DEADLY ACCURACY WITH THE BOW AND ARROW!

LIMOUSINE AFTER LIMOUSINE PULLS UP BEFORE THE *GAYFORD MANSION....*

THE REASON: WEALTHY THOMAS GAYFORD IS HOLDING ONE OF HIS INTERNATIONALLY FAMOUS PARTIES....

HAVE FUN, FOLKS! I'M FOOTING THE BILLS!

LATER--AS THE GUESTS LINE UP AROUND A BANQUET TABLE....

YOU'LL NEVER KNOW JUST HOW GLAD I AM TO HAVE ALL OF YOU HERE. YOU SEE, I HAVE HERE AN ANONYMOUS NOTE, SIGNED *"THE ARCHER."* IT IT PROPHESIES THAT SINCE I HAVE FAILED TO PAY A DEMANDED RANSOM, I SHALL DIE TONIGHT.

WHAT?

SURELY YOU'RE JOKING!

NOT AT ALL. BUT THE JOKE'S ON *"THE ARCHER!"* I'VE POSTED GUARDS ABOUT THE PLACE. IT WILL BE IMPOSSIBLE FOR HIM TO ENTER!

BUT UNKNOWN TO GAYFORD --AT THAT VERY MOMENT ONE OF THE GUARDS LIES STILL IN DEATH...!

A GREEN-CLAD FIGURE LAUNCHES ITSELF FROM THE LIMB OF A HIGH TREE TO A BALCONY ON THE SIDE OF THE MANSION....

A TOAST, FRIENDS-- TO "THE ARCHER"-- WHO MISSED HIS MARK!

LOOK!

UP THERE!

AAAGH HHH!!

GET "THE ARCHER"!

HE'S GONE!

CALL THE POLICE!!

EDITORIAL OFFICE OF THE DAILY PLANET....

WHERE IN BLAZES ARE LOIS LANE AND CLARK KENT?

THEY'RE NOT TO BE FOUND ANYWHERE, MR. WHITE!

FINE THING! JUST WHEN THE BIGGEST NEWS STORY OF THE YEAR IS BREAKING, THEY HAVE TO PLAY HIDE-AND-SEEK!

ER-- MR. WH- WHITE...

YES?

I'LL BE GLAD TO COVER THE STORY FOR YOU.

YOU'LL COVER IT?

I--I'D LIKE TO BECOME A REAL REPORTER--LIKE CLARK KENT, AND IF YOU'D ONLY GIVE ME A CHANCE...

HMM...YOU'D PROBABLY DO A BETTER JOB THAN CLARK, AT THAT. TELL YOU WHAT I'LL DO, KID. COME BACK AGAIN IN FIVE OR TEN YEARS.....AND I MAY GIVE YOU A BREAK....

T-TEN YEARS? --THAT'S A LONG TIME!

CLARK AND LOIS RETURN TO THE NEWSPAPER OFFICE....

SO HERE YOU ARE! WHERE HAVE YOU TWO BEEN?

OUT LOOKING FOR MATERIAL --BUT NOT A THING IS STIRRING!

NOTHING, EH? GET DOWN TO THE GAYFORD MANSION! -- THOMAS GAYFORD HAS BEEN SLAIN BY A MYSTERIOUS PERSON NAMED "THE ARCHER." HE REFUSED TO PAY THE AMOUNT DEMANDED!

WHAT --?!

"THE ARCHER!" SOUNDS MELO-DRAMATIC!

--AND EXCITING!

YOU, EH? IT DOESN'T TAKE YOU LONG TO SHOW UP WHEREVER NEWS IS BEING MADE!

THAT'S OUR BUSINESS!

HAVE YOU ANY IDEA WHO THIS "ARCHER" MAY BE, CASEY?

NONE AT ALL--YET, BUT WE HAVE SOME INTERESTING CLUES.

3

WHY DON'T YOU COOK UP A NEW COME-BACK?

THAT ONE'S A LITTLE SHOP-WORN!

QUIET, YOU TWO--OR I'LL HAVE YOU RUN OFF THE PLACE!

AT THAT MOMENT----

A NOTE--PINNED TO THE WALL BY THE ARROW!

WHAT DOES IT SAY?

KEEP BACK. THIS IS CONFIDENTIAL POLICE BUSINESS!

WELL--??

NO HARM IN LETTING YOU KNOW. "THE ARCHER" SAYS HE KILLED GAYFORD TO SHOW THAT HE MEANS BUSINESS WHEN HE MAKES HIS DEMANDS!

QUICK, A TELEPHONE!

AS THEY DRIVE OFF, CLARK'S QUICK EYES NOTE....

("-AN ARROW--STREAKING DOWN TOWARD US!-")

SWIFTLY, CLARK RAISES HIS HAND SO THAT THE ARROW BOUNCES OFF BEFORE IT REACHES LOIS....

WHAT WAS THAT NOISE?

I DIDN'T HEAR ANYTHING!

BUT THEN--AS THEY SPEED DOWN AN INCLINE... CLARK MAKES ANOTHER STARTLING DISCOVERY....

("-THE BRAKES--THEY DON'T WORK--!-")

CLARK'S X-RAY VISION REVEALS TO HIM THAT THE BRAKES OF HIS CAR HAVE BEEN TAMPERED WITH....

4

("-COMING AROUND THAT CURVE AHEAD--A TRUCK! THERE'S SURE TO BE A COLLISION--UNLESS...!-")

CAREFUL, CLARK!

SWIFTLY CLARK FOCUSES HIS EYES HYPNOTICALLY UPON LOIS LANE SO THAT SHE IS SWIFTLY AND PAINLESSLY RENDERED UNCONSCIOUS....

SHE'S OUT!

NO TIME TO CHANGE TO MY *SUPERMAN* COSTUME!

AS THE TRUCK HURTLES TOWARD HIM, KENT HEAVES HIS ROADSTER UP...!

HOPE THE TRUCK DRIVER DOESN'T GET A GOOD LOOK AT ME!

...AND VAULTS OVER THE ONCOMING TRUCK, ROADSTER AND ALL...!

THAT DOES IT!

THERE! THE BRAKES ARE OKAY AGAIN! BUT NOW TO START DRIVING AGAIN!

I--I MUST HAVE FALLEN ASLEEP!

YOU CERTAINLY DON'T FIND MY COMPANY VERY INTERESTING!

GOODNIGHT, LOIS.-- PLEASANT DREAMS!

I DOUBT IF I'LL SLEEP A WINK--NOT WITH *"THE ARCHER"* LOOSE...!

ONE THING I KNOW DEFINITELY--*"THE ARCHER"* DISLIKES INQUISITIVE REPORTERS!

WHEN CLARK REACHES HIS APARTMENT....

THIS DEMANDS FURTHER INVESTIGATION--FROM **SUPERMAN!**

SHORTLY AFTER, THE COLORFUL *MAN OF TOMORROW* HURTLES THRU THE DARK SKY...

TRACKING DOWN SOMEONE AS COLD AND CRUEL AS *"THE ARCHER"* WILL BE NO CINCH!

AND LATER--HE ALIGHTS ATOP THE BALCONY OUTSIDE THE *GAYFORD MANSION,...*

ONE CLUE HE'S *SURE* TO HAVE LEFT BEHIND!

HIS FOOTPRINTS! MY MICROSCOPIC VISION MAKES THEM APPEAR AS CLEAR AS SIGN POSTS!

SUPERMAN LEAPS DOWN TO THE ROAD BELOW AND FAILS TO SIGHT SHADOWS CREEPING TOWARD HIM...

AND HERE'S WHERE HE STOOD WHEN HE TAMPERED WITH MY CAR'S BRAKES!

SUDDENLY, SEVERAL POLICEMEN SPRING AT THE *MAN OF STEEL...*

IT'S **SUPERMAN!**

GRAB HIM!

A MOMENT BEFORE THE POLICE REACH HIM, **SUPERMAN** DIVES AT THE GROUND AND BURROWS OUT OF VIEW...!

I'D BETTER EXIT!

STOP HIM!

6

AN INSTANT LATER HE POPS OUT OF THE GROUND BEHIND THE OFFICERS...

WERE YOU GENTLEMEN PAGING ME?

THERE HE IS!

DON'T LET HIM GET AWAY!

BUT OFF RACES **SUPERMAN** SO SWIFTLY THAT HE IS OUT OF VIEW IN MOMENTS...!

IT WOULD BE USELESS TO ATTEMPT TO REASON WITH THEM!

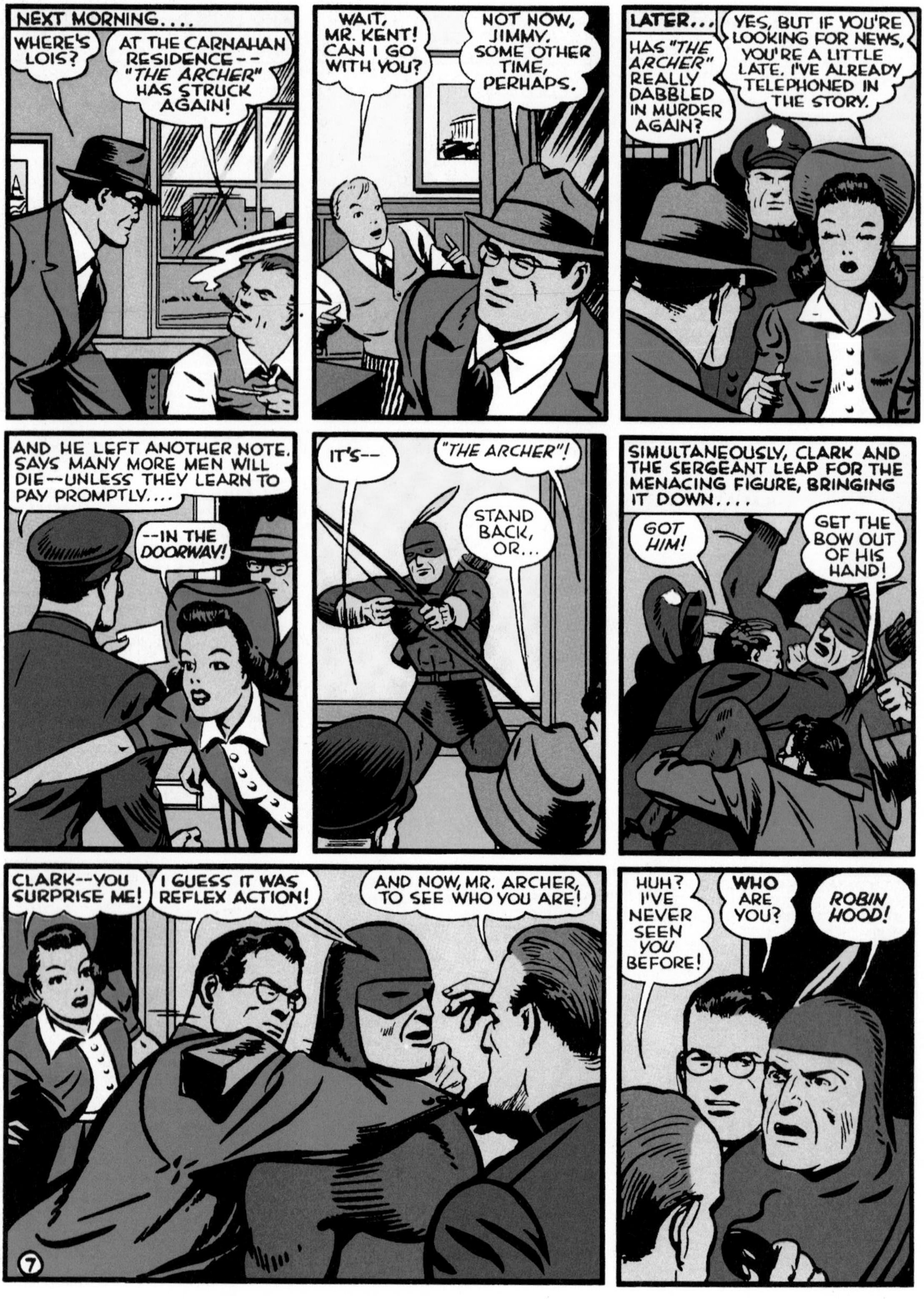
NEXT MORNING....
WHERE'S LOIS?
AT THE CARNAHAN RESIDENCE-- "THE ARCHER" HAS STRUCK AGAIN!
WAIT, MR. KENT! CAN I GO WITH YOU?
NOT NOW, JIMMY. SOME OTHER TIME, PERHAPS.
LATER...
HAS "THE ARCHER" REALLY DABBLED IN MURDER AGAIN?
YES, BUT IF YOU'RE LOOKING FOR NEWS, YOU'RE A LITTLE LATE. I'VE ALREADY TELEPHONED IN THE STORY.
AND HE LEFT ANOTHER NOTE. SAYS MANY MORE MEN WILL DIE--UNLESS THEY LEARN TO PAY PROMPTLY....
--IN THE DOORWAY!
IT'S--
"THE ARCHER"!
STAND BACK, OR...
SIMULTANEOUSLY, CLARK AND THE SERGEANT LEAP FOR THE MENACING FIGURE, BRINGING IT DOWN....
GOT HIM!
GET THE BOW OUT OF HIS HAND!
CLARK--YOU SURPRISE ME!
I GUESS IT WAS REFLEX ACTION!
AND NOW, MR. ARCHER, TO SEE WHO YOU ARE!
7
HUH? I'VE NEVER SEEN YOU BEFORE!
WHO ARE YOU?
ROBIN HOOD!

THIS-- "THE ARCHER"? --I WONDER...

I HEARD A RADIO NEWS FLASH AND HURRIED OVER TO DEMONSTRATE MY SKILL WITH THE BOW AND ARROW!

LATER--AT HEADQUARTERS....

REMEMBER TO MENTION IN THE PAPER THAT IT WAS ME WHO CAPTURED THIS DANGEROUS CRIMINAL.

IF YOU ASK ME, I THINK THIS FELLOW IS A HARMLESS NUT WHO IMAGINES HIMSELF TO BE THE REAL "ARCHER"!

AMOS KENDRICK, THE JEWELER, CALLED.--HE CLAIMS TO HAVE RECEIVED A THREAT FROM "THE ARCHER"!

PAY NO ATTENTION TO HIM. HE'S GOT NOTHING TO WORRY ABOUT NOW THAT "THE ARCHER" IS BEHIND BARS.

("-I'D BETTER EXIT!-")

FAR FROM THE POSSIBILITY OF SCRUTINY, CLARK REMOVES HIS OUTER GARMENTS....

IT'S MY PERSONAL OPINION THAT KENDRICK MAY BE VERY MUCH IN DANGER!

SHORTLY AFTER...THE MAN OF TOMORROW ALIGHTS ATOP THE ROOF OF KENDRICK'S RESIDENCE...

NOW TO MAKE USE OF MY X-RAY VISION!

WHAT THE MAN OF STEEL SIGHTS...

WHY DON'T THE POLICE ARRIVE? THIS SUSPENSE IS DRIVING ME MAD!

⑧

SUDDENLY-- IN THRU THE WINDOW SPEEDS A DEADLY SHAFT...!

IN A TWINKLING, SUPERMAN RIPS AN OPENING IN THE ROOF....

NO TIME TO SEARCH FOR ANOTHER ENTRANCE!

DOWN PLUMMETS THE *MAN OF TOMORROW* AS THE ARROW NEARS ITS GOAL....

A RACE, EH?

...KNOCKING IT ASIDE IN THE NICK OF TIME...

—AND CLOSE, TOO!

WHAT --??

YOU WON'T GET ME! KEEP BACK!

PUT DOWN THAT GUN! WANT TO HURT YOUR-SELF?

BUT KENDRICK FIRES IN UNREASONING TERROR...!

THE BULLETS— THEY GLANCED OFF YOU LIKE PEAS...!

YOU'D BE BETTER OFF WITH A PEA-SHOOTER, AT THAT!

THIS DELAY HAS GIVEN *"THE ARCHER"* AMPLE TIME TO SLIP AWAY!

THEN-- YOU AREN'T HE!

9

NO SIGN OF HIM! *"THE ARCHER"* MADE GOOD HIS ESCAPE!

SOMETIME LATER....

I MESSED UP A BEAUTIFUL OPPORTUNITY TO SNARE "THE ARCHER," MIGHT AS WELL CHANGE NOW.

THIS NOTE CAME FOR MR. KENT, THE MESSENGER SAID IT WAS ABOUT "THE ARCHER."

THANKS, I'LL TAKE IT, JIMMY.

HM-MM! IT SAYS FOR CLARK TO COME TO BINSTON AND ANNEX AVENUES IF HE WANTS TO KNOW WHO "THE ARCHER" IS! WHAT A BREAK FOR ME!

CLARK ENTERS THE DAILY PLANET EDITORIAL OFFICE TWO MINUTES LATER....

CONGRAT-ULATIONS, CLARK! THIS IS YOUR LUCKY DAY!

YES?

A TIP HAS COME IN THAT THERE'S A BIG STORY BREWING AT 1411 WINGATE ROAD! I'D COVER IT MYSELF, ONLY IT'S TOO SENSATIONAL.

THANKS, LOIS. I CERTAINLY APPRECIATE YOUR GENEROSITY.

BUT AS CLARK CHANGES TO HIS IDENTITY AS SUPERMAN...

THIS UNSELFISHNESS ON LOIS' PART IS ALMOST TOO MUCH FOR ME, IT'S RATHER UNUSUAL FOR A REPORTER TO PASS UP A GOOD STORY!

WAIT TILL CLARK FINDS OUT WHAT I'VE UNCOVERED WHILE HE'S ON A WILD-GOOSE CHASE!

⑩

UNKOWN TO LOIS, JIMMY THE OFFICE BOY CONCEALS HIMSELF IN THE TRUNK AT THE REAR OF HER CAR....

IF I WAITED FOR A CHANCE TO BE HANDED TO ME, IT MAY NEVER COME! I'VE GOT TO BE LIKE LOIS-- MAKE MY OPPORTUNITIES!

WHEN LOIS REACHES BINSTON AND ANNEX AVENUES....

I DON'T SEE ANYONE! CAN THAT NOTE HAVE BEEN A HOAX?

WHAT ARE YOU DOING HERE?--I EXPECTED A MALE REPORTER!

SO YOU'RE THE ONE WHO WROTE THE NOTE! IT WAS IMPOSSIBLE FOR KENT TO COME, BUT YOU NEEDN'T HESITATE ABOUT LETTING ME KNOW WHO "THE ARCHER" IS!

I SHALL EXPECT TO BE WELL PAID FOR THIS INFORMATION.--WHILE LOOKING THRU MY MASTER'S PAPERS --SECRETLY, NATURALLY--I CAME ACROSS EVIDENCE THAT POSITIVELY IDENTIFIES HIM AS A CRIMINAL!

I'LL PAY YOU ANY REASONABLE AMOUNT. BUT TELL ME--WHO IS HE?

MY MASTER IS --YAAA-AAA!

NO! OH-HHH!

AS ANOTHER ARROW CUTS THRU THE AIR, LOIS' FIGURE IS THRUST ASIDE JUST IN TIME....

MISS LANE, QUICK! --WE'VE GOT TO HIDE IN THE WOODS!

JIMMY!

LOIS AND JIMMY FLEE THRU THE WOODS IN FRANTIC HASTE....

HURRY!

HE'S CLOSE BEHIND!

11

RUTHLESSLY, "THE ARCHER" STALKS HIS HUMAN PREY...!

I'LL OVERTAKE THEM IN A MOMENT!

MEANWHILE....

THIS IS 1411 WINGATE ROAD, ALL RIGHT. -- BUT THERE'S NOTHING HERE EXCEPT AN EMPTY LOT! IF THIS IS LOIS' IDEA OF A JOKE...!

SUPERMAN RETURNS TO THE DAILY PLANET IN HIS IDENTITY AS CLARK KENT....

THIS NOTE ON LOIS' DESK EXPLAINS EVERYTHING! SHE SENT ME OUT TO NO-MAN'S-LAND SO SHE'D HAVE AN OPPORTUNITY TO INVESTIGATE THAT TIP ABOUT "THE ARCHER" WITHOUT INTERFERENCE FROM ME!

ONCE AGAIN AS SUPERMAN, CLARK SPEEDS TOWARD BINSTON AND ANNEX AVENUES....

FOOLISH GIRL! SHE MAY BE GETTING INTO TERRIBLE DANGER!

HE ALMOST GOT ME --AGAIN!

BENEATH THAT LEDGE -- A PERFECT HIDING PLACE!

LOIS AND JIMMY HUDDLE IN SILENT TERROR BENEATH THE LEDGE, UNAWARE THAT "THE ARCHER" APPEARS ATOP THE LEDGE BEHIND THEM AND TAKES CAREFUL AIM,...

DOWN FLASHES AN ARROW TOWARD LOIS' UNPROTECTED BACK...!

BUT FROM A GREAT HEIGHT, SUPERMAN SIGHTS LOIS' DANGER..

GOT TO OVERTAKE THAT ARROW!

12

NECK AND NECK!

THE *MAN OF TOMORROW* SWOOPS DOWN BEHIND LOIS, RECEIVING THE ARROW UPON HIS OWN SUPER-TOUGH SKIN....

SUPER-MAN!

WHAT A GENIUS YOU ARE, LOIS--FOR GETTING INTO TROUBLE!

OFF RACES *"THE ARCHER"* IN FRANTIC FLIGHT....

IF I CAN ONLY REACH MY CAR...!

UP WITH YOU!

FLUNG BY THE *MAN OF STEEL'S* TREMENDOUSLY POWERFUL MUSCLES, THE HUGE BOULDER SMASHES THE CRIMINAL'S AUTO TO BITS!

LET GO!

THAT MASK IS COMING OFF!

IT'S QUIGLEY--THE FAMOUS BIG-GAME HUNTER!

I--I THOUGHT HUNTING HUMAN BEINGS WOULD PROVE MORE PROFITABLE!

ANY KID COULD TELL YOU THAT CRIME DOESN'T PAY, MR. QUIGLEY.

I'LL BIND HIM FOR YOU--THEN SEE TO IT THAT POLICE GET HERE PROMPTLY!

13

LATER--AT THE *DAILY PLANET*...

TELL ME, JIMMY--HOW DOES IT FEEL TO GET YOUR FIRST BY-LINE?

SWELL. AND I OWE IT TO BOTH OF YOU!

LET SOME OF THE CREDIT GO TO *SUPERMAN,* JIMMY.

THE END

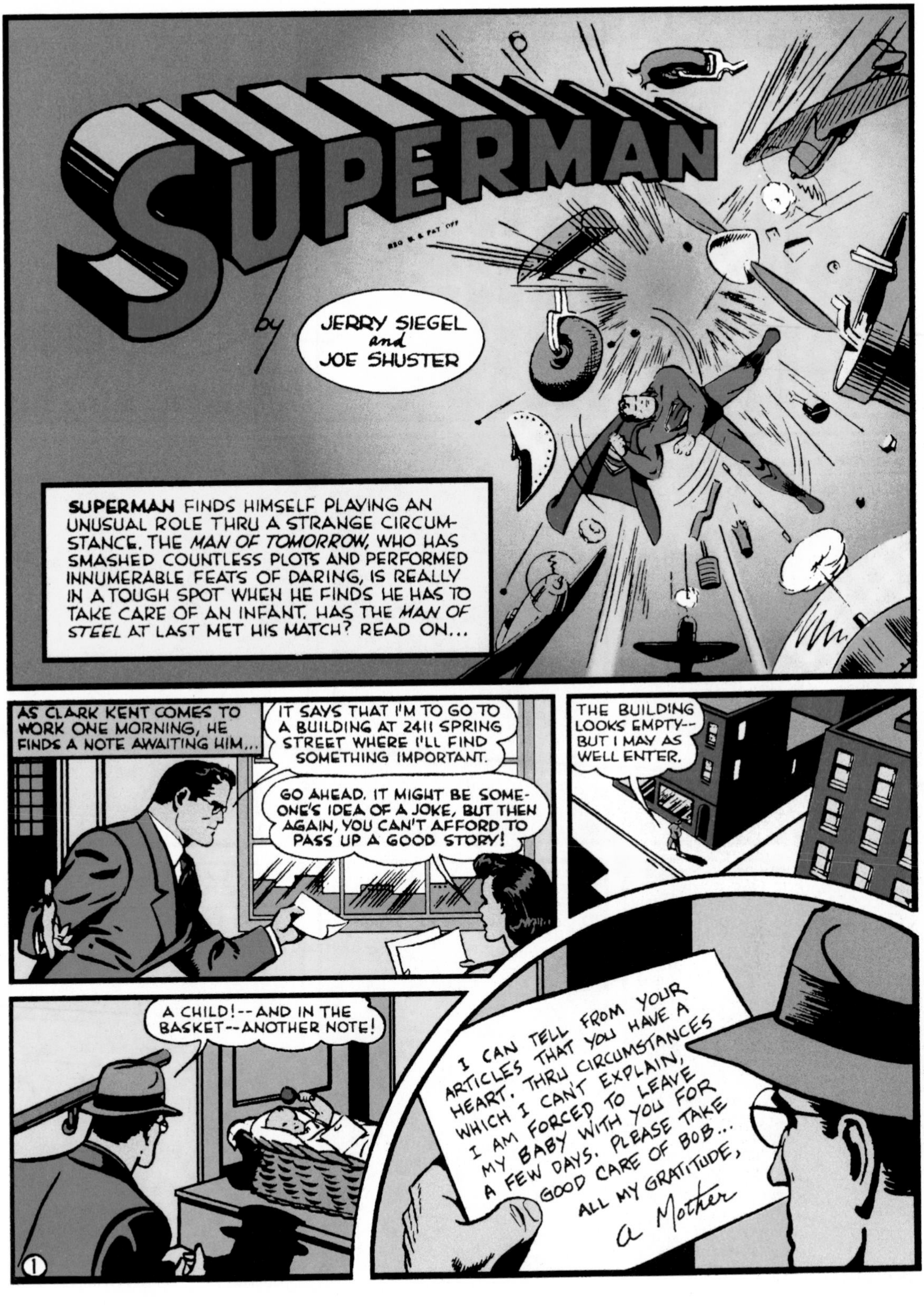
SUPERMAN
REG U.S. PAT OFF
by
JERRY SIEGEL and JOE SHUSTER
SUPERMAN FINDS HIMSELF PLAYING AN UNUSUAL ROLE THRU A STRANGE CIRCUMSTANCE. THE MAN OF TOMORROW, WHO HAS SMASHED COUNTLESS PLOTS AND PERFORMED INNUMERABLE FEATS OF DARING, IS REALLY IN A TOUGH SPOT WHEN HE FINDS HE HAS TO TAKE CARE OF AN INFANT. HAS THE MAN OF STEEL AT LAST MET HIS MATCH? READ ON...
AS CLARK KENT COMES TO WORK ONE MORNING, HE FINDS A NOTE AWAITING HIM...
IT SAYS THAT I'M TO GO TO A BUILDING AT 2411 SPRING STREET WHERE I'LL FIND SOMETHING IMPORTANT.
GO AHEAD. IT MIGHT BE SOMEONE'S IDEA OF A JOKE, BUT THEN AGAIN, YOU CAN'T AFFORD TO PASS UP A GOOD STORY!
THE BUILDING LOOKS EMPTY-- BUT I MAY AS WELL ENTER.
A CHILD!--AND IN THE BASKET--ANOTHER NOTE!
I CAN TELL FROM YOUR ARTICLES THAT YOU HAVE A HEART. THRU CIRCUMSTANCES WHICH I CAN'T EXPLAIN, I AM FORCED TO LEAVE MY BABY WITH YOU FOR A FEW DAYS. PLEASE TAKE GOOD CARE OF BOB... ALL MY GRATITUDE, A Mother
1

WHEN CLARK RETURNS TO THE NEWSPAPER OFFICE....

OF ALL PEOPLE, WHY DID SHE HAVE TO CHOOSE ME?

ISN'T IT CUTE? DON'T WORRY, CLARK. I THINK YOU'LL MAKE A WONDERFUL SUBSTITUTE MOTHER. AND BESIDES, THE NOTE SAID IT WOULD BE FOR ONLY A FEW DAYS.

THIS IS DEFINITE: EITHER I HAVE YOUR HELP, OR I WON'T GO THRU WITH IT! WHAT DO I KNOW ABOUT CHILDREN?

YOU'LL SOON FIND OUT! —I'LL BE GLAD TO HELP!

LATER--CLARK'S APARTMENT....

WHAT NOW?

FIRST DASH OUT TO THE DRUGSTORE AND PURCHASE ALL THE ITEMS ON THIS LIST. AND HURRY!

AFTER CLARK HAS GONE, LOIS ANSWERS A KNOCK AT THE DOOR.

COULD I INTEREST YOU IN SOME TOYS FOR A CHILD OF--SAY--TWO YEARS?

NOT INTERESTED.

YOU DO HAVE A CHILD IN THERE, DON'T YOU?

THAT'S NO AFFAIR OF YOURS. WILL YOU PLEASE LEAVE?

WHAT'S THE TROUBLE, LOIS?

THIS SALESMAN. HE WAS TRYING TO FORCE HIS WAY INTO THE APARTMENT.

I WAS JUST GOING.

I WONDER WHY THAT SALESMAN WAS SO ANXIOUS TO LEARN WHETHER THERE WAS A CHILD IN HERE?

EXCUSE ME, LOIS. I FORGOT SOME OF THE ITEMS.

ATOP THE APARTMENT BUILDING, CLARK CHANGES TO SUPERMAN...

THAT FELLOW'S ACTIONS WERE HIGHLY SUSPICIOUS! I'D BETTER TRAIL HIM!

LEAPING THRU THE SKY, THE *MAN OF STEEL* KEEPS THE "SALESMAN" IN VIEW....

HE'S ENTERING THAT BUILDING!

ALIGHTING OUTSIDE AN OFFICE WINDOW, **SUPERMAN** IS ON THE ALERT.

PERHAPS I CAN LEARN A CLUE AS TO THE IDENTITY OF THE BABY'S MOTHER...

WITHIN THE OFFICE....
WAS THE KID IN THERE?

I COULDN'T SWEAR TO IT. I'D KNOW FOR SURE, BUT THAT REPORTER HAD TO COME BACK IN TIME TO SPOIL IT FOR ME.

WE'LL GO THERE THIS AFTER-NOON WHEN HE'LL BE OUT.

I GET IT! AND WHEN HE COMES BACK, HE'LL FIND THE CHILD GONE!

BUT I'LL BE WAITING FOR THEM! RIGHT NOW I'D BETTER GET BACK TO THE APARTMENT BEFORE LOIS GETS SUSPICIOUS.

LATER....

I'VE GOT TO LEAVE NOW, BUT REMEMBER TO FOLLOW MY INSTRUCTIONS.

I WON'T FORGET.

③

BUT NO SOONER HAS LOIS LEFT, THAN....

WAA-AAA AAA-AA....!

STOP, BOB... PLEASE, STOP... GOSH--WHAT CAN I DO--? WHY DID LOIS HAVE TO LEAVE?

PERHAPS IT WOULD STOP CRYING IF I COULD AMUSE IT. I HAVE IT-- ACROBATICS!

CLARK SPINS THRU THE AIR IN A SUCCESSION OF DIZZY SOMERSAULTS....

...BALANCES ON ONE FINGER...

WHAT CAN I DO? NOTHING SEEMS TO PLEASE HIM!

I GIVE UP... WAIT--!

SWIFTLY, KENT REMOVES HIS OUTER GARMENTS, REVEALING HIMSELF AS-- SUPERMAN...

THIS IS A JOB FOR SUPERMAN!

4

THE INFANT STOPS CRYING, LOOKS ON WITH INTEREST...

AN INSTANT LATER, SUPERMAN AND CHILD STREAK OUT THRU THE APARTMENT WINDOW....

HE'S NO LONGER CRYING! THIS MAY WORK.

NOW SIT THERE-- AND WATCH!

SEE-- IT'S EASY!

EASY AS PIE!

IT LIKES IT! LOOK AT THE BIG GRIN ON ITS FACE!

OH-OH! THOSE TWO MEN-- ENTERING THE APARTMENT BUILDING!--TIME FOR US TO GET BACK!

I HEAR IT INSIDE ---A BABY!

UNLOCK THAT DOOR WITH A MASTER KEY! WE'LL HAVE THAT KID IN A MINUTE!

IT TAKES BUT A MOMENT FOR THE "SALESMAN" TO UNLOCK THE DOOR. THE TWO ENTER STEALTHILY....

THERE IT IS-- ON THE BED...

QUICK! GET IT!

COME ON, KID. WE'RE GOING ON A LITTLE TRIP.

WHA --???

DON'T TOUCH THAT BABY!

SUPERMAN!

KEEP AWAY!

AND DENY MYSELF THE PLEASURE OF GIVING YOU FELLOWS WHAT YOU DESERVE?

--NOT A CHANCE!

HEY!

YOU'RE NOT GONNA DROP US, ARE YOU!?!

NOW TELL ME WHO THAT BABY'S MOTHER IS--AND WHY YOU WANTED TO SNATCH IT.

WE... W-WE DON'T KNOW-- HONEST!

OVER THE TELEPHONE, SOME MYSTERIOUS GUY OFFERED US PLENTY TO GET THE KID FOR HIM. HE SAID CLARK KENT HAD IT.

6

REMEMBER--IF I FIND YOU ANNOYING THE BABY OR ITS MOTHER AGAIN, I'LL MAKE IT A POINT TO ATTEND TO YOU!

WE WON'T FORGET!

MEANWHILE -- CRAWLING FROM THE BED, THE INFANT CRAWLS OUT UPON THE LEDGE OUTSIDE THE WINDOW OF CLARK'S APARTMENT, AND PEERS CURIOUSLY TOWARD THE STREET FAR BELOW....

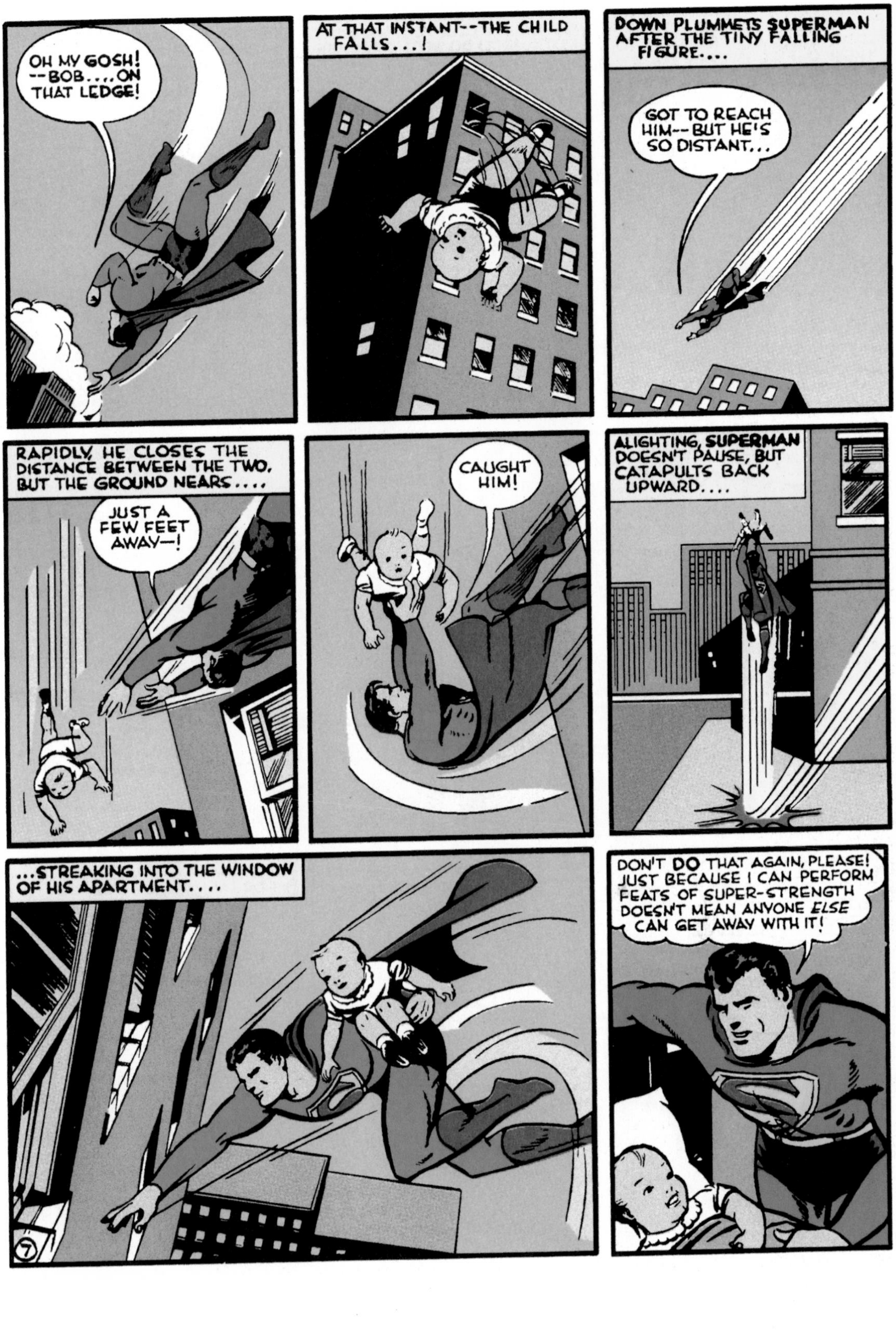
OH MY GOSH! --BOB....ON THAT LEDGE!
AT THAT INSTANT--THE CHILD FALLS...!
DOWN PLUMMETS SUPERMAN AFTER THE TINY FALLING FIGURE....
GOT TO REACH HIM--BUT HE'S SO DISTANT...
RAPIDLY, HE CLOSES THE DISTANCE BETWEEN THE TWO, BUT THE GROUND NEARS....
JUST A FEW FEET AWAY--!
CAUGHT HIM!
ALIGHTING, SUPERMAN DOESN'T PAUSE, BUT CATAPULTS BACK UPWARD....
...STREAKING INTO THE WINDOW OF HIS APARTMENT....
7
DON'T DO THAT AGAIN, PLEASE! JUST BECAUSE I CAN PERFORM FEATS OF SUPER-STRENGTH DOESN'T MEAN ANYONE ELSE CAN GET AWAY WITH IT!

THE THUGS, WHO HAD ATTEMPTED TO SEIZE BOB, RETURN TO THEIR OFFICE IN TIME TO RECEIVE A TELEPHONE CALL...

DID YOU SUCCEED?

WITH **SUPERMAN** ON OUR TAIL, WE DIDN'T HAVE A CHANCE.

NO. NO -- I TELL YOU. WE WANT NOTHING TO DO WITH THIS CASE ANY LONGER. NOT FOR **ANY** AMOUNT OF MONEY!

VERY WELL. IN THAT CASE, I'LL HAVE TO ALTER MY PLANS.

SHORTLY AFTER, CLARK ANSWERS A KNOCK AT HIS DOOR....

ANYTHING I CAN DO FOR YOU?

YES--YOU CAN GIVE ME BACK MY BABY.

THEN--YOU'RE BOB'S MOTHER?

MY BABY-- MY BABY...!

YOU'RE OBVIOUSLY IN TROUBLE. IF THERE'S ANY WAY I CAN HELP...

THANK YOU VERY MUCH, BUT --I'LL MANAGE TO WORK THINGS OUT MY OWN WAY. MEANWHILE, I WANT TO THANK YOU FOR BEING SO GOOD TO MY BOY--YOU'RE A WONDERFUL MAN.

AFTER WOMAN AND CHILD DEPART....

GOSH--THE PLACE DOESN'T SEEM THE SAME WITHOUT BOB. I WAS BECOMING VERY ATTACHED TO HIM....BUT,....HE BELONGS WITH HIS MOTHER.

8

AT THAT MOMENT....

I'VE COME FOR MY CHILD.

WHAT?--WILL YOU PLEASE REPEAT THAT!!

WHERE'S BOB? NOTHING'S HAPPENED TO HIM!!

ANOTHER WOMAN CAME SEVERAL MINUTES AGO-- CLAIMED SHE WAS BOB'S MOTHER-- AND TOOK HIM AWAY WITH HER!

MY POOR BABY-- I SHOULD HAVE KNOWN I COULDN'T WIN AGAINST THEM.

EXPLAIN, PLEASE! YOU MEAN TO SAY THAT OTHER WOMAN WAS A FAKE-- THAT YOU'RE THE REAL MOTHER! BUT WHY...??

I'LL EXPLAIN. I'M CLARA PIERSON. MY HUSBAND, CHARLES PIERSON, WAS AN INVENTOR WORKING ON AN IMPORTANT WARTIME INVENTION WHEN THESE AGENTS OF A FOREIGN GOVERNMENT TRIED TO TORTURE HIS SECRET FROM HIM. HE DIED.

SINCE THEN THEY'VE BEEN AFTER ME, BELIEVING I KNOW THE SECRET OF MY HUSBAND'S INVENTION. IN TERROR THAT THEY WOULD STRIKE AT ME THRU MY CHILD, I LEFT HIM IN YOUR CARE AND TOOK TO HIDING-- BUT IT APPEARS I'VE FAILED.

IT'S MY FAULT...

IT'S CERTAIN THAT THE ONLY REASON THEY'VE TAKEN YOUR CHILD IS TO GET THAT INFORMATION FROM YOU. LET ME ACCOMPANY YOU TO YOUR HOME. THEY'RE SURE TO CONTACT YOU, AND WHEN THEY DO-- PERHAPS I CAN HELP.

I'M SO GRATEFUL TO YOU...

THEY ENTER THE PIERSON RESIDENCE TO FIND THE TELEPHONE RINGING....

YES?

COME TO 819 OAK STREET IF YOU WANT TO SEE YOUR BABY AGAIN ALIVE!

WHEN THEY REACH THE OAK STREET ADDRESS....

GET RID OF THIS MEDDLER!

DON'T HARM HIM!

THEY DON'T DARE --THEY'VE HEARD OF THE POWER OF THE PRESS.

YEAH? GET MOVIN', YOU!

GET INTO THAT CAR!

YOU-- YOU'RE REALLY NOT GOING TO...TO...

KILL YOU? YOU CATCH ON QUICK!

SWIFTLY THE AUTO DRIVES OUT INTO THE COUNTRY ON ITS DEADLY MISSION....

LET ME GO-- I PROMISE NOT TO INTERFERE AGAIN!

YOU'RE A LITTLE TOO LATE.

STOP THE CAR!

WHAT ARE YOU GOING TO DO-- LYNCH ME?

NO--WE'VE A CUTER IDEA!

TYING THE ROPE TO THE LIMB OVERHEAD, THE THUGS WALK BACK TO THEIR AUTO, LEAVING CLARK STANDING ON TIPTOE....

HEY!-- YOU CAN'T LEAVE ME LIKE THIS!

DON'T WORRY, --WE'LL BE RIGHT BACK!

THE TERRIBLE PURPOSE OF THE HEARTLESS SPIES IS REVEALED AS THEIR AUTO STREAKS TOWARD CLARK AT FULL SPEED....

SO THAT'S IT...THEY INTEND TO MAKE IT LOOK AS THO I WERE THE VICTIM OF A HIT-AND-RUN DRIVER!

AN INSTANT BEFORE THE CAR REACHES HIM, CLARK PROPELS HIMSELF UP INTO THE AIR IN A GIANT SWING THAT CARRIES HIM OVER THE LIMB....

THEY'RE DUE FOR A SURPRISE--!

--THEN DOWN HE CRASHES INTO THE ONCOMING AUTOMOBILE, KICKING IT BACK THRU THE AIR!

10

EASILY, CLARK FREES HIMSELF FROM HIS BONDS....

THAT FINISHED THEM! THEIR LITTLE JAUNT INTO THE COUNTRY HAD AN UNEXPECTED ENDING!

SWIFTLY REMOVING HIS OUTER GARMENTS, CLARK TRANSFORMS HIMSELF TO DYNAMIC **SUPERMAN.**

GOT TO GET BACK IN A HURRY--MRS. PIERSON IS IN NEED OF HELP!

MEANWHILE--

LEILA, YOU CAN BRING IN THE CHILD.

BOB-- BOB--!

I DESPISE THESE CRUDE METHODS, MRS. PIERSON, BUT THAT INFORMATION YOU POSSESS IS VERY IMPORTANT TO ME. THIS IS MY ULTIMATUM TO YOU--EITHER YOU SUPPLY ME WITH THE DETAILS OF YOUR HUSBAND'S DISCOVERY... OR LEILA WILL LEAVE WITH YOUR BABY--AND YOU'LL NEVER SEE HIM AGAIN!

I HAVE NO ALTERNATIVE--I'LL TELL YOU ANYTHING, ANYTHING --BUT DON'T HARM MY BABY!

THAT'S BETTER. NOW TELL ME WHAT I WANT TO KNOW...

MY HUSBAND'S SECRET NOTES ARE CONCEALED IN BOB'S BABY RATTLE WHICH STILL REMAINS IN CLARK KENT'S APARTMENT.

REMAIN HERE WITH MRS. PIERSON WHILE I GO TO KENT'S APARTMENT. IF WHAT SHE SAYS IS TRUE, HER CHILD WILL BE RESTORED. OTHERWISE...

SHORTLY AFTER THE SPY CHIEF DEPARTS, **SUPERMAN** SWOOPS DOWN TO A POSITION OUTSIDE THE WINDOW. GLANCING IN, HE IS IMMEDIATELY AWARE OF THE SITUATION....

THAT WOMAN WHO PASSED HERSELF OFF AS BOB'S MOTHER --KEEPING THE **REAL** MRS. PIERSON CAPTIVE!

(11)

SPRINGING IN, **SUPERMAN** CATCHES LEILA OFF-GUARD...

I'LL TAKE THAT!

WHA --??

SUPERMAN!

AFTER THE **MAN OF TOMORROW** BINDS AND GAGS LEILA....

I'M HERE TO HELP YOU. QUICK, TELL ME WHERE THE SPY CHIEF IS.

HE'S GONE TO CLARK KENT'S APARTMENT AFTER THE BABY RATTLE IN WHICH IS HIDDEN THE PLANS OF MY HUSBAND'S INVENTION!

GET IN TOUCH WITH THE POLICE! I'LL ATTEND TO THE SPY CHIEF!

THANK YOU--!

MEANWHILE, AS LOIS CLIMBS THE STAIRS TO CLARK'S APARTMENT...

IT'S TIME I STOPPED IN TO SEE HOW BOB AND CLARK ARE GETTING ALONG.

THAT MAN-- BREAKING INTO CLARK'S ROOM..!

SNOOPING, EH?

GET IN THERE!

JUST WHAT I WANT!

A BABY RATTLE! --NOW I KNOW YOU'RE MAD!

I'LL TAKE THAT, PLEASE!

SUPER- MAN--!

BACK-- OR I SHOOT THE GIRL!

HELPLESS TO INTERFERE, SUPERMAN FOLLOWS HIGH IN THE SKY AS THE SPY CHIEF DRIVES OFF WITH THE HELPLESS LOIS....

HE'LL MAKE ONE FALSE MOVE-- AND THEN..!

BELIEVING HE HAS SUCCEEDED IN ELUDING THE MAN OF STEEL, THE SPY CHIEF HURLS LOIS FROM THE SPEEDING CAR....

I DON'T NEED YOU ANY LONGER!

EEE- EEE!

SWOOPING LOW, **SUPERMAN** CATCHES LOIS BEFORE SHE STRIKES THE PAVEMENT....

GUESS WHO?

SPEEDING ONTO AN ADJACENT AIRFIELD, THE SPY HURRIES INTO A WAITING PLANE AND COMMENCES TO TAKE OFF AS THE *MAN OF TOMORROW* RACES DOWN THE FIELD IN PURSUIT....

TRYING TO GIVE ME THE SLIP, EH?

SEIZING THE TAIL OF THE RISING PLANE, **SUPERMAN** HEAVES IT BACK ONTO *TERRA FIRMA*....

YOU'RE REMAINING RIGHT HERE!

CRASHING INTO THE PLANE'S SIDE, THE *MAN OF TOMORROW* EMERGES MOMENTS LATER WITH A BADLY FRIGHTENED CAPTIVE...

AND NOW--WE'LL HEAD BACK TO YOUR HEAD-QUARTERS.

THRU THE AIR STREAK THE TWO...

YEE-EOW! L-L-LET ME GO!

THAT WOULD BE TOO SIMPLE A SOLUTION TO YOUR TROUBLES.

STREAKING IN THRU THE WINDOW OF THE SPY CHIEF'S APARTMENT, **SUPERMAN** DEPOSITS THE CULPRIT IN THE MIDST OF A SWARM OF POLICE...

HERE'S THE BIG BOY THE FEDERAL MEN WILL BE INTERESTED IN. YOU'LL FIND THE BABY RATTLE AND THE PLANS IN HIS POCKET.

IF WE COULD ONLY DRAFT YOU INTO THE FORCE!

I OWE YOU SO MUCH!

13

DAYS LATER....

I'M SO GRATEFUL TO YOU TWO. WITH YOUR HELP OUR GOVERNMENT, INSTEAD OF A FOREIGN POWER, IS IN POSSESSION OF MY DEPARTED HUSBAND'S INVENTION.

AND DON'T FORGET **SUPERMAN**!

THE END

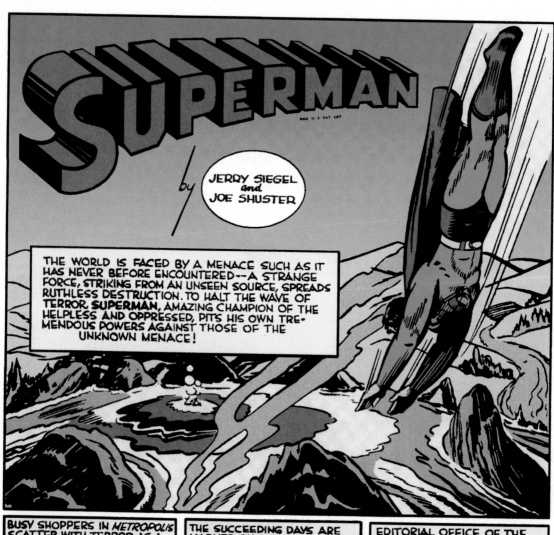

SUPERMAN

REG. U.S. PAT. OFF.

by JERRY SIEGEL and JOE SHUSTER

THE WORLD IS FACED BY A MENACE SUCH AS IT HAS NEVER BEFORE ENCOUNTERED--A STRANGE FORCE, STRIKING FROM AN UNSEEN SOURCE, SPREADS RUTHLESS DESTRUCTION. TO HALT THE WAVE OF TERROR, **SUPERMAN**, AMAZING CHAMPION OF THE HELPLESS AND OPPRESSED, PITS HIS OWN TREMENDOUS POWERS AGAINST THOSE OF THE UNKNOWN MENACE!

BUSY SHOPPERS IN *METROPOLIS* SCATTER WITH TERROR AS A HUGE DEPARTMENT STORE COLLAPSES....

THE SUCCEEDING DAYS ARE MARKED BY THE COLLAPSE OF OTHER GREAT STRUCTURES....

EDITORIAL OFFICE OF THE *DAILY PLANET*....

NO ONE CAN UNDERSTAND HOW ALL THESE DISASTERS COULD HAVE OCCURRED.

IF THERE'S A MORE SINISTER STORY BEHIND THIS AFFAIR THAN IS APPARENT, I WANT YOU TO GET IT!

ATOP THE *DAILY PLANET* BUILDING, CLARK KENT REMOVES HIS OUTER GARMENTS, TRANSFORMING HIMSELF TO **SUPERMAN**...

IT'S ENTIRELY POSSIBLE ANOTHER DISASTER MAY BE IMPENDING--AND IF IT IS--I WANT TO BE READY!

DURING THE NEXT HALF HOUR, SUPERMAN LEAPS THRU THE SKY OVER THE CITY, KEEPING PATROL....

NOTHING --YET!

BUT WAIT! DOWN THERE!

THE *EXCHANGE BUILDING* COMMENCES QUIVERING. ITS OCCUPANTS BEGIN TO POUR OUT OF IT FRANTICALLY, AWARE OF THE DESTRUCTION CERTAIN TO FOLLOW....

I MAY BE IN TIME TO PREVENT THE LOSS OF LIVES!

SUPERMAN PITS HIS COLOSSAL STRENGTH AGAINST THE SIDE OF THE TREMBLING BUILDING, STEADYING IT SLIGHTLY....

HURRY! I CAN'T KEEP IT UP MUCH LONGER!

②

ONCE NO ONE ELSE EMERGES FROM THE EDIFICE, **SUPERMAN** RETREATS A SHORT DISTANCE....

I'VE DONE WHAT I CAN. NOW LET IT FALL!

BUT AS **SUPERMAN** SURVEYS THE DOOMED BUILDING, A STARTLED EXCLAMATION LEAVES HIS LIPS AS HIS AMAZING X-RAY VISION BRINGS TO HIM AN UN-EXPECTED SCENE...

BACK THERE IN THE BUILDING!

WHAT THE *MAN OF TOMORROW* SIGHTS....

GET US OUT OF THIS BUILDING!

THE ELEVATOR DOESN'T RESPOND TO THE CONTROLS!

WE'LL ALL DIE!

ONLY A FEW SECONDS LEFT IN WHICH TO ACT!

THE *MAN OF STEEL* SMASHES CLEAR THRU THE SIDE OF THE BUILDING....

HATE TO BE DESTRUCTIVE-- BUT THIS BUILDING IS ABOUT TO COLLAPSE ANYWAY.

REACHING IN, **SUPERMAN** SNAPS THE ELEVATOR'S THICK CABLES WITH HIS BARE HANDS....

THE BUILDING --FALLING...!

SUPERMAN LEAPS OUT AND AWAY, THE ELEVATOR CAR HELD OVERHEAD, AS THE *EXCHANGE BUILDING* CRASHES TO TOTAL DESTRUCTION...!

MADE IT!

AN INSTANT LATER, HE IS SPRINGING OFF WITH THE GRATEFUL CRIES OF THE RESCUED PEOPLE RINGING IN HIS EARS....

WE OWE OUR LIVES TO YOU!

HURRAY, SUPERMAN!

A SHORT DISTANCE AWAY, **SUPERMAN** TURNS TO SURVEY THE WRECKAGE ONCE MORE. HIS VISION, MORE POWERFUL THAN ORDINARY SIGHT, NOTES--

A RAY--FAINTLY EMERGING FROM THE GROUND WHERE THE SKYSCRAPER STOOD!

AND NOW --IT'S GONE!!

③

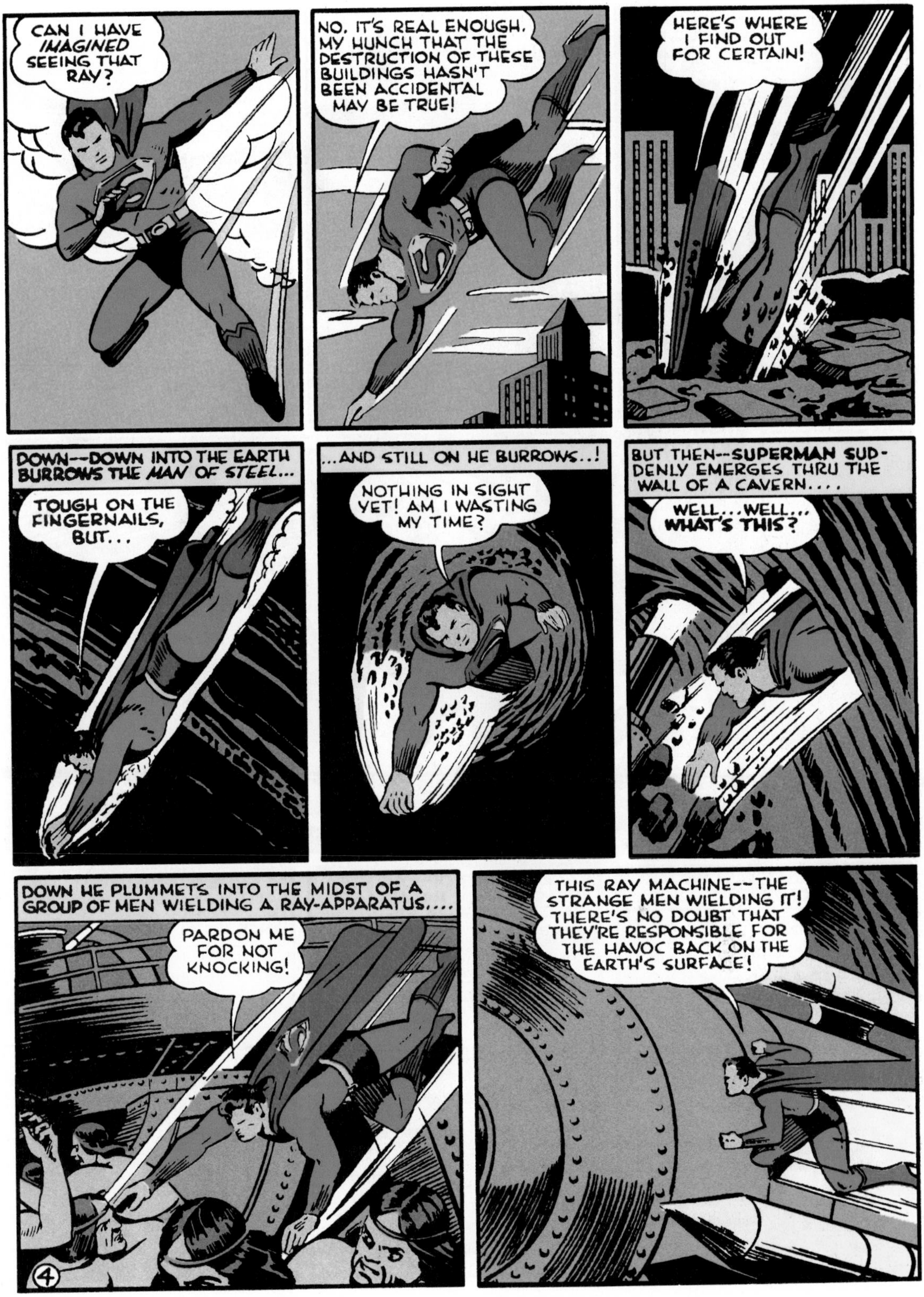
CAN I HAVE IMAGINED SEEING THAT RAY?
NO, IT'S REAL ENOUGH. MY HUNCH THAT THE DESTRUCTION OF THESE BUILDINGS HASN'T BEEN ACCIDENTAL MAY BE TRUE!
HERE'S WHERE I FIND OUT FOR CERTAIN!
DOWN--DOWN INTO THE EARTH BURROWS THE MAN OF STEEL...
TOUGH ON THE FINGERNAILS, BUT...
...AND STILL ON HE BURROWS..!
NOTHING IN SIGHT YET! AM I WASTING MY TIME?
BUT THEN--SUPERMAN SUDDENLY EMERGES THRU THE WALL OF A CAVERN....
WELL...WELL... WHAT'S THIS?
DOWN HE PLUMMETS INTO THE MIDST OF A GROUP OF MEN WIELDING A RAY-APPARATUS....
PARDON ME FOR NOT KNOCKING!
4
THIS RAY MACHINE--THE STRANGE MEN WIELDING IT! THERE'S NO DOUBT THAT THEY'RE RESPONSIBLE FOR THE HAVOC BACK ON THE EARTH'S SURFACE!

BUT AS **SUPERMAN** STRIDES TOWARD THE APPARATUS, THE MEN IN CHARGE OF THE MECHANISM TURN THE WEAPON UPON HIM...

NEXT INSTANT, THE RAY BLASTS AT THE *MAN OF TOMORROW* IN FULL FORCE. HE STAGGERS UNDER THE POWERFUL IMPACT....

WHEW!-- THAT'S NO PLAYTHING!

FORWARD BATTLES **SUPERMAN** AGAINST THE TERRIBLE FORCE OF THE RAY...!

IF IT'S POWERFUL ENOUGH TO SHATTER A SKYSCRAPER, YOU CAN IMAGINE WHAT IT MAY DO TO ME!

BUT ONE WELL-DELIVERED BLOW EXPLODES THE MECHANISM INTO FRAGMENTS...!

THAT'S MORE LIKE IT!

THE MEN CLOSE IN WITH SQUEALS OF ANGER....

A DOZEN TO ONE! THAT'S THE WAY I LIKE MY ODDS!

BACK FLY HIS OPPONENTS, PROPELLED BY THE *MAN OF STEEL'S* POWERFUL FISTS!

AS **SUPERMAN** SURVEYS THE FALLEN FIGURES OF HIS FOES, THERE COMES AN UNEXPECTED VOICE FROM BEHIND....

FURTHER VIOLENCE IS UNNECESSARY!

WHAT --??

YOU SPEAK ENGLISH!

YOU MAY CALL ME KYACK. COME WITH ME AND I WILL OFFER YOU AN EXPLANATION FOR ALL THAT HAS OCCURRED.

KYACK SHOWS **SUPERMAN** THE WONDERS OF AN UNDERWORLD CIVILIZATION....

THE BUILDINGS—ANCIENT! HOW LONG HAS THIS CAVERN CITY BEEN IN EXISTENCE?

FOR CENTURIES. BUT COME INTO MY HUMBLE HOME. I WILL TELL YOU MORE.

OUR RACE ONCE POPULATED THE EARTH IN ABUNDANCE. THEN CAME THE ICE-AGE!

GO ON.

MOST OF US PERISHED UNDER THE IRRESISTIBLE APPROACH OF THE COLOSSAL GLACIERS. BUT THE MOST INTELLIGENT OF US, THE SCIENTISTS, RETREATED DEEP INTO THE EARTH TOWARD ITS WARM CENTER.

WE BUILT THIS RETREAT, EQUIPPED IT WITH ALL THE MARVELS OUR SCIENTIFIC INGENUITY COULD FASHION.

WERE YOU EVER IN TOUCH WITH THE OUTER WORLD?

ONLY THRU OBSERVATION.

WHY HAVE YOU SOUGHT TO DESTROY BUILDINGS ON THE EARTH'S SURFACE?

⑥

PREPARATIONS FOR AN INVASION. YOU SEE—AFTER ALL THESE CENTURIES WE ARE ABOUT TO RETURN TO THE EARTH'S SURFACE ONCE MORE—AND AGAIN ASSUME THE RULE OF THE EARTH THAT WAS ONCE OURS.

BUT YOU DON'T TAKE *ME* INTO YOUR CONSIDERATION!

DIDN'T I—?

WHAT —!!

DOWN PLUMMETS **SUPERMAN!**

NEATLY TRICKED!

--CRASHING TO THE FLOOR OF A CHAMBER FAR BELOW!

SUPERMAN WHIRLS AT THE SOUND OF A GREAT ROAR....

IT LOOKS AS THO THEY BROUGHT ALONG SOME OF THEIR PRE-HISTORIC PLAYMATES TO THIS UNDERWORLD HIDEAWAY!

AS THE GREAT BEAST CHARGES, **SUPERMAN** AGILELY EVADES IT....

SIMPLE AS PIE!

THEN--AS HE SEIZES ITS TAIL....

UP WITH YOU!

--THEN DOWN!

THE WINNER!

⑦

THAT SOUNDED LIKE A CRY FOR HELP! -- IS THIS ANOTHER TRAP?

SUPERMAN AVAILS HIMSELF OF HIS ASTOUNDING X-RAY VISION....

WHAT GOES ON?

THRU THE SOLID WALL THE MAN OF TOMORROW SIGHTS TWO MEN WEARING KYACK'S COLORS ABOUT TO THROW A YOUNG MAN INTO THE CRATER OF A VOLCANO....

CLEAR THRU THE WALL CRASHES SUPERMAN...!

LET GO OF HIM!

TOO LATE! THE YOUTH IS HURLED INTO THE VOLCANO!

DOWN AFTER THE FALLING FIGURE LEAPS SUPERMAN!

THERE MAY STILL BE A CHANCE TO SAVE HIM!

OVERTAKING THE FALLING YOUNG MAN, SUPERMAN SEIZES HIM....

GOT YOU!

BUT THE BOILING LAVA NOW LOOMS ONLY INCHES AWAY!

8

BACK SUPERMAN HURLS HIS BURDEN...

YOU'D BETTER FIND A COOLER PLACE TO REST!

--TO SAFETY--!

BUT THEN—THE *MAN OF STEEL* DISAPPEARS BENEATH THE SURFACE OF THE LAVA...!

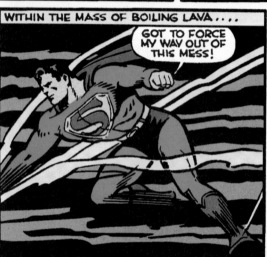

WITHIN THE MASS OF BOILING LAVA....

GOT TO FORCE MY WAY OUT OF THIS MESS!

THE STRONGARM MEN SEIZE THE YOUNG MAN IN PREPARATION TO THROWING HIM BACK INTO THE CRATER.

NO! DON'T DO IT!

SUDDENLY-- OUT OF THE FIERY CRATER BURSTS THE FIGURE OF SUPERMAN...!

BETTER DO AS HE SAYS!

THE GUARDS FLEE IN TERROR AT THE SIGHT OF THIS AMAZING BEING WHO HAS SURVIVED CONTACT WITH THE INCREDIBLY HOT LAVA....

YOU--YOU'RE STILL ALIVE!

YES-- BUT I MUST ADMIT I WAS IN A HOT SPOT!

BUT TELL ME-- WHO ARE YOU?

I AM TULAN-- LEADER OF THE UNDER-GROUND CIVILIZATION!

IF THAT IS SO, THEN HOW IS IT THAT THOSE MEN WERE ATTEMPTING TO KILL YOU?

KYACK HAD THEM KIDNAP ME, THEN SPREAD THE LIE THAT I HAD SLAIN MY-SELF. I FAVOR LIVING HERE IN PEACE--BUT KYACK DEMANDS THAT THE PEOPLE OF THE OUTER WORLD BE ATTACKED!

IS THERE ANY WAY I CAN HELP GET YOU BACK INTO POWER?

I'M SURE THAT IF THE COUNCIL KNEW I AM REALLY ALIVE, THEY'D QUICKLY ATTEND TO SCHEMING KYACK!

THAT'LL BE SIMPLE ENOUGH! FOLLOW ME!

WHAT AMAZING STRENGTH!

THERE'S THE COUNCIL CHAMBER! BUT HERE COME KYACK'S MEN!

I'LL MAKE SHORT WORK OF THEM!

AS SIMPLE AS THAT!

WITHIN THE COUNCIL CHAMBER...

I INSIST THAT MY WAY IS THE RIGHT WAY! WE MUST GO THRU WITH MY PLANS! EARTH MUST BE CONQUERED!

CONSTERNATION REIGNS AS TULAN AND **SUPERMAN** BURST INTO THE ROOM. . . .

TULAN-- ALIVE!

BUT I THOUGHT --!!

THAT YOUR HENCH-MEN HAD SLAIN ME? THEY FAILED!

KYACK INFORMED US THAT YOU HAD SLAIN YOURSELF-- CAST YOURSELF INTO THE FIERY PIT WHILE DESPONDENT! THEN HOW CAN IT BE THAT YOU LIVE?

KYACK LIED! HE HAD HIS MEN CAPTURE TULAN. THEY WOULD HAVE SLAIN HIM IF I HADN'T INTERFERED IN TIME!

DON'T BELIEVE THEM!

KYACK IS PLACED UNDER ARREST....

YOU HAVE COMMITTED A TERRIBLE DEED-- PLOTTING AGAINST OUR RULER,

YOU WILL BE CONFINED TO A CELL WHILE WE PONDER YOUR FATE!

IMPRISON ME-- BUT I'LL STILL HAVE MY VENGEANCE!

I'M SORRY YOUR RECEPTION IN OUR LAND WASN'T MORE HOSPITABLE,

IT'S QUITE ALL RIGHT. AS LONG AS MY FRIENDS ON EARTH ARE LEFT UNDISTURBED, I'VE NOTHING TO COMPLAIN ABOUT.

LATER--KYACK FUMES IN HIS CELL....

IF IT WEREN'T FOR THE INTERFERENCE OF THIS INTERLOPER FROM THE OUTER WORLD, MY PLANS WOULD HAVE SUCCEEDED!

FIGURES ABRUPTLY SPRING ON THE GUARDS...

I KNEW I COULD COUNT ON YOU!

WE'LL SOON HAVE YOU FREE, MASTER!

SHALL WE NOW ATTEND TO THE STRONG ONE FROM THE OUTER WORLD?

NO TIME FOR THAT NOW! WE'VE GOT TO BEGIN THE ATTACK AS PLANNED!

KYACK AND HIS MEN ENTER THEIR FLEET OF BORE-VESSELS...

THEN--OFF FOR THE SURFACE OF EARTH SETS THE ARMADA...!

--EMERGING IN THE VERY CENTER OF *METROPOLIS*...!

THEN COMMENCES A CAMPAIGN OF RUTHLESS DESTRUCTION....

MEANWHILE,....

WHAT IS IT?

KYACK HAS ESCAPED! HIS MEN ARE ATTACKING THE SURFACE-WORLD!

YOU MAY USE ONE OF MY BORE-VESSELS IF YOU DESIRE!

THANKS, TULAN, BUT THAT WON'T BE NECESSARY!

LEAPING UP TO THE CAVERN ROOF, *SUPERMAN* DEPARTS...

AMAZING!

GOOD LUCK TO YOU, *MAN OF STEEL!* MAY RELATIONS BETWEEN OUR TWO WORLDS FOREVER REMAIN PEACEFUL!

⑫

MINUTES LATER, **SUPERMAN** EMERGES THRU THE EARTH TO THE SURFACE....

NOW TO SEE WHAT KYACK IS UP TO!

WHAT **SUPERMAN'S** TELESCOPIC VISION REVEALS....

RACING IN AT TERRIFIC SPEED, THE *MAN OF STEEL* SMASHES THE INVADERS LEFT AND RIGHT...

I WON'T REST TILL YOU'RE ALL DESTROYED!

WHEN ONLY THE COMMANDING VESSEL REMAINS...

THIS DEADLY RAY WILL STOP HIM!

FORWARD, **SUPERMAN** BATTLES AGAINST THE RAY--EXERTING EVERY OUNCE OF ENERGY AGAINST ITS POWERFUL FORCE--!

GOT TO-- MAKE IT--!

⑬

LATER....

WE'VE **SUPERMAN** TO THANK FOR SAVING THE WORLD FROM THOSE STRANGE INVADERS!

... AND FOR GIVING US A FIRST-RATE STORY!

THE END

No. 4

WINTER ISSUE

WORLD'S FINEST COMICS

15¢

A SUPERMAN PUBLICATION DC IND

96 THRILLING PAGES!

SUPERMAN
BATMAN
AND
ROBIN

ZATARA
SANDMAN
RED, WHITE & BLUE

SUPERMAN

by JERRY SIEGEL and JOE SHUSTER

CONFRONTED BY AN OBSOLETE AND DANGEROUS STREET RAILWAY SITUATION, THE CRUSADING *MAN OF TOMORROW* LAUNCHES A CAMPAIGN TO MODERNIZE PUBLIC TRANSPORTATION IN *METROPOLIS* BEFORE LIVES ARE LOST. THE EXPOSURE OF EVIL INFLUENCES BEHIND THE SERIES OF DISASTROUS ACCIDENTS TO ANCIENT STREET CARS CAUSES **SUPERMAN** TO BRING INTO USE ALL HIS MIGHTY, STUPENDOUS POWERS... AND ONCE AGAIN THE DYNAMIC DEFENDER OF JUSTICE TRIUMPHS OVER SINISTER ODDS!

IT'S JUST LIKE YOU TO OFFER TO DRIVE ME TO WORK--THEN TAKE ME ON A STREET CAR..

I'M SORRY, LOIS, BUT I'D COMPLETELY FORGOTTEN THAT I LEFT MY AUTO IN A GARAGE FOR REPAIRS.

AVON STREET

124

I HAVEN'T BEEN ON A STREET CAR FOR A LONG TIME...ALMOST FORGOT HOW BROKEN-DOWN AND ANCIENT THEY ARE IN THIS TOWN...

YOU'D THINK THAT WITH ITS HUGE REVENUE, THE CAR COMPANY COULD AFFORD TO GIVE ITS CUSTOMERS THE BEST.

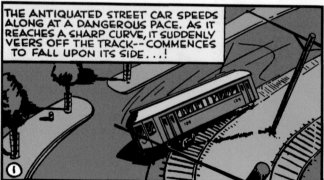

THE ANTIQUATED STREET CAR SPEEDS ALONG AT A DANGEROUS PACE. AS IT REACHES A SHARP CURVE, IT SUDDENLY VEERS OFF THE TRACK--COMMENCES TO FALL UPON ITS SIDE...!

("-DERAILED....! GOT TO ACT FAST OR THE PASSENGERS WILL BE INJURED! BUT HOW CAN I DO IT WITHOUT REVEALING MY TRUE IDENTITY AS **SUPERMAN**?-")

ACTING SO SWIFTLY THAT HIS TREMENDOUS FEAT OF STRENGTH GOES UNNOTICED, CLARK SHOVES HIS HAND THRU THE WINDOW SO THAT IT STRIKES THE PAVEMENT FIRST, HOLDING THE ENTIRE LENGTH OF THE CAR RIGID ABOVE THE GROUND, CUSHIONING THE FALL....

CAREFULLY HE LOWERS IT TO THE PAVEMENT SO THAT LITTLE DAMAGE IS DONE. THEN....

ARE YOU INJURED?

A LITTLE SHAKEN... BUT I'LL BE ALL RIGHT. HELP THE OTHERS!

AS THE REMAINING PASSENGERS EMERGE TO SAFETY, CLARK OVERHEARS AN INTERESTING BIT OF CONVERSATION....

THANK HEAVEN NO ONE WAS HURT!

IT'S A WONDER THIS ACCIDENT DIDN'T HAPPEN LONG AGO. THESE OLD BUGGIES SHOULD HAVE BEEN DISCARDED YEARS AGO.

LATER--AT THE *DAILY PLANET*...

GO TO IT, CLARK!

IT'S ABOUT TIME THE ROTTEN CONDITION OF THE STREET CARS WAS EXPOSED!

HM-MM...THE RAILWAY COMPANY WON'T LIKE THIS...

BUT IT'S THE UNVARNISHED TRUTH...!

THE CITIZENS OF THIS CITY ARE ENTITLED TO A FORM OF PUBLIC TRANSPORTATION THAT WILL NOT BE A DAILY MENACE TO THEIR LIVES!

STREET CAR ACCIDENTS CONTINUE; PLANET DEMANDS TRACTION REFORM

1941

THIS IS HUGH MANTON, PRESIDENT OF THE *METROPOLIS RAILWAY COMPANY*. THAT STORY IN THE *PLANET* IS GROSS LIBEL, WHITE!

MANTON IS BOILING. WE'RE LIABLE TO HAVE A SUIT ON OUR HANDS.

THEN I'D BETTER GET PROOF FOR OUR CHARGES!

WAIT FOR ME!

THE TWO *DAILY PLANET* REPORTERS ROAM THE STREETS UNTIL THEY COME UPON THE SCENE OF A REPAIR CREW WORKING UPON A STREET CAR WHICH HAS BROKEN DOWN IN SERVICE...

THAT OUGHT TO MAKE A GOOD PICTURE!

--AND IT WILL!

HEY, LOOK!

SOMEONE SNAPPING PICTURES!

FOLLOW ME--!

WHAT'S THE IDEA?

WE'RE REPORTERS TAKING PICTURES FOR THE *DAILY PLANET.*

QUICK, CLARK! GIVE ME THE CAMERA!

AS ONE OF THE WORKERS SNATCHES FOR THE CAMERA, LOIS RACES OFF WITH IT....

SMASH THAT CAMERA!

DON'T LET HER GET AWAY!

STEPPING INTO AN ALLEY, CLARK SWIFTLY PEELS OFF HIS OUTER GARMENTS....

LOIS NEEDS MY AID-- AND I CAN HELP HER BETTER AS **SUPERMAN.**

I'VE GOT IT!

BREAK IT--!

DON'T YOU DARE!

STREAKING IN, **SUPERMAN** CATCHES THE FALLING CAMERA BEFORE IT CAN BE SMASHED ON THE PAVEMENT....

THIS EVIDENCE IS TOO IMPORTANT TO BE DESTROYED!

IT'S-- SUPERMAN!

RUN FOR IT!

3

OVERTAKING THE FLEEING REPAIR CREW, **SUPERMAN** HURLS THEM INTO THEIR TRUCK...

STAY THERE UNTIL YOU LEARN TO BEHAVE!

SNATCHING UP LOIS, **SUPERMAN** SPEEDS OVER THE CITY TO THE NEWSPAPER BUILDING....

RUSH THAT PICTURE AND OTHERS INTO PRINT!

THANKS!

DAILY PLANET

STREET CARS ANTIQUATED; CAR RIDERS ENDANGERED

WHAT YOU'RE USING

WHAT THE CITY NEEDS

DAN BRANSOM TO SEE YOU.

BRANSOM...THE PROMINENT CIVIC REFORMER! SHOW HIM IN!

I'VE WANTED TO CONGRATULATE YOU FOR A LONG TIME, YOUNG MAN. YOUR CAMPAIGN AGAINST THE RAILWAY COMPANY EXACTLY COINCIDES WITH MY ATTITUDE, AND I WANT YOU TO KNOW THAT I'LL BACK YOU TO THE LIMIT.

FINE!

TOGETHER, THE TRIO VISIT THE CITY'S MAYOR....

ALL THE *PLANET'S* READERS ARE BEHIND US, MAYOR.

WE INSIST YOU DO SOMETHING ABOUT THE TERRIBLE CONDITION OF THE STREET CARS.

I'LL BRING THE SUBJECT TO THE ATTENTION OF CITY COUNCIL.

THE SUCCEEDING DAYS ARE FILLED WITH WRANGLING BETWEEN COUNCIL AND THE REPRESENTATIVES OF THE STREET CAR COMPANY....

THOSE STREET CARS ARE GOOD FOR AT LEAST ANOTHER TEN YEARS!

IT'S NO SECRET THAT YOU YOURSELF, MANTON, NEVER RIDE ONE OF YOUR STREETCARS.-- IS IT BECAUSE YOU'RE AFRAID TO?

IF THINGS CONTINUE LIKE THIS, WE'LL NEVER GET ANY PLACE.

IT'S A LITTLE TOO EARLY TO BE DISCOURAGED.

WE'VE GOT TO SEE THIS THING THRU!

④

WHEN THE DISCOURAGED CLARK RETURNS TO THE NEWSPAPER OFFICE....

TELEPHONE CALL FOR YOU.

I'LL TAKE IT.

STREET CAR 112 RUNNING ON GAYFORTH AVENUE IS GOING TO MEET WITH AN "ACCIDENT"! ....(CLICK!)

WHAT'S--? HE HUNG UP--!

THIS CALL MIGHT HAVE BEEN FROM A HARMLESS CRANK-- BUT I CAN'T AFFORD TO TAKE ANY CHANCES!

THERE IT IS --BELOW-- CAR NUMBER 112...!

AT THAT MOMENT....

UNDER THE FALLING STREET CAR STREAKS THE MAN OF TOMORROW AT SUPER-SPEED...

WILL I MAKE IT IN TIME?

112

CATCHING THE MASSIVE BULK OF THE GREAT VEHICLE WITH HANDS AND FEET....

...HE LOWERS IT CAREFULLY, GENTLY TO THE PAVEMENT....

THAT DOES IT!

⑤

HM-MM! EVIDENCE OF SABOTAGE...!

GRAB HIM! --HE DERAILED THE CAR!

IT WOULD BE USELESS TO CORRECT THAT MISTAKEN IMPRESSION.

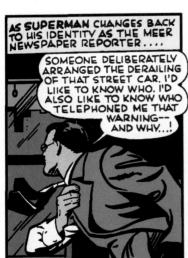

AS SUPERMAN CHANGES BACK TO HIS IDENTITY AS THE MEEK NEWSPAPER REPORTER....

SOMEONE DELIBERATELY ARRANGED THE DERAILING OF THAT STREET CAR. I'D LIKE TO KNOW WHO. I'D ALSO LIKE TO KNOW WHO TELEPHONED ME THAT WARNING-- AND WHY...!

I DON'T BELIEVE THOSE REPORTS THAT SUPERMAN FORCED THE STREET CAR OFF THE TRACKS.

NATURALLY ANYTHING YOUR FAIR-HAIRED BOY DOES IS OKAY WITH YOU.

ANOTHER TELEPHONE CALL FOR YOU, MR. KENT.

("-IT'S THE SAME VOICE THAT TELEPHONED THE WARNING!-")

I'M BREAKING WITH MY BOSS-- MEET ME IN A BLUE SEDAN PARKED AT THE CORNER OF 8TH AND WILSON STREETS, AND I'LL GIVE YOU A STORY THAT'LL MAKE THE FRONT PAGES.

I'LL BE THERE!

MOMENTS LATER-- THE FIGURE OF SUPERMAN STREAKS UP INTO THE SKY FROM ATOP THE DAILY PLANET BUILDING...

AT LAST-- A BREAK!

THERE IT IS-- THE BLUE SEDAN! THIS MAY BE A TRAP-- BUT HERE'S WHERE I FIND OUT!

SUPERMAN! --BUT-- WHERE'S CLARK KENT?

I INTERCEPTED YOUR TELEPHONE CALL AND BEAT HIM HERE!

AS I UNDER-STAND IT, YOU'RE READY TO REVEAL WHO IS SABOTAGING THE STREET-CARS--AND WHY...

THAT'S RIGHT. I'M PLENTY BURNED UP AT THE BOSS. HE PROMISED ME PLENTY, BUT IS WELCHING. I'LL GET EVEN WITH HIM!

WHO IS YOUR BOSS?

YOU'LL BE PLENTY SURPRISED TO FIND OUT!

AT THAT INSTANT, SUPERMAN'S SUPER-ACUTE HEARING DETECTS--

("-TICKING!-")

THE *MAN OF STEEL'S* AMAZING X-RAY EYESIGHT REVEALS TO HIM THAT THERE IS A TIME-BOMB CONCEALED WITHIN THE CAR...!

BEFORE **SUPERMAN** CAN ACT TO PREVENT IT, THERE IS A TREMENDOUS EXPLOSION...!

NOTHING LEFT OF THE CAR BUT TWISTED WRECKAGE. ANOTHER MOMENT AND I'D HAVE LEARNED VALUABLE INFORMATION,--THE SLAIN THUG'S BOSS MUST HAVE KNOWN HE WAS GOING TO SQUEAL AND PLACED THE TIME-BOMB IN THE CAR!

7

LATER--AT THE *PLANET* OFFICE...

I'VE LEARNED ONE OF THE RECENTLY DERAILED STREETCARS WAS SABOTAGED!

THAT'S ODD!--BRANSOM IS COMING SOON. HE OUGHT TO BE INTERESTED, TOO, IN THIS NEW DEVELOPMENT!

THE SABOTAGE OF THE STREET CAR SEEMS TO INDICATE THAT MANY OF THESE RECENT ACCIDENTS HAVE BEEN DELIBERATE.

BUT WHO COULD HOPE TO PROFIT BY SUCH TERRORISTIC METHODS IS WHAT PUZZLES ME--UNLESS IT'S SOME FANATIC WHO HAS A GRUDGE AGAINST THE RAILWAY COMPANY.

SHORTLY AFTER...

I JUST GOT MY CAR OUT OF THE GARAGE--I'D LIKE TO SEE IF IT'S IN GOOD RUNNING CONDITION.

THANKS FOR LETTING ME COME ALONG FOR THE RIDE.

THAT CAR BEHIND--IT'S BEEN FOLLOWING US FOR THE LAST HALF HOUR...

PROBABLY JUST YOUR IMAGINA-TION.

ABRUPTLY-- THE PURSUING CAR VEERS SHARPLY TOWARD CLARK'S ROADSTER, FORCING HIM TOWARD THE RAIL....

LOOK OUT--!

THEY'RE DOING IT DELIBERATELY!

TRIUMPHANTLY, THE MURDER CAR DRIVES SWIFTLY AWAY....

CLARK ACTS SO SWIFTLY THAT LOIS IS UNAWARE OF WHAT OCCURS....

("-SHE MUSTN'T WITNESS WHAT FOLLOWS!-")

OUT OF THE FALLING AUTO DIVES CLARK--!

GOT TO REACH THE GROUND FIRST!

ALIGHTING, HE WHIRLS, CATCHES THE AUTO, THEN LOWERS IT SAFELY TO THE EARTH....

THERE!

WH-WHAT HAPPENED --??

IF SUPERMAN HADN'T COME AND CAUGHT THE CAR, YOU AND I WOULD BE GONERS. HE CAME AND WENT LIKE A SHOT!

BUT WHY SHOULD ANYONE WANT TO SLAY US?

HE MUST KNOW THAT YOU AND I ARE ENDEAVORING TO LEARN WHO IS RESPONSIBLE FOR THE DESTRUCTION OF STREET CARS!

NEGOTIATIONS BETWEEN CITY COUNCIL AND THE RAILWAY COMPANY DRAG ON ENDLESSLY...

NO! NO! NO!

WE'LL NEVER GET ANYWHERE UNLESS THE PRESIDENT OF THE RAILWAY COMPANY IS MORE REASONABLE!

SO A FAIR OUTCOME OF THE PROCEEDINGS ALL DEPENDS ON MANTON SHOWING A MORE SENSIBLE ATTITUDE, EH? PERHAPS I CAN DO SOMETHING ABOUT THAT!

9

THAT EVENING...AS MANTON IS ABOUT TO RETIRE....

HOW DARE YOU BREAK IN LIKE THIS?

YOU'RE NOT ADDRESSING YOUR BOARD OF DIRECTORS NOW, MANTON. GET DRESSED --AND I MEAN PRONTO!

I ABSOLUTELY REFUSE TO DO ANYTHING OF THE KIND!

VERY WELL, THEN YOU CAN COME AS YOU ARE!

WHAT ARE YOU GOING TO DO WITH ME?

YOU NEEDN'T WORRY ABOUT YOUR PRECIOUS HIDE. ALL I'M GOING TO DO IS SHOW YOU SOME OF THE MISERY YOU'VE CAUSED.

LOOK IN THERE-- WHAT DO YOU SEE?

A FAMILY-- THEY SEEM TO BE MOURNING. HAS SOMEONE DIED...?

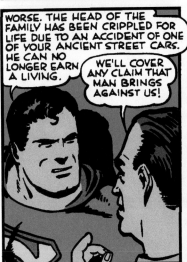

WORSE. THE HEAD OF THE FAMILY HAS BEEN CRIPPLED FOR LIFE DUE TO AN ACCIDENT OF ONE OF YOUR ANCIENT STREET CARS. HE CAN NO LONGER EARN A LIVING.

WE'LL COVER ANY CLAIM THAT MAN BRINGS AGAINST US!

TRUE, PERHAPS--- BUT YOU CAN'T BRING BACK HIS SOUND LIMBS.

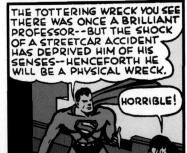

THE TOTTERING WRECK YOU SEE THERE WAS ONCE A BRILLIANT PROFESSOR--BUT THE SHOCK OF A STREETCAR ACCIDENT HAS DEPRIVED HIM OF HIS SENSES--HENCEFORTH HE WILL BE A PHYSICAL WRECK.

HORRIBLE!

I--I NEVER BEFORE REALIZED LIVES AND LIMBS ARE WORTH MORE THAN MERE DOLLARS AND CENTS!

BE SURE YOU REMEMBER THAT AT COUNCIL MEETING TOMORROW!

⑩

NEXT DAY....

BUT I'VE OFFERED TO BEGIN REPLACING STREET CARS WITH MODERN BUSES AND CONTINUE TO DO SO AS CIRCUM- STANCES PERMIT...

THAT SOUNDS REASONABLE...

I DISAGREE! TOSS OUT ALL THE STREET CARS AND REPLACE ALL OF THEM WITH BUSES AT ONCE. ALL OR NOTHING!

BRANSOM DELIBERATE- LY GUMMED UP THE PROCEEDINGS WHEN REFORM WAS DEFI- NITELY IN SIGHT--I'M GOING TO TRAIL HIM AND TRY TO LEARN WHAT THIS MEANS!

AS BRANSOM'S AUTO TURNS INTO THE DRIVEWAY OF HIS HOME, **SUPERMAN** ALIGHTS ATOP THE HOUSE, UNSEEN....

NOW TO KEEP HIM UNDER OBSERVATION WITH MY X-RAY VISION AND SUPER-SENSITIVE HEARING!

THE "REFORMER" LOSES NO TIME IN PLACING A TELEPHONE CALL...

YOUR INSTRUCTIONS ARE AS FOLLOWS, PETE-- WE'VE GOT TO STRIKE QUICKLY, DEVASTATINGLY --FIX IT SO THAT ALMOST EVERY CAR LEAVING CAR BARN K-14 WILL BE SMASHED...

I'LL TAKE CARE OF BRANSOM LATER. RIGHT NOW I'VE GOT TO SEE TO IT THAT PETE DOESN'T SUCCEED IN HIS RUTHLESS WORK!

DOWN PLUMMETS THE *MAN OF TOMORROW* AS THE STREET CARS START LEAVING CAR BARN K-14!

NOT A MINUTE TOO EARLY!

DROPPING DOWN BEFORE THE FOREMOST CAR, **SUPERMAN** PITS HIS STRENGTH AGAINST IT, FORCING THE VEHICLE TO A STOP....

SORRY, BUT YOU GO NO FURTHER!

THEN-- LIFTING ITS MIGHTY BULK, HE PLACES IT CROSS-WISE ON THE TRACKS....

THERE! THAT SHOULD BOTTLE THEM UP!

HEY! WHAT --??

11

I'M NOT DOING THIS TO PLAGUE YOU.-- IF YOU EXAMINE EACH OF YOUR CARS, YOU'LL FIND SOME DAMAGE HAS BEEN DONE TO THEM SO THAT THEY'LL BE DERAILED!

IF THAT'S TRUE, WE OWE YOU OUR LIVES!

PETE MAKES A BREAK FOR IT...

SUPERMAN! --(G-GULP!)-- I--I'D BETTER MAKE TRACKS!

YOU'RE COMING WITH ME, PETE!

AWK! NO!

ALIGHTING BESIDE A MAN-OF-THE-STREET RADIO INTERVIEWER, SUPERMAN SHOVES HIM ASIDE...

MIND IF I BORROW THE MIKE FOR A MOMENT? LADIES AND GENTLEMEN-- **SUPERMAN** SPEAKING. MAY I INTRODUCE TO YOU AN UNSAVORY GENT NAMED PETE, WHO HAS SOMETHING TO CONFESS.

GO AHEAD, PETE! CONFESSION IS GOOD FOR THE SOUL!

I WAS HIRED BY BRANSOM TO SABOTAGE STREET CARS. HE WANTED THEM REPLACED WITH BUSES IMMEDIATELY BECAUSE HE PLANNED TO GET A COMMISSION ON THE SALE OF THE BUSES AN' CLEAN UP!

PETE--SQUEALING--I'VE GOT TO FLEE--GET AWAY...!

BUT LOIS, DRIVING BY, HAS ALSO HEARD THE BROADCAST ON HER CAR-RADIO....

BRANSOM--ABOUT TO TAKE A RUN-OUT POWDER!

STOP WHERE YOU ARE, BRANSOM!

JUST WHAT I NEEDED-- A GETAWAY CAR! GET BACK IN THERE!

MINUTES LATER--AS **SUPERMAN** ARRIVES...

BRANSOM GONE.... LOIS' POCKETBOOK--SHE'S IN DANGER!

THRU THE SKY STREAKS **SUPERMAN** AT SUPER-SPEED IN FRANTIC SEARCH....

BRANSOM'S DANGEROUS! HE TRIED TO MURDER LOIS AND ME ONCE BEFORE. HE WON'T HESITATE TO TRY AGAIN!

12

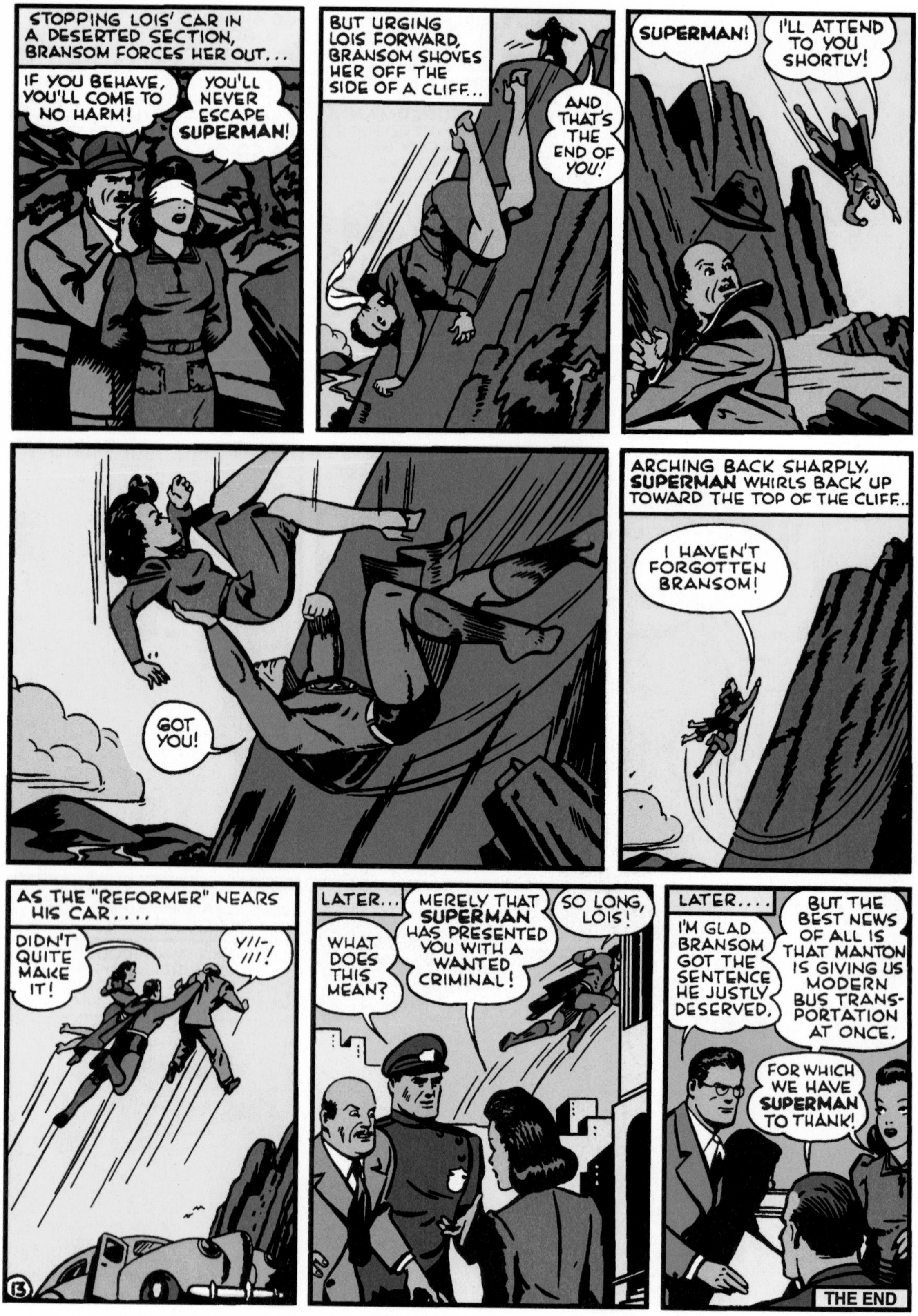
STOPPING LOIS' CAR IN A DESERTED SECTION, BRANSOM FORCES HER OUT...
IF YOU BEHAVE, YOU'LL COME TO NO HARM!
YOU'LL NEVER ESCAPE SUPERMAN!
BUT URGING LOIS FORWARD, BRANSOM SHOVES HER OFF THE SIDE OF A CLIFF...
AND THAT'S THE END OF YOU!
SUPERMAN!
I'LL ATTEND TO YOU SHORTLY!
GOT YOU!
ARCHING BACK SHARPLY, SUPERMAN WHIRLS BACK UP TOWARD THE TOP OF THE CLIFF...
I HAVEN'T FORGOTTEN BRANSOM!
AS THE "REFORMER" NEARS HIS CAR....
DIDN'T QUITE MAKE IT!
Y!!-!!!!
13
LATER...
WHAT DOES THIS MEAN?
MERELY THAT SUPERMAN HAS PRESENTED YOU WITH A WANTED CRIMINAL!
SO LONG, LOIS!
LATER....
I'M GLAD BRANSOM GOT THE SENTENCE HE JUSTLY DESERVED.
BUT THE BEST NEWS OF ALL IS THAT MANTON IS GIVING US MODERN BUS TRANSPORTATION AT ONCE.
FOR WHICH WE HAVE SUPERMAN TO THANK!
THE END

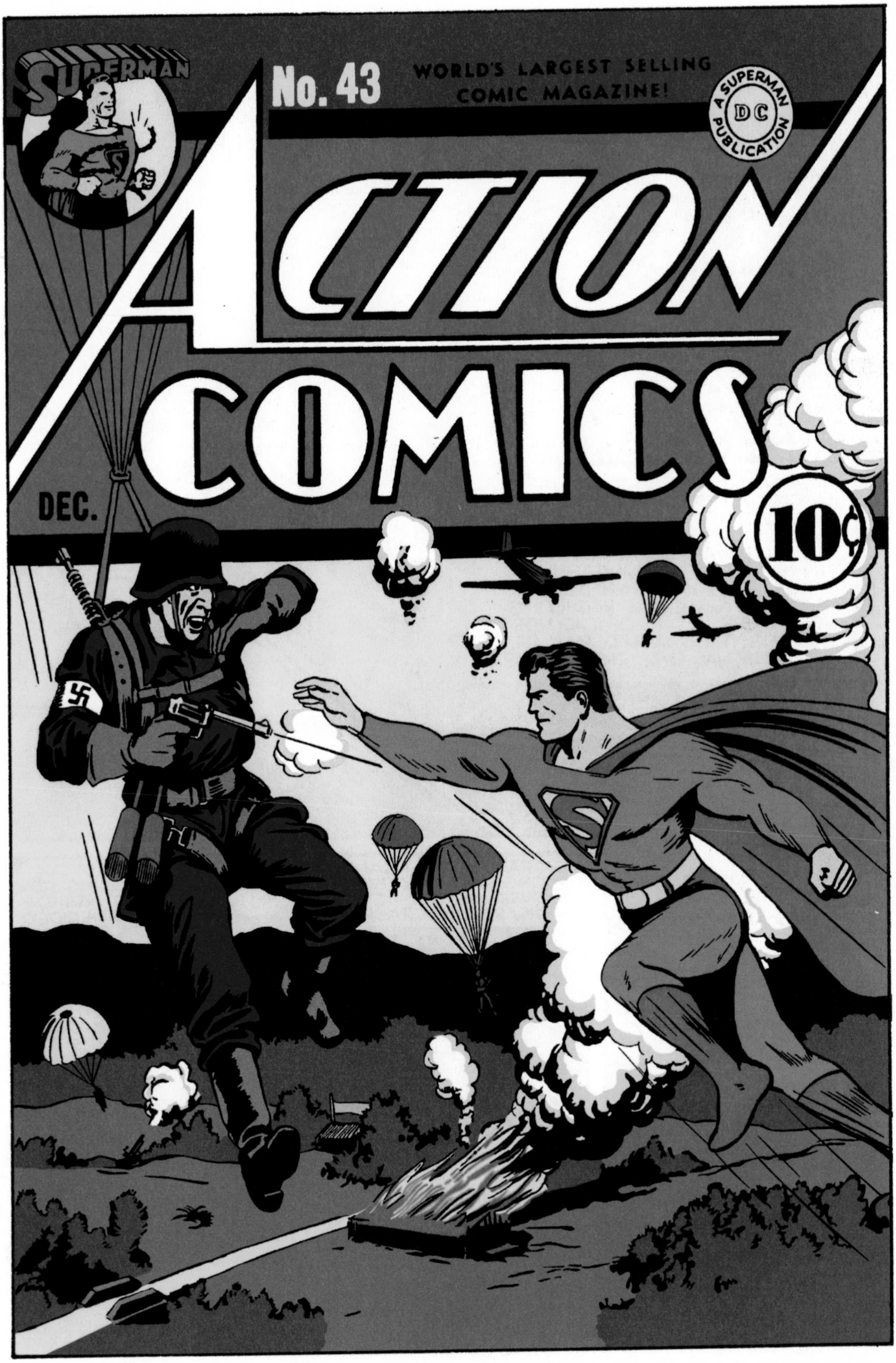
SUPERMAN
No. 43
WORLD'S LARGEST SELLING COMIC MAGAZINE!
A SUPERMAN DC PUBLICATION
ACTION COMICS
DEC.
10¢

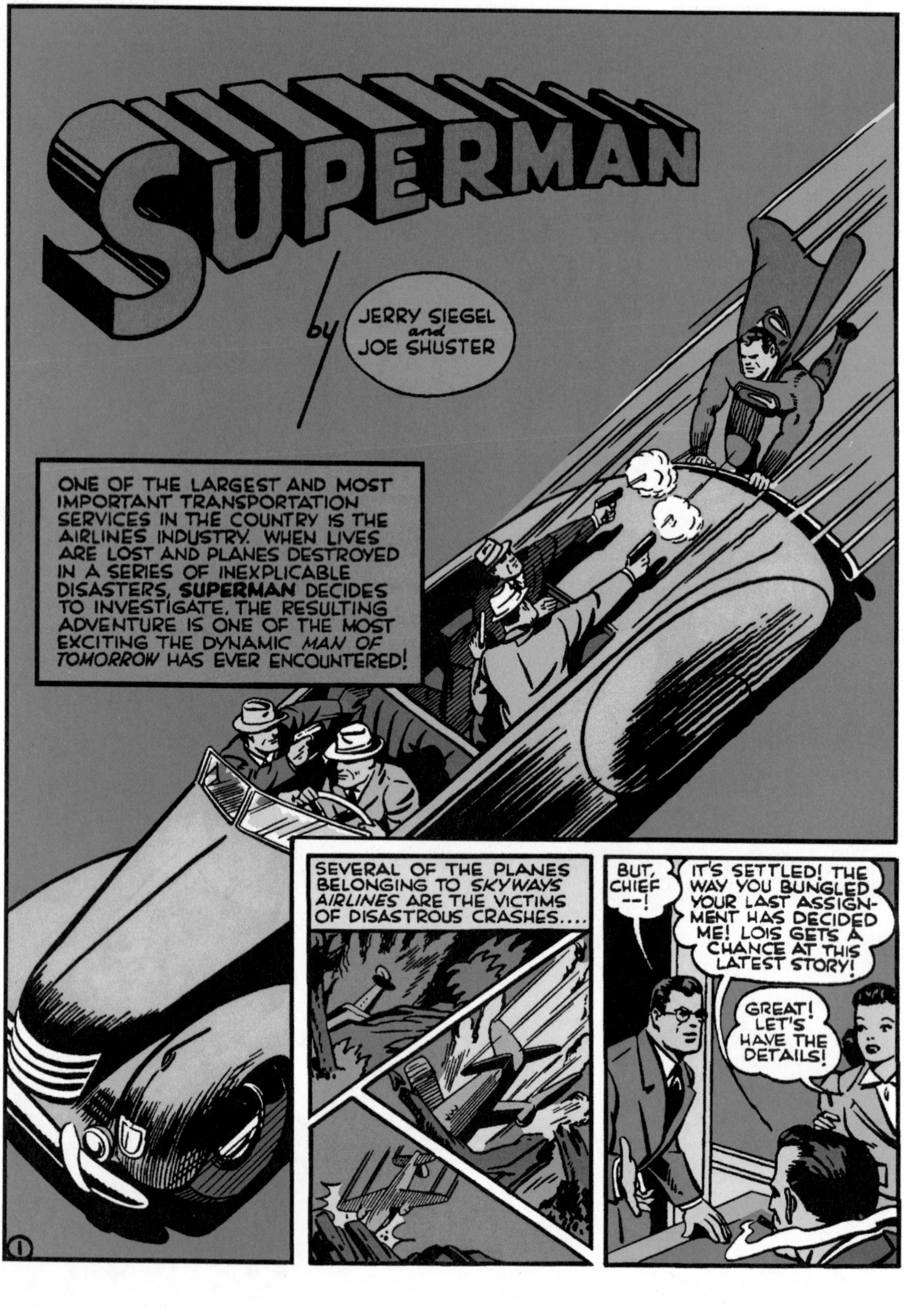
SUPERMAN
by JERRY SIEGEL and JOE SHUSTER
ONE OF THE LARGEST AND MOST IMPORTANT TRANSPORTATION SERVICES IN THE COUNTRY IS THE AIRLINES INDUSTRY. WHEN LIVES ARE LOST AND PLANES DESTROYED IN A SERIES OF INEXPLICABLE DISASTERS, SUPERMAN DECIDES TO INVESTIGATE. THE RESULTING ADVENTURE IS ONE OF THE MOST EXCITING THE DYNAMIC MAN OF TOMORROW HAS EVER ENCOUNTERED!
1
SEVERAL OF THE PLANES BELONGING TO SKYWAYS AIRLINES ARE THE VICTIMS OF DISASTROUS CRASHES....
BUT, CHIEF --!
IT'S SETTLED! THE WAY YOU BUNGLED YOUR LAST ASSIGNMENT HAS DECIDED ME! LOIS GETS A CHANCE AT THIS LATEST STORY!
GREAT! LET'S HAVE THE DETAILS!

EVERY NEWSPAPER IN TOWN IS TRYING TO LOCATE AVERY THORNTON, MANAGER OF *SKYWAYS*. BUT HE'S NOT TO BE FOUND!

BUT I'VE BEEN TIPPED OFF WHERE HE IS. AND I WANT YOU TO INTERVIEW HIM, THO HE MAY NOT WANT TO TALK. THINK YOU CAN HANDLE IT, LOIS?

ALL I ASK IS A CHANCE!

FINE... HERE'S THE ADDRESS.

SO HE'S IN *BRENTVILLE*. THAT'S QUITE A DISTANCE AWAY. I'LL FLY THERE IN ONE OF THE *SKY-WAYS* PLANES.

NO, LOIS! THOSE PLANES HAVE BEEN CRASHING STEADILY!

BUT THINK WHAT A SWELL STORY IT WOULD MAKE IF SOMETHING *DID* HAPPEN TO ME. "PLANET REPORTER STRICKEN WHILE ON TRACK OF STORY"! TA-TA! SEE YOU ON THE FRONT PAGE!

BUT, LOIS--!

HURRYING OFF TO A SECLUDED SPOT, CLARK SWIFTLY REMOVES HIS OUTER GARMENTS, TRANSFORMING HIMSELF TO DYNAMIC **SUPERMAN**!

I'VE GOT TO SEE TO IT THAT THAT HEADSTRONG GIRL MEETS NO HARM!

LOIS ENTERS THE *BRENTVILLE-*BOUND PLANE AND IT TAKES OFF ON ITS JOURNEY....

②

...WITH THE MAN OF STEEL IN SWIFT PURSUIT....

I HOPE MY FEARS HAVE NO FOUNDATION!

AS TIME SLOWLY PASSES...

NOTHING HAPPENED YET--PERHAPS I HAVE NO CAUSE FOR NERVOUSNESS!

BUT AT THAT MOMENT-- IN THE PILOT'S CABIN...!

ONE OF THE PILOTS IS CRIT- ICALLY INJURED BY THE EXPLOSION-- THE OTHER FINDS THAT THE CONTROLS DO NOT RESPOND....

WE'LL CRASH!

DOWN PLUNGES THE AIR- CRAFT TOWARD APPARENTLY CERTAIN DOOM...!

IT'S HEADED TOWARD THAT HIGH MOUNTAIN- PEAK! THERE'S SURE TO BE A CRASH!

SWOOPING UNDER THE PLANE, **SUPERMAN** SHOVES IT SLIGHT- LY UPWARD SO THAT IT MISS- ES THE MENACING PEAK BY INCHES....

THAT'S WHAT I CALL A CLOSE SQUEEZE!

③

BUT AS THE PLANE SWERVES DOWN TOWARD A GREAT TREE....

HEADED FOR TROUBLE AGAIN!

STREAKING IN, **SUPERMAN** SMASHES DOWN THE HUGE TREE BEFORE THE AIRPLANE CAN STRIKE IT....

AS THE PLANE'S NOSE TURNS SHARPLY DOWN TOWARD THE GROUND, **SUPERMAN** STREAKS BENEATH IT....

STRAIGHTEN UP!

...AND CATCHING THE PLANE, LOWERS ITS MIGHTY BULK TO SAFETY...!

THERE YOU ARE!

TERRIFIED PASSENGERS POUR FROM THE GROUNDED PLANE....

EEE-EEE! WHO--?

DON'T BE AFRAID. IT'S **SUPERMAN**. WE OWE OUR LIVES TO HIM!

LET ME INTO THE PLANE!

AS **SUPERMAN** ENTERS THE PILOT'S-ROOM, THE PILOT JUMPS TO THE CONCLUSION THAT THIS STRANGELY-COSTUMED FIGURE IS IN SOME WAY RESPONSIBLE FOR THE DISASTER....

AS THE BULLET BOUNCES HARMLESSLY OFF HIM, THE *MAN OF TOMORROW* SNATCHES THE GUN FROM THE PILOT AND CRUSHES IT IN HIS BARE HAND!

SHOULDN'T PLAY WITH DANGEROUS TOYS! DON'T YOU REALIZE, MAN? I'VE COME TO **HELP** YOU!

I RECOGNIZE YOU NOW, YOU'RE **SUPERMAN**! I--I'M SORRY!

HM-MMM! HE'S IN PRETTY BAD CONDITION--OUGHT TO BE RUSHED TO A HOSPITAL!

BUT HOW CAN WE WHEN THE PLANE'S CONTROLS HAVE BEEN DESTROYED?

THAT, MY FRIEND, IS STRICTLY **MY** PROBLEM! JUST YOU SIT TIGHT--AND LEAVE THE REST TO ME!

GET BACK INTO THE PLANE --THE TRIP IS GOING TO BE RESUMED!

THIS IS OUTRAGEOUS! I'VE A BIG BUSINESS DEAL AT STAKE! I CAN'T AFFORD TO REACH *BRENTVILLE* LATE!

IF **SUPERMAN** HAS IN MIND WHAT I THINK HE HAS, YOU HAVE NOTHING TO WORRY ABOUT.

ONCE THE PASSENGERS HAVE RE-ENTERED THE PLANE, **SUPER MAN** HOISTS IT OVERHEAD....

NOW TO IMPROVE ON NATURE!

DOWN THE FIELD RACES THE *MAN OF TOMORROW* AT TERRIFIC SPEED....

THIS IS ALMOST FUN!

THEN--UP HE LEAPS, CLEARING THE SURROUNDING MOUNTAIN RANGE....

WE'RE OFF!

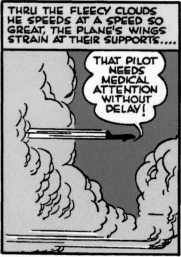

THRU THE FLEECY CLOUDS HE SPEEDS AT A SPEED SO GREAT, THE PLANE'S WINGS STRAIN AT THEIR SUPPORTS....

THAT PILOT NEEDS MEDICAL ATTENTION WITHOUT DELAY!

VERY SHORTLY AFTER.... AT THE *BRENTVILLE* AIRPORT....

L-LOOK! THE *METROP-OLIS* PLANE!

BUT THERE MUST BE SOME MISTAKE! IT COULDN'T HAVE ARRIVED SO SOON!

LOWERING THE PLANE TO THE FIELD, **SUPERMAN** STREAKS UP--UP--AND AWAY....

NOW TO MAKE TRACKS!

⑤

AS THE INJURED PILOT IS RUSHED TO A DOCTOR, LOIS TELEGRAPHS WHITE...

WILL MY EDITOR BE PLEASED TO GET *THIS!*

LATER--**SUPERMAN** OBSERVES LOIS ENTER THE HOME WHERE AVERY THORNTON IS REPORTED TO BE STAYING....

IF ANYONE CAN GET A STATEMENT FROM THORNTON, IT'S LOIS!

PLEASE BE SEATED. MR. THORNTON WILL SEE YOU SOON. WHOM SHALL I SAY IS CALLING?

BUT THE BUTLER, ONCE HE IS ALONE, TELEPHONES THE POLICE INSTEAD....

COME TO THE HOME OF AVERY THORNTON AT ONCE! URGENT!

SUPERMAN HAS BEEN AVAILING HIMSELF OF HIS X-RAY VISION....

SOMETHING DEFINITELY WRONG GOING ON HERE! --I'D BETTER GLANCE INTO THORNTON'S STUDY!

WHAT **SUPERMAN'S** SUPER-SENSORY SIGHT REVEALS TO HIM....

THORNTON--MURDERED! I'VE GOT TO GET LOIS OUT OF THERE BEFORE SHE GETS INTO TROUBLE!

YOU AGAIN! HOW DID YOU KNOW I CAME HERE?

THAT'S UNIMPORTANT. WHAT DOES COUNT IS THAT YOU MUST GET OUT OF HERE!

I CAME HERE FOR AN INTERVIEW-- AND I'M NOT GOING TO LEAVE UNTIL I GET IT!

GOING TO BE STUBBORN, EH?

MAYBE YOU'LL CHANGE YOUR MIND WHEN YOU GLANCE THRU THIS DOOR!

THORNTON --DEAD!

SIRENS WAIL AND POLICE CARS TURN INTO THE DRIVEWAY LEADING TO THE MANSION....

I'VE GOT TO GET YOU OUT OF HERE-- BEFORE YOU'RE IMPLICATED IN THE CRIME!

THAT BUTLER-- DID HE KNOW ABOUT THE CRIME ALL THE TIME?

BETTER REMAIN OUT OF SIGHT FOR A WHILE!

WAIT! LET ME THANK YOU!

MOMENTS LATER....LOIS ENCOUNTERS CLARK....

YOU-- WHERE DID YOU COME FROM?

I GOT WORRIED-- FLEW TO BRENTVILLE TO SEE THAT YOU CAME TO NO HARM.

STOP THAT MAN, CLARK!

WHO --??

GEE...I DID STOP HIM!

OO-OOF!

NICE WORK, CLARK!

WHO IS HE?

HE'S THE BUTLER WHO ADMITTED ME INTO THORNTON'S HOME...HE OBVIOUSLY KNEW THE AIRLINE MANAGER WAS SLAIN AND TRIED TO FRAME ME --ELSE WHY WOULD HE BE FLEEING FROM THE POLICE?

I--I DON'T KNOW WHAT YOU'RE TALKING ABOUT!

⑦

YOU'RE GOING TO TELL ME THE TRUTH-- AND FAST-- OR I PULL THE TRIGGER!

SHE WOULDN'T!

WOULDN'T SHE?--I WOULDN'T BE TOO SURE OF THAT!

WELL.....DO I HAVE TO FIRE?

NO! I'LL TALK! I WAS PLANTED IN THORN-TON'S HOME WITH INSTRUCTIONS TO KILL HIM. WHEN YOU CAME ALONG, IT WAS A PERFECT OPPORTUNITY FOR ME TO PIN THE KILLING ON YOU!

WHO PLANTED YOU IN THORN-TON'S HOME?

IT WAS--

LOOK OUT, LOIS!

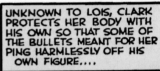

YAAA-AAA!

DOWN DIVES AN AIRPLANE, MACHINE-GUNNING THE BUTLER BEFORE HE CAN TELL MORE!

I OWE YOU MY LIFE!

D-DON'T MENTION IT!

UNKNOWN TO LOIS, CLARK PROTECTS HER BODY WITH HIS OWN SO THAT SOME OF THE BULLETS MEANT FOR HER PING HARMLESSLY OFF HIS OWN FIGURE....

AS THE PLANE STREAKS OFF...

HE'S DEAD!

WHOEVER HIRED HIM TO KILL THORNTON WAS AFRAID HE'D TALK!

RAISE YOUR HANDS!

WHAT --!!

GET INTO THE CAR!

BUT--!

AS THE CAR DRIVES OFF....

WHAT'LL WE DO WIT' 'EM NOW, BOSS?

DESTROY THEM!

WHO, US?

8

LATER-- THE CAR STOPS BESIDE A TOWER ON THE SIDE OF A STEEP CHASM....

BUT YOU CAN'T DO THIS TO US! WE'RE REPORTERS!

KEEP MOVIN'!

NO SENSE TRYING TO REASON WITH THEM!

NO SOONER DO THEY ENTER THE ROOM IN THE TOWER THAN THEY ARE SECURELY BOUND...

THERE! THAT'LL HOLD 'EM!

THEN LET'S GET GOING!

ARE--ARE YOU ALL RIGHT?

YES, BUT THERE'S NO TELLING WHAT THOSE FIENDS PLAN!

MEANWHILE....

HURRY WITH THAT WOOD!

THAT OUGHTA BE ENOUGH!

THOSE TWO REPORTERS WROTE THEIR OWN OBITUARIES WHEN THEY DECIDED TO POKE INTO THIS CASE!

A MOMENT LATER, THE TOWER'S FOUNDATIONS ARE AFLAME...!

THEY'LL GIVE WAY ANY MINUTE!

DON'T I KNOW IT!

("-SMOKE! I SMELL SMOKE! I'VE GOT TO GET US OUT OF HERE BEFORE IT'S TOO LATE!-")

⑨

IN HER FRANTIC EFFORTS TO FREE HERSELF, LOIS ONLY SUCCEEDS IN KNOCKING HERSELF UNCONSCIOUS....

UH--HHH!

A TOUGH BREAK FOR LOIS...BUT IT GIVES ME A CHANCE TO GO INTO ACTION!

THE DANGER OF REVEALING HIS TRUE IDENTITY GONE, CLARK BURSTS HIS BONDS WITH AN EASY FLEX OF HIS SUPER-STRONG MUSCLES...

THAT'S BETTER!

SWIFTLY, HE FREES LOIS....

EVERY SECOND COUNTS!

...THEN REMOVES HIS OUTER GARMENTS, TRANSFORMING HIMSELF TO -- SUPERMAN!

GOT TO GET LOIS OUT OF HERE!

HURLING HIMSELF AGAINST THE DOOR, THE MAN OF STEEL KNOCKS IT CLEAR OFF....

CLEAR THE ROAD!

BUT AT THAT INSTANT, THE FOUNDATIONS GIVE WAY....

DOWN OFF THE CLIFF PLUNGES THE TOWER, CRASHING TO SMITHEREENS ON THE ROCKS FAR BELOW!

181

WELL...THAT'S THE END OF THEM!

GOOD RIDDANCE!

BUT--AS THE TOWER FELL, **SUPERMAN** HAD SEIZED LOIS AND LEAPT OUT INTO SPACE...

HERE GOES..!

...ALIGHTING SAFELY ON A SMALL LEDGE ON THE CLIFF'S SIDE...!

NOT A VERY SECURE FOOTHOLD ...BUT BETTER THAN NONE AT ALL!

AS THE THUGS DRIVE OFF....

THE BOSS OUGHT TO BE HIGHLY PLEASED!

AND WHY NOT? WHEN WE'RE ASSIGNED A JOB, WE GUARANTEE SATISFACTION!

UP THE SIDE OF THE ALMOST PERPENDICULAR CLIFF RACES THE *MAN OF TOMORROW* WITH HIS LOVELY BURDEN!

GOING UP--!

AS LOIS REVIVES....

SUPERMAN! YOU MUST HAVE SAVED ME! --B-BUT WHERE'S CLARK?

I'VE ALREADY REMOVED HIM TO SAFETY. I SUGGEST YOU GO TO A HOTEL AND COMPOSE YOURSELF.

BUT AS FOR ME-- I'VE A SCORE TO SETTLE WITH THOSE THUGS!

11

OVERTAKING THE GANGSTERS' CAR, **SUPERMAN** TEARS ITS SIDE COMPLETELY OPEN...!

HEY!! WHAT--?

MOVE OVER, BOYS! I'M COMING IN!

LEAPING WITHIN THE CAR, **SUPERMAN** DELIBERATELY SPEEDS IT ACROSS A RAILROAD TRACK, DIRECTLY IN FRONT OF A TRAIN....

COME WITH ME!

FORWARD HE RACES ALONG THE RAILROAD TRACK, A FEW FEET AHEAD OF THE SPEEDING TRAIN....

ARE YOU BOYS GOING TO TELL ME WHO YOUR BOSS IS, OR DO I HAVE TO LET THAT SPEEDING TRAIN RUN INTO US?

WE'RE MEMBERS OF THE DUTCH O'LEARY GANG!

STOP IT! STOP IT!

I SUGGEST YOU FELLOWS CONTINUE GOING OUT OF TOWN--AND **STAY OUT!**

DON'T WORRY!

AS LONG AS YOU'RE HERE, **NOTHING** COULD MAKE US COME BACK!

AS LOIS SENDS A TELEGRAM TO WHITE, THE HOTEL'S DESK CLERK MAKES A SURREPTITIOUS TELEPHONE CALL....

WILL PERRY BE STARTLED TO GET **THIS!**

LATER--AS LOIS RELAXES IN HER ROOM, SHE IS CHLOROFORMED BY A MAID....

THE ROAD CLEAR?

SHE'S OUT!

ARRIVING AT DUTCH O'LEARY'S HANGOUT, **SUPERMAN** FINDS THE PLACE EMPTY. BUT AS HE LOOKS THRU DUTCH'S PAPERS, HE DISCOVERS....

PRESS CLIPPING...THAT PROVES DUTCH WAS ONCE A PILOT EMPLOYED BY **SKYWAYS**--BUT WAS DISCHARGED FOR RECKLESSNESS AFTER A CRASH. THINGS ARE BEGINNING TO SHAPE UP.

⑫

WHEN LOIS RETURNS TO CONSCIOUSNESS...

HERE SHE IS, DUTCH, LOOKS LIKE THE BOYS SLIPPED UP.

BUT I WON'T! THERE'S NO TELLING WHAT THE BUTLER TOLD HER. I'LL TAKE HER UP IN MY PRIVATE PLANE!

SUPERMAN PATIENTLY AWAITS DUTCH'S ARRIVAL. BUT AS THE THUG WHO HAD BROUGHT LOIS TO DUTCH ARRIVES, **SUPERMAN** SEIZES HIM....

WHA--??

THAT'S WHAT **I** WANT TO KNOW, WHAT'S GOING ON?

AFTER SUBMITTING THE THUG TO A SERIES OF TYPICAL **SUPERMAN** ACROBATIC STUNTS....

NOW WILL YOU TELL ME?

YES! YES!—BUT DON'T DO ANY MORE OF THEM NOSE DIVES!

IT WAS DUTCH WHO HAD THOSE PLANES WRECKED, BEFORE HE BECAME A SUCCESSFUL GAMBLER HE WAS FIRED BY *SKYWAYS*—HAS ALWAYS HELD A GRUDGE AGAINST THEM. THIS WAS HIS WAY OF GETTING EVEN...!

AND WHERE CAN I FIND DUTCH?

IN HIS PLANE, HE'S TAKEN A GIRL REPORTER UP IN IT AND IS GOING TO KILL HER!

IT MUST BE LOIS!

AT THAT MOMENT—LOIS IS HURLED FROM DUTCH'S PLANE...

EEE-EEE!

BARELY IN TIME!

YOU S-SAID IT!

PLACING LOIS SAFELY ON THE GROUND, **SUPERMAN** LEAPS BACK INTO THE AIR. AS DUTCH'S PLANE STREAKS AT HIM, MACHINE GUNS BLASTING....

ROAD-HOG!

13

SWOOPING DOWN, **SUPERMAN** LIFTS THE UNINJURED DUTCH FROM THE FALLING WRECKAGE.

CAN'T LET YOU DIE LIKE THIS WHEN A SPOT IS ALREADY RESERVED FOR YOU IN THE ELECTRIC CHAIR!

NO! LET ME GO! I'LL PAY YOU ANYTHING!

LATER...IN *METROPOLIS*....

A FINE THING! I GO THRU ALL SORTS OF UNNERVING EXPERIENCES—AND **YOU** GET THE STORY INTO PRINT FIRST!

BLAME **SUPERMAN**. HE BROUGHT ME STRAIGHT BACK TO *METROPOLIS*.

SORRY, LOIS—BUT DEADLINES DON'T PLAY FAVORITES.

THE END

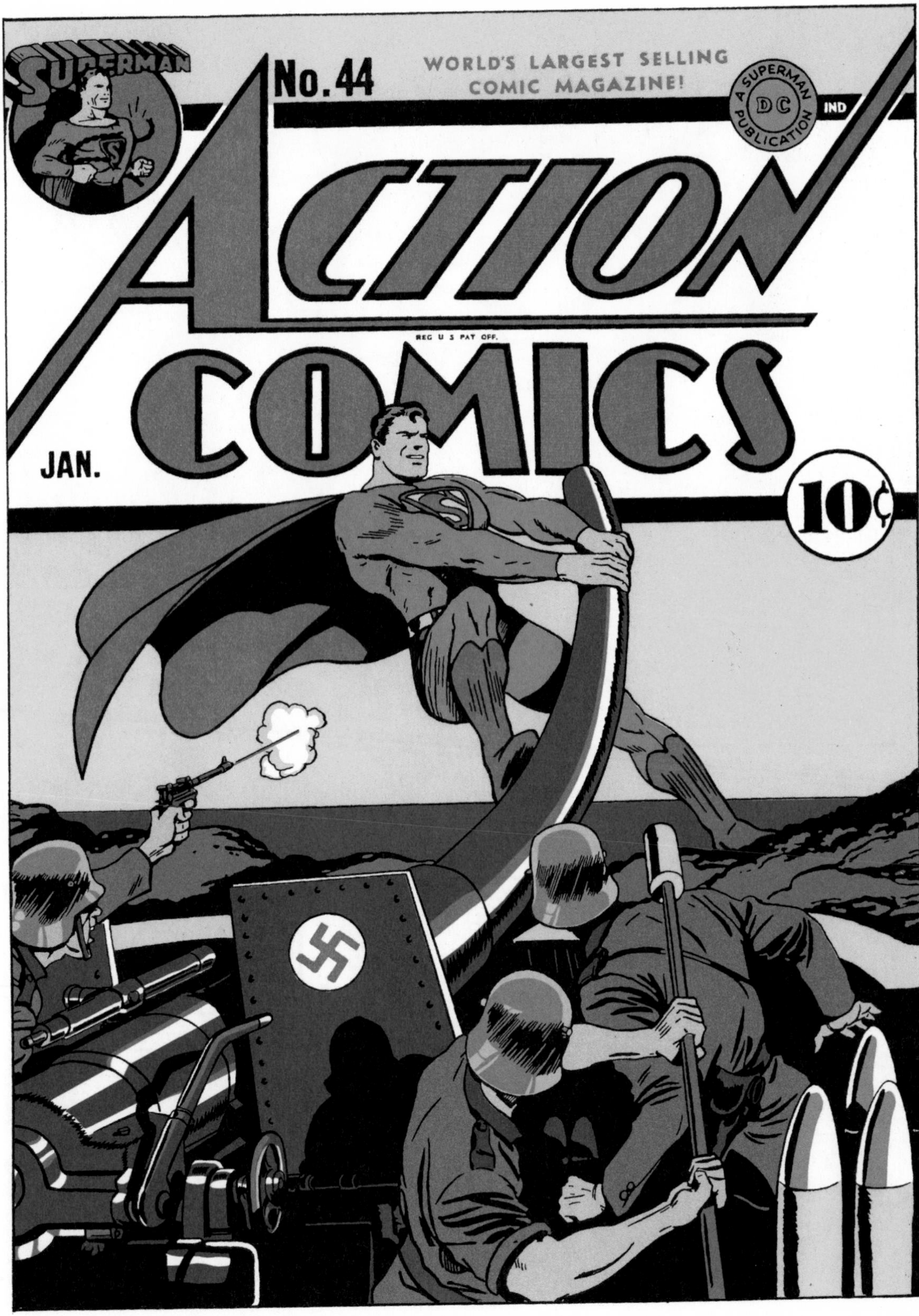
SUPERMAN
No. 44
WORLD'S LARGEST SELLING
COMIC MAGAZINE!
A SUPERMAN DC PUBLICATION
IND
ACTION
REG U S PAT OFF.
COMICS
JAN.
10¢

SUPERMAN

by JERRY SIEGEL and JOE SHUSTER

IN ONE OF HIS MOST ASTONISHING ADVENTURES, THE DARING SUPER-POWERFUL *MAN OF TOMORROW* ENCOUNTERS A MAN FROM THE PREHISTORIC PAST! THE RESULT IS A MYSTERY OF UNFATHOMABLE COMPLEXITIES -- WHICH ONLY THE KEEN MIND OF MIGHTY **SUPERMAN** CAN PIERCE!

HURRY OVER TO THE *METROPOLIS MUSEUM OF NATURAL HISTORY*, YOU TWO! PROFESSOR STEFFENS HAS SOMETHING STARTLING TO REVEAL.

DON'T TELL ME HE'S DISCOVERED ANOTHER OLD POT?

THAT WOULD BE JUST TOO, *TOO* THRILLING!

THINGS HAVE BEEN PRETTY DULL LATELY-- AND NOW *THIS* TO TOP IT OFF!

EVEN MY LOVELORN COLUMN IS EXCITING BY COMPARISON!

BUT AS CLARK AND LOIS ENTER THE MUSEUM'S AUDITORIUM, THEIR BORED EXPRESSIONS VANISH....

WHAT --?!

GOOD HEAVENS!

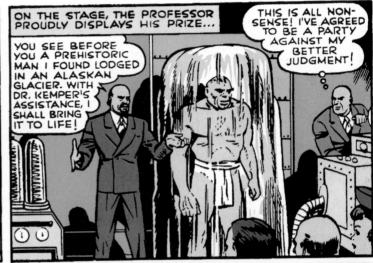

ON THE STAGE, THE PROFESSOR PROUDLY DISPLAYS HIS PRIZE...

YOU SEE BEFORE YOU A PREHISTORIC MAN I FOUND LODGED IN AN ALASKAN GLACIER. WITH DR. KEMPER'S ASSISTANCE, I SHALL BRING IT TO LIFE!

THIS IS ALL NON-SENSE! I'VE AGREED TO BE A PARTY AGAINST MY BETTER JUDGMENT!

AT LEAST, THIS MAY BE AMUSING.

SOMEHOW I CAN'T LAUGH ABOUT IT-- IT'S TOO EERIE!

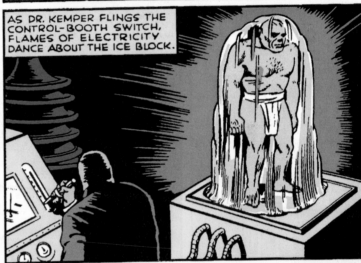

AS DR. KEMPER FLINGS THE CONTROL-BOOTH SWITCH, FLAMES OF ELECTRICITY DANCE ABOUT THE ICE BLOCK.

PROFESSOR STEFFENS LOOKS ON, HIS FACE A FROZEN MASK OF EXPECTANCY....

IT MUST COME TO LIFE-- IT MUST...!

②

SUDDENLY SPLINTERS FLY... THE GROTESQUE FIGURE OF THE DAWN MAN STIRS...!

IT LIVES! IT LIVES!

187

CLARK AND LOIS DASH FOR THE TELEPHONE BOOTH....

PARDON ME, BUT--LADIES FIRST, YOU KNOW!

SO HELP ME, WHITE--IT'S TRUE.... A PREHISTORIC MAN BROUGHT TO LIFE AFTER SPENDING *CENTURIES* LOCKED IN A GLACIER!

MY OPPORTUNITY TO SLIP AWAY AND CHANGE TO **SUPERMAN.** NO TELLING WHAT VIOLENCE THAT CREATURE MIGHT CAUSE.

BUT BEFORE CLARK CAN GET AWAY....

NO YOU DON'T! WE'RE GOING BACK THERE--WHETHER YOU'RE SCARED OR NOT--AND NOT MISS A THING!

CLARK AND LOIS HAVE TO BATTLE THEIR WAY THRU THE TERRIFIED AUDIENCE STREAMING OUT....

IS THAT THE WAY TO TREAT A LADY?

THE TWO REPORTERS FIND THE PROFESSOR AND DOCTOR ARGUING HEATEDLY....

NO! NO! THE MOVEMENT IS A REFLEX ACTION CAUSED BY THE APPLICATION OF ELECTRICITY!

...AS THE CREATURE BREAKS **FREE**...

LOOK-- IT **IS** ALIVE!

HELP! HELP!

LET ME OUTA HERE!

YOWW!

3

THE HEAVY-SET PRIMORDIAL LOOKS ABOUT IN DAZED, UNCOMPREHENDING FASHION...

BUT THEN--AS IT SIGHTS THE THREE HUMANS--IT ADVANCES, SNARLING....

BACK!

IT MAY THINK US ENEMIES!

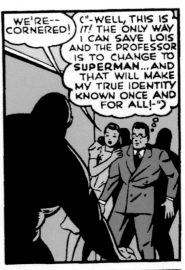
WE'RE-- CORNERED!

("--WELL, THIS IS *IT!* THE ONLY WAY I CAN SAVE LOIS AND THE PROFESSOR IS TO CHANGE TO SUPERMAN...AND THAT WILL MAKE MY TRUE IDENTITY KNOWN ONCE AND FOR ALL!--")

BUT AS THE MONSTER-MAN SIGHTS LOIS, ITS DEMEANOR CHANGES. IT SITS DOCILELY BESIDE HER....

THAT-- CERTAINLY WAS A TENSE MOMENT!

IT WANTS TO BE FRIENDLY.

CAREFUL, LOIS!

YOU CAN LEAVE NOW, I'M SURE I CAN KEEP HIM UNDER CONTROL. AND ONCE AGAIN I WANT TO THANK BOTH OF YOU FOR YOUR AID.

IT WAS NOTHING!

LISTEN TO HIM! I TAME THE BEAST --AND CLARK TAKES THE CREDIT!

AS THEY DRIVE BACK TOWARD THE *DAILY PLANET*....

NOW WE REALLY HAVE A STORY!

YOU--YOU CAN *KEEP* THAT KIND OF STORY!

④

NO! COME BACK!

STREET TRAFFIC DISORGANIZES AT SIGHT OF THE WEIRD PREHISTORIC MAN...

WHEN THE TWO REPORTERS REACH THEIR DESTINATION...

OH-OH! DON'T LOOK NOW, BUT I THINK WE HAVE COMPANY!

THE PREHISTORIC MAN!

CAN YOU BEAT IT? HE'S FOLLOWING ME AROUND LIKE A PET DOG!

HERE COME THE POLICE!

YOU CAN PUT YOUR GUNS AWAY. OUR FRIEND HERE IS HARMLESS. WE'LL TAKE HIM RIGHT BACK TO THE MUSEUM!

D-DID YOU HAVE TO INSIST HE GO BACK IN MY CAR?

IT WAS THE ONLY WAY I WAS SURE I COULD KEEP HIM UNDER CONTROL!

THANK HEAVEN YOU BROUGHT HIM BACK! I WAS WORRIED HE MIGHT CAUSE SOME DAMAGE.

THE SITUATION IS WELL IN HAND.

SEE THAT YOU KEEP THAT OVERGROWN MONKEY BEHIND BARS WHERE HE CAN'T HURT ANYONE!

THIS IS CERTAINLY GOING TO MAKE SWELL READING!

NO DOUBT. BUT THE PREHISTORIC MAN IS A NOVELTY THE PUBLIC WILL SOON FORGET ABOUT.

BUT CLARK IS MISTAKEN! FOR LATER THAT DAY, PROFESSOR STEFFENS MAKES A FRANTIC CALL TO POLICE HEADQUARTERS

COME TO THE MUSEUM--AT ONCE! SOMETHING TERRIBLE HAS HAPPENED --TERRIBLE!

AS CLARK KENT IS ABOUT TO DEPART FOR HOME, A LAST-MINUTE TIP-OFF CAUSES HIM TO FORGET EVERYTHING BUT THE NEWS ITEM...!

WHAT'S THAT--?! THE DAWN MAN HAS KILLED DR. KEMPER!?!

CLARK AND LOIS ARRIVE AT THE MUSEUM TO FIND THE POLICE IN CHARGE...

KEMPER AND I BECAME INVOLVED IN AN ARGUMENT. THE PREHISTORIC MAN HAD BECOME ATTACHED TO ME AND FIRST THING I KNEW HE HAD CRUSHED KEMPER'S SKULL!

HE WAS ONLY ACTING OUT OF LOYALTY.

BUT MURDER IS STILL MURDER!

AS STEFFENS AND HIS COMPANION ARE BEING DRIVEN TO THE STATION...

OUT... GET US OUT OF HERE!

THE PATROL WAGON'S REAR DOOR FLIES OPEN....

STEFFENS ESCAPES POLICE WITH DAWN MAN!

THEN--UNEXPECTEDLY--A SERIES OF CRIMES IS COMMITTED BY THE PREHISTORIC MAN....

PREHISTORIC MAN TURNED CRIMINAL! IF ONLY WE HAD THE DETAILS!

I'LL TRY TO GET THOSE DETAILS FOR YOU, CHIEF!

IF I DON'T BEAT YOU TO IT!

BUT WHEN HE IS ALONE, THE MEEK REPORTER TRANSFORMS HIMSELF TO THE DYNAMIC PERSONALITY OF SUPERMAN!

THAT PREHISTORIC MAN IS A DEFINITE MENACE...I CAN'T PERMIT HIS VIOLENCES TO CONTINUE.

191

SUPERMAN'S POWERFUL MUSCLES LAUNCH HIM HIGH INTO THE SKY...

ALL I NEED IS ONE CLUE TO SET ME ON THAT CREATURE'S TRAIL!

MEANWHILE -- AS A STOREKEEPER CLOSES SHOP, HE FAILS TO SIGHT A MONSTROUS SHADOW FORMING ON THE WALL BEHIND HIM....

ALL THIS TALK ABOUT A PRE-HISTORIC MAN RUNNING AROUND ....NONSENSE...

BUT A SUDDEN INSTINCT WARNS THE STOREKEEPER. HE WHIRLS....

THE DAWN MAN!

Y!!- !!!!!!

SUPERMAN'S KEEN EYES PICK OUT THE FIGURE OF THE RUNNING DAWN MAN...

AS THE MONSTER-MAN FLEES WITH THE DAY'S RECEIPTS....

POLICE-- GET ME THE POLICE!

7

THE MAN OF STEEL'S SUPER-SENSITIVE HEARING PICKS UP A POLICE BROADCAST OF THE CRIME. IN AN INSTANT, HE IS ON THE SCENE....

THE PREHISTORIC MAN DIVES INTO A WAITING CAR....

RAPIDLY, THE *MAN OF TOMORROW* CLOSES IN ON THE FLEEING AUTO...

I'LL OVERTAKE IT IN ANOTHER MOMENT!

DELIBERATELY, THE AUTO CRASHES A FRUIT VENDOR'S CART!

STREAKING IN, THE *MAN OF TOMORROW* CATCHES THE FALLING FRUIT....

JUST LIKE A BALL GAME!

...THEN SWIFTLY REPLACES IT IN THE VESTIGES OF THE CART...!

BUSINESS AS USUAL!

THANK YOU-- THANK YOU!

BUT AS SUPERMAN RACES ON....HE FINDS THE CAR-- GONE...!

8

THERE IT IS!

BUT THERE'S NO ONE INSIDE!

SWIFTLY THE *MAN OF STEEL* SCANS THE SURROUNDING BUILDINGS WITH HIS AMAZING X-RAY VISION....

HM-MMM!

SUPERMAN SIGHTS THE OBJECT OF HIS SEARCH IN A NEARBY OFFICE....

UP-- UP...!

BUT AS HE REACHES THE WINDOW SILL, UNEXPECTED MACHINE-GUN BLASTS CAUSE HIM TO LOSE HIS GRIP....

⑨

WHAT A WAY TO RECEIVE A GUEST!

SUPERMAN STRIKES EARTH WITH TERRIFIC FORCE...!

CONTACT!

BUT UP HE POPS, UNINJURED!

JUST LIKE A BOUNCING BALL!

THEN UP AGAIN HE STREAKS!

THIS TIME I'M PREPARED!

ONLY TO DISCOVER....

THEY'RE GONE!

BUT SUPERMAN'S SHARP EYES NOTE A SMALL PIECE OF CLOTH CAUGHT ON A NAIL...

I'D RECOGNIZE THAT ANYWHERE-- A PIECE OF THE MATERIAL FROM PROFESSOR STEFFENS'S SUIT!

MEANWHILE....

I THINK I'LL STOP IN AT THE MUSEUM OF NATURAL HISTORY. I MAY FIND A CLUE AS TO THE PROFESSOR'S HIDEOUT.

LATER--IN THE MUSEUM, LOIS REGARDS A LIFELIKE EXHIBIT OF THE PREHISTORIC MAN...

I COULD ALMOST SWEAR IT WAS REAL!

10

SEIZE HER!

IT IS ALIVE!

ROUGH HANDS SEIZE THE GIRL REPORTER AND DRAG HER THRU A SECRET PANEL INTO A HIDDEN CHAMBER...

DR. STEFFENS!

PERMIT ME TO INTRODUCE DUKE BRADY, A MAN OF INFLUENCE IN THE UNDER-WORLD WHO HAS SEEN FIT TO JOIN FORCES WITH ME.

TOO BAD, LADY, THAT YOU CAN'T KEEP AWAY FROM THINGS THAT DON'T CONCERN YOU!

THE PRE-HISTORIC MAN! THEN— THIS OTHER ONE...

A FAKE, YOU SEE, MISS LANE, IT WAS *I* WHO KILLED DR. KEMPER IN THE HEAT OF ALTERCATION. DUKE WAS ABLE TO HIDE ME FROM THE POLICE.

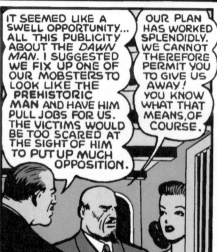

IT SEEMED LIKE A SWELL OPPORTUNITY... ALL THIS PUBLICITY ABOUT THE *DAWN MAN.* I SUGGESTED WE FIX UP ONE OF OUR MOBSTERS TO LOOK LIKE THE PREHISTORIC MAN AND HAVE HIM PULL JOBS FOR US. THE VICTIMS WOULD BE TOO SCARED AT THE SIGHT OF HIM TO PUT UP MUCH OPPOSITION.

OUR PLAN HAS WORKED SPLENDIDLY. WE CANNOT THEREFORE PERMIT YOU TO GIVE US AWAY! YOU KNOW WHAT THAT MEANS, OF COURSE.

SUPERMAN RETURNS TO THE *DAILY PLANET* AS CLARK KENT....

LOIS? SHE'S GONE TO THE METROPOLIS MUSEUM OF NATURAL HISTORY... PROBABLY ON A WILD-GOOSE CHASE.

THANKS!

ONCE AGAIN CLARK CHANGES TO HIS IDENTITY AS THE MIGHTY *MAN OF TOMORROW...*

I'D BETTER KEEP AN EYE ON THAT GIRL....

TOWARD THE MUSEUM STREAKS *SUPERMAN*....

HER ABILITY TO GET INTO MISCHIEF IS ABSOLUTELY AMAZING!

OKAY, PUGSY! GET TO WORK!

WH-WHAT IS HE GOING TO D-DO?

KILL YOU, MY DEAR! AND WHEN YOUR BODY IS FOUND, THE PRE-HISTORIC MAN WILL GET THE BLAME!

SIGHTING LOIS IN PERIL, THE REAL *DAWN MAN* GROWLS ANGRILY, THEN IN AN UNEXPECTED BURST OF STRENGTH, RIPS OPEN HIS CAGE!

THE DAWN MAN!

STOP HIM!

PUGSY DIES BEFORE THE ATTACK OF THE REAL *DAWN MAN* WHO HAS LEAPT TO LOIS'S AID...

YAAA-AAA-AA

STOP IT! LET HIM GO!

AS THE *PREHISTORIC MAN* CRUSHES THE PROFESSOR...

THEY'RE KILLED!

AND SHE'S NEXT!

SUPERMAN'S X-RAY VISION INSTANTLY ACQUAINTS HIM WITH THE SITUATION.....HE CRASHES THRU THE WALL...

SPEED!

BEATING THE BULLETS TO THEIR TARGET, SUPERMAN REMOVES LOIS TO SAFETY...

THAT'S NO PLACE FOR A LADY!

RUNNING BACK, HE DASHES FULL INTO THE GUN FIRE...!

HE KEEPS COMING!

KEEP FIRING!

BUT IT WON'T BE FOR LONG!

CRASHING INTO THE THUGS, SUPERMAN BRUSHES ASIDE THEIR PUNY OPPOSITION...

YOU'LL HAVE TO DO BETTER THAN THAT, BOYS!

BUT RACING THRU THE SECRET PANEL, DUKE BRADY SEIZES LOIS....

LET GO OF ME!

OH, NO! NOT WHILE YOU CAN PROVIDE ME WITH A SHIELD!

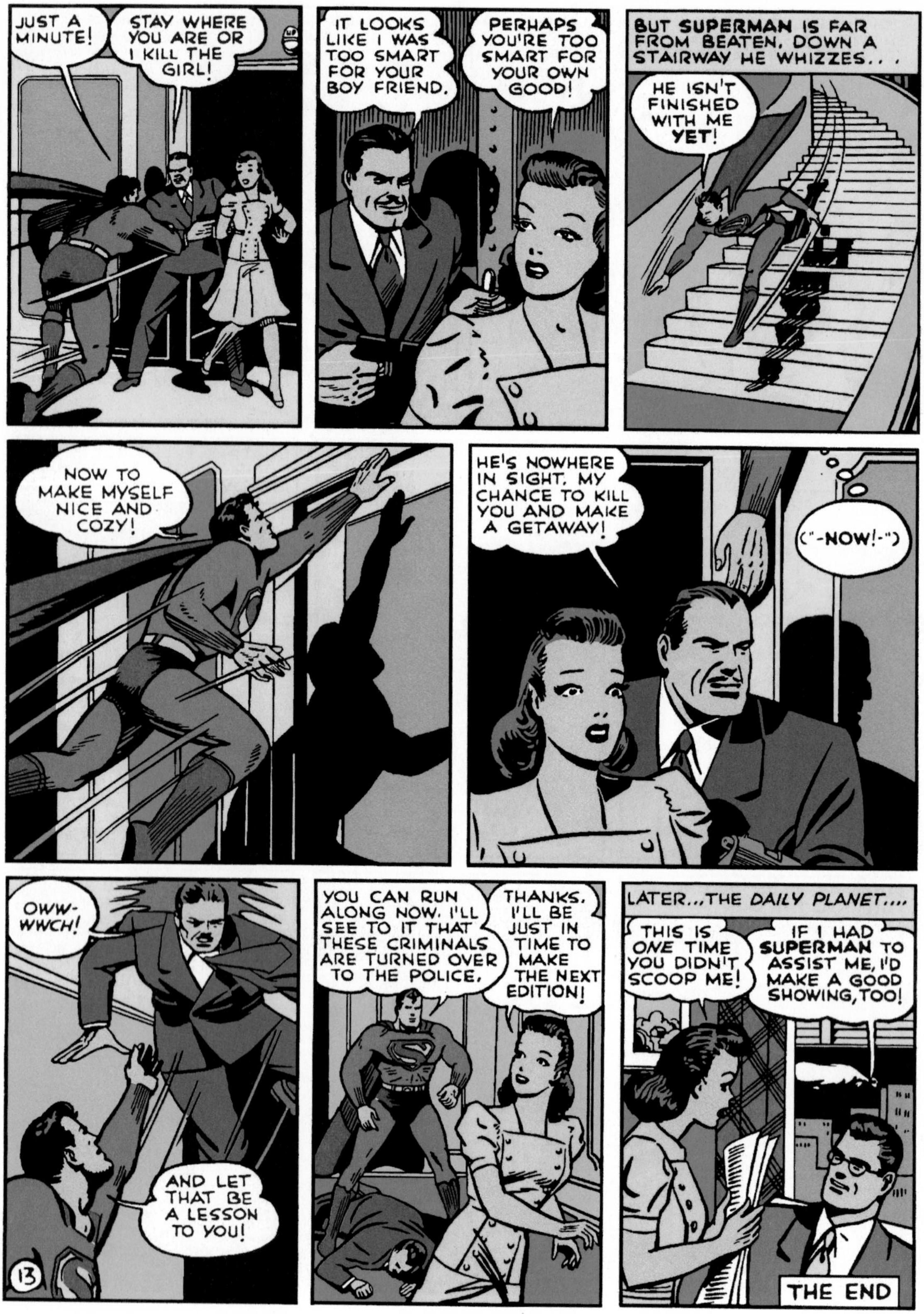
JUST A MINUTE!
STAY WHERE YOU ARE OR I KILL THE GIRL!
IT LOOKS LIKE I WAS TOO SMART FOR YOUR BOY FRIEND.
PERHAPS YOU'RE TOO SMART FOR YOUR OWN GOOD!
BUT SUPERMAN IS FAR FROM BEATEN. DOWN A STAIRWAY HE WHIZZES. . .
HE ISN'T FINISHED WITH ME YET!
NOW TO MAKE MYSELF NICE AND COZY!
HE'S NOWHERE IN SIGHT. MY CHANCE TO KILL YOU AND MAKE A GETAWAY!
("-NOW!-")
OWW-WWCH!
AND LET THAT BE A LESSON TO YOU!
13
YOU CAN RUN ALONG NOW. I'LL SEE TO IT THAT THESE CRIMINALS ARE TURNED OVER TO THE POLICE.
THANKS. I'LL BE JUST IN TIME TO MAKE THE NEXT EDITION!
LATER...THE DAILY PLANET....
THIS IS ONE TIME YOU DIDN'T SCOOP ME!
IF I HAD SUPERMAN TO ASSIST ME, I'D MAKE A GOOD SHOWING, TOO!
THE END

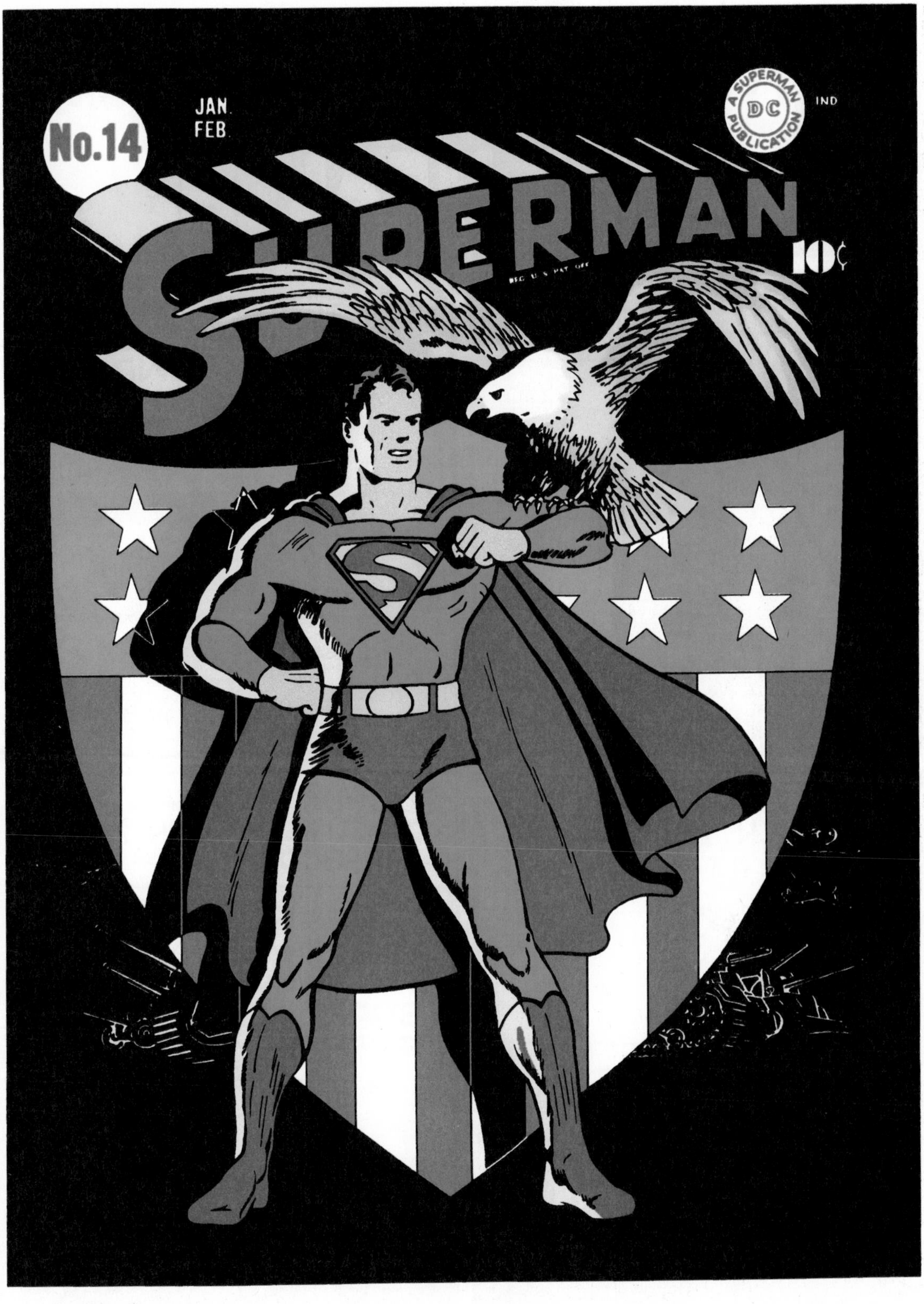
No.14
JAN.
FEB.
SUPERMAN
10¢
A SUPERMAN DC PUBLICATION
IND

SUPERMAN'S TIPS FOR SUPER-HEALTH:

① EXERCISE REGULARLY

② GET SUFFICIENT REST AND PLENTY OF FRESH AIR

③ STAY OUTDOORS AS MUCH AS POSSIBLE

④ BUT ABOVE ALL, CONSUME VITAMIN-RICH FOOD!

THERE'S NOTHING LIKE CEREALS, MILK, AND FRUIT TO GIVE YOU THAT **SUPERMAN ENERGY!**

SUPERMAN

REG U S PAT OFF

by JERRY SIEGEL *and* JOE SHUSTER

IN HIS LONG AND EXCITING CAREER, **SUPERMAN**, AMAZING *MAN OF TOMORROW*, HAS ENCOUNTERED MANY CUNNING PLOTTERS. BUT NOW HE MEETS A CRIMINAL WHO USES ESPECIALLY PUZZLING MEANS TO FURTHER HIS EVIL DESIGNS--AND THE *MAN OF STEEL* IS CALLED UPON TO DEMONSTRATE THAT HE NOT ONLY POSSESSES THE MOST POWERFUL PHYSIQUE IN THE WORLD, BUT HAS A SUPER-ABUNDANCE OF GREY MATTER AS WELL!

I'M SORRY, CLARK--BUT YOU'LL HAVE TO COVER THE CONCERT RUDOLPH KRAZINSKI IS GIVING AT *MONMOUTH HALL*. THE MUSIC EDITOR IS ILL.

BUT WHY *ME*?

I'LL TAKE THAT ASSIGNMENT, CHIEF! I'M INTERESTED IN THE BETTER THINGS OF LIFE EVEN IF CLARK ISN'T!

LOIS ATTENDS THE CONCERT --AND IS ENTHRALLED BY KRAZINSKI'S MASTERFUL PLAYING...

BRILLIANT!

LATER-- I SEE YOU SURVIVED THE PERFORMANCE!

MAY I HAVE AN ERASER? WAIT, I'LL LOOK IN MY POCKETBOOK.

IT--IT'S *GONE*!

GONE? *WHAT'S* GONE? --THE ERASER?

NO... MY PAY ENVELOPE! I'M CERTAIN IT WAS IN MY POCKETBOOK WHEN I WENT TO THE CONCERT.

HEAR ABOUT THE EXCITEMENT AT POLICE HEADQUARTERS?

MANY OF THE PEOPLE WHO WERE AT KRAZINSKI'S CONCERT HAVE TELEPHONED IN THAT THEY WERE MYSTERIOUSLY ROBBED.

HEAR THAT, LOIS?

YOU BET I DO!

CLARK ACCOMPANIES LOIS. AT THE HALL THEY ENCOUNTER AN OLD ACQUAINTANCE -- SERGEANT CASEY...

CASEY! I'VE A COMPLAINT TO MAKE!

I KNOW-- YOU'VE BEEN ROBBED!

BUT HOW COULD THESE ROBBERIES HAVE BEEN COMMITTED? I COULD SWEAR THAT NO ONE CAME NEAR MY POCKETBOOK.

THAT'S WHAT ALL THE OTHERS CLAIM!--THE PLACE MUST'VE BEEN JAMMED WITH EXPERT PICKPOCKETS!

LOIS AND CLARK STAND BY AS CASEY QUESTIONS KRAZINSKI...

YOU NOTICED NOTHING?

NOT A THING! HOW HUMILIATING THIS ALL IS....I WON'T BE ABLE TO FACE MY AUDIENCE TOMORROW!

THEY SAY LIGHTNING NEVER STRIKES TWICE IN THE SAME PLACE. BUT JUST THE SAME I'M GOING TO BE ON HAND FOR TOMORROW EVENING'S PERFORMANCE -- JUST IN CASE.

OKAY IF I GO WITH YOU?

I'M SORRY...BUT I SEEM TO RECALL THAT YOU'RE NOT INTERESTED IN THE FINE ARTS!

BUT, LOIS--!

NEXT NIGHT...

ONE TICKET, PLEASE.

("THE NERVE OF CLARK--ASKING TO GO WITH ME ONLY BECAUSE HE SCENTED A STORY.-")

BUT AS LOIS ENTERS THE HALL, CLARK KENT HURRIES TO THE BOX-OFFICE...

THAT YOUNG LADY WHO JUST ENTERED...I'D LIKE THE SEAT NEXT TO HER, PLEASE.

SERGEANT CASEY! DON'T TELL ME *YOU'VE* TAKEN AN INTEREST IN CLASSICAL MUSIC?

I'M HERE PURELY ON BUSINESS. NOTHING WILL GET PAST ME, YOU CAN BE SURE!

CLARK!

IN PERSON! MIND IF I SIT DOWN?

YOU SEE, LOIS-- YOU ATTRACT ME SO POWERFULLY, I JUST COULDN'T STAY AWAY FROM YOU...

AT THAT MOMENT, A BURST OF APPLAUSE HERALDS KRAZINSKI AS HE ENTERS THE PLATFORM, TAKES HIS BOWS....

ISN'T HE A BIT PREMATURE? THEY MIGHT NOT APPLAUD AFTER THEY HEAR HIS PLAYING.

BUT AS KRAZINSKI COMMENCES TO PLAY WITH A SURE TOUCH OF A MASTER PIANIST, CLARK IS FORCED TO CONFESS TO HIMSELF THE PIANIST HAS A REMARKABLE COMMAND OF HIS ART...

THE TUNE SLOWS IN TEMPO, IS LULLING, PEACEFUL IN EFFECT. BUT SERGEANT CASEY CONTINUES TO EYE THOSE ABOUT HIM SUSPICIOUSLY...

IF THERE'S A PICKPOCKET IN THE HOUSE, ALL HE NEED DO IS MAKE ONE FALSE MOVE!

ABRUPTLY, CLARK IS STARTLED BY A LOUD SNORE BEHIND HIM...

THE FELLOW BEHIND US HAS-- *WHAT!*-- SHE'S ASLEEP, TOO!

CLARK LOWERS HIS EYELIDS, PRETENDING SLUMBER, AND FOR A GOOD REASON--FOR THO KRAZINSKI PLAYS RAPTUROUSLY, THE ENTIRE AUDIENCE IS ASLEEP!

CEASING PLAYING, KRAZINSKI MEDITATIVELY REGARDS THE SLEEPING AUDIENCE, THEN REMOVES TWO COTTON PLUGS FROM HIS EARS...

AS THE PIANIST SIGNALS....

IN RESPONSE, SEVERAL TOUGH-LOOKING INDIVIDUALS AMONG THE AUDIENCE RISE AND ALSO REMOVE PLUGS FROM THEIR EARS.

LET'S GET BUSY!

WE'VE GOT TO MAKE IT FAST!

BOY--WHAT A SWEET RACKET!

UNDER THE DIRECTION OF RUDOLPH KRAZINSKI, THE HIRELINGS SYSTEMATICALLY AND THOROUGHLY LOOT THE AUDIENCE....

GEE... THIS IS LIKE TAKING CANDY FROM A BABY-- ONLY EASIER!

WE OUGHT TO GET QUITE A HAUL!

HEY--WHAT'RE YA DOIN'?

REPLACING THE MONEY WE STOLE FROM THIS YOUNG LADY YESTERDAY, SHE MADE A FAVORABLE IMPRESSION UPON ME.

WOTSA IDEA?

I DO AS I PLEASE-- DO YOU UNDERSTAND THAT--OR MUST I MAKE IT CLEARER...?

NOT... NOT THE DEATH-TUNE!

WELL, WELL! IF IT AIN'T MY OLD PAL, SERGEANT CASEY!--I SWORE I'D GET EVEN WITH HIM!

YOU FOOL! WITH MILLIONS TO BE MADE--YOU WANT TO SPOIL IT BY PETTY VENGEANCE!

THO HIS EYELIDS HAVE REMAINED CLOSED, CLARK'S X-RAY VISION HAS ENABLED HIM TO VIEW ALL THAT HAS OCCURRED....

("--AMAZING! KRAZINSKI HYPNO-TIZED THE AUDIENCE WITH MUSIC SO THAT HIS HENCHMEN COULD ROB THEM! I'D SMASH THE SET-UP RIGHT NOW, BUT I THINK I'D BETTER LEARN MORE ABOUT IT FIRST!--")

BUT IN DEFIANCE OF HIS CHIEF'S ORDERS, ONE OF THE THUGS HAS SLUNG THE UNCONSCIOUS CASEY OVER HIS SHOULDER AND CARRIED HIM OFF....

ARE YOU NUTS? IF KRAZINSKI FINDS OUT, I'D HATE TO BE IN YOUR SHOES!

I'LL WORRY ABOUT THAT LATER!

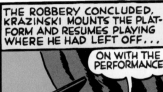

THE ROBBERY CONCLUDED, KRAZINSKI MOUNTS THE PLATFORM AND RESUMES PLAYING WHERE HE HAD LEFT OFF....

ON WITH THE PERFORMANCE!

SLOWLY THE MEASURED TEMPO INCREASES, AND AS IT DOES, THE AUDIENCE COMES OUT OF ITS SLUMBER, TOTALLY UNAWARE OF ANY LAPSE OF TIME....

ISN'T IT SOOTHING?

HE'S A MASTER --A GENIUS!

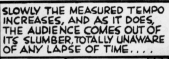

BUT THE MAN WHO HAD BEEN SEATED BESIDE SERGEANT CASEY GETS A MINOR SHOCK...

I COULD HAVE *SWORN* THERE WAS SOMEONE SEATED THERE A MOMENT AGO...BUT IT MUST HAVE BEEN MY IMAGINATION!

AT THE CONCLUSION OF THE PROGRAM, AFTER KRAZINSKI TAKES HIS BOWS, LOIS MAKES A STARTLING DISCOVERY....

WH-WHAT--? --MY MONEY!

CLARK, IF THIS IS YOUR IDEA OF A PRACTICAL JOKE--!

IT MUST HAVE BEEN IN YOUR POCKETBOOK ALL THE TIME!

ABRUPTLY--PANDEMONIUM REIGNS IN THE AUDIENCE AS THE ABSENCE OF VALUABLES IS DISCOVERED....

EEE-EEK! MY NECKLACE!

MY WATCH --IT'S GONE!

POLICE REACH THE SCENE A FEW MINUTES LATER....

NO SIGN OF CASEY!

HE WAS TO BE HERE ON THE JOB--HE'S FALLEN DOWN MISERABLY!

MINUTES LATER--AS KRAZINSKI DRIVES OFF, CLARK KENT DIVESTS HIMSELF OF HIS OUTER GARMENTS...

HE'S HEADED FOR HIS GANG'S HEADQUARTERS-- THEREFORE, I TRAIL HIM!

A STRANGE, COSTUMED FIGURE-- SWOOPING DOWN TO THE ROAD...!

SUPERMAN! I'VE GOT TO DODGE HIM-- AND *QUICK!* I HAVE IT! THEY'RE BLASTING ON THE MOUNTAIN ROAD AHEAD...!

AS THE SPEEDING AUTO TURNS A CURVE THAT LEADS ONTO A NARROW ROAD ON THE SIDE OF A MOUNTAIN, ITS DRIVER LEAPS FREE OF IT....

DANGER
BLAST

SUPERMAN-- LANDING ATOP THE CAR! I DIDN'T LEAVE A MOMENT TOO EARLY!

--EMPTY!

AT THAT MOMENT-- A MEMBER OF THE NIGHT SHIFT BLASTING CREW FORCES DOWN THE PLUNGER OF A DYNAMITE DETONATOR!

IN RESPONSE-- THE ENTIRE SIDE OF THE MOUNTAIN EXPLODES-- THEN COLLAPSES UPON BOTH AUTO AND *MAN OF TOMORROW!*

TAXI!

THAT CALLED FOR FAST THINKING! I WON'T BE TROUBLED BY **SUPERMAN** ANY MORE!

BUT THE NOTED PIANIST ERRS! --FOR THE MIGHTY MASS OF BOULDERS COMMENCES TO MOVE, ERUPT....

AND A MOMENT LATER, THE MIGHTY *MAN OF STEEL* BURROWS HIS WAY INTO VIEW!

THIS LITTLE EPISODE HAS ALLOWED KRAZINSKI TO MAKE A COMPLETE GETAWAY...PERHAPS!

MEANWHILE... WH-WHERE--? SAY! HOW'D I GET HERE?! I WAS WATCHING THE CONCERT WHEN...

NEVER MIND HOW YOU GOT HERE, COPPER! WHAT MATTERS IS THAT YOU'RE GONNA LEAVE HERE FEET FIRST--AND I EVEN AN OLD SCORE...!

DON'T SHOOT!

I TOLD YOU TO LEAVE THAT COP ALONE!

UH-HHH!

STAY HERE AND WATCH THE PRISONER. YOU OTHERS GO TO YOUR STATIONS UNTIL *THE TIME!*

SO YOU'RE THE ONE TO BLAME FOR THE ROBBERIES!

AFTER THE OTHERS DEPART...

BETTER NOT SHOOT! YOUR BOSS WON'T LIKE IT!

BUT IT WILL BE TOO LATE TO DO ANYTHING ABOUT IT!

FORTUNATELY, I NOTED THE LICENSE OF THAT CAR...

FORCING OPEN A WINDOW OF THE AUTO LICENSE BUREAU, **SUPERMAN** ENTERS....

DR 703... IF THAT DOESN'T LEAD ME TO THE SCHEMING PIANIST-- *NOTHING* WILL!

JAMES NOONAN-- 411 DYSART ROAD...!

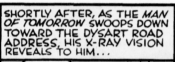

SHORTLY AFTER, AS THE *MAN OF TOMORROW* SWOOPS DOWN TOWARD THE DYSART ROAD ADDRESS, HIS X-RAY VISION REVEALS TO HIM...

CASEY --IN DANGER!

AS THE THUG FIRES, IN THRU THE WALL CRASHES....

SUPERMAN!

RIGHT--AS YOU'LL SOON LEARN TO YOUR DISMAY!

RACING THE BULLET, **SUPERMAN** OVERTAKES IT AND MOVES SERGEANT CASEY ASIDE TO SAFETY BEFORE IT REACHES HIM!

KEEP AWAY-- DON'T COME ANY CLOSER!

YOU MAY AS WELL STOP FIRING.

Panel 1: LET GO--! / NOT JUST YET-- YOU'RE COMING WITH ME!

Panel 2: ONCE AGAIN YOU'VE SAVED MY LIFE! / MIND IF I BORROW YOUR PRISON-ER?

Panel 3: CAREFUL! DON'T DROP ME --! / THIS IS JUST A TASTE OF WHAT'S COMING IF YOU DON'T TELL ME KRAZINSKI'S PLAN!

Panel 4: HE'S GOING TO BLOT OUT THE PRESIDENT'S SPECIAL BROAD-CAST WHEN EVERYONE WILL BE LISTENING--INSTEAD EVERYONE WILL HEAR HIS PIANO PLAYING AND BE HYPNOTIZED TO SLEEP--EXCEPT HIS GANGSTERS, WHO WILL LOOT THE TOWN! / WHAT AN AMAZING SCHEME! BUT I'LL SEE TO IT THAT IT DOESN'T WORK!

Panel 5: AS THE TREACHEROUS THUG SEEKS TO SHOVE **SUPERMAN** OFF THE CLIFF, THE *MAN OF STEEL* SIDESTEPS AND THE CRIMINAL PLUNGES TO HIS DOOM! / MISSED ME--! / YAA-AAA!

Panel 6: MEANWHILE -- IN ONE OF THE MANY LOCATIONS WHERE GANGSTERS WAIT IMPATIENTLY... / HE'LL BE ON THE AIR ANY MINUTE, NOW--PUT THE PLUGS IN YOUR EARS! / BOY, HOW SIMPLE IT'LL BE TO PULL A JOB WHEN HALF THE TOWN IS FAST ASLEEP!

Panel 7: IN HIS SECRET STUDIO, KRAZINSKI LIKEWISE PLACES PLUGS IN HIS EARS, THEN COMMENCES TO PLAY....

Panel 8: THROUGHOUT *METROPOLIS*, HUNDREDS OF THOUSANDS OF LISTENERS TUNE IN TO HEAR A "FIRESIDE CHAT"--INSTEAD, THEY HEAR LULLING, HYPNOTIC PIANO PLAYING--AND IN A MATTER OF MOMENTS ARE FAST ASLEEP! / LOANS

AS **SUPERMAN**'S SUPER-SENSITIVE HEARING PICKS UP THE BROADCAST, HE STREAKS THRU THE AIR TOWARD ITS SOURCE...

IT SEEMS TO BE COMING FROM THAT DIRECTION!

BUT AS HE SIGHTS AN IMPENDING ACCIDENT BELOW, DOWN HE PLUMMETS....

THOSE TWO AUTOS-- ABOUT TO COLLIDE!

ALIGHTING BETWEEN THE TWO HURTLING CARS, **SUPERMAN** FORCES THEM APART SO THAT THE CRASH IS AVERTED...!

A CLOSE CALL!

THE DRIVER'S ASLEEP AT THE WHEEL...RADIO'S GOING... BROADCASTING KRAZINSKI'S INSIDIOUS MUSIC...I'VE GOT TO STOP THAT CROOKED MUSICIAN BEFORE HE CAUSES UNTOLD DAMAGE!

BUT THEN--THE *MAN OF STEEL*'S AMAZING TELESCOPIC VISION REVEALS TO HIM A SERIES OF ROBBERIES BEING PERPETRATED UPON DOZING, HELPLESS MEN...

SPEEDING TO THE CRIMES HE HAS SIGHTED, **SUPERMAN** ATTENDS TO THE THUGS IN RECORD TIME...

KEEP 'EM FLYING!

THEN-- ONCE AGAIN THE *MAN OF STEEL* RESUMES HIS SEARCH...

KRAZINSKI IS AT THE BOTTOM OF THIS-- HE MUST HAVE HIS HIRED THUGS SIMULTANEOUSLY PULLING DOZENS OF CRIMES. IF I CAN FOLLOW THE RADIO WAVES TO THEIR SOURCE... LOCATE HIM .

A STRONG WAVE OF ELECTRICAL ENERGY EMANATING FROM BELOW...YET THERE'S NO KNOWN RADIO STATION THERE! I'LL INVESTIGATE!

BUT AS **SUPERMAN** ENTERS THRU A DOOR ON THE ROOF, HE IS MET BY A GREAT BLAST OF ELECTRICITY...

A TRAP!

BUT WHAT'S A COUPLE MILLION VOLTS OF ELECTRICITY TO ME? HM-MM! IT'S OBVIOUS SOMEONE DOESN'T WANT TO BE INTERRUPTED!

SUPERMAN'S X-RAY VISION INFORMS HIM HE HAS COME TO THE END OF HIS SEARCH..!

AS THE STEEL BUCKLES AND GIVES WAY, THE CRIMINAL PIANIST PLAYS ON, THO SWEAT COVERS HIS BROW...

SOMEONE-- SOMETHING --TRYING TO BREAK IN...!

SUPERMAN! BUT I THOUGHT...

THAT YOU HAD DESTROYED ME? GUESS AGAIN!

YOU CAN STOP PLAYING THAT PIANO RIGHT NOW. THE GAME'S UP, KRAZINSKI!

AS THE *MAN OF TOMORROW* ADVANCES, KRAZINSKI FURIOUSLY ATTACKS THE PIANO KEYS....

YOU RECKON WITHOUT THE POWER OF HYPNOSIS!

THE PIANIST PLAYS LIKE A MAN GONE MAD! DEXTEROUSLY, HIS FINGERS FLY OVER THE KEYS AT HURRICANE SPEED, BEATING OUT A WEIRD, ENCHANTING MELODY!

SUPERMAN HALTS AS THE MUSIC SEEMS TO ASSAULT HIM LIKE A SOLID OBJECT...

THESE NOTES --PARALYZING ME...!

A MOMENT LATER, THE *MAN OF STEEL* STANDS RIGID, COMPLETELY UNDER THE POWER OF THAT HYPNOTIC MUSIC!

I'VE **WON!**

MIGHTILY, THE *MAN OF TOMORROW* CONCENTRATES, TRYING TO THROW OFF THE INSIDIOUS SPELL!

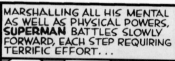

MARSHALLING ALL HIS MENTAL AS WELL AS PHYSICAL POWERS, **SUPERMAN** BATTLES SLOWLY FORWARD, EACH STEP REQUIRING TERRIFIC EFFORT...

STOP... STOP!

I'VE-- GOT TO GO--ON!

HE SUCCEEDS IN FREEING HIMSELF! LEAPING IN, HE SMASHES THE BROADCASTING APPARATUS!

MADE IT!

YOU'VE SMASHED MY COSTLY APPARATUS!

AS THE BROADCAST IS CUT OFF THE AIR, THE VICTIMS OF KRAZINSKI'S HYPNOTIC PIANO PLAYING ABRUPTLY AWAKEN...

WH--WHAT?

LOOK-- BANDITS!

CAUGHT OFF GUARD, KRAZINSKI'S HIRELINGS ARE QUICKLY OVER-WHELMED AND CAPTURED...

YOU SEE--YOUR LAST ATTEMPT AT RESISTANCE FAILED.--YOU MIGHT AS WELL GIVE UP.

YOU MAY HAVE RUINED MY PLOT-- BUT YOU'LL NEVER GET ME!

SWIFTLY, KRAZINSKI'S FINGERS FLY OVER THE PIANO KEYS, STRIKING A CERTAIN COMBIN-ATION OF BIZARRE NOTES...!

A PIERCING SHRIEK LEAVES THE PIANIST--HE CRASHES DOWN UPON THE KEYS....

YAA-AAA!

DEAD!--SLAIN BY THOSE BRIEF NOTES OF MUSIC. HE LITERALLY WILLED HIM-SELF TO DIE...!

CASEY--IF YOU LEAVE HEAD-QUARTERS AND DASH TO THE FOLLOWING ADDRESS, YOU'LL FIND KRAZINSKI THERE, DEAD --THE MAN WHO TRIED TO HYPNOTIZE A CITY--THEN ROB IT WHILE IT SLEPT!

THANKS, SUPERMAN! THE WAY I FUMBLED THE INVESTIGATION GOT ME IN TROUBLE WITH MY SUPERIORS-- BUT DISCOVERING KRAZINSKI SHOULD PUT ME BACK IN THEIR GOOD GRACES!

LATER...

KRAZINSKI-- A CRIMINAL HYPNOTIST! WHERE IN THE WORLD DID YOU GET YOUR FACTS?

THAT'S MY SECRET, LOIS, I HAVE A FORMULA OF MY VERY OWN.

THE END

213

SUPERMAN

by JERRY SIEGEL and JOE SHUSTER

MOST OF THE COMFORTS AND NECESSITIES OF MODERN-DAY CIVILIZATION WERE ORIGINATED BY YOUNG, "IMPRACTICAL" DREAMERS. SOMETIMES THE DISCOVERIES OF THE INVENTORS BROUGHT THEM FAME AND FORTUNE. BUT OFTEN THE FRUITS OF THEIR LABORS WERE ANNEXED BY UNSCRUPULOUS SCHEMERS. SUPERMAN COMES UP AGAINST SUCH A SITUATION-- AND DEALS OUT SUPER-JUSTICE AS ONLY THE MAN OF TOMORROW CAN!

HOW IT STARTED IS NEVER LEARNED --BUT SUDDENLY A TENEMENT BUILDING IN THE SLUM SECTION OF METROPOLIS CATCHES FIRE AND BURNS WITH THE SPEED OF A TINDER-BOX...THE SAFETY OF THE SURROUNDING TENEMENTS IS JEOPARDIZED....

1

A TENEMENT FIRE ON MAGNOLIA STREET! COVER IT!

YOU BET!

WAIT FOR ME!

BUT CLARK DELIBERATELY FALLS BACK, THEN DODGES INTO AN EMPTY ROOM WHERE HE SWIFTLY REMOVES HIS OUTER GARMENTS....

LIVES MAY BE IN DANGER!

SUPERMAN REACHES HIS DESTINATION IN MOMENTS...

IS EVERYONE SAFELY OUT?

NO! SEVERAL PEOPLE ARE TRAPPED ON THE THIRD FLOOR!

UP TOWARD THE THIRD FLOOR CATAPULTS THE MAN OF STEEL LIKE A ROCKET....

I THOUGHT I MIGHT BE OF HELP!

....CRASHING IN THRU A WINDOW OUT OF VIEW OF THE GAPING CROWD...!

YOU'VE NOTHING TO FEAR, FOLKS!

NOTHING? WE MAY BE BURNED ALIVE!

HELP US GET OUT OF HERE!

DOWN PLUMMETS SUPERMAN TO THE PAVEMENT WITH SEVERAL PEOPLE UNDER HIS ARM....

THERE YOU ARE! NOW TO ATTEND TO THE OTHERS!

②

FLASHING BACK AND FORTH AT BEWILDERING SPEED, SUPERMAN TRANSFERS ALL THE TRAPPED TENEMENT TENANTS TO SAFETY....

THANKS!

WE OWE OUR LIVES TO YOU!

THERE'S STILL THAT FIRE TO ATTEND TO!

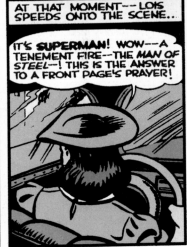

AT THAT MOMENT -- LOIS SPEEDS ONTO THE SCENE..

IT'S SUPERMAN! WOW -- A TENEMENT FIRE -- THE MAN OF STEEL --! THIS IS THE ANSWER TO A FRONT PAGE'S PRAYER!

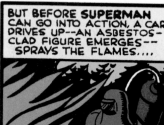
BUT BEFORE **SUPERMAN** CAN GO INTO ACTION, A CAR DRIVES UP--AN ASBESTOS-CLAD FIGURE EMERGES---SPRAYS THE FLAMES....

WHO IS HE?

I'M SURE I DON'T KNOW. HE'S OBVIOUSLY NOT A MEMBER OF THE FIRE-DEPARTMENT.

BEFORE THE ONSLAUGHT OF THE STRANGE POWDER, FLAMES RAPIDLY VANISH...!

IT'S WORK-ING!

THIS RATES AN INTER-VIEW!

CARE-FUL, LOIS!

I'D LIKE TO KNOW WH-- LOOK OUT!!

DOWN TOWARD THE TWO FIGURES HURTLES A GREAT FLAMING RAFTER...!

RACING IN, **SUPERMAN** SMASHES THE MENACING OBJECT ASIDE BEFORE IT CAN DO ANY HARM...!

STILL JOHNNY-ON-THE-SPOT!

AND A LUCKY THING FOR YOU!

③

RACING OFF TO A STORE ROOM, **SUPERMAN** SWIFTLY CHANGES BACK TO HIS IDENTITY AS CLARK KENT....

BETWEEN THE FIRE DEPARTMENT AND THAT MIRACULOUS FIRE-FIGHTER, THERE'S NOTHING LEFT FOR **SUPERMAN** TO DO HERE. BUT THERE SEEMS TO BE A NEWS STORY FOR CLARK KENT!

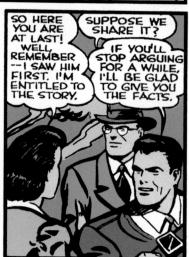
SO HERE YOU ARE AT LAST! WELL, REMEMBER --I SAW HIM FIRST. I'M ENTITLED TO THE STORY.

SUPPOSE WE SHARE IT?

IF YOU'LL STOP ARGUING FOR A WHILE, I'LL BE GLAD TO GIVE YOU THE FACTS.

THAT'S AN EXCELLENT IDEA. WHO ARE YOU, AND HOW DID YOU MANAGE TO CONTROL THOSE FLAMES SO QUICKLY?

I'M CHET FARNS-WORTH. FOR THE LAST SEVERAL YEARS I'VE BEEN PERFECT-ING A POWDER WHICH WOULD ALMOST INSTANTLY EXTIN-GUISH FLAMES. I BELIEVE I'VE SUCCEEDED AT LAST!

AND I THINK YOU HAVE SUCCEEDED-- ADMIRABLY! HAVE YOU EVER MARKETED ONE OF YOUR DISCOVERIES?

NOT YET-- BUT I HAVE HIGH HOPES.

I THINK YOU'VE GOT SOMETHING IN THIS POWDER, CHET. I KNOW SOMEONE WHO I BELIEVE COULD BE INTERESTED IN IT.

LATER--CLARK SPEAKS TO A MANUFACTURER FRIEND OF HIS....

AND I THINK IT WOULD BE WORTH YOUR WHILE TO LOOK AT THIS YOUNG MAN'S DISCOVERY.

THERE'LL BE NO HARM IN LOOK-ING AT IT, CLARK.

BUT MEANWHILE, LOIS' WRITE-UP OF THE TENEMENT FIRE HAS ALREADY APPEARED,....

YOUNG INVENTOR DISCOVERS FIRE EXTINGUISHING POWDER

LATER--WHEN CLARK KENT REACHES CHET'S APARTMENT, ACCOMPANIED BY HIS FRIEND...

CHET, THIS IS--

GOOD NEWS, CLARK! I'VE SOLD MY DISCOVERY!

THEN THERE'S NO NEED FOR ME TO REMAIN FURTHER. GOODBYE, KENT!

CLARK, THIS IS JIM BALDWIN, THE MAN I'VE SIGNED WITH. HE'S GOING TO MAKE MY DREAMS COME TRUE!

BALDWIN? I THINK I'VE HEARD THE NAME BEFORE...

AND WHO HASN'T HEARD OF BALDWIN, THE FAMOUS PROMOTER! THIS YOUNG MAN IS GOING PLACES!

BUT AS CLARK DEPARTS....

I RECALL NOW WHAT I HEARD ABOUT BALDWIN....HE'S SHARP, UNSCRUPULOUS..... I HOPE FOR HIS SAKE, AS WELL AS CHET'S, THAT HE GIVES FARNSWORTH A SQUARE DEAL!

SEVERAL WEEKS LATER....

REMEMBER THE YOUNG INVENTOR WE ENCOUNTERED AT THAT TENEMENT FIRE? HAVE YOU ANY IDEA HOW HE IS MAKING OUT?

FARNSWORTH SHOULD BE MAKING OUT PRETTY WELL.

THAT'S AN IDEA. I THINK I'LL DROP IN ON CHET AND SAY HELLO.

BUT AS CLARK GLANCES UP TOWARD THE INVENTOR'S APARTMENT, HIS TELESCOPIC VISION BRINGS HIM A SIGHT THAT CAUSES HIM TO STIFFEN IN ASTONISHMENT....

WELL...!

WHAT CLARK HAS SEEN....

RACING INTO AN ALLEY, KENT SWIFTLY STRIPS OFF HIS OUTER GARMENTS....

THIS IS A JOB FOR SUPERMAN!

UP TOWARD THE WINDOW OF CHET'S APARTMENT STREAKS A COLORFULLY COSTUMED FIGURE...

LUCKY FOR CHET THAT I DECIDED TO DROP IN!

5

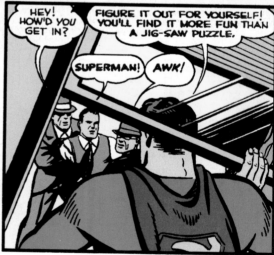

HEY! HOW'D YOU GET IN?

FIGURE IT OUT FOR YOURSELF! YOU'LL FIND IT MORE FUN THAN A JIG-SAW PUZZLE.

SUPERMAN!

AWK!

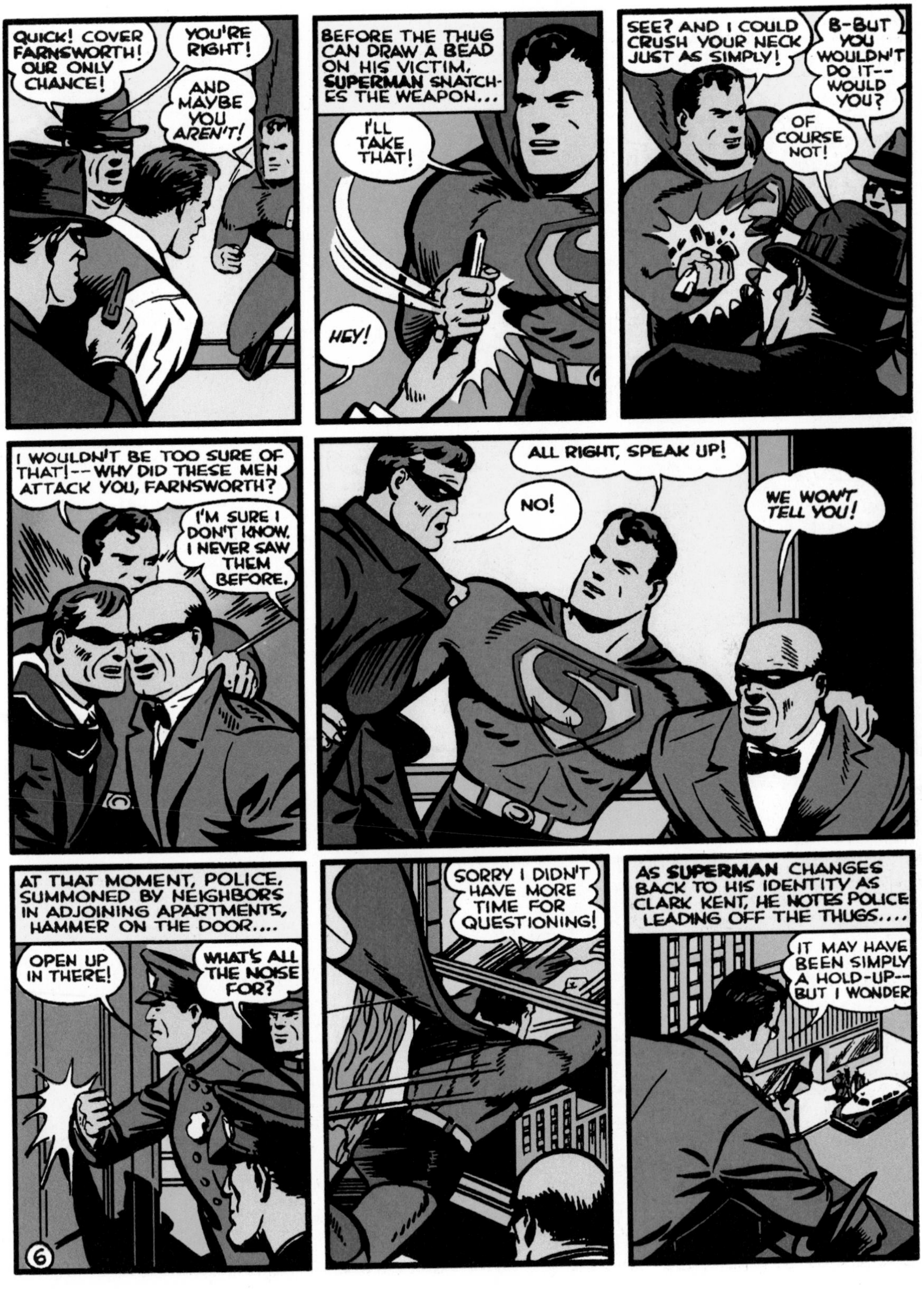
QUICK! COVER FARNSWORTH! OUR ONLY CHANCE!
YOU'RE RIGHT!
AND MAYBE YOU AREN'T!
BEFORE THE THUG CAN DRAW A BEAD ON HIS VICTIM, SUPERMAN SNATCHES THE WEAPON...
I'LL TAKE THAT!
HEY!
SEE? AND I COULD CRUSH YOUR NECK JUST AS SIMPLY!
B-BUT YOU WOULDN'T DO IT-- WOULD YOU?
OF COURSE NOT!
I WOULDN'T BE TOO SURE OF THAT!-- WHY DID THESE MEN ATTACK YOU, FARNSWORTH?
I'M SURE I DON'T KNOW. I NEVER SAW THEM BEFORE.
ALL RIGHT, SPEAK UP!
NO!
WE WON'T TELL YOU!
AT THAT MOMENT, POLICE, SUMMONED BY NEIGHBORS IN ADJOINING APARTMENTS, HAMMER ON THE DOOR....
OPEN UP IN THERE!
WHAT'S ALL THE NOISE FOR?
6
SORRY I DIDN'T HAVE MORE TIME FOR QUESTIONING!
AS SUPERMAN CHANGES BACK TO HIS IDENTITY AS CLARK KENT, HE NOTES POLICE LEADING OFF THE THUGS....
IT MAY HAVE BEEN SIMPLY A HOLD-UP-- BUT I WONDER

SHORTLY AFTER....CLARK ENTERS CHET'S APARTMENT...

WHAT'S ALL THE EXCITEMENT?

TWO THUGS ATTACKED ME. I CAN THANK **SUPERMAN** FOR SAVING ME FROM THEM!

BUT WHY SHOULD ANYONE WANT TO HARM YOU?

THAT'S WHAT I CAN'T FIGURE OUT!

ATOP AN ADJOINING BUILDING, A WAITING THUG SEES HIS OPPORTUNITY....

NOW'S MY CHANCE!

HE'LL BE CRUSHED FLATTER'N A PANCAKE!

BUT INSTINCTIVELY GLANCING UP, CLARK SIGHTS THE HEAVY MISSILE STREAKING DOWN TOWARD HIS COMPANION...

("-WHAT--!!-")

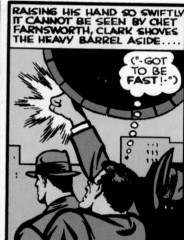

RAISING HIS HAND SO SWIFTLY IT CANNOT BE SEEN BY CHET FARNSWORTH, CLARK SHOVES THE HEAVY BARREL ASIDE....

("-GOT TO BE FAST!-")

...SO THAT IT CRASHES HARMLESSLY TO THE PAVEMENT BESIDE THEM...!

LOOK OUT!

⑦

IF YOU HADN'T SHOVED ME ASIDE IN TIME...!

I--I SCARCELY KNEW WHAT I WAS DOING!

("-SOMEONE WANTS TO DESTROY CHET! I INTEND TO FIND OUT *WHO* AND *WHY*!-")

SHORTLY AFTER--CLARK CHANGES TO-- **SUPERMAN!**

I'D BETTER CONTINUE TO WATCH OVER CHET!

PURSUING THE YOUNG INVENTOR FROM A VANTAGE POINT HIGH IN THE SKY, THE *MAN OF STEEL* OBSERVES HIM ENTER AN OFFICE BUILDING...

HE'S CALLING ON BALDWIN!

ALIGHTING ON A LEDGE OUTSIDE BALDWIN'S OFFICE WINDOW, **SUPERMAN** PREPARES TO GET AN EARFUL....

I DON'T WANT TO MISS THIS!

WITHIN THE OFFICE....

FIFTY DOLLARS! BUT I THOUGHT YOU WERE MAKING GREAT PROGRESS!

SORRY, KID. BE PATIENT. IT TAKES TIME TO WORK UP SOMETHING LIKE THIS. YOU'LL MAKE PLENTY LATER.

I DON'T BELIEVE YOU! I THINK YOU'RE HOLDING OUT ON ME!-- YOU CAN'T REPRESENT ME ANYMORE!

NOT SO FAST, YOUNGSTER --YOU'RE SPEAKING TO THE MAN WHO *OWNS* THAT DISCOVERY!

OWNS IT?-- WHAT DO YOU MEAN?

THIS PAPER--A PHOTOSTAT OF THE AGREEMENT YOU SIGNED. WHEN YOU ACCEPTED THAT "ADVANCE" AND SIGNED THIS PAPER, YOU FORFEITED ALL RIGHTS TO YOUR DISCOVERY.

BUT-- BUT THAT'S **NOT** FAIR!

BE A GOOD LAD AND MAYBE YOU'LL MAKE SOME MONEY OUT OF THIS. BUT ANY TIME YOU RAISE A KICK YOU'LL BE OUT!

8

THERE GOES CHET-- BEATEN--DISCOURAGED! POOR KID! HE DIDN'T REALIZE THE TYPE OF OBSTACLES THAT LIE IN THE PATH OF A YOUNG INVENTOR!

SHORTLY AFTER.... CHET RETURNS TO HIS APARTMENT, HIS FACE SET GRIMLY....

WHAT'S THE USE OF INVENTING SOMETHING IF YOU CAN'T ENJOY THE FRUITS OF YOUR DISCOVERY.

FARNSWORTH SMASHES THE INSTRUMENTS IN HIS SMALL LABORATORY....

I'LL NEVER INVENT ANOTHER THING IN MY LIFE!

RIGHT, BUD!

HOW DID YOU GET IN?

YOU'RE COMING WITH US!

CHET FARNSWORTH IS FORCED INTO THE HOODLUMS' AUTO...

WHERE ARE YOU TAKING ME?

ON A ONE-WAY RIDE!

THAT'S WHAT THEY THINK!

SAY YOUR PRAYERS, KID!

HERE'S WHERE YOU GET YOURS!

GUESS AGAIN!

SUPERMAN!

THE THUGS SCRAMBLE ERECT AND DASH OFF IN FRANTIC FLIGHT....

IT'S THE MAN OF TOMORROW!

WE HAVEN'T A CHANCE AGAINST *HIM*!

BUT EASILY OVERTAKING THEM, *SUPERMAN* LEAPS ALOFT WITH THEM UNDER HIS ARMS....

HEY! LEGGO!

YOU'RE HURTING ME!

LISTEN TO ME-- BOTH OF YOU!

YOU SEE THAT TREE AHEAD? I CAN DASH ALL OF US AGAINST IT.

YOU WOULDN'T DO IT!

THAT WOULD BE MURDER!

MAKE UP YOUR MINDS--TELL ME WHO HIRED YOU TO BUMP OFF FARNSWORTH-- OR THE BOTH OF YOU WILL SOON BE *MEMORIES*!

WE'LL TALK-- WE'LL TALK!

THE TREE-- WE'LL HIT IT--!

ARCHING SHARPLY, *SUPER-MAN* NARROWLY MISSES THE TREE....

WHO?

JIM BALDWIN!

THANKS FOR THE INFORMATION, BOYS! TA-TA!

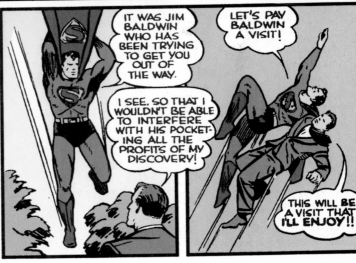

IT WAS JIM BALDWIN WHO HAS BEEN TRYING TO GET YOU OUT OF THE WAY.

I SEE. SO THAT I WOULDN'T BE ABLE TO INTERFERE WITH HIS POCKET-ING ALL THE PROFITS OF MY DISCOVERY!

LET'S PAY BALDWIN A VISIT!

THIS WILL BE A VISIT THAT I'LL ENJOY!!

10

BUT WHEN THEY REACH BALDWIN'S OFFICE...

HE'S GONE!

LET'S TRY HIS HOME!

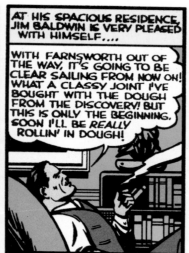

AT HIS SPACIOUS RESIDENCE, JIM BALDWIN IS VERY PLEASED WITH HIMSELF....

WITH FARNSWORTH OUT OF THE WAY, IT'S GOING TO BE CLEAR SAILING FROM NOW ON! WHAT A CLASSY JOINT I'VE BOUGHT WITH THE DOUGH FROM THE DISCOVERY! BUT THIS IS ONLY THE BEGINNING, SOON I'LL BE REALLY ROLLIN' IN DOUGH!

THIS IS THE PLACE. WHEW! IT'S QUITE A MANSION!

BOUGHT WITH YOUR MONEY!

AS BALDWIN'S BUTLER IS ABOUT TO OPEN THE DOOR, BALDWIN SEES WHO HIS VISITORS ARE....

DON'T OPEN THAT DOOR! BOLT IT!

AS YOU SAY, SIR!

UNSOCIABLE CRITTER! BUT HE'S GOING TO SEE US WHETHER HE WANTS TO OR NOT!

YOU CAN'T BREAK IN HERE! I'LL HAVE THE LAW ON YOU!

FOR A GUY THAT DABBLES IN MURDER, YOU CERTAINLY HAVE DEVELOPED A SUDDEN AFFECTION FOR LAW AND ORDER!

EEEEEE! WHAT ARE YOU GOING TO DO WITH ME?

YOU'LL FIND OUT!

MEANWHILE-- IN ONE OF THE MANSION'S ROOMS, A CANDLE-HOLDER UPSETS, QUICKLY, DRAPES CATCH FIRE!

YOU'VE GYPPED FARNSWORTH OUT OF THE FRUITS OF HIS DISCOVERY-- THERE'S NO REASON FOR ME TO HANDLE YOU GENTLY.

DON'T!

WILL YOU RELINQUISH FARNSWORTH'S RIGHTS TO HIM...THE RIGHTS YOU STOLE THRU TRICKERY?

NO!

LOOK-- THE HOUSE IS AFIRE!

EVERY CENT I'VE GOT IN THE WORLD IS TIED UP IN THAT MANSION! DO SOMETHING! STOP THE FIRE!

I COULD STOP IT EASILY-- BUT ONLY FOR A CONSIDERATION. IF I SAVE THE HOME, WILL YOU RESTORE CHET'S RIGHTS TO HIM?

YES! YES! BUT STOP THAT FIRE!

BUT FIRST WRITE A COMPLETE RELEASE OF ALL RIGHTS TO CHET.

YOU'D BETTER HURRY WHILE YOUR HOME IS STILL INTACT!

NO SOONER DOES BALDWIN SIGN THAN **SUPERMAN** RACES ABOUT THE MANSION WITH SUCH TERRIFIC SPEED THAT A VACUUM IS CREATED-- AND THE FIRE GOES OUT....

THE MANSION IS SAVED --BUT--I'M RUINED...

AND LET ME WARN YOU. IF YOU TRY TO HARM CHET AGAIN, I'LL ATTEND TO YOU WITHOUT MERCY!

12

SUPERMAN LEAVES CHET FARNSWORTH SAFELY ATOP HIS APARTMENT BUILDING....

GOODBYE! AND THANKS FOR ALL YOU'VE DONE FOR ME!

JUST KEEP UP THE GOOD WORK!

LATER--AT THE *DAILY PLANET* EDITORIAL OFFICE....

YOUR STORIES REGARDING CHET FARNSWORTH WERE FINE. BUT HOW DID YOU MANAGE TO GET ALL THOSE FACTS WHEN I FAILED TO?

FIGURE IT OUT!

THE END

SUPERMAN

REG. U. S. PAT OFF

by JERRY SIEGEL and JOE SHUSTER

SENT TO COVER WHAT APPEARS TO BE A HAIR-BRAINED ASSIGNMENT, LOIS LANE GIVES UP IN DISGUST, BUT CLARK KENT, SCENTING A POSSIBLE GRAIN OF TRUTH, INVESTIGATES IN HIS IDENTITY AS DYNAMIC SUPERMAN AND STUMBLES UPON AN INCREDIBLE SECRET...THE VERY FATE OF THE WORLD HANGS IN THE BALANCE AS SUPERMAN EXPLORES "THE UNDER-SEA CITY"!!

EDITORIAL OFFICE OF THE PLANET...

WHILE YOU REMAINED OUT TO LUNCH AN HOUR OVERTIME, ALL THE OTHER PAPERS IN TOWN SCOOPED US ON THE MAYOR'S RESIGNATION! BUT--I'VE AN ASSIGNMENT WHICH WILL GIVE YOU A CHANCE TO REDEEM YOURSELVES!

WE'LL MAKE IT UP TO YOU!

WHAT IS IT?

I GOT A PHONE CALL FROM CHET FURNALL, A FISHERMAN OUT ON THE BAY. HE CLAIMS TO HAVE SEEN A MERMAID. COVER THE STORY!

A--A MERMAID?

COME ON, LOIS!

DO YOU THINK WE'RE BEING RIBBED?

WE'LL SOON KNOW!

WHEN THE PUZZLED REPORTERS REACH FURNALL'S COTTAGE...

DID I SEE A REAL LIVE MERMAID? YOU CAN BET YOUR LIFE I DID!

TELL US ABOUT IT!

PLEASE DO!

FURNALL'S STORY... "I WAS OUT FISHIN' THIS MORNING, SEE, WHEN ALL OF A SUDDEN A MERMAID POPS OUTA THE WATER AND GIVES ME THE GLAD-EYE...!"

G-GLORY BE!!

"--TRIED TO MAKE UP TO ME, SHE DID-- BUT I LET HER KNOW I WOULDN'T STAND FOR NO SHENANIGANS...!"

OFF WITH YOU, YOU OVERGROWN HERRING!

I'VE HEARD TELL OF THESE MERMAIDS! THEY AIN'T TO BE TRUSTED! I TELL YOU, NEXT TIME I MEET UP WITH HER, I'LL FINISH HER FOR GOOD!

LET'S GO, CLARK!

THANKS--BUT WE'VE GOT TO BE GOING NOW!

OF ALL THE CRUMMY ASSIGNMENTS! HAVING US INTERVIEW A LUNATIC!

CALM DOWN, LOIS!

LOOK HERE, PERRY! WHAT'S THE IDEA OF HAVING US WASTE OUR TIME ON A MADMAN?

YOU DESERVE TO BE DISCIPLINED!

SO THAT'S IT! YOU DIDN'T BELIEVE HIS STORY YOURSELF!

SHORTLY AFTER.... IN AN EMPTY STOREROOM, CLARK KENT CHANGES TO HIS IDENTITY AS-- **SUPERMAN**!

FURNALL'S STORY MAY BE A FAKE--BUT I INTEND TO LOOK INTO THIS FURTHER!

TOWARD THE BAY RACES THE *MAN OF TOMORROW* AT TERRIFIC SPEED....

A MERMAID --LIVING-- BREATH-ING...I MUST BE PRETTY GULLIBLE!

LATER--ATOP A HIGH CLIFF, **SUPERMAN** MAKES USE OF HIS TELESCOPIC VISION...

FURNALL-- FISHING AGAIN!

SHE'D BETTER NOT SHOW UP AND START ANY MONKEY BUSINESS AGAIN-- I'M READY FOR HER THIS TIME!

A SUDDEN DISTURBANCE IN THE WATER--SOMETHING COMING TO THE SURFACE....

THE MERMAID!!

3

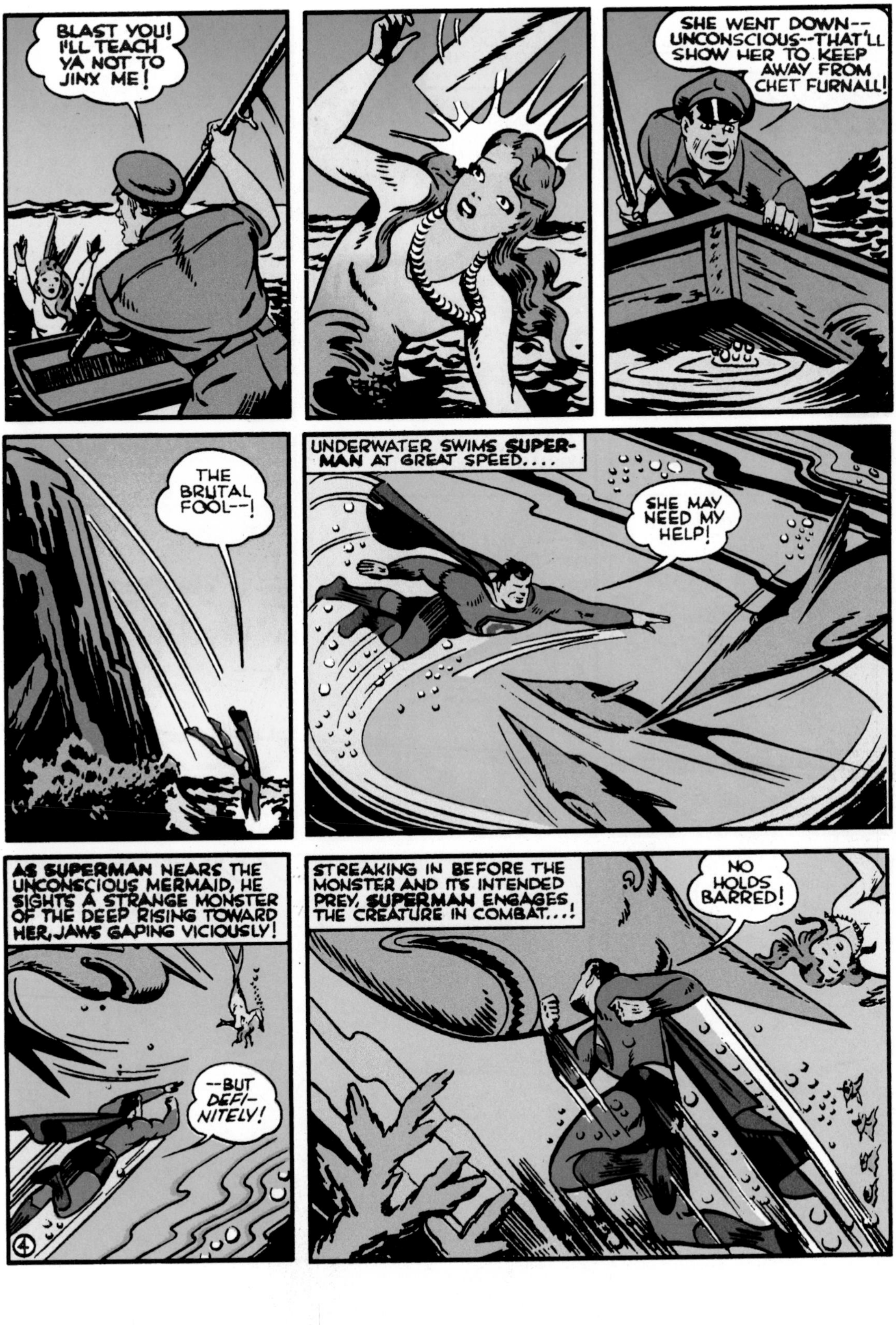
BLAST YOU! I'LL TEACH YA NOT TO JINX ME!
SHE WENT DOWN-- UNCONSCIOUS--THAT'LL SHOW HER TO KEEP AWAY FROM CHET FURNALL!
THE BRUTAL FOOL--!
UNDERWATER SWIMS SUPERMAN AT GREAT SPEED....
SHE MAY NEED MY HELP!
AS SUPERMAN NEARS THE UNCONSCIOUS MERMAID, HE SIGHTS A STRANGE MONSTER OF THE DEEP RISING TOWARD HER, JAWS GAPING VICIOUSLY!
--BUT DEFI-NITELY!
4
STREAKING IN BEFORE THE MONSTER AND ITS INTENDED PREY, SUPERMAN ENGAGES THE CREATURE IN COMBAT...!
NO HOLDS BARRED!

IRON JAWS CLAMP DOWN UPON THE *MAN OF STEEL'S* ARM....

HUNGRY, EH?

BUT **SUPERMAN** EASILY FORCES THE POWERFUL JAWS APART.....

I'M NOT INCLINED TO FURNISH YOU WITH A MEAL RIGHT NOW!

GET WHAT I MEAN?

REVIVING, THE MERMAID HAS MADE FOR THE WATER'S SURFACE, BUT FURNALL IS READY....

I CAME PREPARED TO FINISH YOU OFF!

DOWN TOWARD THE HELPLESS MERMAID STREAKS THE DEADLY HARPOON--!

BUT **SUPERMAN** STREAKS IN IN TIME TO RECEIVE THE HARPOON UPON HIS OWN IMPERVIOUS SKIN....

FURNALL, I'M GETTING TO POSITIVELY DISLIKE YOU!

THEREFORE-- SCRAM!

⑤

PROPELLED BY THE *MAN OF TOMORROW'S* SHOVE, THE ROWBOAT WHIZZES ACROSS THE WATER AT GREAT SPEED AND DUMPS ITS CARGO UNCEREMONIOUSLY ON THE SHORE!

EEE EEE!

SHOREWARD SWIMS **SUPERMAN** WITH HIS FAIR BURDEN....

COME ALONG!

GLADLY!

SUPERMAN'S ADVANCED INTELLECT INSTANTLY COMPREHENDS THE MERMAID'S STRANGE LANGUAGE....

CAN YOU UNDERSTAND WHAT I SAY?

YES, EVERY WORD.

THEN, I'LL TELL YOU MY STORY. I'M PRINCESS KUELLA OF THE UNDERSEA PEOPLE. MY FATHER'S EVIL ADVISER, AKTHAR, PLANS TO INVADE THE LAND-WORLD UNKNOWN TO KING SAFFRO-- BUT I OVERHEARD HIM PLOTTING WITH HIS HENCHMEN...

I SEE, YOU'VE COME TO WARN THE LAND PEOPLE, THAT'S VERY KIND OF YOU.

MY PEOPLE HAVE LIVED UNDERWATER FOR THOUSANDS OF YEARS--IT IS OUR CUSTOM THAT WHOEVER COMES TO THE SURFACE WORLD MUST DIE,...

THEN YOU IMPERILED YOUR OWN LIFE TO WARN THE PEOPLE OF MY WORLD!

ABRUPTLY, A SHORT DISTANCE AWAY A STRANGE VESSEL SHOOTS TO THE WATER'S SURFACE....

WHO --??

AKTHAR!

A BOLT IS BLASTED TOWARD THE TWO ON THE ROCKS...!

BUT SNATCHING UP KUELLA, **SUPERMAN** LEAPS OUT OF RANGE IN TIME, EVADING THE FORCE OF THE EXPLOSION...

AKTHAR! I'M AFRAID THIS IS GOING TO BE A CASE OF DISLIKE AT FIRST SIGHT!

BUT KUELLA DELIBERATELY TWISTS HERSELF FREE FROM **SUPERMAN**'S PROTECTIVE GRIP...

THEY'RE AFTER ME ALONE. YOU MUST NOT COME TO HARM BECAUSE OF ME!

WAIT, KUELLA!

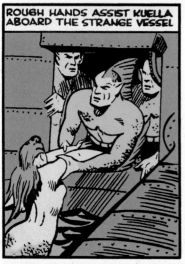

ROUGH HANDS ASSIST KUELLA ABOARD THE STRANGE VESSEL

AS THE VESSEL SUBMERGES, **SUPERMAN** SWIMS RAPIDLY AFTER IT IN PURSUIT....

KUELLA'S IN PERIL!

DOWN—DOWN THEY GO... TO THE OCEAN'S VERY DEPTHS....

NO MAN FROM THE UPPER WORLD HAS EVER PENETRATED THE OCEAN TO THIS DEPTH!

SUDDENLY THERE APPEARS BELOW A FANTASTIC *UNDERSEA CITY!* THE VESSEL LANDS!

INCREDIBLE!

⑦

LET GO OF HER!

YOU SHOULD THINK TWICE BEFORE OPPOSING AKTHAR!

MY FATHER COMES!

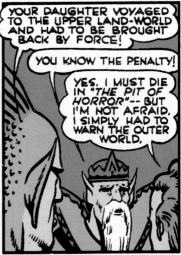

YOUR DAUGHTER VOYAGED TO THE UPPER LAND-WORLD AND HAD TO BE BROUGHT BACK BY FORCE!

YOU KNOW THE PENALTY!

YES, I MUST DIE IN "THE PIT OF HORROR"-- BUT I'M NOT AFRAID. I SIMPLY HAD TO WARN THE OUTER WORLD.

SHE LIES! SHE HAS INVENTED THIS STORY OF PERFIDY ON MY PART TO ESCAPE THE CONSEQUENCES OF HER ACT. I DEMAND SHE BE ABANDONED TO HER FATE!

I HAVE NO ALTERNATIVE!

GUARDS SEIZE SUPERMAN AS KUELLA SWIMS INTO THE "PIT OF HORROR"....

SHE'LL NEVER RETURN --ALIVE!

THEN WHY DO YOU STAND FOR IT?

AN ABRUPT SCREAM FROM THE "PIT OF HORROR"...!

EEE-EEEE!

8

COMING, KUELLA!

INTO THE "PIT OF HORROR" SWIMS THE MAN OF STEEL....

I'M NOT THE KIND TO LET A FRIEND DOWN!

ENTERING THE PIT, SUPERMAN SIGHTS....

KUELLA IN THE GRIP OF AN OCTOPUS!

STREAKING IN TO AID THE PRINCESS, SUPERMAN IS HIMSELF SNATCHED UP BY A MIGHTY TENTACLE....

THIS WILL BE NO CINCH!

STEELY HANDS VERSUS CRUSHING TENTACLES! SUPERMAN LITERALLY RIPS HIS FOE APART!

NO TIME FOR NICETIES!

AND SHORTLY AFTER...

THEY LIVE!

ACCORDING TO LAW, SHOULD A PRISONER EMERGE FROM THE "PIT OF HORROR," HE IS ENTITLED TO FREEDOM!

TRUE! BUT THAT DOESN'T APPLY TO THE INTRUDER FROM THE LAND WORLD, HE MUST PASS "THE TESTS!"

ARE YOU PREPARED TO PASS "THE TESTS"?

BRING THEM ON -- SINGLY OR COLLECTIVELY!

9

THE FIRST TEST IS A RACE BETWEEN MY MAN AND YOU. IF HE OUTSWIMS YOU--AND HE IS THE FASTEST SWIMMER AMONG US--YOUR PENALTY WILL BE DEATH!

WHAT ARE WE WAITING FOR?

AT A GIVEN WORD, THE RACE BEGINS....

NOW!

NOW IT IS!

EASILY, **SUPERMAN** SWIMS CIRCLES ABOUT HIS OPPONENT

DON'T OVERSTRAIN YOURSELF, BUD--YOU'LL BURST A LUNG!

BACK FLASHES THE *MAN OF STEEL* TO THE FINISH LINE BEFORE HIS OPPONENT HAS SCARCELY BEGUN THE RACE...

ANY MORE TESTS TODAY, PAL?

YES, BLAST YOU! AND NEXT TIME YOU'LL FAIL, I GUARANTEE YOU!

YOUR NEXT ASSIGNMENT IS MERELY TO BRING BACK A PURPLE STONE FROM *IKTAK'S CAVERN*...! THAT OUGHT TO BE SIMPLE, EH?

SHOULD IT?

YOU MUST NOT LET AKTHAR DO THIS TO THE STRANGER! IT ISN'T FAIR!

SORRY, DEAR-- BUT IT'S THE LAW!

SHORTLY AFTER....

SO THIS IS *IKTAK'S CAVERN!* THERE ARE PLENTY OF PURPLE STONES ON THE FLOOR. WHAT'S SO TOUGH ABOUT THIS ASSIGNMENT?

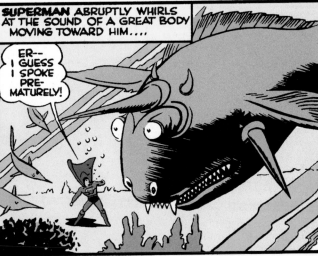

SUPERMAN ABRUPTLY WHIRLS AT THE SOUND OF A GREAT BODY MOVING TOWARD HIM....

ER-- I GUESS I SPOKE PREMATURELY!

AS THE MIGHTY CREATURE OF THE DEEP RUSHES HIM WITH GAPING JAWS, **SUPERMAN** LETS FLY WITH A POWERFUL RIGHT....

RIGHT ON THE KISSER!

⑩

AND SO ENDS THE INTRUDING BRAGGART!

AND HE WAS SUCH A FINE MAN!

BUT NEXT INSTANT....

HERE'S SOME PURPLE STONES FROM *IKTAK'S CAVERNS-* WITH *IKTAK* HIMSELF THROWN IN FOR GOOD MEASURE!

HE'S ALIVE!

YES!

YOU HAVE PASSED *"THE TESTS"* SUCCESSFULLY-- REMAIN HERE IN PEACE!

BUT WHAT ABOUT AKTHAR'S PLANNED INVASION OF THE LAND-WORLD?

("-I'D BETTER SLIP AWAY!-")

OH, NO YOU DON'T!

YEE-EEEK! LET GO!

SUPERMAN SWIMS IN A CIRCLE SO FAST THAT HE AND HIS CAPTIVE CAN BE SEEN ONLY AS A BLUR....

NOW WILL YOU ADMIT THE TRUTH-- OR SHALL WE GO FOR ANOTHER SWIM?

NO--I'LL TELL, YES-- I DID PLAN TO INVADE THE UPPER WORLD!

AND I *STILL* DO! BACK-- OR SHE DIES!

YOU TRAITOR!

IF YOU HARM KUELLA --!!

AKTHAR PLACES **SUPERMAN** UNDER A STRANGE SPELL...

REMAIN THERE --HELPLESS-- WHILE I CONQUER THE LAND-WORLD!

CAN'T-- MOVE...!

11

UP TOWARD THE LAND-WORLD SPEED AKTHAR'S VESSELS AND WARRIORS...!

236

A MIGHTY TOWER POPS INTO VIEW ON THE SEA'S SURFACE. IMMEDIATELY, GREAT BEAM-FORCES STAB AT THE WATERS.

IN RESPONSE, THE OCEAN SWEEPS DOWN UPON THE CITIES....

AKTHAR'S WARRIORS SPREAD HAVOC...!

CONCENTRATING MIGHTILY, SUPERMAN SHAKES OFF AKTHAR'S SPELL....

IF YOU HURRY, YOU MAY BE ABLE TO OVERTAKE THEM!

FREE AT LAST!

I DON'T NEED ANY URGING!

COMING TO THE OCEAN'S SURFACE, SUPERMAN DESTROYS THE MIGHTY METAL TOWER SINGLEHANDED!

AND THAT FINISHES YOU!

IN RESPONSE, THE OCEAN POURS BACK INTO ITS BASIN! SUPERMAN STREAKS THRU THE CITY'S STREETS, ATTENDING TO AKTHAR'S ARMY...

⑫

WITHIN HIS VESSEL, THE CRAVEN AKTHAR SPEEDS BACK TOWARD THE UNDER-SEA CITY....

BEATEN BY YOUR FRIEND! BUT I'LL HAVE MY REVENGE!

YOU'RE BEATEN! AND I'M GLAD-- GLAD!

I'VE STILL GOT A SCORE TO SETTLE WITH AKTHAR!

IN THRU THE SIDE OF THE VESSEL BURSTS THE *MAN OF TOMORROW....*

SUPERMAN!

I'LL DESTROY US ALL!

OUT THRU THE SIDE OF THE VESSEL STREAKS *SUPERMAN* WITH KUELLA....

GOT TO MAKE TRACKS!

AKTHAR MAKES GOOD HIS THREAT. HE EXPLODES HIS VESSEL IN A VIOLENT ERUPTION THAT ENGULFS THE UNDERSEA CITY....

NO, KUELLA!

I CHOOSE TO DIE WITH MY PEOPLE!

A BRAVE GIRL—THE PEOPLE OF THE LAND-WORLD OWE THEIR CONTINUED EXISTENCE TO HER!

13

LATER--IN THE *DAILY PLANET* OFFICE....

THIS STORY IS ABSOLUTELY SENSATIONAL!

AND YOU THOUGHT YOU WERE SENDING LOIS AND ME OUT ON A WILD-GOOSE CHASE.

REMEMBER TO GIVE *SUPERMAN* SOME CREDIT, HE MERELY SAVED ALL OF US FROM DESTRUCTION!

THE END

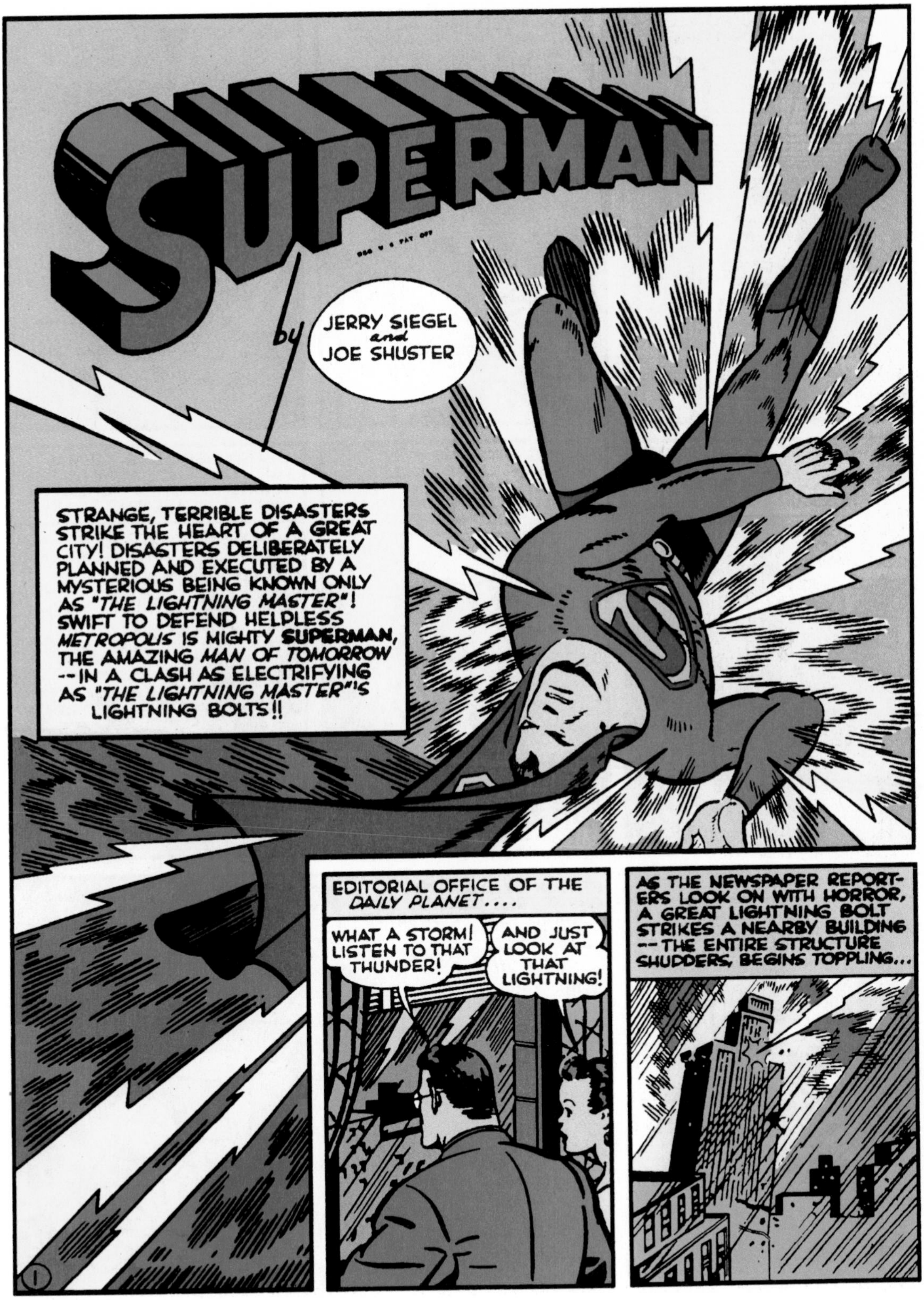
SUPERMAN
by
JERRY SIEGEL and JOE SHUSTER
STRANGE, TERRIBLE DISASTERS STRIKE THE HEART OF A GREAT CITY! DISASTERS DELIBERATELY PLANNED AND EXECUTED BY A MYSTERIOUS BEING KNOWN ONLY AS "THE LIGHTNING MASTER"! SWIFT TO DEFEND HELPLESS METROPOLIS IS MIGHTY SUPERMAN, THE AMAZING MAN OF TOMORROW --IN A CLASH AS ELECTRIFYING AS "THE LIGHTNING MASTER"'S LIGHTNING BOLTS!!
1
EDITORIAL OFFICE OF THE DAILY PLANET....
WHAT A STORM! LISTEN TO THAT THUNDER!
AND JUST LOOK AT THAT LIGHTNING!
AS THE NEWSPAPER REPORTERS LOOK ON WITH HORROR, A GREAT LIGHTNING BOLT STRIKES A NEARBY BUILDING --THE ENTIRE STRUCTURE SHUDDERS, BEGINS TOPPLING...

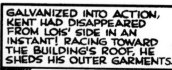
CLARK! DID YOU NOTICE TH-- OH-HH! HE'S **GONE!**

GALVANIZED INTO ACTION, KENT HAD DISAPPEARED FROM LOIS' SIDE IN AN INSTANT! RACING TOWARD THE BUILDING'S ROOF, HE SHEDS HIS OUTER GARMENTS.

A LOT OF PEOPLE MAY BE HURT UNLESS--

--I ACT QUICKLY ENOUGH!

ALIGHTING AT THE FOOT OF THE TOTTERING BUILDING, THE *MAN OF TOMORROW* GLANCES UP TO NOTE....

THE BUILDING --ALREADY COLLAPSING!

RACING WITH THE VERY SPEED OF LIGHT ITSELF, **SUPERMAN** SNATCHES UP A FULL DOZEN PEDESTRIANS IN THE BUILDING'S PATH....

NO TIME FOR FORMAL INTRODUCTIONS!

....AND DEPOSITS THEM A SAFE DISTANCE AWAY AS THE DEBRIS CRASHES TO EARTH WITH A DEAFENING ROAR!

CLOSE, EH?

WE--WE OWE OUR LIVES TO YOU!

LOIS DASHES ONTO THE STREET...

SUPERMAN IN ACTION! I DON'T WANT TO MISS *THIS!*

②

STRUCK BY LIGHTNING, A GREAT TREE CRASHES DOWN TOWARD LOIS' COWERING FIGURE....

STREAKING IN, A MOMENT BEFORE THE TREE CAN REACH THE GIRL REPORTER, THE *MAN OF STEEL* SMASHES IT ASIDE WITH ONE BLOW....

WHAT WOULD I DO WITHOUT YOU TO LOOK AFTER?

I WISH YOU'D MAKE IT A PERMANENT JOB!

THAT'S ODD! THE STORM'S OVER... STOPPED IN INSTANTS!

THEN MY PRESENCE IS NO LONGER REQUIRED!

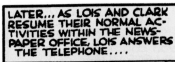

LATER... AS LOIS AND CLARK RESUME THEIR NORMAL ACTIVITIES WITHIN THE NEWSPAPER OFFICE, LOIS ANSWERS THE TELEPHONE....

THIS CALL IS OF UTMOST IMPORTANCE. MAY I SPEAK TO CLARK KENT?

("-THERE'S SOMETHING SINISTER ABOUT THIS VOICE THAT MAKES ME BELIEVE AN IMPORTANT STORY IS POPPING!-")

NO. -- MAY I TAKE THE MESSAGE?

TELL HIM THAT THE DESTRUCTION OF THAT BUILDING BY LIGHTNING WASN'T ACCIDENTAL. AND THAT IF HE WISHES TO LEARN MORE, TO COME TO 918 KENYON AVENUE... ALONE...

I'LL--I'LL TELL HIM!

918 KENYON AVENUE!

THIS IS ONE TIME I'LL SHOW THAT SMART-ALECKY CLARK HE ISN'T THE ONLY ONE TO UNCOVER FRONT PAGE YARNS!

THE DOOR'S OPEN! I--I SUPPOSE IT'S FOOLISH OF ME TO FEEL NERVOUS, BUT--

③

BY ALL MEANS, YOUNG LADY-- COME IN!!

ULP!!

YOU'RE THE YOUNG WOMAN I SPOKE TO OVER THE TELEPHONE, NO DOUBT. WHY HAVE YOU COME? DIDN'T YOU GIVE MY MESSAGE TO KENT?

YOU CAN RELY ON ME!

VERY WELL. YOU'LL DO. LISTEN CLOSELY. THAT LIGHTNING STORM, THE DESTRUCTION OF THAT BUILDING, WAS NOT A WHIM OF NATURE--IT WAS CAUSED BY ME! I'VE GAINED CONTROL OF NATURE'S MOST POWERFUL FORCE-- LIGHTNING!

AND WHO ARE YOU!

YOU MAY CALL ME *"THE LIGHTNING MASTER."* AS TO MY REAL IDENTITY, THAT'S MY OWN AFFAIR! THIS IS WHAT I WANT YOU TO PRINT--UNLESS *METROPOLIS* PAYS ME $300,000, I WILL DESTROY IT!

LET'S SEE WHAT YOU ACTUALLY LOOK LIKE!

YOU LITTLE FOOL! DO YOU REALIZE WHAT YOU'VE DONE? NOW THAT YOU'VE SEEN MY FACE, I CAN'T PERMIT YOU TO LIVE!

I--I DIDN'T THINK OF THAT!

WHAT ARE YOU GOING TO DO TO ME?

BLAST YOU INTO INFINITY, MY DEAR! AND THERE'S NO NEED FOR YOU TO SCREAM--NO ONE WILL HEAR YOU!

④

AFTER *"THE LIGHTNING MASTER"* DEPARTS...

THIS IS MADDEN- ING!--I'VE GOT TO SIT HERE-- KNOWING THAT AT ANY MOMENT I MAY BE BLOWN SKY-HIGH..!

MY ONLY CHANCE-- THAT TELEPHONE-- IF I CAN ONLY REACH IT....

LOIS SUCCEEDS IN KNOCKING THE RECEIVER OFF THE HOOK!

NUMBER, PLEASE...

QUICK, OPERATOR! GET ME CLARK KENT AT THE *DAILY PLANET* IMMEDIATELY! IT'S A MATTER OF *LIFE* AND *DEATH!*

QUIT YOUR KIDDING, LOIS! --I'M IN NO MOOD FOR YOUR PRACTICAL JOKES.

BUT I'M **NOT** FOOLING! A MADMAN, *"THE LIGHTNING MASTER,"* IS ABOUT TO DESTROY ME, DO YOU HEAR?! IF YOU DON'T GET DOWN TO 918 KENYON AVENUE AT ONCE AND FREE ME, I'LL NEVER SPEAK TO YOU AGAIN!

REACHING HIS SECRET LABORATORY, *"THE LIGHTNING MASTER"* IMMEDIATELY HASTENS TO THE CONTROLS OF HIS LIGHTNING MACHINE....

IT'S A PITY TO BLAST SUCH A LOVELY GIRL OUT OF EXISTENCE, BUT I MUST NOT ALLOW HUMAN DECENCY TO INFLUENCE ME.

GLANCING OUT A WINDOW, CLARK NOTES THE SKY DARKENING....

LOOKS LIKE WE'RE IN FOR ANOTHER LIGHTNING STORM. SA-AAY! MAYBE LOIS WASN'T JOKING AT THAT!

5

ATOP THE *DAILY PLANET* BUILDING, CLARK KENT TRANSFORMS HIMSELF TO DYNAMIC **SUPERMAN**....

THE SKY GROWING DARKER WITH EACH MOMENT. I'D BETTER GET TO THAT KENYON AVENUE ADDRESS...

--AND IN A HURRY!

AS THE *MAN OF STEEL* SWOOPS DOWN TOWARD HIS DESTI-NATION, MAKING USE OF HIS X-RAY VISION, LIGHTNING BEGINS TO FLARE OVERHEAD...

LOIS **IS** HELD CAPTIVE IN THERE!

NO TIME TO DELAY!

SUPERMAN! THANK HEAVEN YOU CAME!

I'VE GOT TO GET YOU **OUT** OF HERE!

THE *MAN OF TOMORROW* RIPS APART LOIS'S BONDS IN ONE EASY MOVEMENT....

I'M FREE!

NOT YET--NOT UNTIL YOU'RE MANY MILES AWAY FROM THIS HOUSE!

THUNDER CRASHES DEAFEN-INGLY...LIGHTNING FLARES BLINDINGLY...AS THE *MAN OF TOMORROW* LEAPS AWAY WITH LOIS.

LET'S GET GOING-- BEFORE X MARKS THE SPOT!

NOW!!!

6

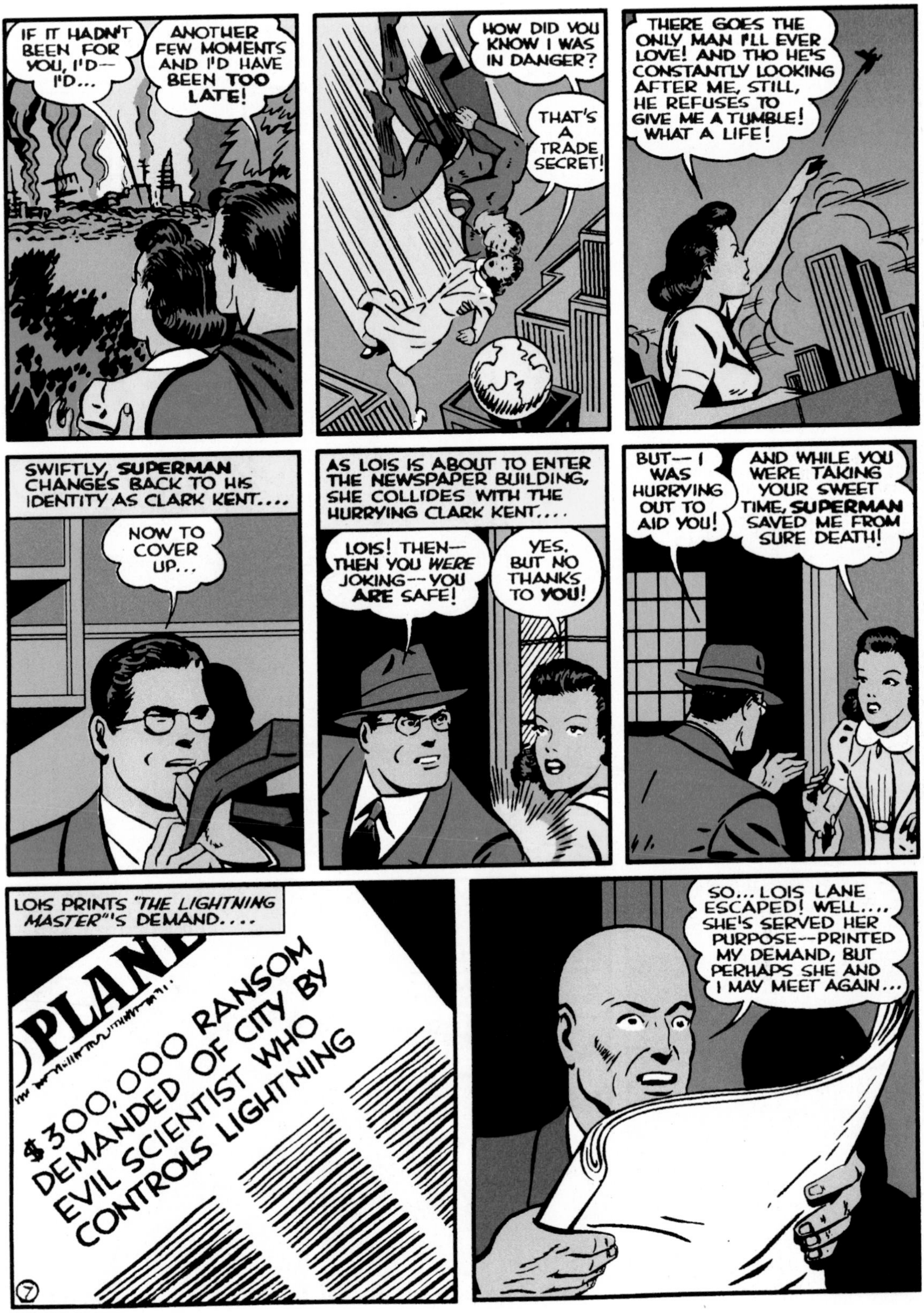
IF IT HADN'T BEEN FOR YOU, I'D-- I'D...
ANOTHER FEW MOMENTS AND I'D HAVE BEEN TOO LATE!
HOW DID YOU KNOW I WAS IN DANGER?
THAT'S A TRADE SECRET!
THERE GOES THE ONLY MAN I'LL EVER LOVE! AND THO HE'S CONSTANTLY LOOKING AFTER ME, STILL, HE REFUSES TO GIVE ME A TUMBLE! WHAT A LIFE!
SWIFTLY, SUPERMAN CHANGES BACK TO HIS IDENTITY AS CLARK KENT....
NOW TO COVER UP...
AS LOIS IS ABOUT TO ENTER THE NEWSPAPER BUILDING, SHE COLLIDES WITH THE HURRYING CLARK KENT....
LOIS! THEN-- THEN YOU WERE JOKING--YOU ARE SAFE!
YES, BUT NO THANKS TO YOU!
BUT-- I WAS HURRYING OUT TO AID YOU!
AND WHILE YOU WERE TAKING YOUR SWEET TIME, SUPERMAN SAVED ME FROM SURE DEATH!
LOIS PRINTS "THE LIGHTNING MASTER"'S DEMAND....
PLANE
$300,000 RANSOM DEMANDED OF CITY BY EVIL SCIENTIST WHO CONTROLS LIGHTNING
SO... LOIS LANE ESCAPED! WELL.... SHE'S SERVED HER PURPOSE--PRINTED MY DEMAND, BUT PERHAPS SHE AND I MAY MEET AGAIN...
7

THE MAYOR IS GOING TO ANSWER *"THE LIGHTNING MASTER"* IN A BROADCAST!

THEN LET'S GET GOING! WE DON'T WANT TO MISS THIS!

THE CITY OF *METROPOLIS* REFUSES TO BE INTIMIDATED! WE WILL NOT PAY ONE CENT OF BLACKMAIL!

I'M GLAD TO SEE THAT THE MAYOR OF OUR CITY HAS BACKBONE!

HE *IS* TAKING A COURAGEOUS STAND.

("—AND PERHAPS A FOOLHARDY ONE!—")

DEFY ME, WILL THEY? I'LL SHOW THEM.... AND IN A MANNER THEY'LL *NEVER* FORGET!

THE SKY DARKENS...THUNDER RUMBLES...LIGHTNING BEGINS TO FLASH ABOVE THE RADIO STATION....

SLIPPING AWAY FROM LOIS, CLARK HURRIES TO THE BUILDING'S ROOF AND SWIFTLY CHANGES TO HIS IDENTITY AS **SUPERMAN**....

SO *"THE LIGHTNING MASTER"* IS UP TO HIS OLD TRICKS!

THAT INSTANT—A GREAT DESTRUCTIVE BOLT OF LIGHTNING IS LAUNCHED TOWARD THE RADIO STATION ON ITS MURDEROUS ERRAND...!

SUPERMAN LEAPS UP TO MEET THE BOLT....!

ONE CHANCE!

AS HE COLLIDES WITH IT, THERE IS A TERRIFIC, BLINDING FLASH. RAPIDLY THE FLARE FADES....

IF I CAN ABSORB THE ELECTRICAL FORCES INTO MY OWN BODY!

ONCE AGAIN, THE *MAN OF TOMORROW* PERFORMS AN AMAZING FEAT. HIS SUPERB BODY HAS ABSORBED THE ELECTRICITY--AND REMAINED--

UNHARMED!

THAT'S STRANGE --HE'S STILL SPEAKING! THE RADIO STATION HASN'T BEEN DESTROYED!

--AND "THE LIGHTNING MASTER" WILL BE TRACKED DOWN AND MADE TO PAY THE FULL PENALTY!

I'D BETTER GIVE MY EQUIPMENT A COMPLETE CHECKING OVER. NO-- I'VE A BETTER IDEA. I CAN *STILL* PROVE MY POWER!

SPEEDING TO THE RADIO STATION, *"THE LIGHTNING MASTER"* CONCEALS HIMSELF NEAR IT....

THIS ELECTRICAL-BOLT GUN WILL SETTLE THE MAYOR'S HASH!

REVERTING TO HIS IDENTITY AS CLARK KENT, THE *MAN OF STEEL* HAD REJOINED LOIS. NOW, AS THEY DEPART FROM THE BUILDING A SHORT DISTANCE BEHIND THE MAYOR...

"THE LIGHTNING MASTER"--KIDNAPPING THE MAYOR!

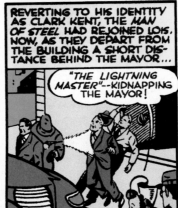

AS THE FIENDISH SCIENTIST DRIVES OFF, HE SENDS ONE LAST ELECTRIC-BOLT BACK TOWARD LOIS....

I SAID I'D KILL YOU WHEN I GOT THE CHANCE... AND I MEANT IT!

CLARK BRINGS LOIS DOWN IN A TACKLE OUT OF THE DESTRUCTIVE BOLT'S PATH...

DOWN, LOIS!

OH-HHH!

SHE'S STUNNED—BUT UNHARMED! MY CHANCE TO CHANGE TO SUPERMAN AND GIVE CHASE!

SUPERMAN —IN PURSUIT!

HE'LL GIVE YOU THE FATE YOU DESERVE!

BUT AS THE SCIENTIST DELIBERATELY SENDS THE AUTO OVER A CLIFF'S EDGE AND LEAPS OUT--

SEE YOU SOON!

THAT'S WHAT YOU THINK!

CAUGHT IT!

UP THE SIDE OF THE CLIFF RACES THE MAN OF STEEL, HIS GREAT BURDEN HELD ALOFT....

I CAN HARDLY WAIT TO GET MY HANDS ON "THE LIGHTNING MASTER"!

BUT SUPERMAN SIGHTS WITHIN THE AUTO....

THIS TERRIBLE EXPERIENCE--MY SIDE--A HEART ATTACK!

10

MUCH AS I HATE TO LET THAT EVIL SCIENTIST GET AWAY, IT'S MORE IMPORTANT THAT I RUSH THE MAYOR TO A HOSPITAL FOR MEDICAL TREATMENT!

AFTER DEPOSITING THE MAYOR AT A HOSPITAL, SUPERMAN RACES OFF....

NOW TO REJOIN LOIS...AS CLARK KENT...!

AS THE DAYS PASS....

PLANET
LIGHTNING MASTER RENEWS THREATS

AND I STILL INSIST THAT THE CITY WON'T PAY THE RANSOM!

I HEAD A COMMITTEE OF BUSINESS MEN. WE'RE GOING TO PAY HIM THAT MONEY OUT OF OUR OWN POCKETS!

WE CAN'T AFFORD TO HAVE OUR PROPERTY DESTROYED.

THIS IS TO INFORM *"THE LIGHTNING MASTER"* THAT $300,000 WILL BE PLACED IN A PACKAGE ON THE *JANSTROM BRIDGE* AT NOON!

LOIS CONCEALS HERSELF ON THE BRIDGE....

A TIGHT SQUEEZE... BUT IT MAY BE WORTH IT!

POLICE, LED BY SERGEANT CASEY, CONCEAL THEMSELVES NEAR THE BRIDGE....

IF THAT SCIENTIST THINKS HE CAN GET AWAY WITH THAT MONEY, HE'S EVEN CRAZIER THAN WE'VE SUSPECTED!

ATOP A DISTANT MOUNTAIN-RIDGE, **SUPERMAN** KEEPS KEEN-EYED VIGIL WITH THE AID OF HIS TELESCOPIC VISION....

A SHOWDOWN IS IMMINENT!

AS A CAR DRIVES ONTO THE BRIDGE AND PARKS, *"THE LIGHTNING MASTER"* EMERGES. POLICE CLOSING SWIFTLY IN...

GET HIM!

BUT AS THEY CHARGE FORWARD THE SCIENTIST TOUCHES A MECHANISM ON HIS CAR, AND INSTANTLY A BARRIER OF ELECTRICITY SURROUNDS THE BRIDGE LIKE A WALL OF FIRE...

FOOLS! TO THINK THEY COULD TRICK ME!

("-NOW'S MY CHANCE TO CAPTURE HIM SINGLE-HANDED!-")

WARNED BY THE SOUND OF HER FOOTSTEPS, *"THE LIGHTNING MASTER"* WHIRLS....

THE LANE GIRL! GOOD! YOU'LL COME IN HANDY AS A HOSTAGE!

AS THE *"LIGHTNING MASTER"* DRIVES SWIFTLY OFF, HIS CAR SURROUNDED BY CRACKING ELECTRICITY, HIS VOICE BOOMS FROM A LOUDSPEAKER

BACK!-- DON'T FOLLOW-- OR THE GIRL DIES!

LOIS CAPTURED --I MIGHT HAVE FORESEEN IT!

RETREAT, *SUPERMAN*-- IF YOU WANT THE GIRL TO LIVE!

YOU WIN!

BUT **SUPERMAN** TRAILS *"THE LIGHTNING MASTER"* FROM A POSITION HIGH IN THE STRATOSPHERE....

SO THAT'S WHERE THE HIDEOUT IS LOCATED!

THEY'LL NEVER FIND ME NOW!

WITH TREMBLING HANDS, THE EVIL SCIENTIST TEARS OPEN THE PACKAGE...ONLY TO SHRIEK WITH RAGE....

TRICKED! I'VE BEEN TRICKED! *BLANK PAPER!*

12

BUT THEY'LL PAY FOR IT DEARLY! I'LL DESTROY *METROPOLIS* COMPLETELY! WHEN I FINISH WITH IT, THERE WON'T BE A STONE LEFT STANDING!

AND AT THE SAME TIME *METROPOLIS* PERISHES, YOU DIE, TOO--IN THE ELECTRIC-CHAIR!

NO.. NO..!!

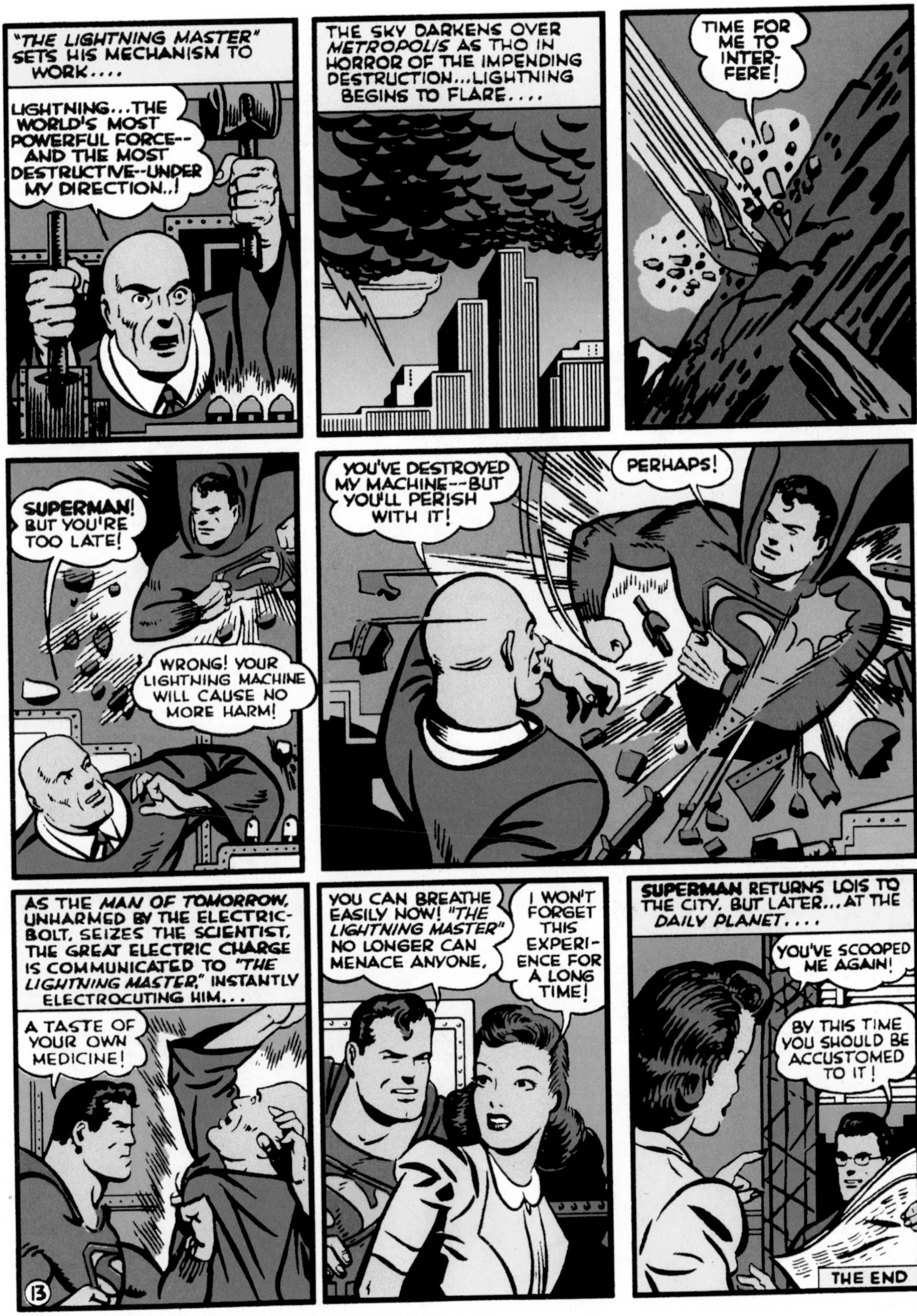

"THE LIGHTNING MASTER" SETS HIS MECHANISM TO WORK....
LIGHTNING...THE WORLD'S MOST POWERFUL FORCE--AND THE MOST DESTRUCTIVE--UNDER MY DIRECTION..!
THE SKY DARKENS OVER METROPOLIS AS THO IN HORROR OF THE IMPENDING DESTRUCTION...LIGHTNING BEGINS TO FLARE....
TIME FOR ME TO INTER-FERE!
SUPERMAN! BUT YOU'RE TOO LATE!
WRONG! YOUR LIGHTNING MACHINE WILL CAUSE NO MORE HARM!
YOU'VE DESTROYED MY MACHINE--BUT YOU'LL PERISH WITH IT!
PERHAPS!
AS THE MAN OF TOMORROW, UNHARMED BY THE ELECTRIC-BOLT, SEIZES THE SCIENTIST, THE GREAT ELECTRIC CHARGE IS COMMUNICATED TO "THE LIGHTNING MASTER," INSTANTLY ELECTROCUTING HIM...
A TASTE OF YOUR OWN MEDICINE!
13
YOU CAN BREATHE EASILY NOW! "THE LIGHTNING MASTER" NO LONGER CAN MENACE ANYONE,
I WON'T FORGET THIS EXPERI-ENCE FOR A LONG TIME!
SUPERMAN RETURNS LOIS TO THE CITY, BUT LATER...AT THE DAILY PLANET....
YOU'VE SCOOPED ME AGAIN!
BY THIS TIME YOU SHOULD BE ACCUSTOMED TO IT!
THE END

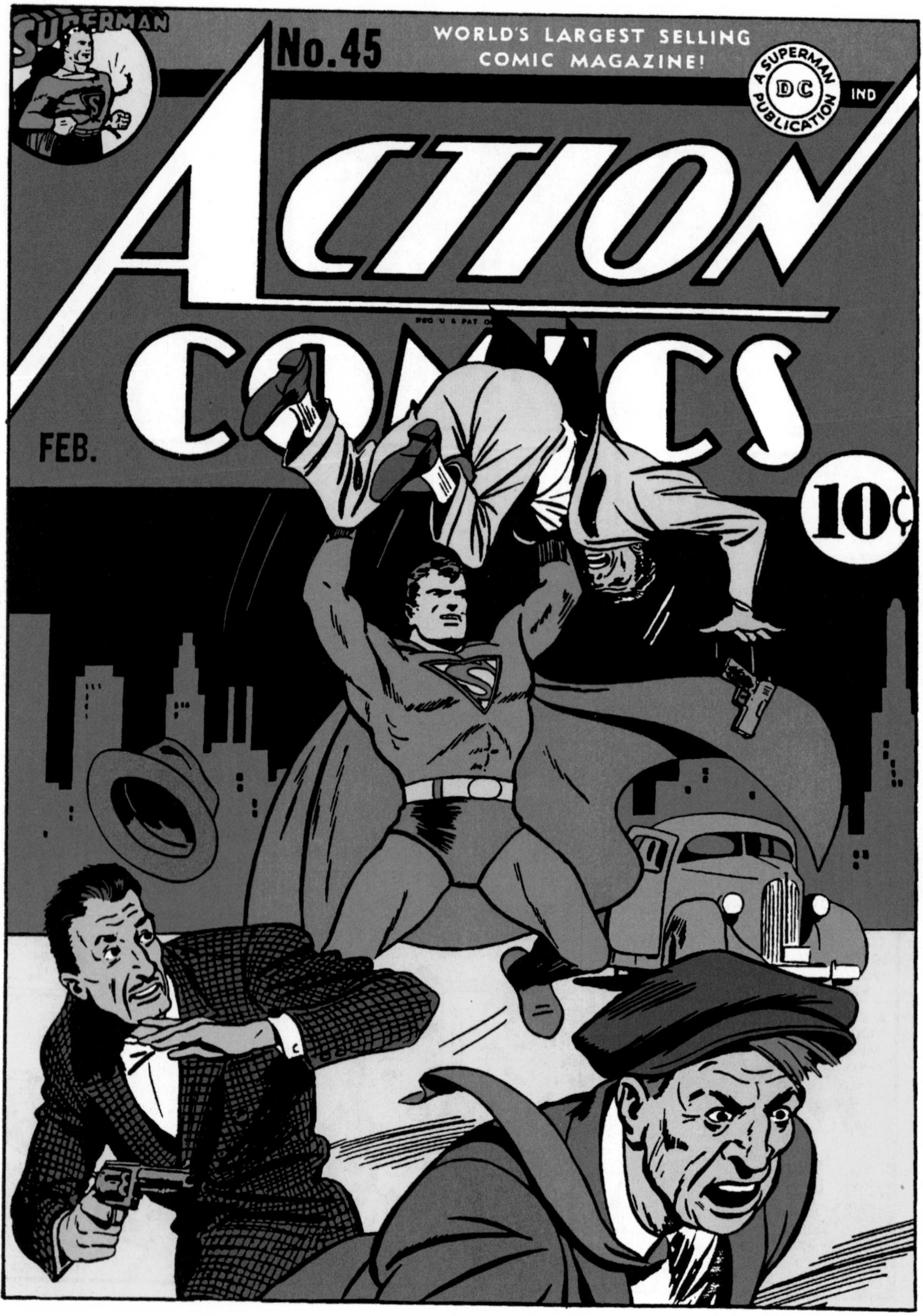
SUPERMAN
No.45
WORLD'S LARGEST SELLING
COMIC MAGAZINE!
A SUPERMAN DC PUBLICATION
IND
ACTION
COMICS
FEB.
10¢

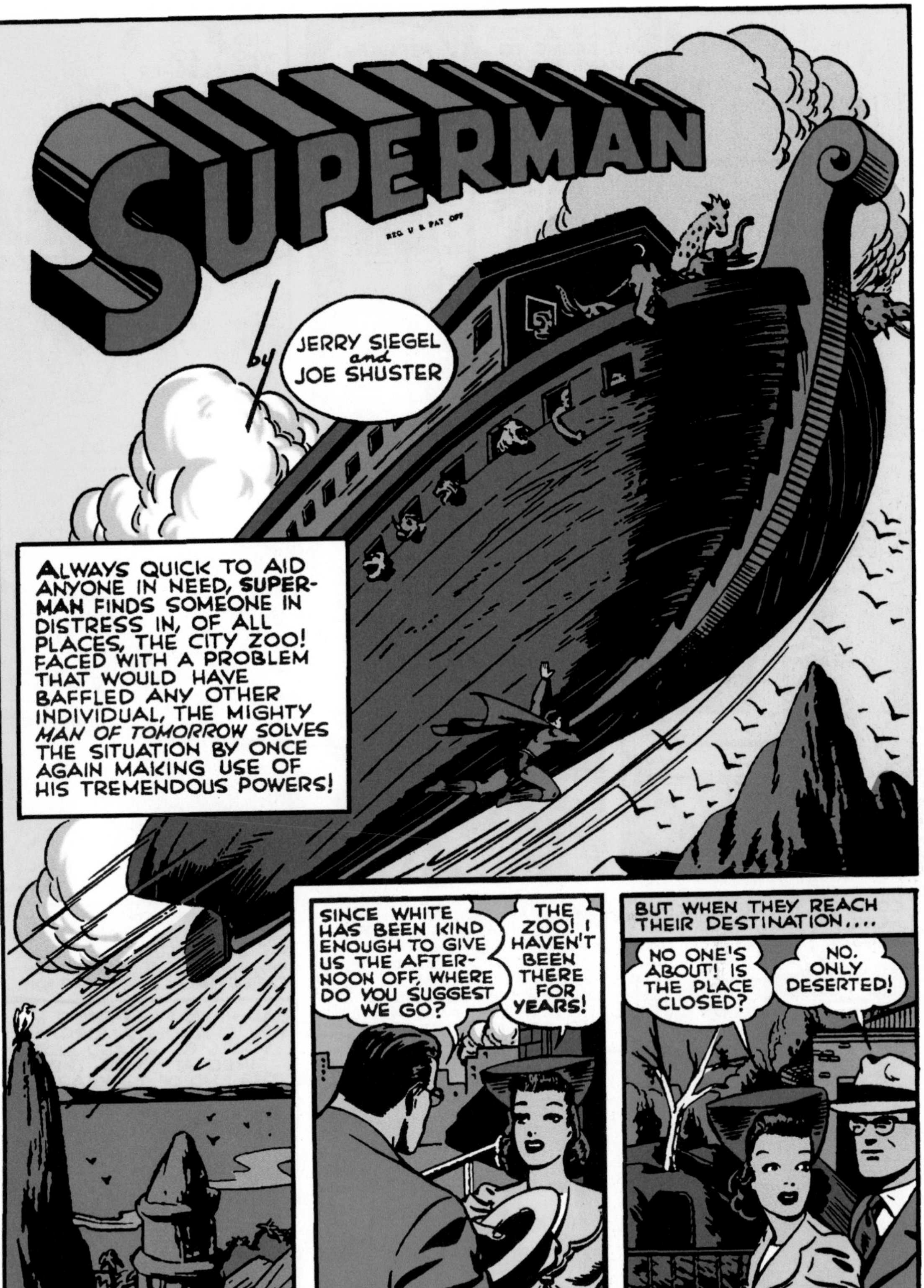
SUPERMAN
REG. U.S. PAT. OFF.
by JERRY SIEGEL and JOE SHUSTER
ALWAYS QUICK TO AID ANYONE IN NEED, SUPERMAN FINDS SOMEONE IN DISTRESS IN, OF ALL PLACES, THE CITY ZOO! FACED WITH A PROBLEM THAT WOULD HAVE BAFFLED ANY OTHER INDIVIDUAL, THE MIGHTY MAN OF TOMORROW SOLVES THE SITUATION BY ONCE AGAIN MAKING USE OF HIS TREMENDOUS POWERS!
1
SINCE WHITE HAS BEEN KIND ENOUGH TO GIVE US THE AFTERNOON OFF, WHERE DO YOU SUGGEST WE GO?
THE ZOO! I HAVEN'T BEEN THERE FOR YEARS!
BUT WHEN THEY REACH THEIR DESTINATION....
NO ONE'S ABOUT! IS THE PLACE CLOSED?
NO. ONLY DESERTED!

THE CAGES.... MOST OF THEM ARE EMPTY...!

WHAT A ZOO! IT SEEMS TO HAVE EVERYTHING BUT ANIMALS!

PERHAPS I CAN EXPLAIN.

AND WHO ARE YOU?

THE ZOO KEEPER.

WELL...IT'S NICE TO KNOW THAT CLARK AND I AREN'T THE ONLY ONES HERE, AFTER ALL!

YES...NOT MANY PEOPLE COME OUT TO THE ZOO ANY MORE. AND WHY SHOULD THEY? THERE'S NOT MUCH TO SEE.

WHY DON'T YOU GET MORE ANIMALS?

I'VE BEEN TRYING TO GET THE CITY COUNCIL TO PURCHASE THEM FOR THE ZOO FOR YEARS, BUT THEY WON'T LISTEN TO ME, AND THE WAR IN EUROPE IS MAKING IT ALMOST IMPOSSIBLE.

THAT'S TOO BAD...

IT REALLY IS, JUST THINK OF WHAT ALL THE CHILDREN IN *METROPOLIS* ARE MISSING.

COME HERE, CHARLES!

IF YOU'LL EXCUSE ME.....THAT'S A MEMBER OF THE CITY COUNCIL....

AS CHARLES AND THE COUNCILMAN WALK OFF....

AND *METROPOLIS* IS SUPPOSED TO BE A MODERN, PROGRESSIVE CITY. IF YOU ASK ME, NO CITY IS COMPLETE WITHOUT AN ADEQUATE ZOO!

BUT CLARK'S ATTENTION IS SUDDENLY DIVERTED, FOR HIS SUPER-SENSITIVE HEARING HAS PICKED UP AN INTERESTING CONVERSATION...

BAD NEWS FOR YOU, CHARLES. YOU'LL BE FIRED AT THE END OF THE WEEK!

FIRED, MR. MORGAN? AND AFTER ALL THESE YEARS?

I'M SORRY FOR YOU, CHARLES, BUT THE COUNCIL BELIEVES THE ZOO A WASTE OF MONEY. WHY, PRACTICALLY NO ONE EVER COMES HERE ANY MORE.

I CAN EXPLAIN...

IT'S ONLY BE-CAUSE THERE'S NOTHING TO SEE! NOW, IF WE HAD A BUNCH OF NEW AND UNUSUAL ANIMALS...

BUT WE HAVEN'T --AND WE CAN'T AFFORD TO BUY ANY! TOO BAD, CHARLES, NOTHING CAN BE DONE ABOUT IT.

("-NOTHING? THAT REMAINS TO BE SEEN!-")

LATER THAT DAY-- CLARK KENT TRANSFORMS HIM-SELF TO A FIGHTING CHAMPION OF JUSTICE WHO IS FAMOUS THE WORLD OVER.

THIS IS DEFINITELY A JOB FOR SUPERMAN!

LATER-- AS THE COLOR-FULLY-COSTUMED FIGURE STREAKS DOWN FROM THE SKY TOWARD THE CITY ZOO...

CHARLES-- ABOUT TO DESTROY HIMSELF...!

AREN'T YOU BEING HASTY?

NO! LET ME FALL!

3

YOU SHOULDN'T HAVE DONE THAT. THAT'S A COWARD'S WAY OUT!

MY JOB GONE...THE END OF MY LIFE'S WORK --THERE'S NOTHING WORTH LIVING FOR...

SUICIDE IS THE HEIGHT OF STUPIDITY! I'M ALMOST TEMPTED NOT TO HELP YOU.

I RECOGNIZE YOU NOW--SUPERMAN!

BUT--WHAT COULD YOU DO FOR ME?

PLENTY!--SEE THAT OLD ABANDONED ARK YOU ONCE USED AS AN EXHIBIT?

MIND IF I BORROW IT?

GO--(GULP!)--GO RIGHT AHEAD!

THANKS! I'LL RETURN IT SOON. MEANWHILE, PROMISE ME NOT TO TRY ANYTHING FOOLISH!

I--I WON'T!

OUT OVER THE OCEAN SPRINGS THE *MAN OF STEEL* WITH HIS CUMBERSOME BURDEN...

QUITE AN ARMFUL!

DROPPING TO THE SEA, HE SWIMS AT GREAT SPEED, SHOVING THE ANCIENT VESSEL BEFORE HIM...

IF THERE'S A QUICKER WAY TO AFRICA, I HAVEN'T HEARD OF IT!

THE *MAN OF STEEL* REACHES THE DARK CONTINENT IN RECORD TIME....

4

UPON REACHING HIS DESTINATION, **SUPERMAN** SETS HIS BURDEN DOWN WITHIN THE JUNGLE.... THEN...AS SHOUTS REACH HIS EARS....

VOICES! ...I'LL INVESTIGATE!

THE *MAN OF TOMORROW* SIGHTS NATIVES, UNDER COMMAND OF A STERN-FACED WHITE MAN, CLOSING IN ON AN ELEPHANT HERD...

HUNTERS!

WARNED BY A STRANGE INSTINCT, THE HERD OF MIGHTY PACHYDERMS PIVOTS AND THUNDERS DOWN UPON THE HUNTING PARTY....

NOW TO PLAY ELEPHANT BOY!

THIS IS AS FAR AS YOU GO!

SUPERMAN SHOVES THE ELEPHANT LEADER BACK -- BACK AGAINST THE REMAINDER OF THE HERD, BRINGING THE STAMPEDE TO A HALT...

CAN'T WE TALK THIS THING OVER?

AS THE TERRIFIED ELEPHANTS FLEE BEFORE THE MIGHT OF THEIR STRANGE OPPONENT, *SUPERMAN* TURNS TO THE HUNTER. BUT THE WHITE MAN URGES THE NATIVES TO ATTACK THE *MAN OF STEEL*...

KILL HIM! KILL! *KILL!*

⑤

AS A SHOWER OF SPEARS GLANCE HARM-LESSLY OFF HIS IMPENETRABLE SKIN....

IS THIS JUNGLE GRATITUDE?-- I THOUGHT WE COULD BE FRIENDS, BUT IF IT'S A SCRAP YOU WANT, I'LL BE THE LAST TO OBJECT!

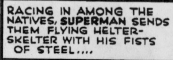

RACING IN AMONG THE NATIVES, **SUPERMAN** SENDS THEM FLYING HELTER-SKELTER WITH HIS FISTS OF STEEL....

THIS IS WHAT I CALL A PUSH-OVER!

AND HERE'S WHERE I CHANGE THE CONTOUR OF YOUR JAW!

STOP! I RECOGNIZE YOU NOW. YOU'RE SUPERMAN!

YOU'VE HEARD OF ME, EH? AND WHO ARE YOU?

FORGIVE MY RASHNESS, I THOUGHT YOU MIGHT BE SOME STRANGE CREATURE OF THE JUNGLE, BUT NOW THAT I REALIZE WHO YOU ARE, I SEE I'VE MADE A TERRIBLE MISTAKE!

I AM COUNT VON HENZEL, YOU HAVE UNWITTINGLY TRESPASSED ON MY JUNGLE DOMAIN, BUT IF YOU'D CARE TO COME TO MY HUMBLE HEADQUARTERS, I SHALL OFFER YOU MY HOSPITALITY.

THANKS, COUNT. I'LL BE GLAD TO ACCEPT!

MOUNTING A TAMED ELEPHANT WITH VON HENZEL, SUPERMAN IS LED THRU THE JUNGLE,....

I PRIDE MYSELF ON BEING A HUNTER OF EXTRAORDINARY SKILL. WHAT ARE YOU DOING HERE IN AFRICA?

IT'S A LONG STORY.

MINUTES LATER....

AND THAT'S HOW IT IS! IF I'M TO BE OF ANY ASSISTANCE TO CHARLES, I'VE GOT TO RETURN WITH A CARGO OF WILD ANIMALS....AND BEFORE THE WEEK IS OVER.

PERHAPS I MAY BE OF SOME ASSISTANCE.

SA-AAY! THAT'S A RATHER ELABORATE LAYOUT TO BE FOUND IN THE CENTER OF A JUNGLE,

I INSIST ON ALL THE COMFORTS!

IT'S GOING TO BE NICE HAVING YOU FOR A VISITOR. I'M ALL ALONE HERE...HAVEN'T SEEN ANOTHER WHITE PERSON IN YEARS!

("-ALONE, EH?-")

THE *MAN OF STEEL* IS PUZZLED, FOR HIS TELESCOPIC VISION SIGHTS A PRETTY WHITE GIRL STARING DOWN IN FRIGHT FROM BEHIND A HEAVILY CURTAINED WINDOW....

NO DOUBT YOU'RE PUZZLED TO BE HANDED A GLASS OF COOL TEA. I HAVE MY OWN REFRIGERATION PLANT HERE.

HOW INTERESTING...AND USEFUL!

VON HENZEL! I...

I THOUGHT I TOLD YOU TO REMAIN IN YOUR ROOM!

YOU SAID YOU WERE ALL ALONE HERE!

YOU SAW ME COME HERE WITH THIS UNEXPECTED VISITOR. YOU TOOK THIS OPPORTUNITY TO BURST IN, WELL, YOU WANTED TO SPEAK TO HIM—WHY DON'T YOU?

I—I'M SORRY TO HAVE DIS-OBEYED YOU, I'LL GO RIGHT BACK TO MY ROOM!

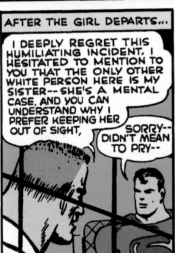

AFTER THE GIRL DEPARTS...

I DEEPLY REGRET THIS HUMILIATING INCIDENT. I HESITATED TO MENTION TO YOU THAT THE ONLY OTHER WHITE PERSON HERE IS MY SISTER—SHE'S A MENTAL CASE, AND YOU CAN UNDERSTAND WHY I PREFER KEEPING HER OUT OF SIGHT.

SORRY—DIDN'T MEAN TO PRY—

AND THIS IS MY TROPHY ROOM!

A WIDE SELECTION OF FEROCIOUS ANIMALS...AS WELL AS HUNTING DECORATIONS AND AWARDS.....—YOU DO TAKE PRIDE IN YOUR HUNTING!

I KNOW JUST THE SPOT WHERE YOU'LL BE ABLE TO FIND A NUMBER OF MOST UNUSUAL SPECIMENS. I'LL BE GLAD TO HAVE MY MEN ACCOMPANY YOU IN THE MORNING ON A HUNTING EXPEDITION. MEANWHILE, WHY DON'T YOU RETIRE?

⑦

LATER....

ALL THE COMFORTS OF HOME! I CERTAINLY WAS LUCKY TO MEET UP WITH COUNT VON HENZEL!

MEANWHILE—DOWNSTAIRS....

NOW?

NOT YET, MAWBI! YOU WILL HAVE AMPLE OPPORTUNITY TOMORROW!

NIGHT--A SHADOW FLITS ALONG THE HALLWAY....

...AND ENTERS THE *MAN OF TOMORROW'S* ROOM!

WHO IS IT?

I HAVEN'T MUCH TIME! I'VE COME TO WARN YOU...!

WARN ME AGAINST WHAT?

YOU'RE IN DREADFUL DANGER, HE.... OH-HHH!

DISOBEY-ING ME AGAIN!

HOW MANY TIMES HAVE I TOLD YOU NOT TO LEAVE YOUR ROOM?

I WON'T DO IT AGAIN! I PROMISE! I PROMISE!

AGAIN I MUST APOLOGIZE. BUT I CAN ASSURE YOU THAT MY SISTER WILL ANNOY YOU NO LONGER! I'LL SEE TO **THAT!**

PLEASE DON'T BE HARSH WITH THE UNFOR-TUNATE GIRL.

NEXT MORNING..., **SUPERMAN** SETS OFF WITH THE EXPEDITION...

GOOD HUNTING-- SORRY I CAN'T ACCOMPANY YOU AT THIS TIME!

I'LL BE BACK SOON...AND WITH ANIMALS FOR **SEVERAL ZOOS!**

8

HE'S GONE! OUR LAST HOPE!

VON HENZEL IS A DEVIL! THERE'S NO USE OPPOSING HIM!

HAVE WE MUCH FURTHER TO GO?

NOT FAR NOW!

DOWN THERE IN VALLEY-- DEVIL ANIMALS...!

THEN LET'S GET GOING!

THE PARTY DESCENDS THE PRECARIOUS SIDE OF THE CLIFF....

PRETTY STEEP!

NOW!

UNNOTICED BY THE *MAN OF TOMORROW*, TWO NATIVES STEAL FORWARD FROM BEHIND IN AN ATTEMPT TO HURL HIM BELOW...BUT AS THEY DO...A FEROCIOUS, STRIPED FIGURE HURTLES TOWARD THEM...

TIGER!!

DUCK!

SPRINGING OVER THE FRIGHTENED NATIVES, *SUPERMAN* MEETS THE ANIMAL IN A HEAD-ON COLLISION....

WHOA!

'ROUND AND 'ROUND *SUPERMAN* SPINS THE HOWLING CAT....

COOL OFF!

HE'LL BEHAVE NOW! LET'S CONTINUE!

AS THEY REACH THE VALLEY....

A SPLENDID OPPORTUNITY -- GONE!

BUT THERE WILL BE OTHERS!

AS THE HUNTING EXPEDITION ADVANCES, SUDDENLY IT COMES UPON A STRANGE ASSORTMENT OF JUNGLE CREATURES....

DEVIL ANIMALS!

I'VE CERTAINLY SEEN NOTHING LIKE THEM BEFORE!

THE FRIGHTENED NATIVES TURN TO RETREAT ONLY TO DISCOVER....

COMPLETELY SURROUNDED!

WE'LL ALL DIE!

PESSIMISTIC, AREN'T YOU?

AS THE JUNGLE ANIMALS CLOSE IN, SUPERMAN STREAKS TOWARD THEM, AN UNLEASHED LIGHTNING BOLT,....

NO TIME TO STAND IDLY BY!

'ROUND THE GREAT CIRCLE HE RUNS, SNATCHING UP THE ANIMALS AS HE GOES... HURLING THEM OVER HIS SHOULDER ONE AFTER THE OTHER...

INTO YOUR PLACES!

... SO THAT THEY TUMBLE INTO THE OPEN CAGES!

THEN...ALONG THE LINE OF CAGES SPEEDS THE MAN OF STEEL, SLAMMING SHUT THE ENTRANCES...

NEATLY TRAPPED, IF I MUST SAY SO MYSELF!

HE'S CAPTURED THEM ALL!

A MIRACLE!

SORRY TO CUT THE EXPEDITION SHORT ....BUT WE'VE ALREADY CAPTURED A SUFFICIENT NUMBER AND VARIETY OF ANIMALS... SUPPOSE WE RETURN NOW.

BUT FIRST-- DRINK TO THE VICTORY OF THE HUNT!!

NO SOONER DOES SUPERMAN DRINK THE CUP'S CONTENTS THAN HE KEELS OVER, TO LIE MOTIONLESS ON THE GROUND,....

WITNESS THE POWER OF THE POTION!

IS HE--??

HE IS--!!

10

LATER...THE EXPEDITION RETURNS TO VON HENZEL'S JUNGLE RETREAT....

YOU'VE ATTENDED TO HIM?

HE IS COMPLETELY HELPLESS! THE WITCH-POTION AFFECTED EVEN SUPERMAN

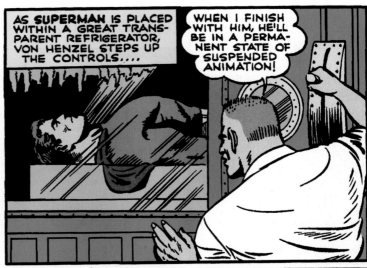

AS SUPERMAN IS PLACED WITHIN A GREAT TRANSPARENT REFRIGERATOR, VON HENZEL STEPS UP THE CONTROLS....

WHEN I FINISH WITH HIM, HE'LL BE IN A PERMANENT STATE OF SUSPENDED ANIMATION!

LATER....

WHY HAVE YOU ORDERED US HERE? YOU KNOW MY BROTHER IS TOO CRITICALLY WOUNDED TO BE MOVED!

I WANT YOU TO WITNESS THE LATEST ADDITION TO MY COLLECTION!

THE COSTUMED STRANGER! YOU'VE DESTROYED HIM!

YES, AS I MUST NOW DESTROY BOTH YOU AND YOUR BROTHER! --WHEN YOU AND HE STUMBLED ONTO MY HOME, YOU THOUGHT YOU HAD FOUND REFUGE AFTER BEING LOST IN THE JUNGLE, BUT YOU DIDN'T KNOW OF MY CONSUMING DESIRE TO HUNT UNUSUAL PREY!

NOW GET IN THERE--AND BE TRANSFORMED INTO IMPERISHABLE STATUES...OR I'LL SHOOT YOU DOWN!

YOU FIEND...!

SUPERMAN HAS BEEN AWARE OF WHAT IS OCCURRING, THO HELPLESS TO ACT. NOW HE GATHERS ALL HIS STRENGTH FOR A GIGANTIC EFFORT....

("-GOT TO FREE MYSELF!-")

11

A TERRIFIC STRAIN-- AT FIRST AN APPARENTLY LOSING BATTLE... THEN..... SUPERMAN MOVES...!!

YOU LIVE!

ONE MOMENT FROM NOW I MAY NOT BE ABLE TO SAY THE SAME FOR YOU!

IN HIS ANXIETY TO ESCAPE, VON HENZEL BACKS AWAY...

KEEP AWAY! KEEP AWAY!

NOT UNTIL I GIVE YOU THE BEATING YOU DESERVE!

THE CRUEL HUNTER TRIPS ...FALLS INTO THE REFRIGERATOR

YA-AA-AAA!

LOOK OUT!

DASHING INTO THE SUB-ZERO COLD OF THE UNUSUAL MECHANISM, SUPERMAN DRAGS FORTH VON HENZEL'S BODY....

HE'S STIFF AS A BOARD...DESTROYED BY HIS OWN FIENDISH MACHINE -- WAIT HERE AN INSTANT!

RACING OUT OF THE BUILDING, SUPERMAN RAISES ALOFT THE CAGES, ONE ATOP THE OTHER, AND RACES TO THE ARK WITH THEM....

TIME TO TRAVEL!

RETURNING TO THE BUILD-ING, HE SNATCHES UP THE GIRL AND HER BROTHER...

WHAT --??

I'VE GOT TO TAKE YOUR BROTHER TO WHERE HE CAN RECEIVE MEDICAL TREAT-MENT!

ABOVE THE JUNGLE STREAKS THE MAN OF TOMORROW, HOLDING THE ARK AND HIS HUMAN PASSENGERS OVER-HEAD....

CIVILIZATION!

DEPOSITING VON HENZEL'S FORMER CAPTIVES BEFORE A HOSPITAL, SUPERMAN SPRINGS OFF....

WHAT A WONDERFUL MAN!

WE OWE HIM OUR LIVES!

⑫

BACK ACROSS THE OCEAN SWIMS SUPERMAN WITH THE LOADED ARK....

AMERICA, HERE I COME!

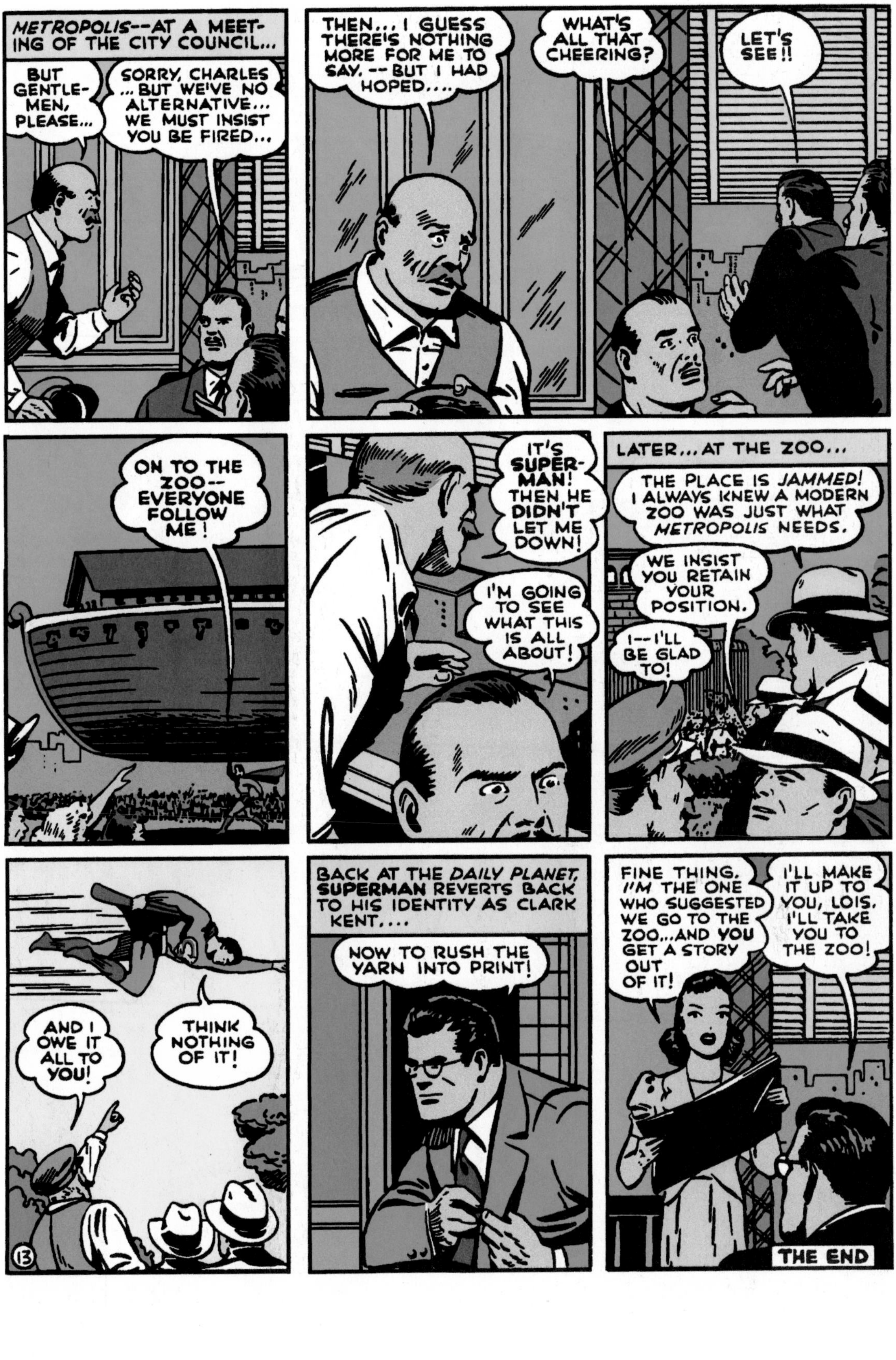
METROPOLIS--AT A MEETING OF THE CITY COUNCIL...
BUT GENTLEMEN, PLEASE...
SORRY, CHARLES ...BUT WE'VE NO ALTERNATIVE... WE MUST INSIST YOU BE FIRED...
THEN... I GUESS THERE'S NOTHING MORE FOR ME TO SAY. -- BUT I HAD HOPED....
WHAT'S ALL THAT CHEERING?
LET'S SEE!!
ON TO THE ZOO-- EVERYONE FOLLOW ME!
IT'S SUPERMAN! THEN HE DIDN'T LET ME DOWN!
I'M GOING TO SEE WHAT THIS IS ALL ABOUT!
LATER... AT THE ZOO...
THE PLACE IS JAMMED! I ALWAYS KNEW A MODERN ZOO WAS JUST WHAT METROPOLIS NEEDS.
WE INSIST YOU RETAIN YOUR POSITION.
I--I'LL BE GLAD TO!
AND I OWE IT ALL TO YOU!
THINK NOTHING OF IT!
13
BACK AT THE DAILY PLANET, SUPERMAN REVERTS BACK TO HIS IDENTITY AS CLARK KENT,...
NOW TO RUSH THE YARN INTO PRINT!
FINE THING. I'M THE ONE WHO SUGGESTED WE GO TO THE ZOO...AND YOU GET A STORY OUT OF IT!
I'LL MAKE IT UP TO YOU, LOIS. I'LL TAKE YOU TO THE ZOO!
THE END

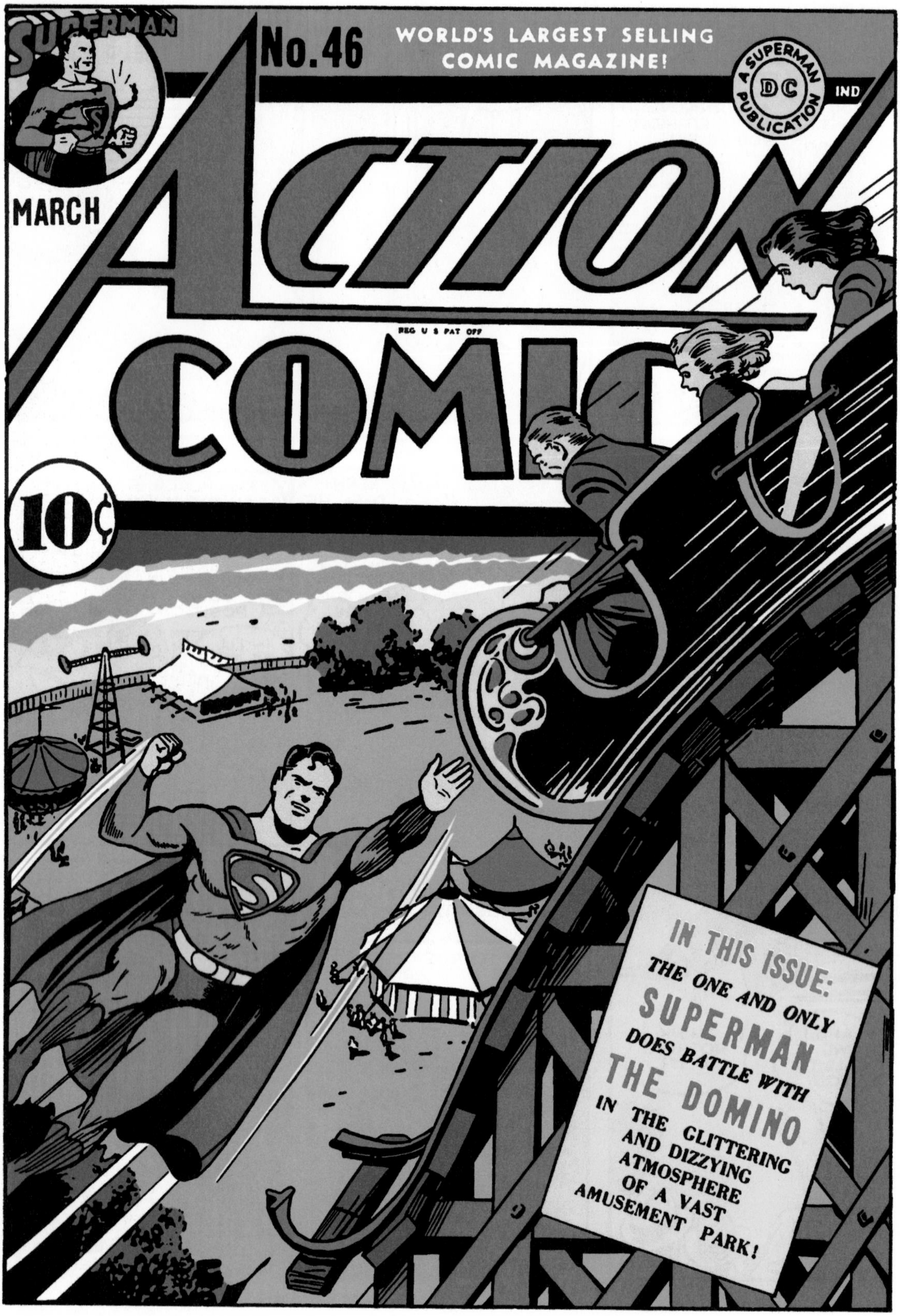
SUPERMAN
No. 46
WORLD'S LARGEST SELLING COMIC MAGAZINE!
A SUPERMAN DC PUBLICATION
IND
MARCH
ACTION COMICS
REG U S PAT OFF
10¢
IN THIS ISSUE:
THE ONE AND ONLY
SUPERMAN
DOES BATTLE WITH
THE DOMINO
IN THE GLITTERING AND DIZZYING ATMOSPHERE OF A VAST AMUSEMENT PARK!

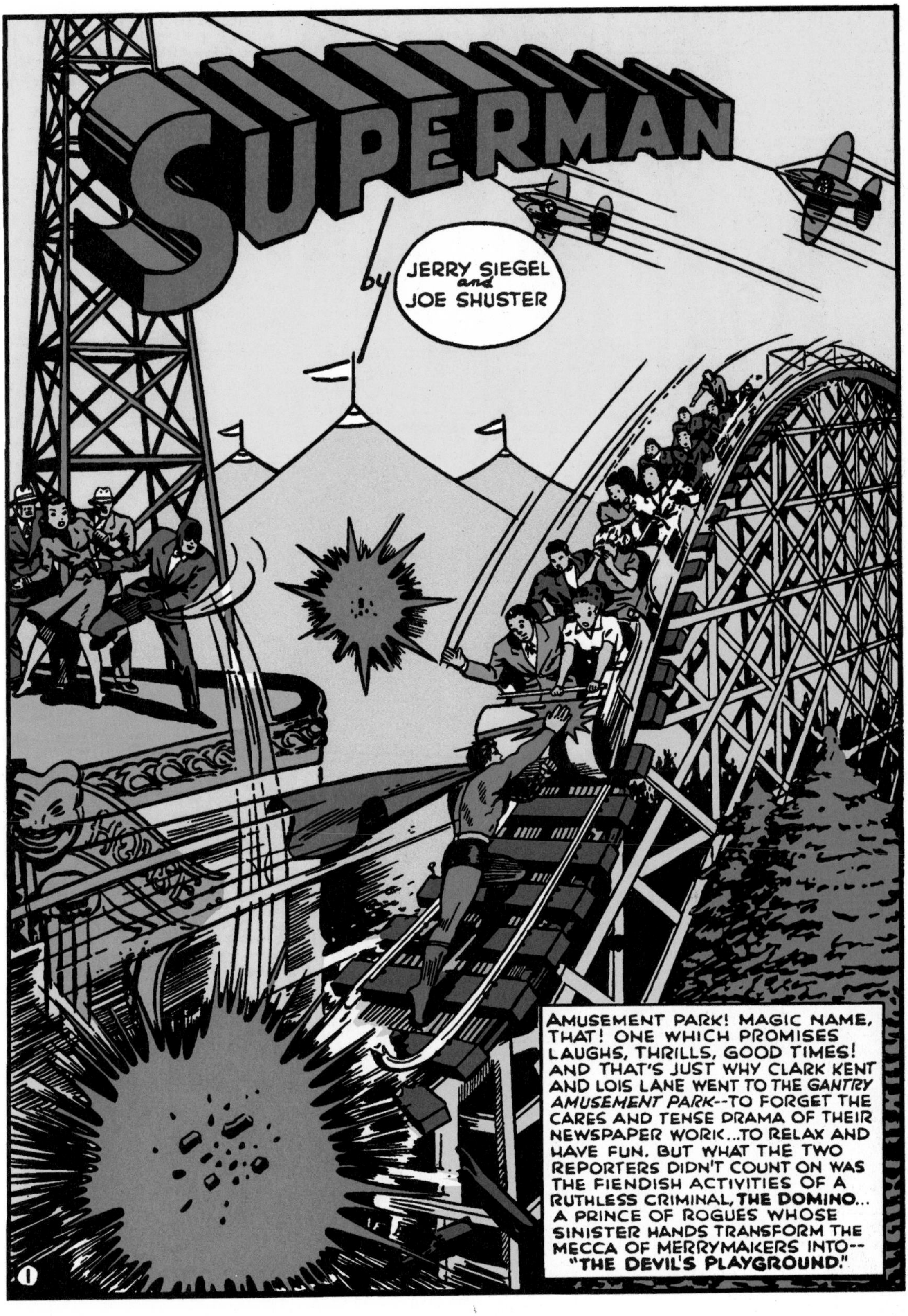
SUPERMAN
by JERRY SIEGEL and JOE SHUSTER
AMUSEMENT PARK! MAGIC NAME, THAT! ONE WHICH PROMISES LAUGHS, THRILLS, GOOD TIMES! AND THAT'S JUST WHY CLARK KENT AND LOIS LANE WENT TO THE *GANTRY AMUSEMENT PARK*--TO FORGET THE CARES AND TENSE DRAMA OF THEIR NEWSPAPER WORK...TO RELAX AND HAVE FUN. BUT WHAT THE TWO REPORTERS DIDN'T COUNT ON WAS THE FIENDISH ACTIVITIES OF A RUTHLESS CRIMINAL, **THE DOMINO**... A PRINCE OF ROGUES WHOSE SINISTER HANDS TRANSFORM THE MECCA OF MERRYMAKERS INTO-- **"THE DEVIL'S PLAYGROUND."**
1

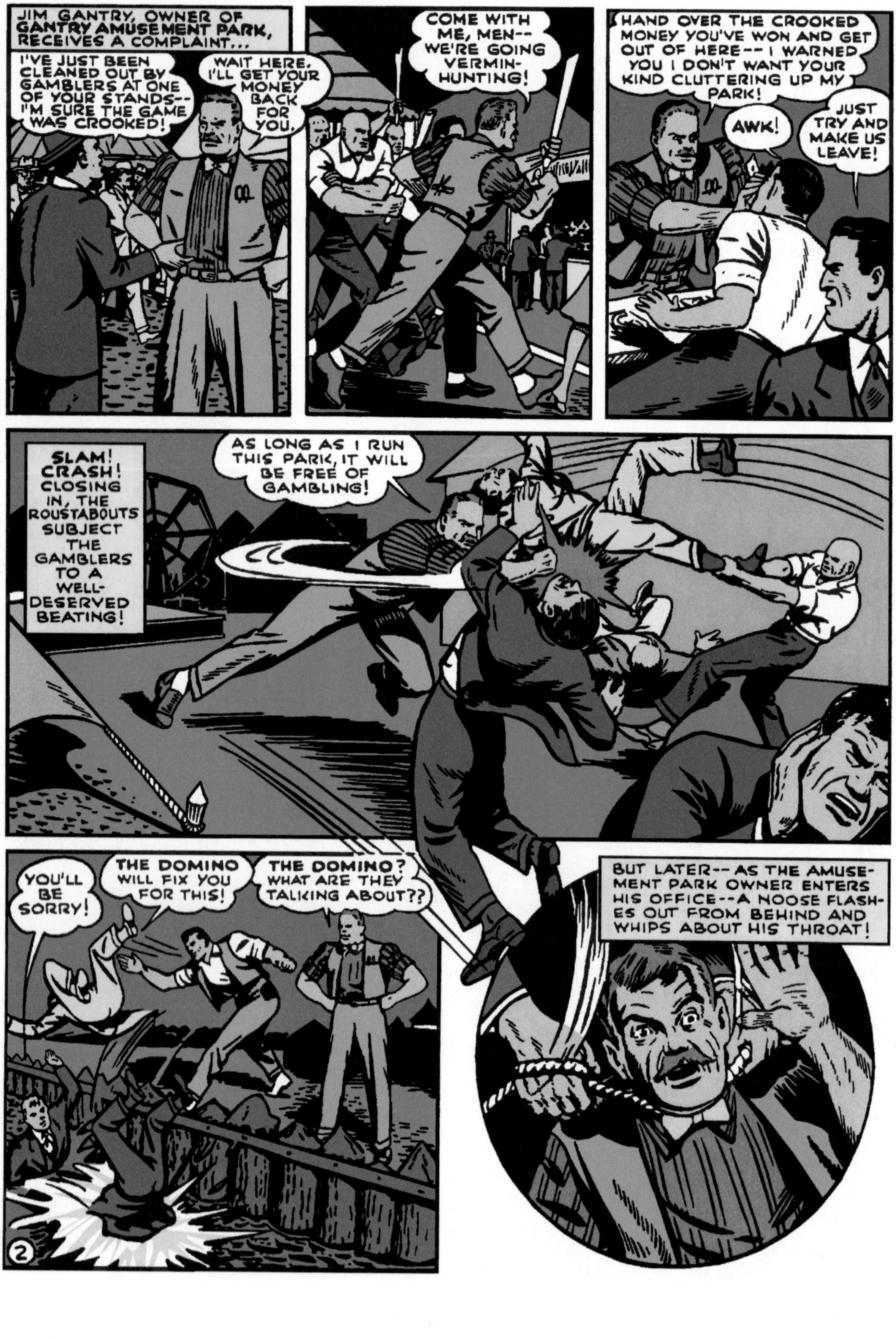
JIM GANTRY, OWNER OF GANTRY AMUSEMENT PARK, RECEIVES A COMPLAINT...
I'VE JUST BEEN CLEANED OUT BY GAMBLERS AT ONE OF YOUR STANDS-- I'M SURE THE GAME WAS CROOKED!
WAIT HERE. I'LL GET YOUR MONEY BACK FOR YOU.
COME WITH ME, MEN-- WE'RE GOING VERMIN-HUNTING!
HAND OVER THE CROOKED MONEY YOU'VE WON AND GET OUT OF HERE-- I WARNED YOU I DON'T WANT YOUR KIND CLUTTERING UP MY PARK!
AWK!
JUST TRY AND MAKE US LEAVE!
SLAM! CRASH! CLOSING IN, THE ROUSTABOUTS SUBJECT THE GAMBLERS TO A WELL-DESERVED BEATING!
AS LONG AS I RUN THIS PARK, IT WILL BE FREE OF GAMBLING!
YOU'LL BE SORRY!
THE DOMINO WILL FIX YOU FOR THIS!
THE DOMINO? WHAT ARE THEY TALKING ABOUT??
2
BUT LATER-- AS THE AMUSEMENT PARK OWNER ENTERS HIS OFFICE-- A NOOSE FLASHES OUT FROM BEHIND AND WHIPS ABOUT HIS THROAT!

PERHAPS THIS WILL MAKE YOU CHANGE YOUR MIND. WILL YOU PERMIT GAMBLING IN YOUR PARK?

THE DOMINO! NO-- I-- I WON'T!

THE NOOSE TIGHTENS...AS JIM GANTRY SLIPS INTO UNCONSCIOUSNESS, THRU A BLACK HAZE HE DIMLY SIGHTS MALEVOLENT EYES GLARING DOWN THRU A DOMINOED MASK AT HIM!

LATER-- WHEN GANTRY REVIVES...

MY THROAT--IT'S STILL BRUISED! THAT ENCOUNTER COULDN'T HAVE BEEN MY IMAGINATION! THE DOMINO, EH? I WON'T PERMIT GAMBLING FOR HIM OR ANYONE!

ISN'T THAT MAN ACTING STRANGELY?

FOR ONCE, FORGET BUSINESS! YOU PROMISED ME A GOOD TIME AND I INTEND TO HAVE IT!

GET IN-- AND STOP ACTING AS THO I'M ASKING YOU TO COMMIT SUICIDE!

THESE THINGS ALWAYS M-MAKE ME DIZZY!

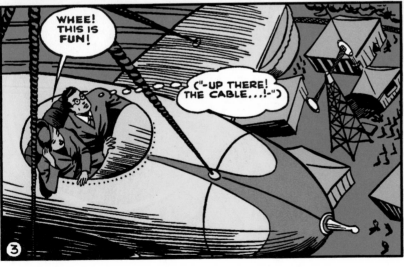

WHEE! THIS IS FUN!

("-UP THERE! THE CABLE...!-")

CLARK'S KEEN TELE-SCOPIC VISION HAS APPRISED HIM OF THE FACT THAT ONE OF THE CABLES SUPPORTING THE PLANE IS STRAINING --ABOUT TO PART!!

③

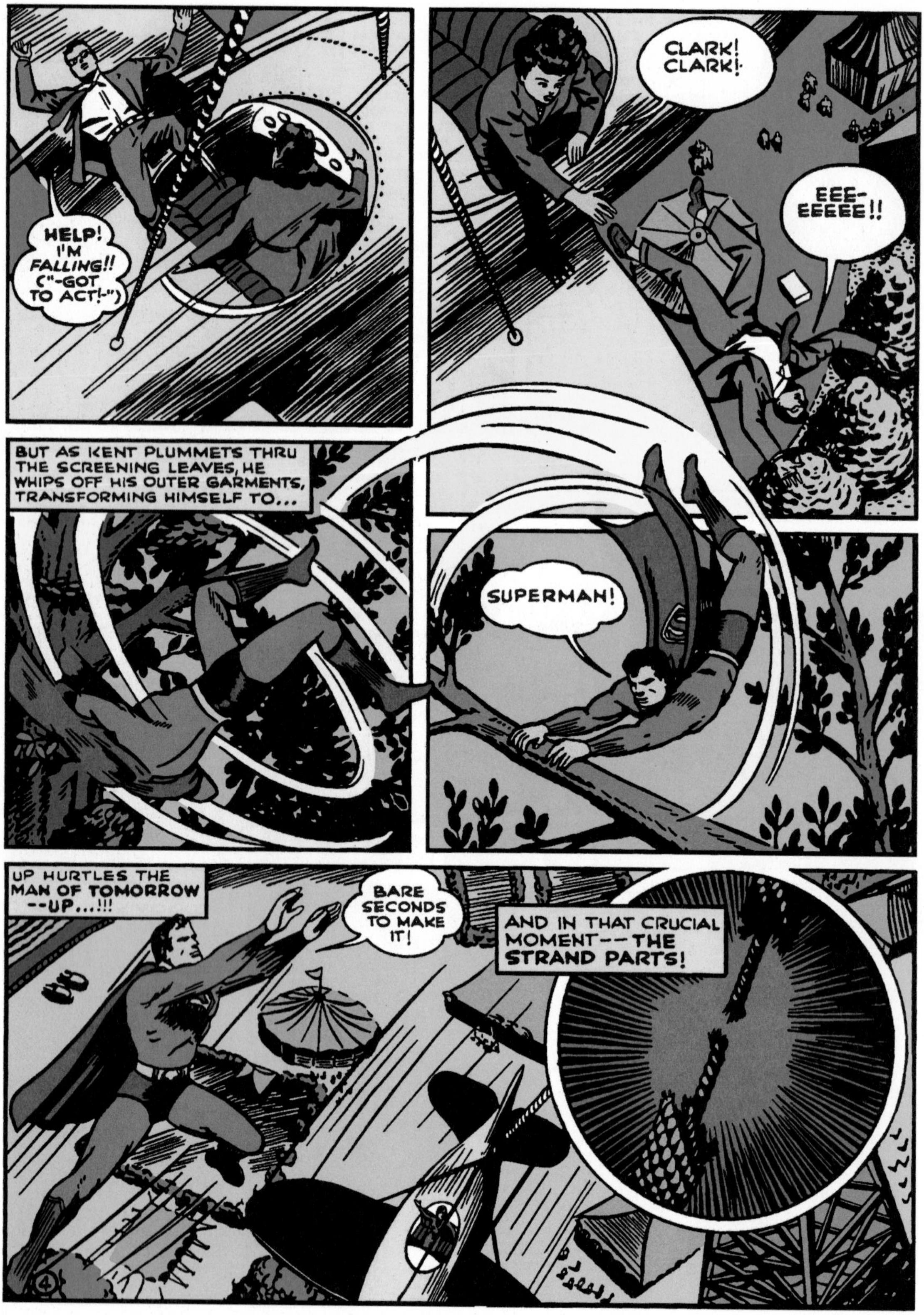
HELP! I'M FALLING!! ("-GOT TO ACT!-")
CLARK! CLARK!
EEE-EEEEE!!
BUT AS KENT PLUMMETS THRU THE SCREENING LEAVES, HE WHIPS OFF HIS OUTER GARMENTS, TRANSFORMING HIMSELF TO...
SUPERMAN!
UP HURTLES THE MAN OF TOMORROW --UP...!!!
BARE SECONDS TO MAKE IT!
AND IN THAT CRUCIAL MOMENT-- THE STRAND PARTS!

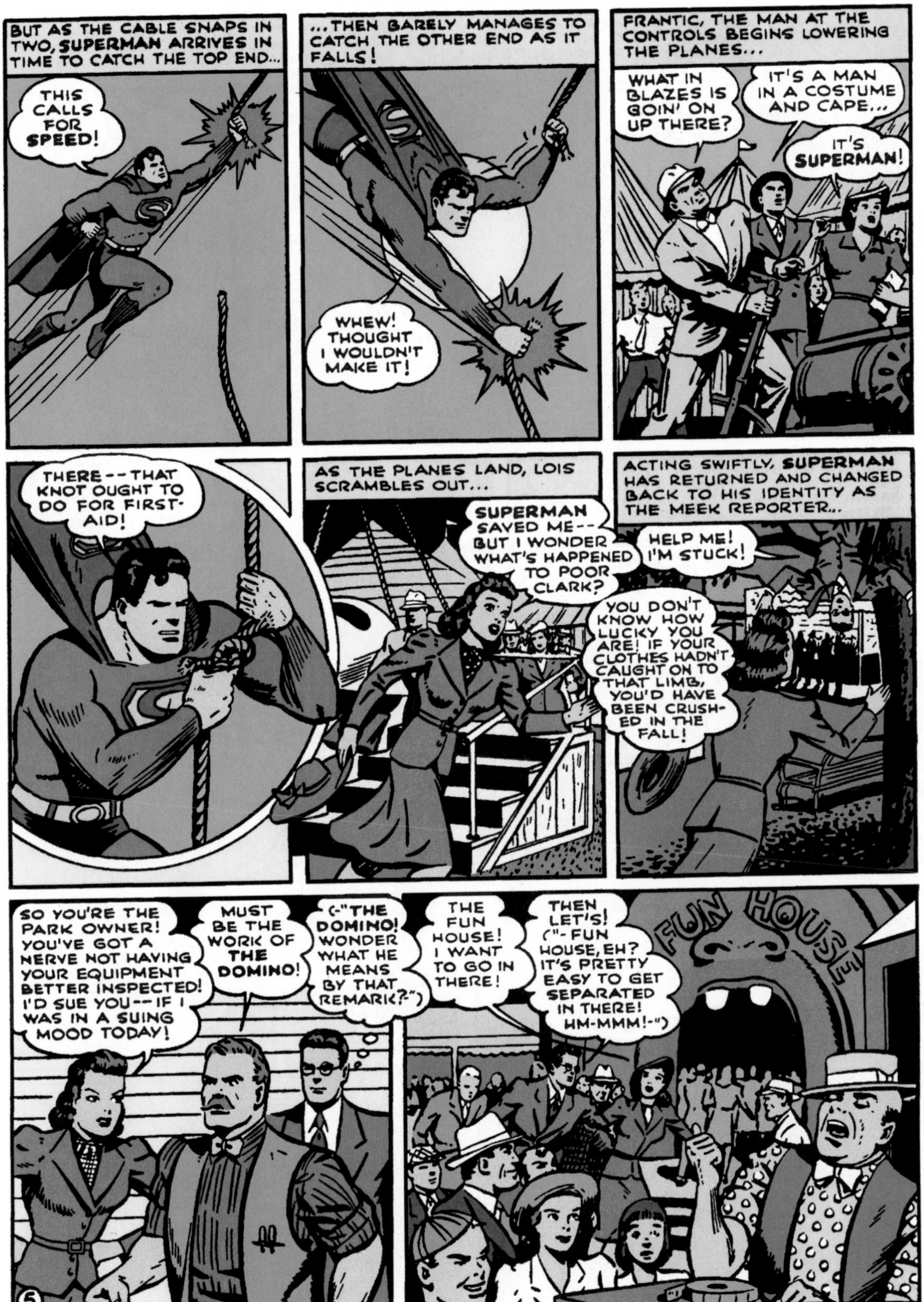
BUT AS THE CABLE SNAPS IN TWO, SUPERMAN ARRIVES IN TIME TO CATCH THE TOP END...
THIS CALLS FOR SPEED!
...THEN BARELY MANAGES TO CATCH THE OTHER END AS IT FALLS!
WHEW! THOUGHT I WOULDN'T MAKE IT!
FRANTIC, THE MAN AT THE CONTROLS BEGINS LOWERING THE PLANES...
WHAT IN BLAZES IS GOIN' ON UP THERE?
IT'S A MAN IN A COSTUME AND CAPE...
IT'S SUPERMAN!
THERE--THAT KNOT OUGHT TO DO FOR FIRST-AID!
AS THE PLANES LAND, LOIS SCRAMBLES OUT...
SUPERMAN SAVED ME--BUT I WONDER WHAT'S HAPPENED TO POOR CLARK?
ACTING SWIFTLY, SUPERMAN HAS RETURNED AND CHANGED BACK TO HIS IDENTITY AS THE MEEK REPORTER...
HELP ME! I'M STUCK!
YOU DON'T KNOW HOW LUCKY YOU ARE! IF YOUR CLOTHES HADN'T CAUGHT ON TO THAT LIMB, YOU'D HAVE BEEN CRUSHED IN THE FALL!
SO YOU'RE THE PARK OWNER! YOU'VE GOT A NERVE NOT HAVING YOUR EQUIPMENT BETTER INSPECTED! I'D SUE YOU--IF I WAS IN A SUING MOOD TODAY!
MUST BE THE WORK OF THE DOMINO!
("THE DOMINO! WONDER WHAT HE MEANS BY THAT REMARK?")
5
THE FUN HOUSE! I WANT TO GO IN THERE!
THEN LET'S! ("-FUN HOUSE, EH? IT'S PRETTY EASY TO GET SEPARATED IN THERE! HM-MMM!-")
FUN HOUSE

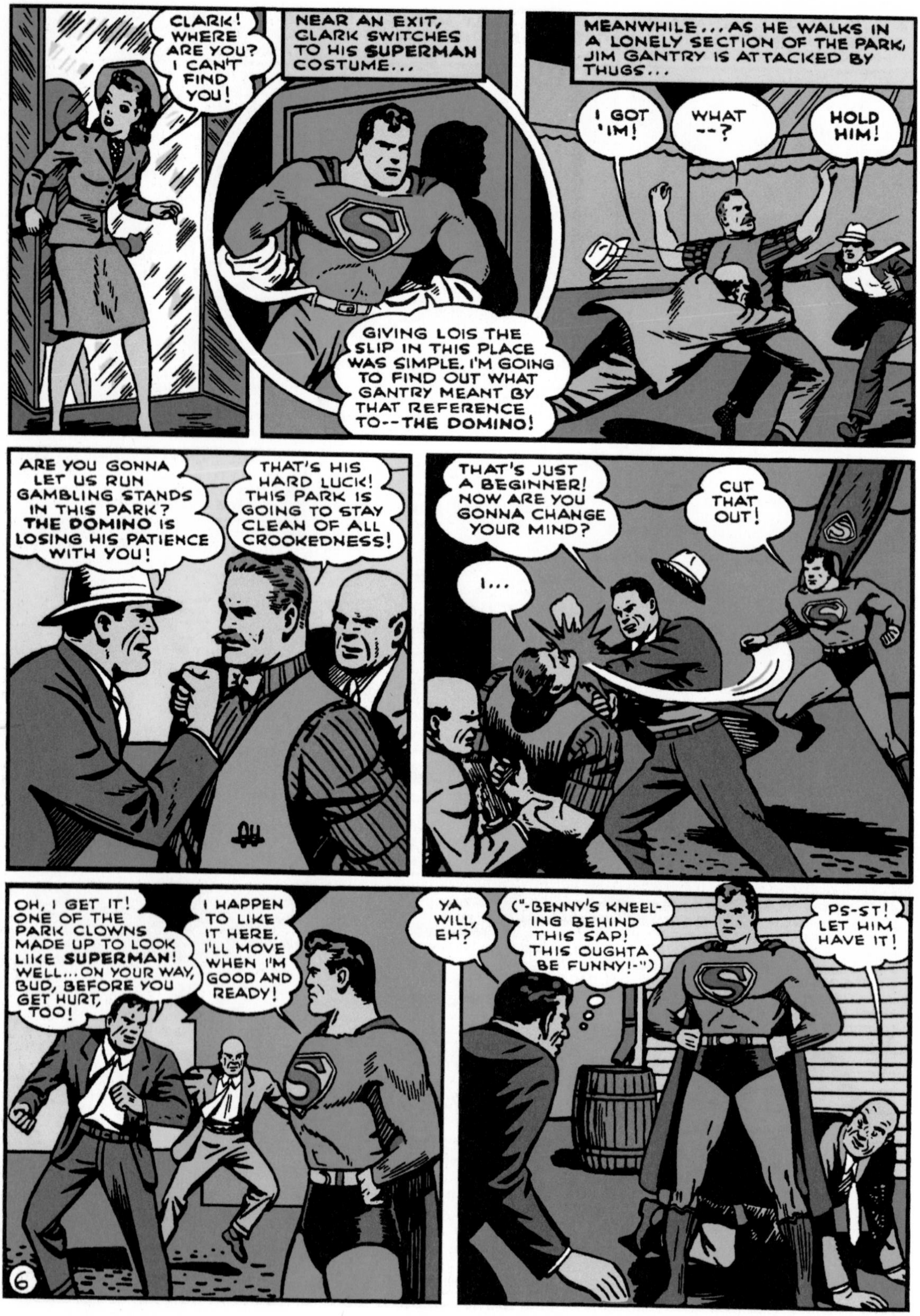

CLARK! WHERE ARE YOU? I CAN'T FIND YOU!
NEAR AN EXIT, CLARK SWITCHES TO HIS SUPERMAN COSTUME...
GIVING LOIS THE SLIP IN THIS PLACE WAS SIMPLE. I'M GOING TO FIND OUT WHAT GANTRY MEANT BY THAT REFERENCE TO--THE DOMINO!
MEANWHILE... AS HE WALKS IN A LONELY SECTION OF THE PARK, JIM GANTRY IS ATTACKED BY THUGS...
I GOT 'IM!
WHAT --?
HOLD HIM!
ARE YOU GONNA LET US RUN GAMBLING STANDS IN THIS PARK? THE DOMINO IS LOSING HIS PATIENCE WITH YOU!
THAT'S HIS HARD LUCK! THIS PARK IS GOING TO STAY CLEAN OF ALL CROOKEDNESS!
THAT'S JUST A BEGINNER! NOW ARE YOU GONNA CHANGE YOUR MIND?
I...
CUT THAT OUT!
OH, I GET IT! ONE OF THE PARK CLOWNS MADE UP TO LOOK LIKE SUPERMAN! WELL...ON YOUR WAY, BUD, BEFORE YOU GET HURT, TOO!
I HAPPEN TO LIKE IT HERE. I'LL MOVE WHEN I'M GOOD AND READY!
6
YA WILL, EH?
("-BENNY'S KNEELING BEHIND THIS SAP! THIS OUGHTA BE FUNNY!-")
PS-ST! LET HIM HAVE IT!

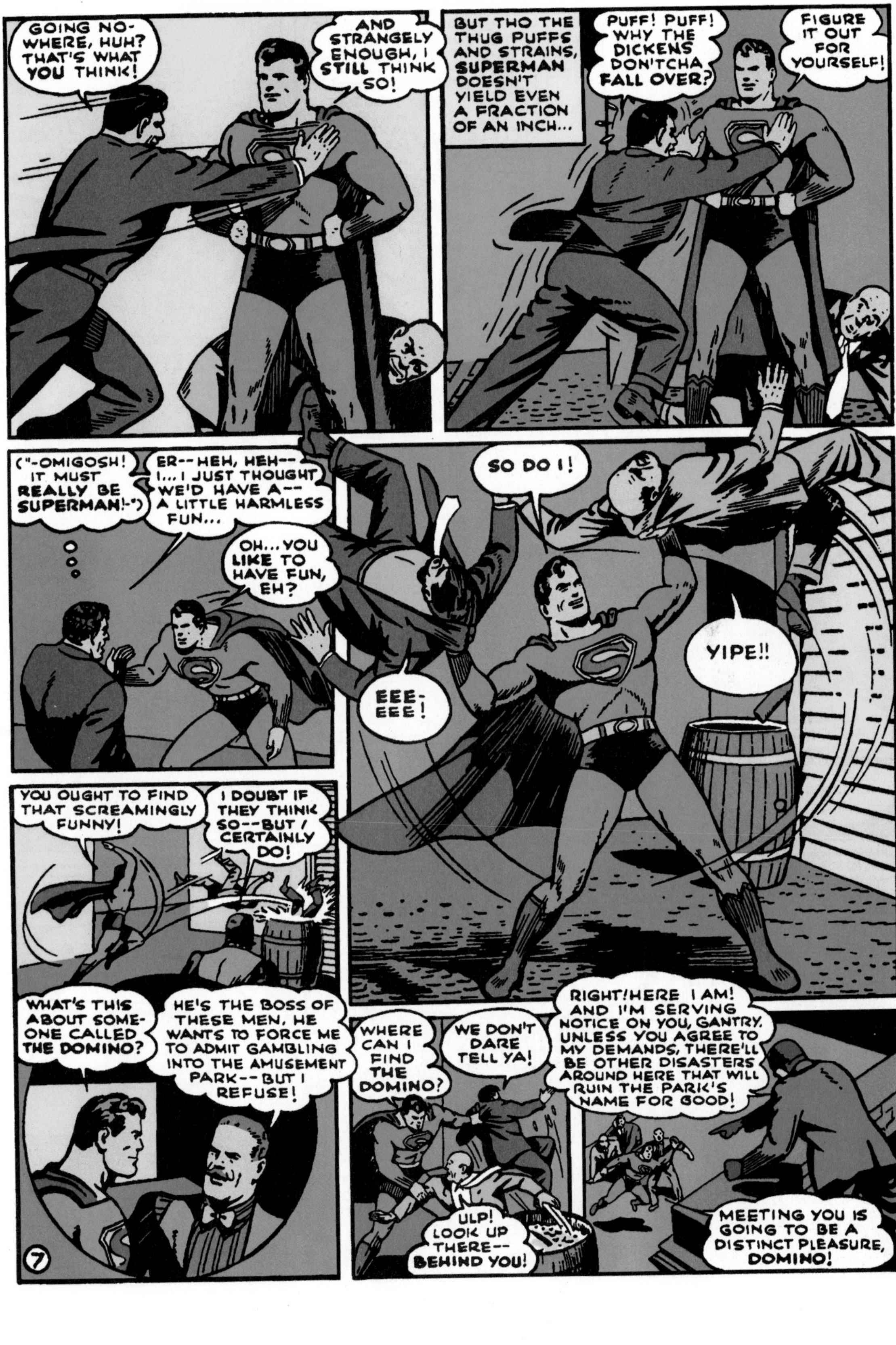
GOING NO-WHERE, HUH? THAT'S WHAT YOU THINK!
AND STRANGELY ENOUGH, I STILL THINK SO!
BUT THO THE THUG PUFFS AND STRAINS, SUPERMAN DOESN'T YIELD EVEN A FRACTION OF AN INCH...
PUFF! PUFF! WHY THE DICKENS DON'TCHA FALL OVER?
FIGURE IT OUT FOR YOURSELF!
("-OMIGOSH! IT MUST REALLY BE SUPERMAN!-")
ER--HEH, HEH--I... I JUST THOUGHT WE'D HAVE A--A LITTLE HARMLESS FUN...
OH... YOU LIKE TO HAVE FUN, EH?
SO DO I!
YIPE!!
EEE-EEE!
YOU OUGHT TO FIND THAT SCREAMINGLY FUNNY!
I DOUBT IF THEY THINK SO--BUT I CERTAINLY DO!
WHAT'S THIS ABOUT SOME-ONE CALLED THE DOMINO?
HE'S THE BOSS OF THESE MEN. HE WANTS TO FORCE ME TO ADMIT GAMBLING INTO THE AMUSEMENT PARK--BUT I REFUSE!
7
WHERE CAN I FIND THE DOMINO?
WE DON'T DARE TELL YA!
ULP! LOOK UP THERE--BEHIND YOU!
RIGHT! HERE I AM! AND I'M SERVING NOTICE ON YOU, GANTRY. UNLESS YOU AGREE TO MY DEMANDS, THERE'LL BE OTHER DISASTERS AROUND HERE THAT WILL RUIN THE PARK'S NAME FOR GOOD!
MEETING YOU IS GOING TO BE A DISTINCT PLEASURE, DOMINO!

A VERY DISTINCT PLEASURE!

BUT AS **SUPERMAN** ALIGHTS ATOP THE BUILDING, THE DOOR SLAMS IN HIS FACE...

LOCKED! I GUESS HE ISN'T ANXIOUS TO MAKE MY ACQUAINTANCE!

BUT WE MUSTN'T LET THAT STAND IN THE WAY OF A BEAUTIFUL FRIENDSHIP!

SO I'M BACK IN THE FUN HOUSE, AGAIN! I'D BETTER LOOK UP LOIS! I'LL BET SHE'S BURNING UP OVER MY ABSENCE!

BUT WHEN SUPERMAN REACHES THE CHUTE'S BOTTOM HE FINDS HIMSELF IN THE MIDST OF MERRYMAKERS...

L-LOOK!!

DON'T MIND ME, FOLKS!

A CHUTE-- THAT'S HOW HE MUST HAVE MADE HIS ESCAPE! WELL, I CAN SHOOT-THE-CHUTES, TOO!

LOIS! WHO'S THAT WITH YOU?

DON'T YOU KNOW HIM? HE'S JEFF FARNHAM, THE SOCIETY PLAYBOY, IF YOU'RE NOT INTERESTED IN MY COMPANY, HE IS!

I'LL SAY I AM!

WHY DON'T YOU RUN ALONG? DON'T YOU KNOW WHEN YOU'VE BEEN JILTED?

BUT LOIS-- I BROUGHT YOU HERE!

I DON'T LIKE TO BE IGNORED!

BUT CLARK'S PROTESTS CEASE AS HE TURNS AND SIGHTS A STARTLING SCENE...

WHAT'S **THIS**?

BESIDE THE *MILL-CHUTE*, TWO OF THE DOMINO'S THUGS ARE CONGRATULATING EACH OTHER...

A SWELL JOB!

THE DOMINO WILL BE PROUD OF US! BUT WE'D BETTER BEAT IT BEFORE THE FIREWORKS START!

STEPPING BETWEEN TWO BUILDINGS, CLARK KENT CHANGES TO SUPERMAN...

UNLESS MY SUPER-SENSITIVE HEARING IS TRICKING ME, THE DOMINO'S HIRELINGS ARE UP TO MISCHIEF!

WAIT A MINUTE! YOU'RE NOT LEAVING YET!

BUT YOU GOT TO LET US GO!

IT'S SURE DEATH IF WE STAY HERE!

EXPLAIN!

WE'VE PLANTED A BOMB AT THE BOTTOM OF THE *MILL-CHUTE*!

WHEN THE NEXT CAR STREAKS DOWN THE CHUTE INTO THE WATER, IT WILL HIT A BOMB AT THE BOTTOM OF THE CHUTE. THEN EVERYTHING WILL GO BLOOIE!

AT THAT VERY INSTANT, A BOAT FILLED WITH GAILY LAUGHING PASSENGERS BEGINS TO HURTLE DOWN THE ALMOST PERPENDICULAR CHUTE...!

SPRINGING IN, SUPERMAN HALTS THE BOAT'S DOWNWARD PLUNGE!

END OF THE RIDE!

BACK UP WITH YOU!

SNATCHING UP THE CONCEALED BOMB, SUPERMAN DESTROYS IT IN HIS BARE HANDS, THEN VAULTS AWAY...

ANOTHER FAILURE FOR THE DOMINO-- AND ANOTHER SCORE FOR ME TO EVEN WHEN I NEXT ENCOUNTER HIM!

⑨

MEANWHILE--AS LOIS AND JEFF RIDE INTO THE *DARK TURNS* CONCESSION....

AND THAT'S A FACT. I SEEM TO HAVE A CHARMED LIFE. EVERY TIME I GET IN TROUBLE, SUPERMAN POPS UP AND--PRESTO!--I'M OUT OF THE SOUP!

SUPERMAN CERTAINLY MUST THINK A LOT OF YOU. I CAN UNDERSTAND WHY!

SUDDENLY, IN THE DARKNESS, A PAIR OF STRONG ARMS SUDDENLY GRASP LOIS.

EEE-EEE! STOP

SHUT UP!!

GET HER OUT OF THE CAR!

I AM THE DOMINO! I OVERHEARD YOUR REMARK ABOUT SUPERMAN'S INTEREST IN YOU, YOU WILL MAKE A VALUABLE HOSTAGE!

WHAT HAVE YOU DONE WITH JEFF?

OKAY, DOMINO!

I'VE LEFT HIM BOUND AND HELPLESS BACK THERE IN THE DARKNESS ALONGSIDE A BOMB. AT THE PROPER MOMENT, HE WILL BE PROJECTED INTO ETERNITY!

YOU-- KILLER...!

EMERGING ON THE ROOF OF THE BUILDING, THE DOMINO LIGHTS A DYNAMITE STICK--THEN TOSSES IT AT THE NEARBY ROLLER COASTER TRACK...

THIS WILL SHOW GANTRY THAT THE DOMINO IS NOT TO BE TRIFLED WITH!

YOU'LL INJURE DOZENS OF INNOCENT PEOPLE!!

THAT'S NO CONCERN OF THE DOMINO!

THE DOMINO STILL UP TO HIS MURDEROUS TRICKS! CUTE FELLA!

10

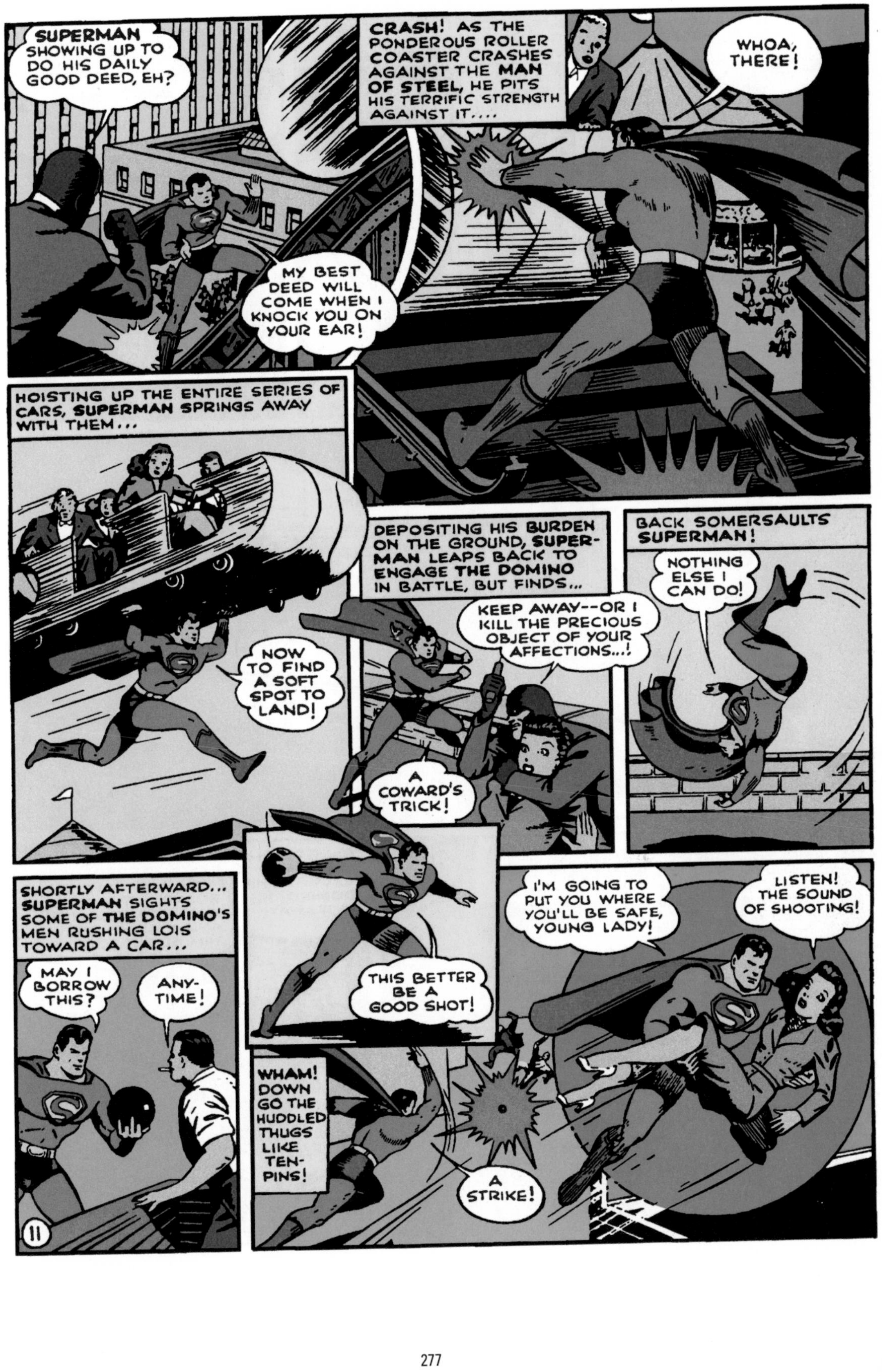

SUPERMAN SHOWING UP TO DO HIS DAILY GOOD DEED, EH?
MY BEST DEED WILL COME WHEN I KNOCK YOU ON YOUR EAR!
CRASH! AS THE PONDEROUS ROLLER COASTER CRASHES AGAINST THE MAN OF STEEL, HE PITS HIS TERRIFIC STRENGTH AGAINST IT....
WHOA, THERE!
HOISTING UP THE ENTIRE SERIES OF CARS, SUPERMAN SPRINGS AWAY WITH THEM...
NOW TO FIND A SOFT SPOT TO LAND!
DEPOSITING HIS BURDEN ON THE GROUND, SUPERMAN LEAPS BACK TO ENGAGE THE DOMINO IN BATTLE, BUT FINDS...
KEEP AWAY--OR I KILL THE PRECIOUS OBJECT OF YOUR AFFECTIONS...!
A COWARD'S TRICK!
BACK SOMERSAULTS SUPERMAN!
NOTHING ELSE I CAN DO!
SHORTLY AFTERWARD... SUPERMAN SIGHTS SOME OF THE DOMINO'S MEN RUSHING LOIS TOWARD A CAR...
MAY I BORROW THIS?
ANY-TIME!
11
THIS BETTER BE A GOOD SHOT!
WHAM! DOWN GO THE HUDDLED THUGS LIKE TEN-PINS!
A STRIKE!
I'M GOING TO PUT YOU WHERE YOU'LL BE SAFE, YOUNG LADY!
LISTEN! THE SOUND OF SHOOTING!

LED BY THE NEFARIOUS DOMINO HIMSELF, BANDITS STAGE A ROBBERY...

QUICK!

THIS STICKUP IS A CINCH!

BUT ANTICIPATING FURTHER TROUBLE, GANTRY HAS SUMMONED THE POLICE...

STOP! STOP OR WE FIRE!

SHOOT AND BE BLASTED!

TAKE TO HIDING ON THE MERRY-GO-ROUND!

A BLISTERING GUN-BATTLE BETWEEN THE DOMINO'S MEN AND THE FORCES OF THE LAW...

DON'T LET THOSE CROOKS ESCAPE!

YOU'VE TRAPPED THE DOMINO!

CHARGING INTO THE MIDST OF THE FRAY, DISREGARDING THE BULLETS THAT BOUND OFF HIS IMPENETRABLE SKIN, STREAKS --SUPERMAN!

SORRY TO INTRUDE!

DARTING IN AND GRASPING THE MERRY-GO-ROUND'S SIDE, SUPERMAN WHIRLS IT AROUND AT A SWIFTLY INCREASING SPEED...

I'LL GIVE THEM THEIR MONEY'S WORTH!

HEY!

STOP!

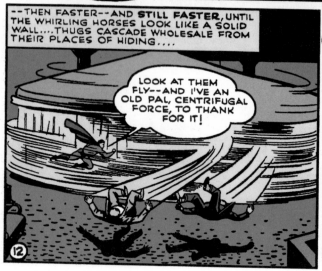

--THEN FASTER--AND STILL FASTER, UNTIL THE WHIRLING HORSES LOOK LIKE A SOLID WALL....THUGS CASCADE WHOLESALE FROM THEIR PLACES OF HIDING....

LOOK AT THEM FLY--AND I'VE AN OLD PAL, CENTRIFUGAL FORCE, TO THANK FOR IT!

12

YOU GOT 'EM ALL--ALL EXCEPT THE DOMINO! HE GOT AWAY!

HEAVENS! I JUST REMEMBERED! JEFF FARNHAM...HELPLESSLY BOUND IN THE DARK TURNS CONCESSION..., AND A BOMB BESIDE HIM ABOUT TO GO OFF...

IN THAT CASE I'D BETTER GO HELP HIM!

NO NEED TO! HERE I AM-- SAFE AND SOUND!

THANK HEAVEN YOU'RE SAFE! BUT HOW'D YOU GET FREE?

I MANAGED TO UNTIE MYSELF, THEN PUT OUT THE BOMB! SIMPLE!

("-MY X-RAY VISION... IT REVEALS SOMETHING INTERESTING IN JEFF'S POCKET!-")

YOU MADE ONE ERROR, JEFF! YOU LEFT AN IMPORTANT BIT OF EVIDENCE IN YOUR POCKET!

A MASK!

TH-THEN-- HE'S THE DOMINO!!

YES--I'M THE DOMINO ALL RIGHT! WHEN I RAN THRU MY FAMILY INHERITANCE, THERE WAS ONLY ONE WAY TO KEEP ME LIVING IN THE MANNER TO WHICH I WAS ACCUSTOMED-- CRIME AND GAMBLING!--IF ANY OF YOU MAKE A MOVE TO STOP ME, I'LL SET OFF THIS DYNAMITE!

BUT A POWERFUL PUFF FROM THE MAN OF STEEL'S POWER- FUL LUNGS EXTINGUISHES THE CIGARETTE LIGHTER...

WHAT--?

NOW IT'S GOING TO BE A MATTER OF BARE FISTS!

I'LL-- OW-WWCH!!

YOU HAD YOUR TURN!

NOW IT'S MINE!

WOTTA SOCK!

BUT IT SERVES HIM RIGHT! THE DOMINO IS A HEARTLESS KILLER!

GOODBYE, LOIS! I HOPE YOU ENJOYED YOUR VISIT TO THE PARK!

I CAME FOR RELAXATION AND GOT A NEWS YARN!

LOIS! I'VE BEEN LOOKING ALL OVER FOR YOU! DO YOU REALIZE WHAT'S BEEN GOING ON HERE? MURDER --EXCITEMENT--FIGHTING...

I KNOW ALL ABOUT IT. AND IF YOU WANT FURTHER DETAILS, YOU CAN READ IT IN THE DAILY PLANET BENEATH MY BYLINE!

THE END

13

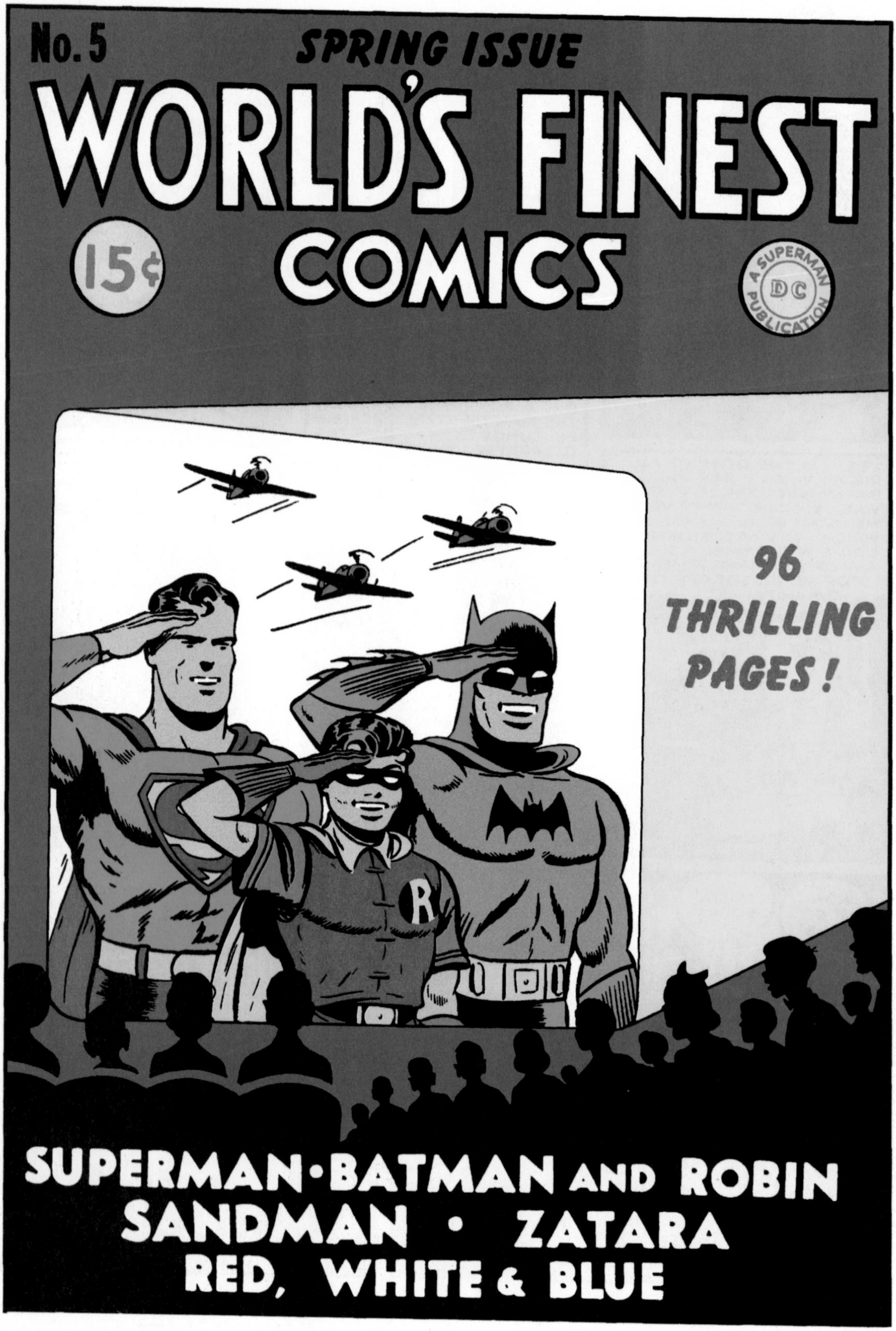
No. 5
SPRING ISSUE
WORLD'S FINEST COMICS
15¢
A SUPERMAN DC PUBLICATION
96 THRILLING PAGES!
SUPERMAN • BATMAN AND ROBIN
SANDMAN • ZATARA
RED, WHITE & BLUE

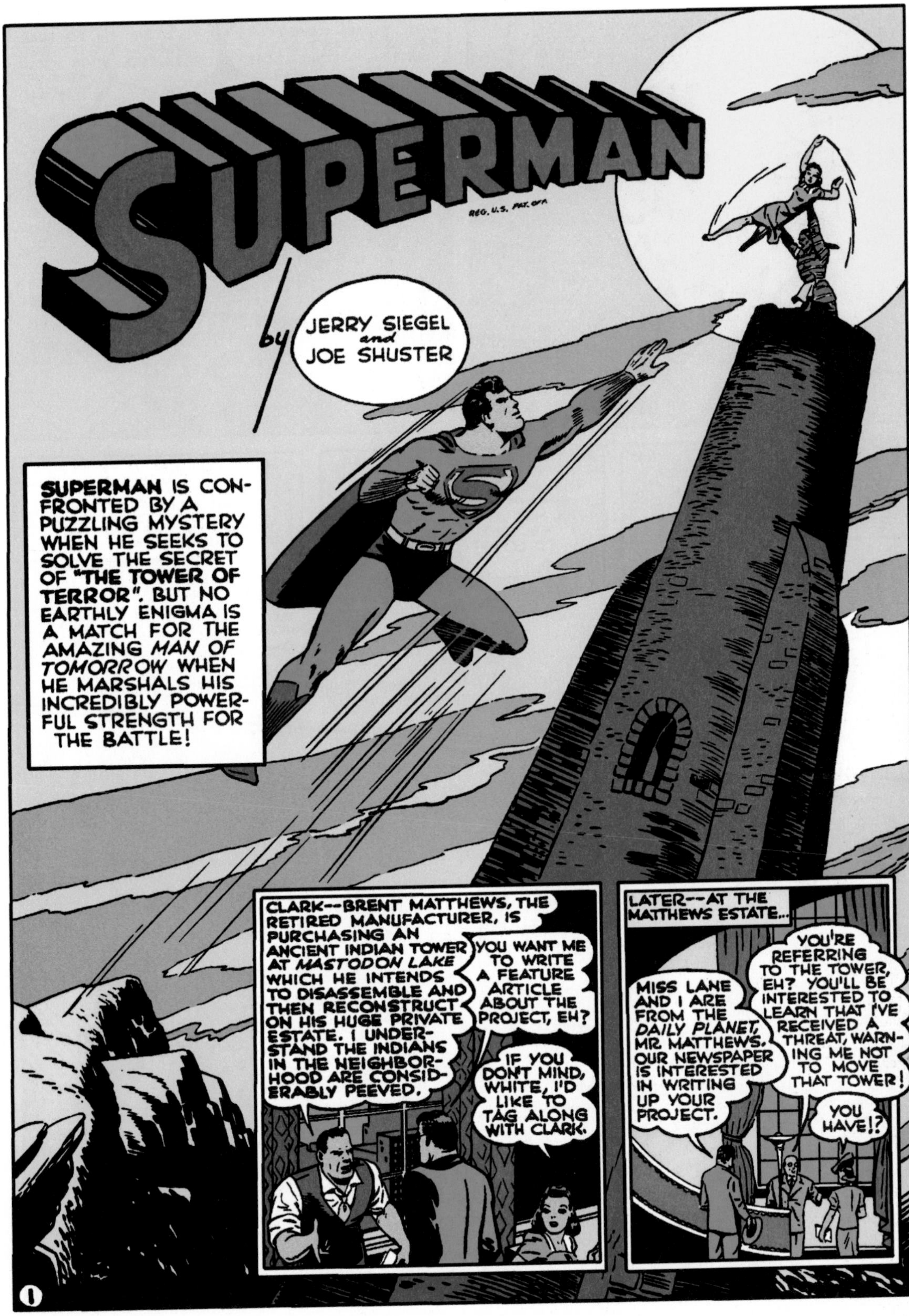
SUPERMAN
REG. U.S. PAT. OFF.
by JERRY SIEGEL and JOE SHUSTER
SUPERMAN IS CONFRONTED BY A PUZZLING MYSTERY WHEN HE SEEKS TO SOLVE THE SECRET OF "THE TOWER OF TERROR". BUT NO EARTHLY ENIGMA IS A MATCH FOR THE AMAZING MAN OF TOMORROW WHEN HE MARSHALS HIS INCREDIBLY POWERFUL STRENGTH FOR THE BATTLE!
CLARK--BRENT MATTHEWS, THE RETIRED MANUFACTURER, IS PURCHASING AN ANCIENT INDIAN TOWER AT MASTODON LAKE WHICH HE INTENDS TO DISASSEMBLE AND THEN RECONSTRUCT ON HIS HUGE PRIVATE ESTATE. I UNDERSTAND THE INDIANS IN THE NEIGHBORHOOD ARE CONSIDERABLY PEEVED.
YOU WANT ME TO WRITE A FEATURE ARTICLE ABOUT THE PROJECT, EH?
IF YOU DON'T MIND, WHITE, I'D LIKE TO TAG ALONG WITH CLARK.
LATER--AT THE MATTHEWS ESTATE...
MISS LANE AND I ARE FROM THE DAILY PLANET, MR. MATTHEWS. OUR NEWSPAPER IS INTERESTED IN WRITING UP YOUR PROJECT.
YOU'RE REFERRING TO THE TOWER, EH? YOU'LL BE INTERESTED TO LEARN THAT I'VE RECEIVED A THREAT, WARNING ME NOT TO MOVE THAT TOWER!
YOU HAVE!?
1

WHEN I AWOKE THIS MORNING, I FOUND THIS ARROW ON MY PILLOW! IT'S AN OMEN MEANT TO WARN ME!

AN INDIAN WAR-ARROW! I GUESS THOSE INDIANS ARE PRETTY SERIOUS IN THEIR OBJECTIONS!

WELL, THOSE IGNORANT SAVAGES CAN'T INTIMIDATE ME! HECK, I DON'T WANT TO DO THEIR SHRINE ANY HARM. I JUST WANT IT DISMANTLED AND SET UP HERE ON MY ESTATE. I WAS JUST ABOUT TO LEAVE FOR MASTODON LAKE. WOULD YOU CARE TO GO ALONG?

WE'D BE VERY PLEASED.

I'D LIKE TO GET A LOOK AT THAT TOWER!

BUT AS THEY REACH MATTHEWS' AUTO, CLARK'S ULTRA-KEEN VISION REVEALS THAT THE CAR HAS BEEN TAMPERED WITH SO THAT A WHEEL IS CERTAIN TO FALL OFF ONCE THE VEHICLE IS IN MOTION!

ON SECOND THOUGHT, I WON'T GO ALONG-- IF YOU DON'T MIND, LOIS CAN HANDLE THIS CAPABLY. THERE ARE OTHER THINGS I MUST DO!

THAT'S PERFECTLY ALL RIGHT WITH ME!

SORRY YOU CAN'T COME ALONG!

AS THE CAR DRIVES OFF, CLARK HURRIES BEHIND SOME SHRUBBERY...

NOT A SECOND TO LOSE!

SAFELY CONCEALED FROM ANY CHANCE OF OBSERVATION, THE NEWSPAPER REPORTER REMOVES HIS CIVILIAN GARMENTS, REVEALING THE COLORFUL COSTUME OF THE ONE AND ONLY SUPERMAN!

THEY'RE HEADED FOR TROUBLE-- UNLESS I ACT QUICKLY!

THE MAN OF STEEL RACES AFTER THE LIMOUSINE AT A PACE SO SWIFT HE RAPIDLY OVERTAKES IT...

THE WHEEL... ALREADY COMING LOOSE...!

AT THAT MOMENT-- THE WHEEL FALLS FROM THE SPEEDING AUTO...!

②

RACING IN WITH INCREDIBLE SPEED, THE *MAN OF STEEL* CATCHES THE TIRE....

NO YOU DON'T!

—THEN—BEFORE THE AXLE CAN STRIKE THE GROUND—SUPERMAN SEIZES THE CAR'S REAR AND KEEPS IT ALOFT...

A TICKLISH JOB!

AND THIS TIME IT WILL STAY ON!

THE MOST ASTOUNDING PHASE OF THE FEAT IS THAT THOSE WITHIN HAVE NO INKLING THAT THEIR LIVES WERE JUST SAVED BY SUPERMAN'S AMAZING SKILL!

HOW SMOOTHLY THE CAR RUNS!

IT OUGHT TO! IT COST ME A SMALL FORTUNE!

LEAPING SKYWARD, THE *MAN OF STEEL* FOLLOWS THE CAR...

NEVER CAN TELL...THEY MAY STILL NEED MY HELP...

DASHING ALONG, KEEPING THE AXLE RAISED ABOVE THE GROUND, SUPERMAN PERFORMS AN ASTONISHING FEAT. HE REPLACES THE WHEEL ON THE SPEEDING CAR, FASTENS IT SECURELY...

WHEN *MASTODON LAKE* IS REACHED....

I AM LEMUEL P. POTTS... SPECIALIST IN INDIAN LORE AT MOSELY MUSEUM, MR. MATTHEWS. I'VE COME TO ADD MY PLEAS TO THOSE OF THE INDIANS. PLEASE LEAVE THEIR SHRINE ALONE!

I'LL DO AS I PLEASE. I WANT THAT TOWER!

YOU WILL PAY FOR YOUR BLASPHEMY!

I'M SORRY YOU FEEL THAT WAY, MATTHEWS, THESE INDIANS ARE A HOT-BLOODED PEOPLE. I'D HATE TO BE THEIR ENEMY.

THREATS DON'T BOTHER ME, THERE ARE STILL POLICE YOU KNOW, AND THIS IS A CIVILIZED COUNTRY!

MATTHEWS WOULD DO WELL NOT TO BE TOO SURE OF HIM- SELF! THAT WHEEL WAS DELIBERATELY LOOSENED! AND THAT WAR-ARROW IS NO LAUGHING MATTER!

③

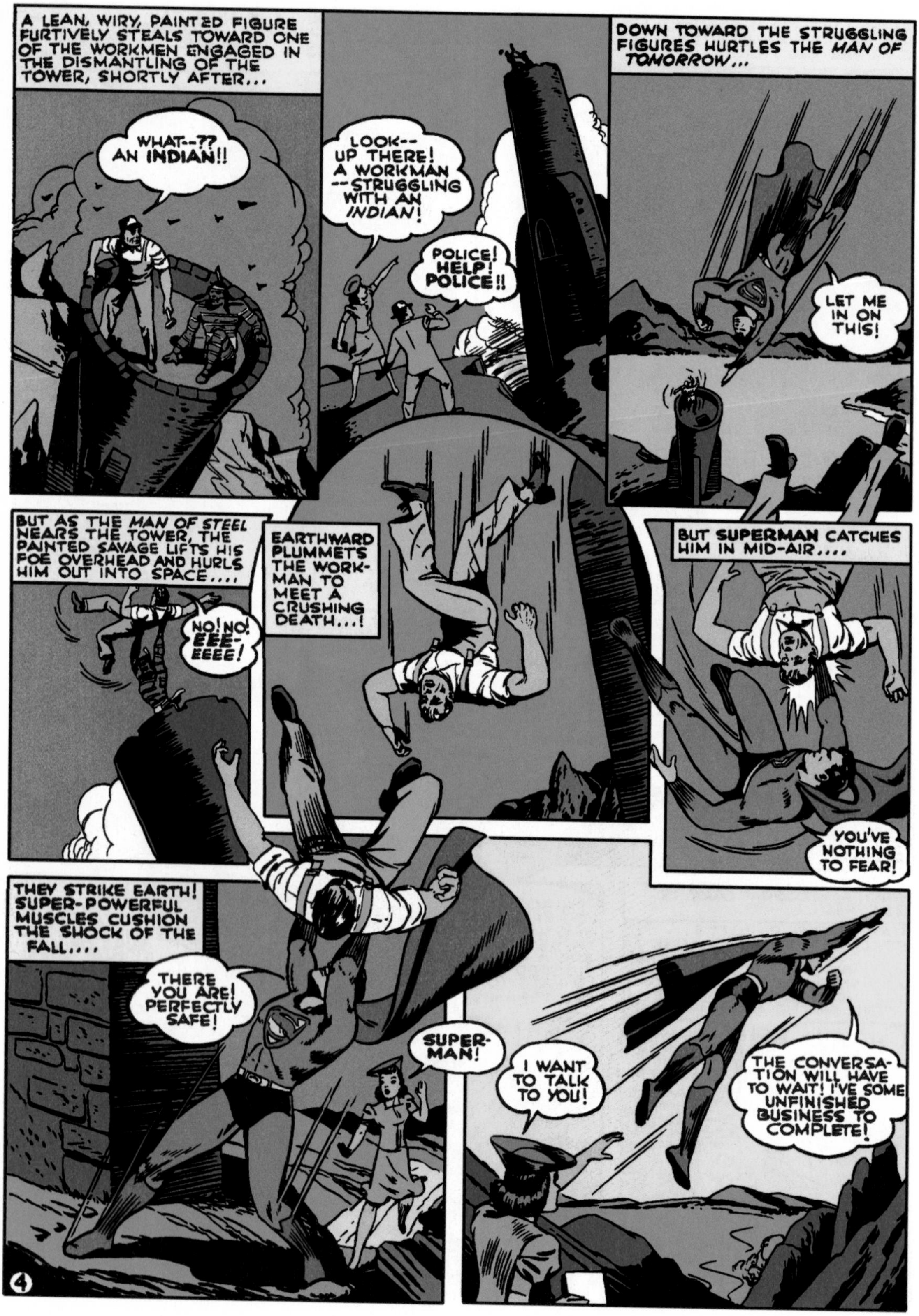
A LEAN, WIRY, PAINTED FIGURE FURTIVELY STEALS TOWARD ONE OF THE WORKMEN ENGAGED IN THE DISMANTLING OF THE TOWER, SHORTLY AFTER...
WHAT--?? AN INDIAN!!
LOOK-- UP THERE! A WORKMAN --STRUGGLING WITH AN INDIAN!
POLICE! HELP! POLICE!!
DOWN TOWARD THE STRUGGLING FIGURES HURTLES THE MAN OF TOMORROW...
LET ME IN ON THIS!
BUT AS THE MAN OF STEEL NEARS THE TOWER, THE PAINTED SAVAGE LIFTS HIS FOE OVERHEAD AND HURLS HIM OUT INTO SPACE....
NO! NO! EEE-EEEE!
EARTHWARD PLUMMETS THE WORKMAN TO MEET A CRUSHING DEATH...!
BUT SUPERMAN CATCHES HIM IN MID-AIR....
YOU'VE NOTHING TO FEAR!
THEY STRIKE EARTH! SUPER-POWERFUL MUSCLES CUSHION THE SHOCK OF THE FALL....
THERE YOU ARE! PERFECTLY SAFE!
SUPER-MAN!
4
I WANT TO TALK TO YOU!
THE CONVERSATION WILL HAVE TO WAIT! I'VE SOME UNFINISHED BUSINESS TO COMPLETE!

BUT AS HE REACHES THE TOWER'S TOP, THE MAN OF STEEL FINDS,...

NO TRACE OF THAT INDIAN!

AS HE REJOINS LOIS AND MATTHEWS...

MR. MATTHEWS, I'D LIKE YOU TO MEET SUPERMAN. I GUESS I DON'T HAVE TO EXPLAIN WHO HE IS... EVERYONE KNOWS THAT BY NOW.

OUCH! MY HAND!

SORRY! FORGOT MYSELF FOR A MOMENT. GLAD TO MEET YOU!

UNNOTICED BY ANYONE, AT THE REAR OF THE TOWER, A SECRET ENTRANCE OPENS AND A FURTIVE FIGURE SLIPS OUT AND AWAY...

THAT INDIAN--THE WAY HE CAME AND DIS- APPEARED! COULD IT HAVE BEEN A GHOST? PERHAPS YOU'D BETTER ABANDON YOUR PROJECT.

I WILL NOT! I BOUGHT THAT TOWER FROM THE COUNTY AND I AIM TO HAVE IT ON MY ESTATE REGARD- LESS OF THE CONSEQUENCES.

JUST WATCH!

SINCE YOUR MIND IS MADE UP, PERHAPS I CAN BE OF SOME HELP TO YOU.

WHAT'S HE UP TO?

I'VE A VAGUE IDEA, AND IF IT IS WHAT I THINK IT IS, YOU'RE IN FOR AN AMAZING SIGHT!

SEIZING THE TOWER'S SIDE, SUPERMAN RIPS IT CLEAR OUT OF THE GROUND....

SIMPLE, EH?

GOOD HEAVENS! L-LOOK!!

THAT'S SUPERMAN FOR YOU!

5

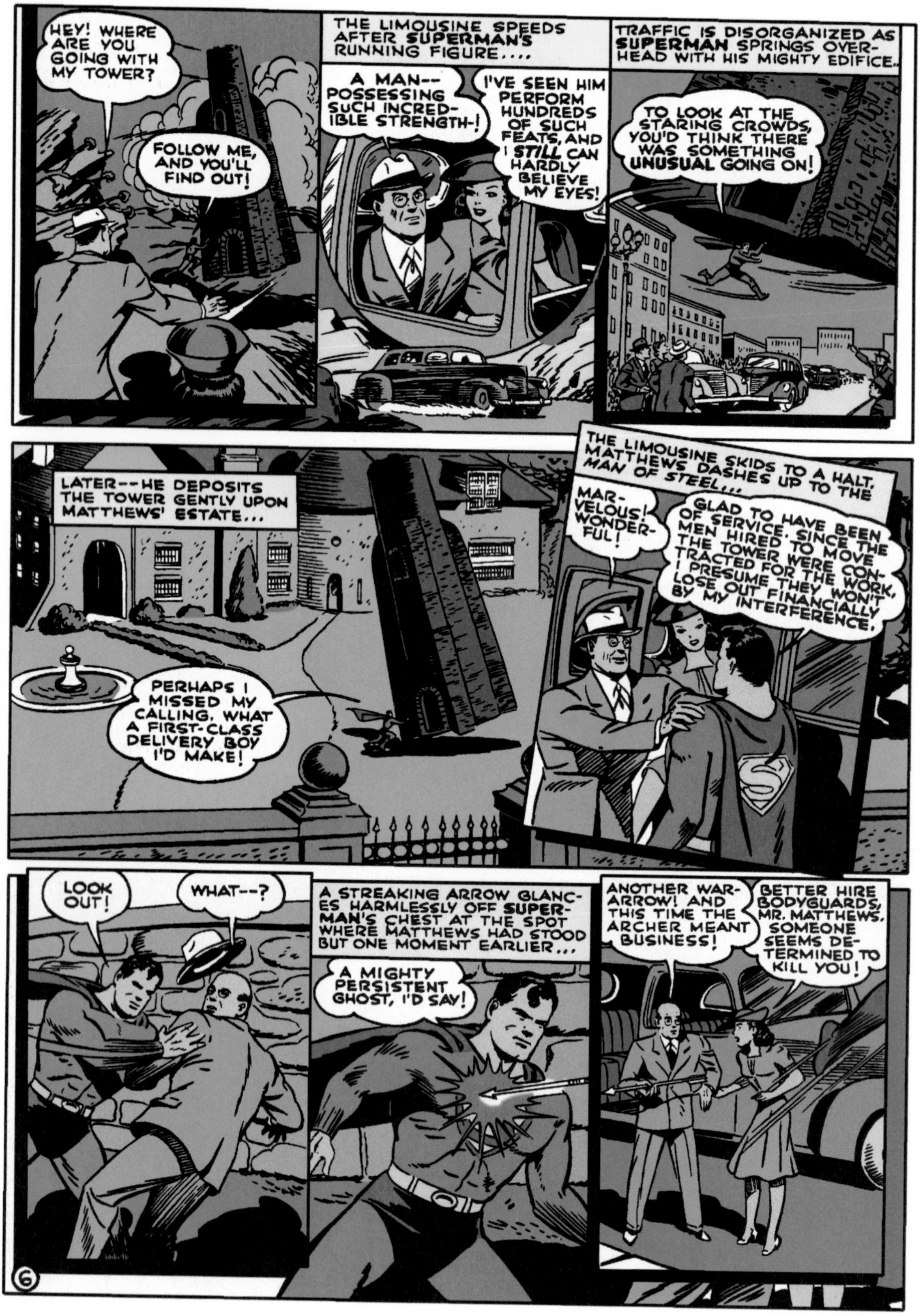
HEY! WHERE ARE YOU GOING WITH MY TOWER?
FOLLOW ME, AND YOU'LL FIND OUT!
THE LIMOUSINE SPEEDS AFTER SUPERMAN'S RUNNING FIGURE....
A MAN-- POSSESSING SUCH INCREDIBLE STRENGTH-!
I'VE SEEN HIM PERFORM HUNDREDS OF SUCH FEATS, AND I STILL CAN HARDLY BELIEVE MY EYES!
TRAFFIC IS DISORGANIZED AS SUPERMAN SPRINGS OVERHEAD WITH HIS MIGHTY EDIFICE.
TO LOOK AT THE STARING CROWDS, YOU'D THINK THERE WAS SOMETHING UNUSUAL GOING ON!
LATER--HE DEPOSITS THE TOWER GENTLY UPON MATTHEWS' ESTATE...
PERHAPS I MISSED MY CALLING. WHAT A FIRST-CLASS DELIVERY BOY I'D MAKE!
THE LIMOUSINE SKIDS TO A HALT. MATTHEWS DASHES UP TO THE MAN OF STEEL...
MARVELOUS! WONDERFUL!
GLAD TO HAVE BEEN OF SERVICE. SINCE THE MEN HIRED TO MOVE THE TOWER WERE CONTRACTED FOR THE WORK, I PRESUME THEY WON'T LOSE OUT FINANCIALLY BY MY INTERFERENCE.
LOOK OUT!
WHAT--?
6
A STREAKING ARROW GLANCES HARMLESSLY OFF SUPERMAN'S CHEST AT THE SPOT WHERE MATTHEWS HAD STOOD BUT ONE MOMENT EARLIER...
A MIGHTY PERSISTENT GHOST, I'D SAY!
ANOTHER WAR-ARROW! AND THIS TIME THE ARCHER MEANT BUSINESS!
BETTER HIRE BODYGUARDS, MR. MATTHEWS. SOMEONE SEEMS DETERMINED TO KILL YOU!

HURTLING BACK AND FORTH ABOVE THE SURROUNDING DISTRICTS, SUPERMAN FINDS NO TRACE OF MATTHEWS' WOULD-BE ASSASSIN...

A SLIPPERY GENT, IF THERE EVER WAS ONE! I'M ALMOST INCLINED TO BELIEVE THAT HE IS A GHOST!

NOW TO CHANGE BACK TO CLARK KENT.

LATER... AT THE *DAILY PLANET*

SO HERE YOU ARE! AND WHY DIDN'T YOU STICK WITH MATTHEWS?

I HAD ALL THE INFORMATION I WANTED.

YOU DID, EH? BUT YOU DIDN'T KNOW THAT MATTHEWS WAS ABOUT TO BE AIDED AND RESCUED BY *SUPERMAN*-- THAT THE TOWER IS HAUNTED BY A JINX! IF IT HADN'T BEEN FOR LOIS, WE'D HAVE MISSED THE STORY ENTIRELY!

I--I'M SORRY!

I SEEM TO BE IN THE DOG-HOUSE.

AND WITH GOOD REASON! YOU'RE SLIPPING, CLARK!

THAT EVENING...

MATTHEWS IS BY NO MEANS OUT OF DANGER!

THRU THE NIGHT HURTLES THE *MAN OF TOMORROW* TOWARD THE MATTHEWS ESTATE...

I'D BETTER KEEP A SHARP LOOKOUT OVER HIM!

7

AS BRENT MATTHEWS RETIRES...

MY HOME SURROUNDED BY GUARDS...AND YET I STILL CAN'T HELP FEELING UNEASY!

MEANWHILE--THE BODYGUARDS FALL VICTIMS TO A TEAM OF VICIOUS THUGS...

GUARDS! GUARDS!

NO USE SHOUTING FOR HELP!

THEY WON'T HEAR YOU!

THE RETIRED MILLION-AIRE IS OVERCOME AFTER A BRIEF, FUTILE STRUGGLE...

MINUTES LATER... SUPERMAN ARRIVES...

THE GUARDS-- UNCONSCIOUS..!

AT THAT INSTANT, A HIGH-POWERED CAR ROARS OUT OF THE DRIVEWAY...

THIS IS ANOTHER TIME MY X-RAY VISION COMES IN HANDY!

THE MAN OF STEEL'S AMAZING VISION ENABLES HIM TO SEE MATTHEWS A PRISONER WITH-IN THE INTERIOR OF THE AUTO...

YOU'LL NEVER GET AWAY WITH THIS!

FUNNY, WE DON'T AGREE WITH YOU!

THEY'RE DUE FOR A BIG SURPRISE!

8

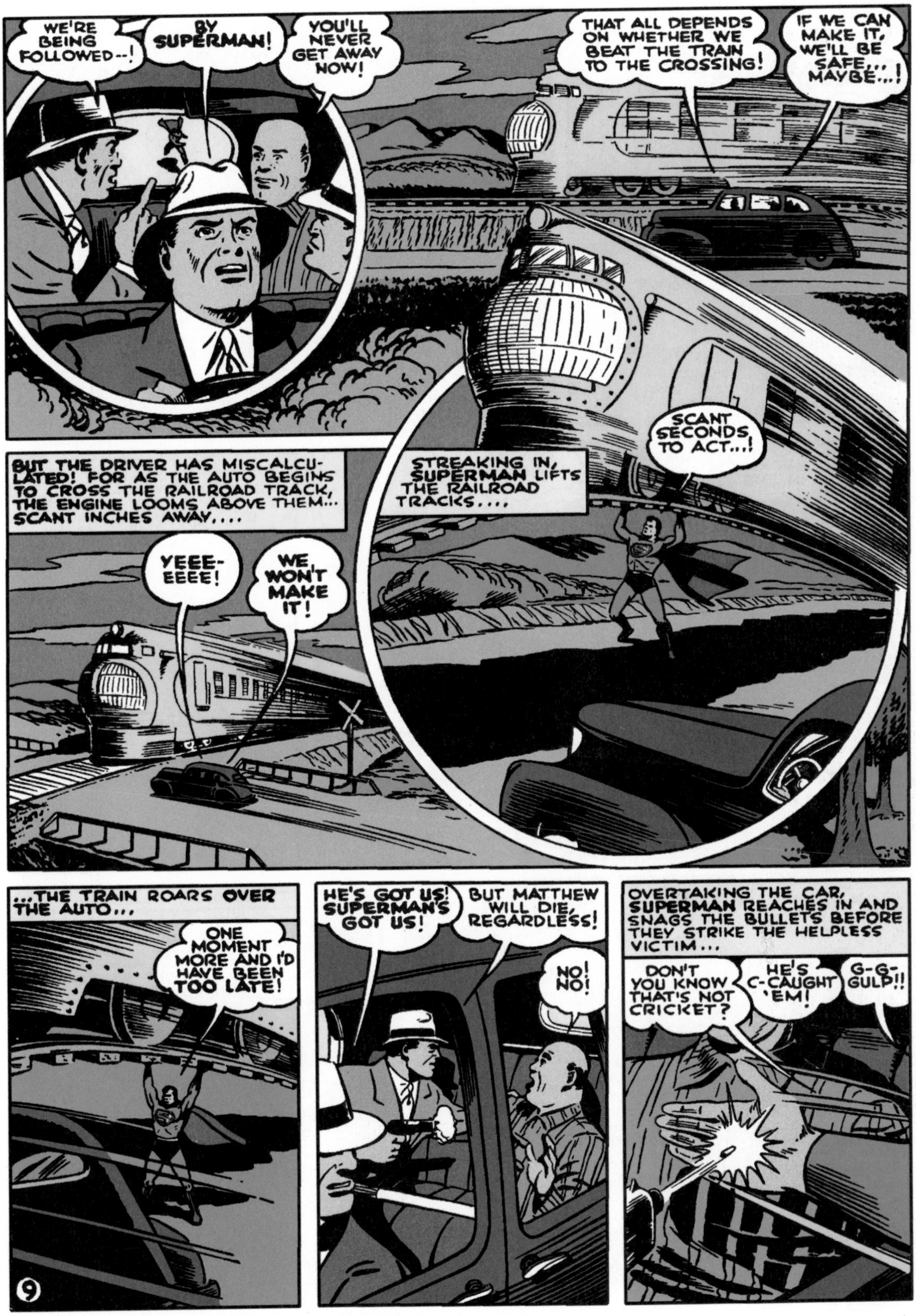
WE'RE BEING FOLLOWED--!
BY SUPERMAN!
YOU'LL NEVER GET AWAY NOW!
THAT ALL DEPENDS ON WHETHER WE BEAT THE TRAIN TO THE CROSSING!
IF WE CAN MAKE IT, WE'LL BE SAFE... MAYBE...!
BUT THE DRIVER HAS MISCALCULATED! FOR AS THE AUTO BEGINS TO CROSS THE RAILROAD TRACK, THE ENGINE LOOMS ABOVE THEM... SCANT INCHES AWAY....
YEEE-EEEE!
WE, WON'T MAKE IT!
STREAKING IN, SUPERMAN LIFTS THE RAILROAD TRACKS....
SCANT SECONDS TO ACT...!
...THE TRAIN ROARS OVER THE AUTO...
ONE MOMENT MORE AND I'D HAVE BEEN TOO LATE!
9
HE'S GOT US! SUPERMAN'S GOT US!
BUT MATTHEW WILL DIE, REGARDLESS!
NO! NO!
OVERTAKING THE CAR, SUPERMAN REACHES IN AND SNAGS THE BULLETS BEFORE THEY STRIKE THE HELPLESS VICTIM...
DON'T YOU KNOW THAT'S NOT CRICKET?
HE'S C-CAUGHT 'EM!
G-G-GULP!!

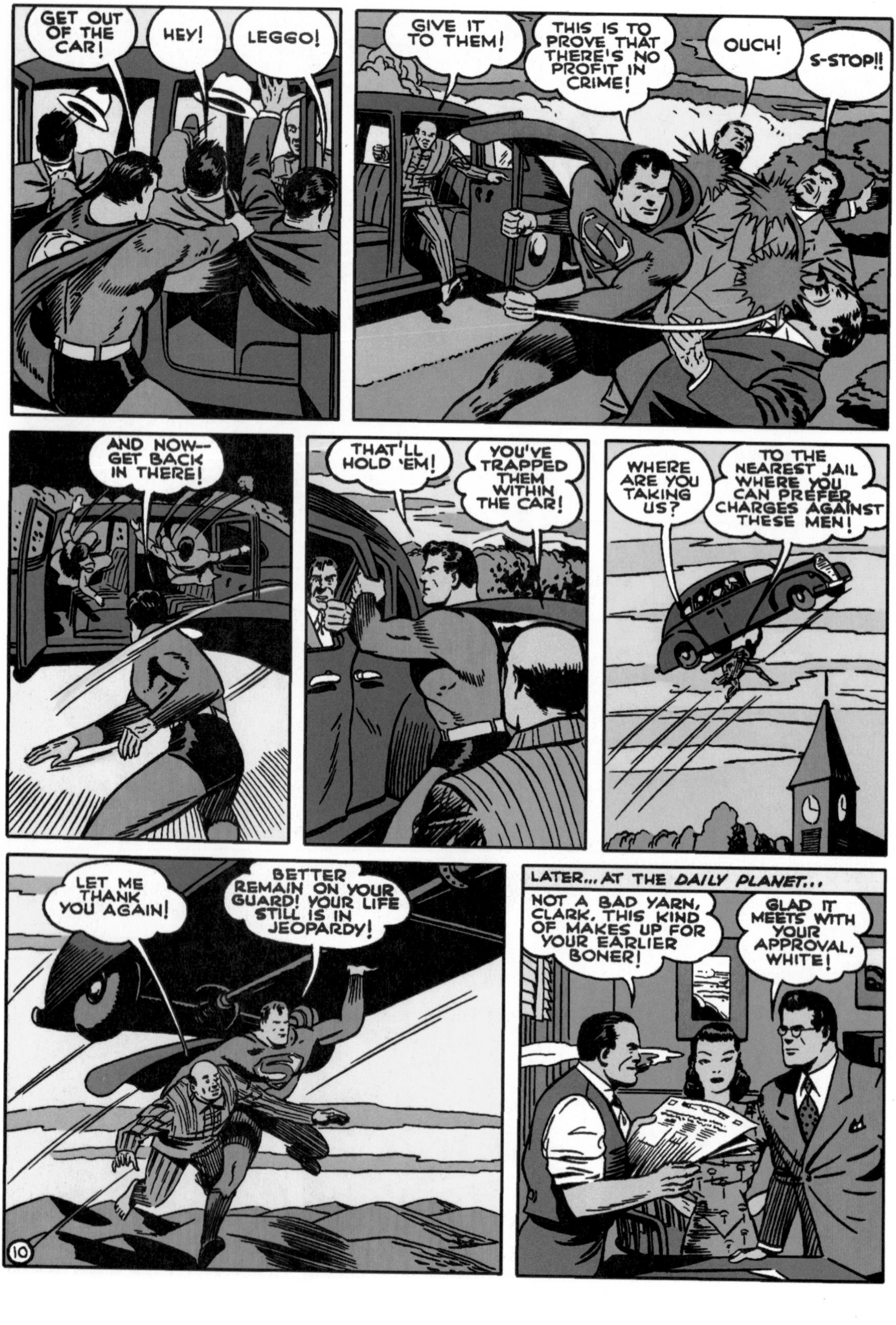

GET OUT OF THE CAR!
HEY!
LEGGO!
GIVE IT TO THEM!
THIS IS TO PROVE THAT THERE'S NO PROFIT IN CRIME!
OUCH!
S-STOP!!
AND NOW-- GET BACK IN THERE!
THAT'LL HOLD 'EM!
YOU'VE TRAPPED THEM WITHIN THE CAR!
WHERE ARE YOU TAKING US?
TO THE NEAREST JAIL WHERE YOU CAN PREFER CHARGES AGAINST THESE MEN!
LET ME THANK YOU AGAIN!
BETTER REMAIN ON YOUR GUARD! YOUR LIFE STILL IS IN JEOPARDY!
10
LATER... AT THE DAILY PLANET...
NOT A BAD YARN, CLARK, THIS KIND OF MAKES UP FOR YOUR EARLIER BONER!
GLAD IT MEETS WITH YOUR APPROVAL, WHITE!

LET'S GO, CLARK! IF WE HURRY TO THE POLICE STATION, WE MAY LEARN WHO HIRED THOSE MEN AND GET AN INKLING OF WHAT THIS IS ALL ABOUT!

A GOOD IDEA! LEAD ON!

BUT MEANWHILE...

ARE YOU GOING TO TELL US WHY YOU KIDNAPPED MATTHEWS?

IT'S AS I TOLD YA... WE WERE PAID TO DO IT!

BUT BY WHOM?

WE'LL --WE'LL TELL YA...!

BUT BEFORE THE THUGS HAVE A CHANCE TO DIVULGE THEIR KNOWLEDGE, ARROWS WHIZ IN THRU THE CELL'S WINDOW!!

AAAGH-HH!

ARROWS!

THE KILLER'S OUTSIDE THE JAIL! GET HIM!

CLARK AND LOIS REACH THE JAIL TO FIND IT IN CONFUSED DISORDER...

WHAT HAPPENED?

TWO PRISONERS... SLAIN BY ARROWS AS THEY WERE ABOUT TO CONFESS!!

NO YOU DON'T! I'M PHONING IN THIS STORY!

THIS IS ONE TIME I WISH I WEREN'T A GENTLEMAN!

("-THE INDIAN'S STRUCK AGAIN!-")

TOUGH IT HAD TO HAPPEN JUST WHEN THEY WERE ABOUT TO TALK, ISN'T IT? I'M GOING TO CALL ON MATTHEWS FOR A STATEMENT. WANT TO COME ALONG?

NOTHING DOING! I'M NO NIGHT OWL LIKE YOU BIRDS... I'M GOING HOME AND SLEEP!

THIS AFFAIR POSITIVELY GETS ALL THE MORE SPOOKY AS IT GOES ALONG! I WONDER IF MATTHEWS HAS BEEN HOLD-ING ANYTHING OUT ON US?

ONCE AGAIN MATTHEWS RETIRES....

WHAT A HECTIC EVENING! THANK HEAVEN THE FIRE-WORKS ARE OVER!

AS MATTHEWS TURNS, HE STIFFENS WITH TERROR...

AN INDIAN!

AN UNEQUAL BATTLE...!

WALKING INTO THE MATTHEWS ESTATE, LOIS UNEXPECTEDLY COMES FACE TO FACE WITH THE PAINTED SAVAGE AND HIS CAPTIVE....

OH-HHH!

THE GIRL REPORTER TURNS TO RUN. BUT AS A BROWN ARM ENCIRCLES HER, SHE FAINTS IN TERROR...

I CAN'T GET TO SLEEP—WORRYING ABOUT LOIS...SHE HAS A BETTER APTITUDE FOR GETTING INTO TROUBLE THAN ANYONE I'VE EVER KNOWN...I'D BETTER CHANGE TO SUPERMAN...

12

THRU THE DARK NIGHT HURTLES THE POWERFUL *MAN OF TOMORROW*. BUT AS HE REACHES THE MATTHEWS ESTATE EVEN HIS PERFECT CONTROL OF EXPRESSION IS SHATTERED BY THE AMAZING SIGHT BELOW....

GOOD GRIEF! WHAT GOES ON DOWN THERE--???

SEATED CROSS-LEGGED BEFORE THE GREAT TOWER, PLAYING A WEIRD TUNE ON A STRANGE INSTRUMENT--THE FIGURE OF AN AMERICAN INDIAN, AND AS HE SWAYS IN RHYTHM TO THE FANTASTIC TUNE, THE MIGHTY TOWER SWAYS IN UNISON...

SWOOPING DOWN, THE *MAN OF TOMORROW* SNATCHES UP THE UNCONSCIOUS FIGURES OF LOIS AND MATTHEWS FROM THE TOP OF THE DANGEROUSLY STRAINING TOWER...

THAT MUSIC... CRUMBLING THE TOWER AS A GLASS SHATTERS FROM THE NOTE OF A VIOLIN! THE TOWER CAN'T LAST MUCH LONGER!

DEPOSITING THEM A SAFE DISTANCE AWAY, HE RACES TOWARD THE SOLITARY FIGURE...

YOU'LL PLAY ANOTHER TUNE BEFORE I'M FINISHED WITH YOU!

BUT AS THE INDIAN TURNS TO FLEE-- WITH A MIGHTY ROAR, THE TOWER COLLAPSES UPON THE TWO FOES...

AS MATTHEWS AND LOIS LANE REVIVE, SUPERMAN DIGS HIMSELF FREE FROM THE WRECKAGE...

THE INDIAN... CRUSHED... DYING...

BEND OVER... LISTEN...

CLOSER SCRUTINY OF THE "INDIAN" REVEALS AN ASTONISHING SECRET...

LEMUEL P. POTTS!

JUST A WEEK AGO-- I LEARNED FROM AN OLD MANUSCRIPT THAT ANCIENT INDIAN VALUABLES WERE HIDDEN IN THE TOWER. I KNEW THAT IF THE TOWER WAS DISMANTLED, THE TREASURE I WANTED WOULD BE DISCLOSED BEFORE I COULD GET AT IT...SO...I STIRRED UP THE INDIANS AGAINST MATTHEWS...THEN..DONNED THIS DISGUISE...I.....I.... AHH-HHH...

MY WORD! IF I HAD ONLY KNOWN...!

WHERE ARE YOU GOING?

TO RUSH THIS STORY INTO PRINT!

STRANGE... BUT I'VE A PECULIAR FEELING THAT CLARK KENT IS GOING TO BEAT YOU TO IT AGAIN!

THE END

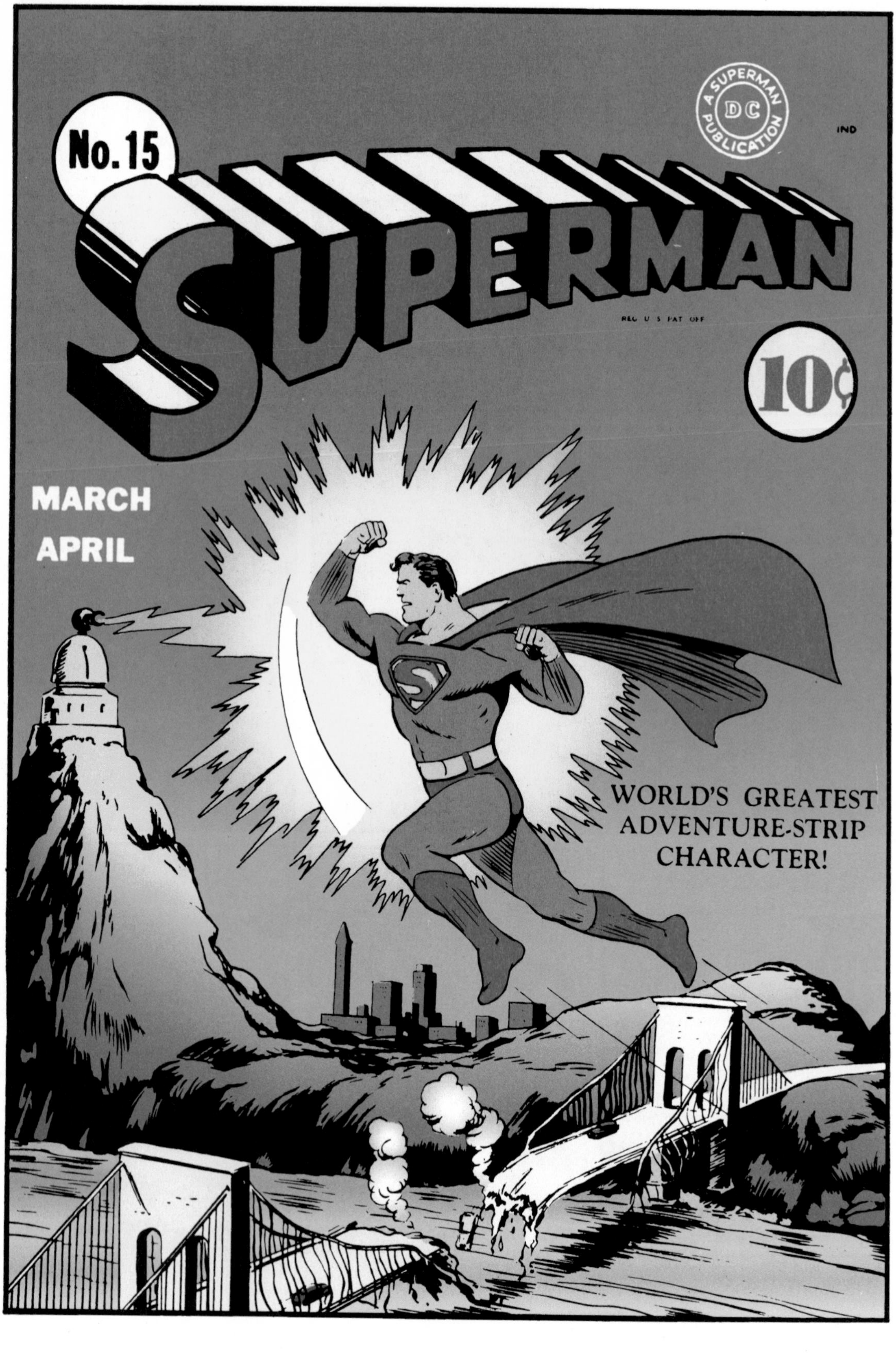
No. 15
A SUPERMAN DC PUBLICATION
IND
SUPERMAN
REG U S PAT OFF
10¢
MARCH
APRIL
WORLD'S GREATEST
ADVENTURE-STRIP
CHARACTER!

Attaining SUPER-HEALTH
A FEW HINTS FROM SUPERMAN!

THE SECRET OF BUILDING POWERFUL MUSCULAR CONTROL IS *REGULAR, DAILY, EXERCISE!* HOWEVER **AVOID OVERSTRAIN!**

DON'T WEAKEN IN YOUR DETERMINATION TO EXERCISE DAILY. -- ITS HARD WORK TO STIFFEN SOFT MUSCLES INTO *SINEWS OF STEEL* -- *BUT BOY, IT'S WORTH IT!*

> I GAVE UP EXERCISING AFTER A FEW DAYS

> *I* DIDN'T!

IN UNITY THERE IS **STRENGTH!** FORM *EXERCISE CLUBS* WITH YOUR CLOSE PALS SO THAT YOU'LL ALL BENEFIT!

> ALL TOGETHER, FELLAS!

DON'T SLOUCH! KEEP YOUR HEAD HIGH, SHOULDERS BACK, CHIN IN AND CHEST OUT. YOU'LL BE SURPRISED AT THE CONFIDENCE YOU GAIN IN YOURSELF.

> I DON'T LIKE JOHNNY. MY! LOOK HOW TERRIBLE HE SLOUCHES WHEN HE WALKS!

> LARRY STRIDES SO STRAIGHT AND MANLY. I THINK HE'S **WONDERFUL!**

A WELL-ROUNDED DIET IS, OF COURSE, ESSENTIAL, FRUITS, VEGETABLES, AND *PLENTY OF MILK* ARE ADVISABLE

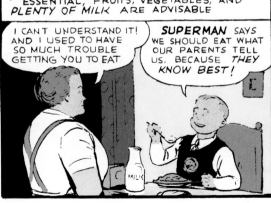

> I CAN'T UNDERSTAND IT! AND I USED TO HAVE SO MUCH TROUBLE GETTING YOU TO EAT

> *SUPERMAN* SAYS WE SHOULD EAT WHAT OUR PARENTS TELL US, BECAUSE *THEY KNOW BEST!*

MENTAL HEALTH IS INEXTRICABLY LINKED WITH PHYSICAL HEALTH. ALWAYS DO THE RIGHT AND JUST THING -- HELP OTHERS, KEEP YOUR CONSCIENCE CLEAR. . . . THAT'S *SUPER-LIVING!*

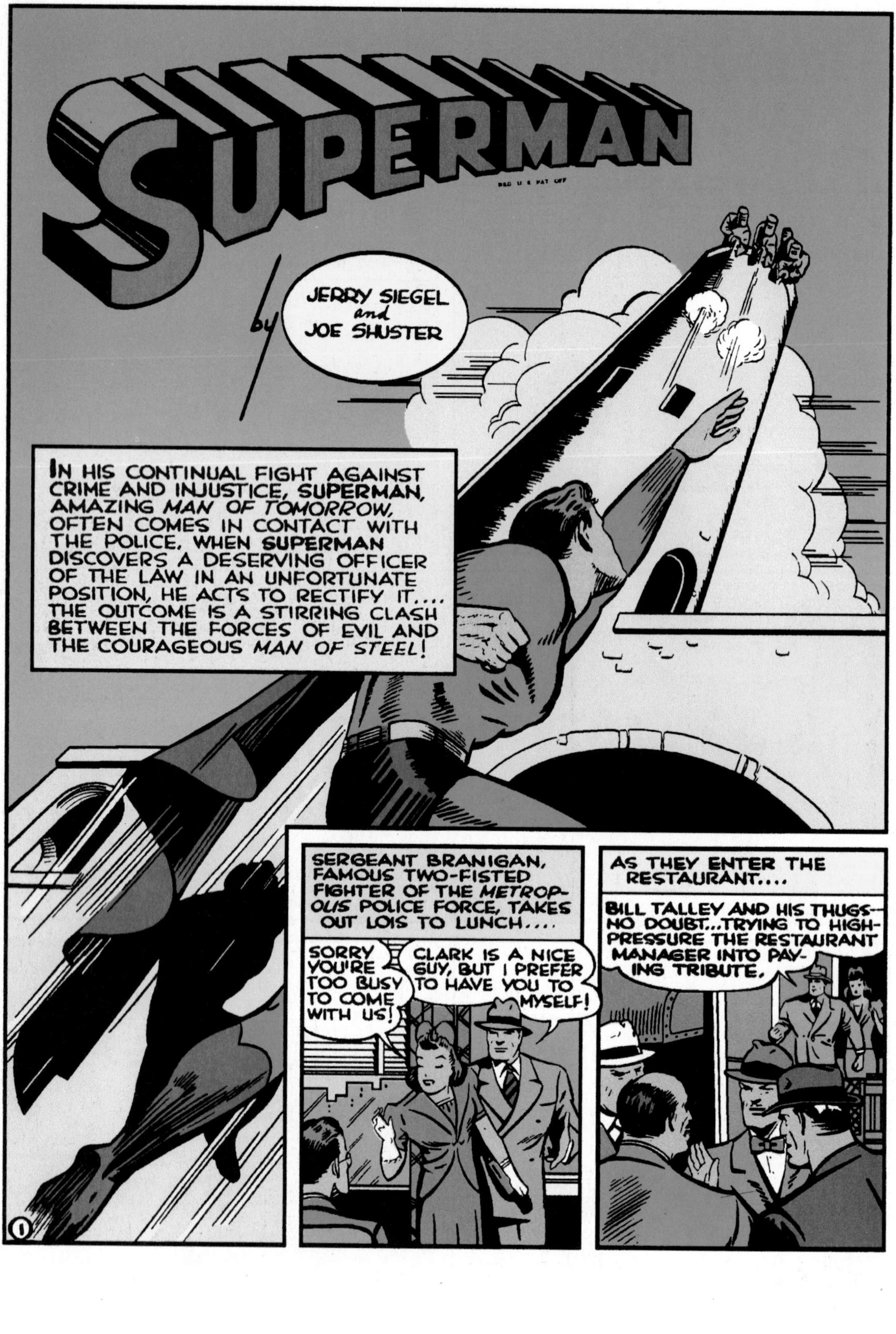
SUPERMAN
by
JERRY SIEGEL and JOE SHUSTER
IN HIS CONTINUAL FIGHT AGAINST CRIME AND INJUSTICE, SUPERMAN, AMAZING MAN OF TOMORROW, OFTEN COMES IN CONTACT WITH THE POLICE. WHEN SUPERMAN DISCOVERS A DESERVING OFFICER OF THE LAW IN AN UNFORTUNATE POSITION, HE ACTS TO RECTIFY IT.... THE OUTCOME IS A STIRRING CLASH BETWEEN THE FORCES OF EVIL AND THE COURAGEOUS MAN OF STEEL!
1
SERGEANT BRANIGAN, FAMOUS TWO-FISTED FIGHTER OF THE METROPOLIS POLICE FORCE, TAKES OUT LOIS TO LUNCH....
SORRY YOU'RE TOO BUSY TO COME WITH US!
CLARK IS A NICE GUY, BUT I PREFER TO HAVE YOU TO MYSELF!
AS THEY ENTER THE RESTAURANT....
BILL TALLEY AND HIS THUGS--NO DOUBT...TRYING TO HIGH-PRESSURE THE RESTAURANT MANAGER INTO PAYING TRIBUTE.

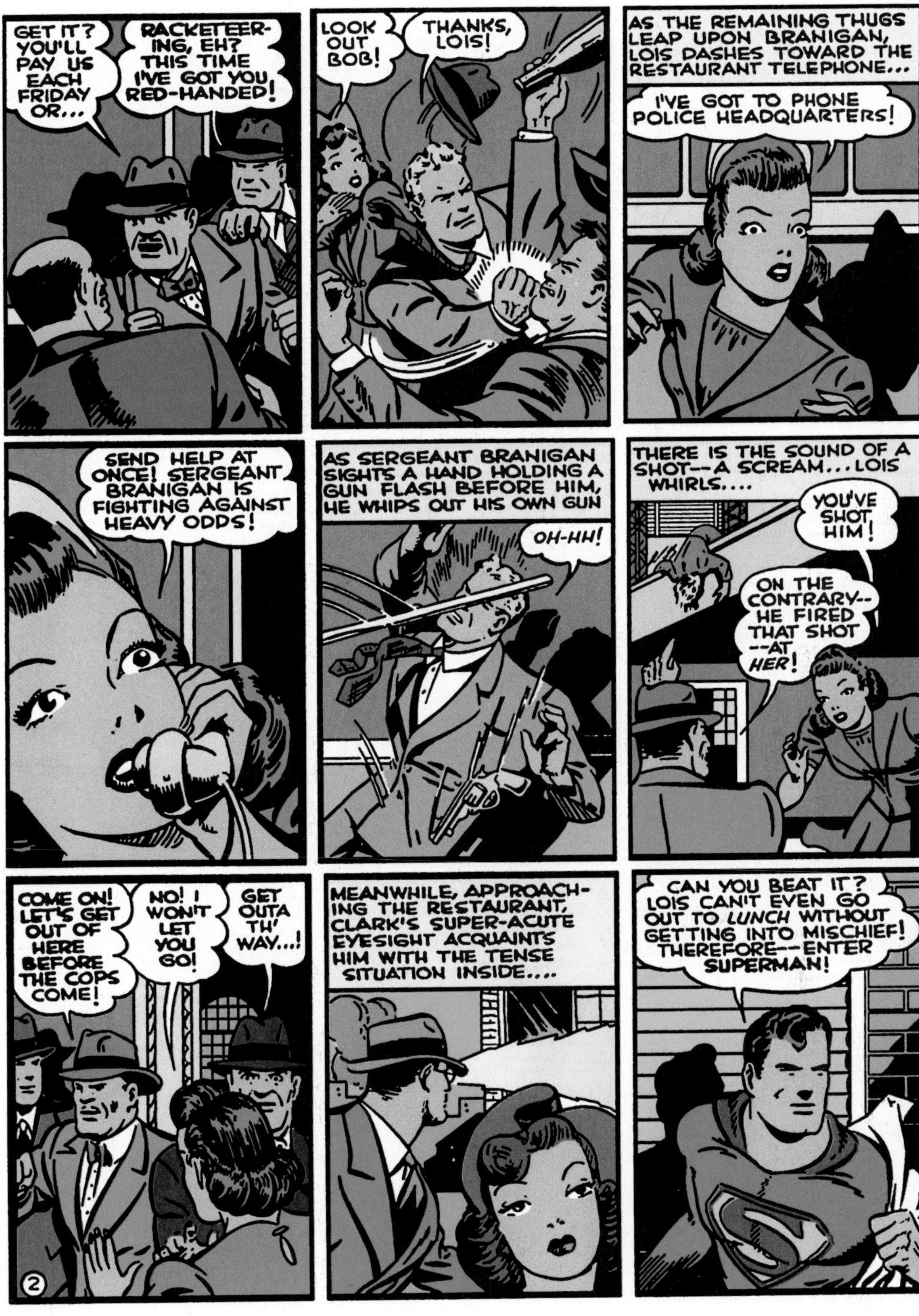
GET IT? YOU'LL PAY US EACH FRIDAY OR...
RACKETEERING, EH? THIS TIME I'VE GOT YOU RED-HANDED!
LOOK OUT BOB!
THANKS, LOIS!
AS THE REMAINING THUGS LEAP UPON BRANIGAN, LOIS DASHES TOWARD THE RESTAURANT TELEPHONE...
I'VE GOT TO PHONE POLICE HEADQUARTERS!
SEND HELP AT ONCE! SERGEANT BRANIGAN IS FIGHTING AGAINST HEAVY ODDS!
AS SERGEANT BRANIGAN SIGHTS A HAND HOLDING A GUN FLASH BEFORE HIM, HE WHIPS OUT HIS OWN GUN
OH-HH!
THERE IS THE SOUND OF A SHOT--A SCREAM... LOIS WHIRLS....
YOU'VE SHOT HIM!
ON THE CONTRARY--HE FIRED THAT SHOT --AT *HER*!
COME ON! LET'S GET OUT OF HERE BEFORE THE COPS COME!
NO! I WON'T LET YOU GO!
GET OUTA TH' WAY...!
2
MEANWHILE, APPROACHING THE RESTAURANT, CLARK'S SUPER-ACUTE EYESIGHT ACQUAINTS HIM WITH THE TENSE SITUATION INSIDE....
CAN YOU BEAT IT? LOIS CAN'T EVEN GO OUT TO *LUNCH* WITHOUT GETTING INTO MISCHIEF! THEREFORE--ENTER SUPERMAN!

BILL TALLEY SWINGS A WICKED BLOW AT LOIS....

I'LL TEACH YOU TO STEP ASIDE WHEN I ORDER YOU TO!

BUT AS HIS FIST STRIKES AN UNYIELDING PALM, HE SHRIEKS WITH PAIN....

OWW! MY HAND!

SURPRISED?

THE THUGS SEEK TO RACE ABOUT THE *MAN OF STEEL*, BUT *SUPERMAN* IS TOO FAST FOR THEM....

WHERE'S BRANIGAN? WHAT HAPPENED?

BILL TALLEY AND HIS MEN GANGED UP ON HIM, SUPERMAN PREVENTED THEIR ESCAPE,

THANKS, *SUPERMAN!* I'LL REPAY THE FAVOR SOME TIME,

I MAY REMIND YOU OF THAT PROMISE!

AS BRANIGAN REVIVES...

I TELL YOU, BOB BRANIGAN SHOT THAT WOMAN!

MY EYES -- I CAN'T SEE!

SOMETHING'S WRONG WITH BRANIGAN'S EYES, TAKE HIM TO THE HOSPITAL,

MY EYES... MY EYES...

OKAY IF I TRAIL ALONG?

AT POLICE HEADQUARTERS...

SORRY TO TELL YOU THIS, LOIS-- BUT THAT SLAIN WOMAN—WHOSE IDENTITY WE HAVEN'T YET BEEN ABLE TO TRACE-- WAS KILLED BY A BULLET FIRED FROM SERGEANT BRANIGAN'S GUN, LOOKS BAD FOR HIM.

BUT THIS IS AWFUL! I'M SURE BOB DIDN'T MEAN TO KILL ANYONE DELIBERATELY! IT WAS A TERRIBLE ACCIDENT!

③

AND LATER--AT THE *PLANET*...

IT'S BAD ENOUGH BOB HAS LOST HIS EYESIGHT, HE MAY BE ACCUSED OF MURDER.

WE'LL GO TO THAT INQUIRY, LOIS. IF THERE'S ANYTHING WE CAN DO, HE CAN COUNT ON US!

AT THE INQUIRY....

I WAS IN THE RESTAURANT WITH SOME OF THE BOYS, SEE, MINDIN' MY OWN BUSINESS WHEN IN COMES BRANIGAN WITH THE REPORTER DAME. I GUESS HE DIDN'T LIKE MY FACE 'CAUSE HE STARTED A FIGHT WITH ME FOR NO REASON.

AND DID YOU SEE SERGEANT BRANIGAN SHOOT THIS WOMAN?

WITH MY OWN EYES, I SAW IT! HE GOT SO SORE AT ME, SEE, HE PULLED OUT HIS GUN AND FIRED. BUT I DUCKED, THE WOMAN GOT IT!

BILL TALLEY IS LYING! SERGEANT BRANIGAN DIDN'T PICK A FIGHT. HE SAW TALLEY TRYING TO INTIMIDATE THE RESTAURANT MANAGER AND INTERFERED, I'M POSITIVE BOB WOULDN'T KILL AN INNOCENT...

WE'RE NOT INTERESTED IN YOUR OPINIONS, MISS LANE!

DID YOU OR DID YOU NOT KILL THIS WOMAN!

I--I DON'T KNOW. I REMEMBER PULLING OUT MY GUN TO DEFEND MYSELF. THEN EVERYTHING WENT BLACK.

SERGEANT BRANIGAN...THE INQUIRY COMMITTEE FINDS THAT YOU DID NOT SLAY THIS WOMAN DELIBERATELY.... BUT MAY HAVE DONE SO ACCIDENTALLY WHILE MISUSING YOUR POWERS AS A POLICE OFFICER. FOR THAT REASON YOU WILL NOT STAND TRIAL FOR MURDER--BUT YOU ARE HEREWITH SERVED NOTICE THAT YOU ARE NO LONGER A MEMBER OF THE POLICE DEPARTMENT.

WHAT A SHAME. IT'S BAD ENOUGH BRANIGAN HAD TO LOSE HIS EYESIGHT, BUT ON TOP OF THAT HE'S BEEN DISMISSED IN DISGRACE.

I'VE AN IDEA HOW WE CAN AID HIM.

LATER....

WE KNEW YOU'D WANT TO GO ON SUPPORTING YOURSELF, BOB, SO WE'VE ARRANGED A SMALL BUSINESS FOR YOU.

I--I DON'T DESERVE TO HAVE GOOD FRIENDS LIKE YOU TWO.

I'M SURE YOU'D STAND BY US, BOB, IF WE'D BE IN THE SAME SPOT.

LATER THAT DAY....

HEY, BOSS! THAT BLIND COP HAS OPENED A STAND IN THE ALLENTON.

I THINK I'LL DROP OVER AND SEE HOW BOB IS DOING!

ANYTHING I CAN DO FOR YOU GENTLEMEN?

HA! HA! NEVER THOUGHT I'D HEAR YOU CALLING ME AND TH' BOYS *GENTLEMEN*.

THIS IS KILLIN' ME!

BILL TALLEY! WHAT ARE YOU DOING HERE?

IT OCCURRED TO US THAT SEEING YOU'RE A BLIND MAN, YOU MIGHT NEED PROTECTION.

PROTECTION? FROM *WHAT*??

WELL, NOW-- SUPPOSE A COUPLE OF HARD GUYS WERE TO SHOVE YOUR STAND AROUND, YOU OUGHT TO BE WILLING TO PAY TO PREVENT THAT!

I WON'T PAY YOU ONE CENT!

TOO BAD-- FOR YOU! GET TO WORK, BOYS!

THIS IS WHAT I CALL EASY WORK.

TALLEY IN THERE-- ANNOYING BOB--!

I'VE BEEN LONGING TO GET ANOTHER CRACK AT TALLEY.

300

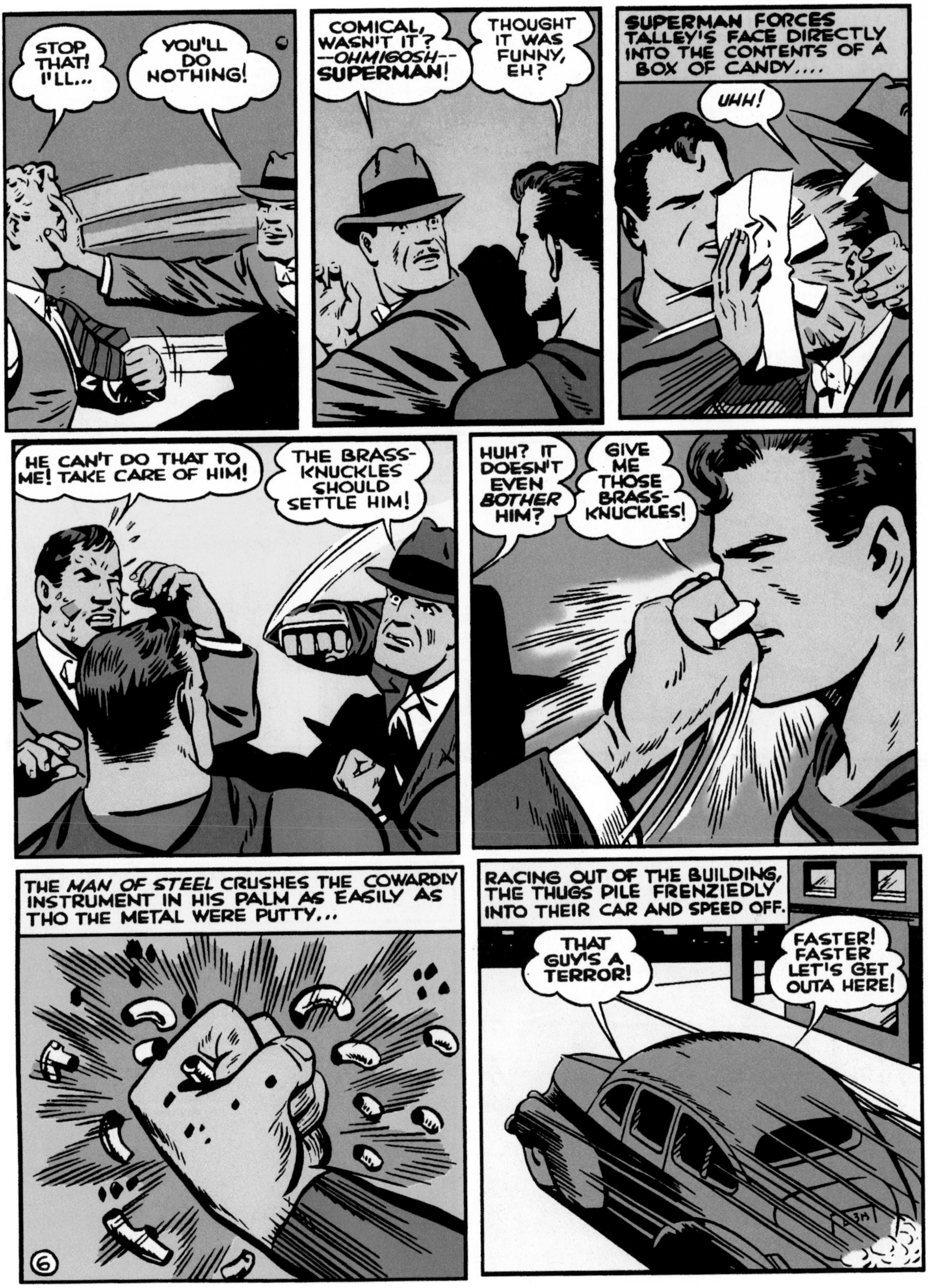
STOP THAT! I'LL...
YOU'LL DO NOTHING!
COMICAL, WASN'T IT? --OHMIGOSH-- SUPERMAN!
THOUGHT IT WAS FUNNY, EH?
SUPERMAN FORCES TALLEY'S FACE DIRECTLY INTO THE CONTENTS OF A BOX OF CANDY....
UHH!
HE CAN'T DO THAT TO ME! TAKE CARE OF HIM!
THE BRASS-KNUCKLES SHOULD SETTLE HIM!
HUH? IT DOESN'T EVEN BOTHER HIM?
GIVE ME THOSE BRASS-KNUCKLES!
THE MAN OF STEEL CRUSHES THE COWARDLY INSTRUMENT IN HIS PALM AS EASILY AS THO THE METAL WERE PUTTY...
6
RACING OUT OF THE BUILDING, THE THUGS PILE FRENZIEDLY INTO THEIR CAR AND SPEED OFF.
THAT GUY'S A TERROR!
FASTER! FASTER LET'S GET OUTA HERE!

RACING ABOUT WITH INCREDIBLE SWIFTNESS, SUPERMAN RETRIEVES THE FALLEN OBJECTS...

WHAT A FIRST-RATE CUSTODIAN I'D MAKE!

EVERYTHING'S ALL RIGHT NOW, I'LL TRY TO CONVINCE THOSE MEN IT WOULDN'T PAY TO ANNOY YOU FURTHER!

THANK YOU. I CAN'T TELL YOU HOW MUCH THIS MEANS TO ME...

AND NOW FOR A LITTLE HEART-TO-HEART TALK WITH BILL AND THE BOYS!

WHEW! THANK GOODNESS WE'VE SHAKEN THAT SUPERHUMAN HOODOO!

B-BUT WE HAVEN'T!

SWIFTLY, SUPERMAN OVERTAKES THE CAR....

IN JUST ANOTHER MOMENT...!

PULL OVER!

WH-WHAT'LL I DO, BOSS?

DON'T MIND HIM! KEEP DRIVING!

⑦

A SUDDEN SPURT OF SPEED, AND THE MAN OF STEEL RACES AHEAD OF THE AUTO, WHIRLS, THEN FACES IT....

I GUESS IT WILL TAKE MORE THAN JUST TALK TO STOP THEM!

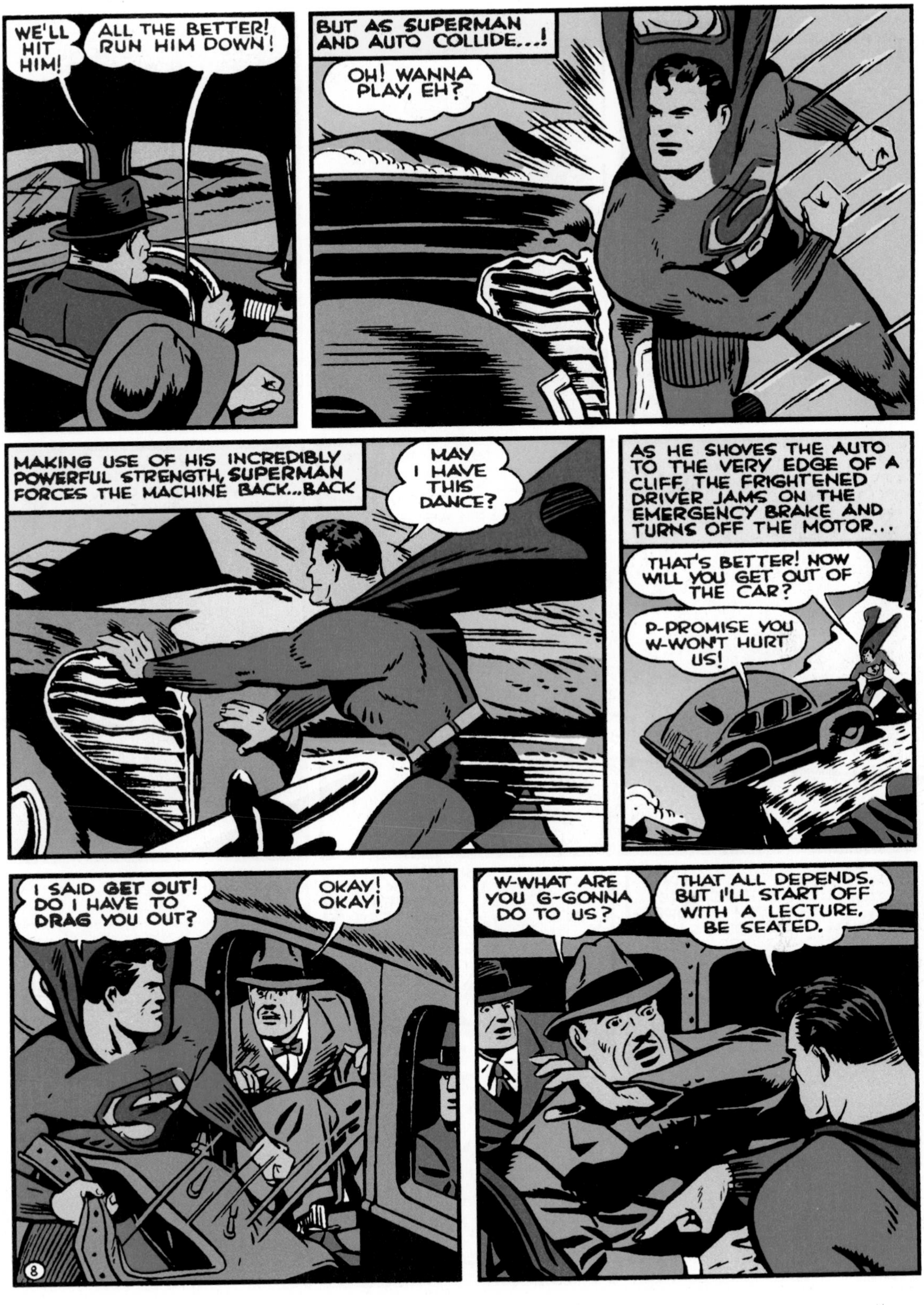
WE'LL HIT HIM!
ALL THE BETTER! RUN HIM DOWN!
BUT AS SUPERMAN AND AUTO COLLIDE...!
OH! WANNA PLAY, EH?
MAKING USE OF HIS INCREDIBLY POWERFUL STRENGTH, SUPERMAN FORCES THE MACHINE BACK...BACK
MAY I HAVE THIS DANCE?
AS HE SHOVES THE AUTO TO THE VERY EDGE OF A CLIFF, THE FRIGHTENED DRIVER JAMS ON THE EMERGENCY BRAKE AND TURNS OFF THE MOTOR...
THAT'S BETTER! NOW WILL YOU GET OUT OF THE CAR?
P-PROMISE YOU W-WON'T HURT US!
I SAID GET OUT! DO I HAVE TO DRAG YOU OUT?
OKAY! OKAY!
8
W-WHAT ARE YOU G-GONNA DO TO US?
THAT ALL DEPENDS. BUT I'LL START OFF WITH A LECTURE. BE SEATED.

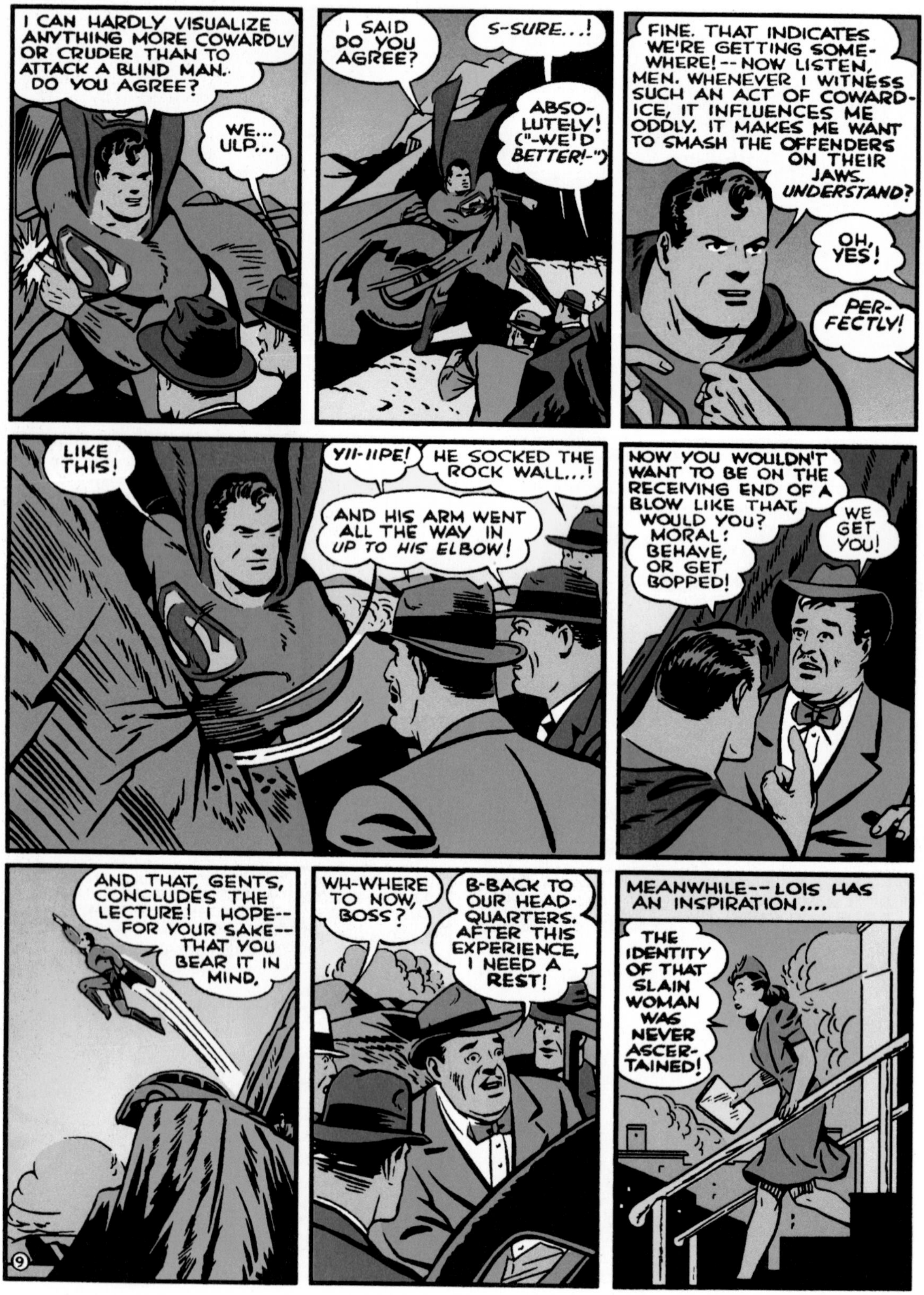
I CAN HARDLY VISUALIZE ANYTHING MORE COWARDLY OR CRUDER THAN TO ATTACK A BLIND MAN.. DO YOU AGREE?
WE... ULP...
I SAID DO YOU AGREE?
S-SURE...!
ABSOLUTELY! ("-WE'D BETTER!-")
FINE. THAT INDICATES WE'RE GETTING SOMEWHERE! --NOW LISTEN, MEN. WHENEVER I WITNESS SUCH AN ACT OF COWARDICE, IT INFLUENCES ME ODDLY. IT MAKES ME WANT TO SMASH THE OFFENDERS ON THEIR JAWS. UNDERSTAND?
OH, YES!
PERFECTLY!
LIKE THIS!
YII-IIPE!
HE SOCKED THE ROCK WALL...!
AND HIS ARM WENT ALL THE WAY IN UP TO HIS ELBOW!
NOW YOU WOULDN'T WANT TO BE ON THE RECEIVING END OF A BLOW LIKE THAT, WOULD YOU? MORAL: BEHAVE, OR GET BOPPED!
WE GET YOU!
AND THAT, GENTS, CONCLUDES THE LECTURE! I HOPE--FOR YOUR SAKE--THAT YOU BEAR IT IN MIND.
9
WH-WHERE TO NOW, BOSS?
B-BACK TO OUR HEADQUARTERS. AFTER THIS EXPERIENCE, I NEED A REST!
MEANWHILE--LOIS HAS AN INSPIRATION....
THE IDENTITY OF THAT SLAIN WOMAN WAS NEVER ASCERTAINED!

As Lois is about to enter the "Bureau of Missing Persons"....

It's really a waste of time to come here. If it had been possible to trace that woman, it would've been done already. --Wait!

The dress that woman wore--I remember now--a new style introduced only a few days ago at KENDALL, INC.! Hmmm...

When Lois reaches the department store....

That model didn't sell well. I have a list of twenty charge account sales I can give you, tho.

But as Lois visits home after home....

My wife still alive? I -- I'm afraid she is.

Thank you...

The last address on the list. Are my feet aching!

There was a Miss Reynolds living here, yes. But she left the boarding house some time ago. I can give you her new address.

I'd appreciate it.

But as Lois is about to approach the home the boarding-house landlady indicated she is halted by Jimmy Olsen, the DAILY PLANET office boy who happens to be passing by...

⑩

I wouldn't go in THERE if I were you, Miss Lane!

Why not, Jimmy?

That's the home of Bill Talley, the notorious gangster!

Oh, golly-gosh! This is even more than I could have hoped for!

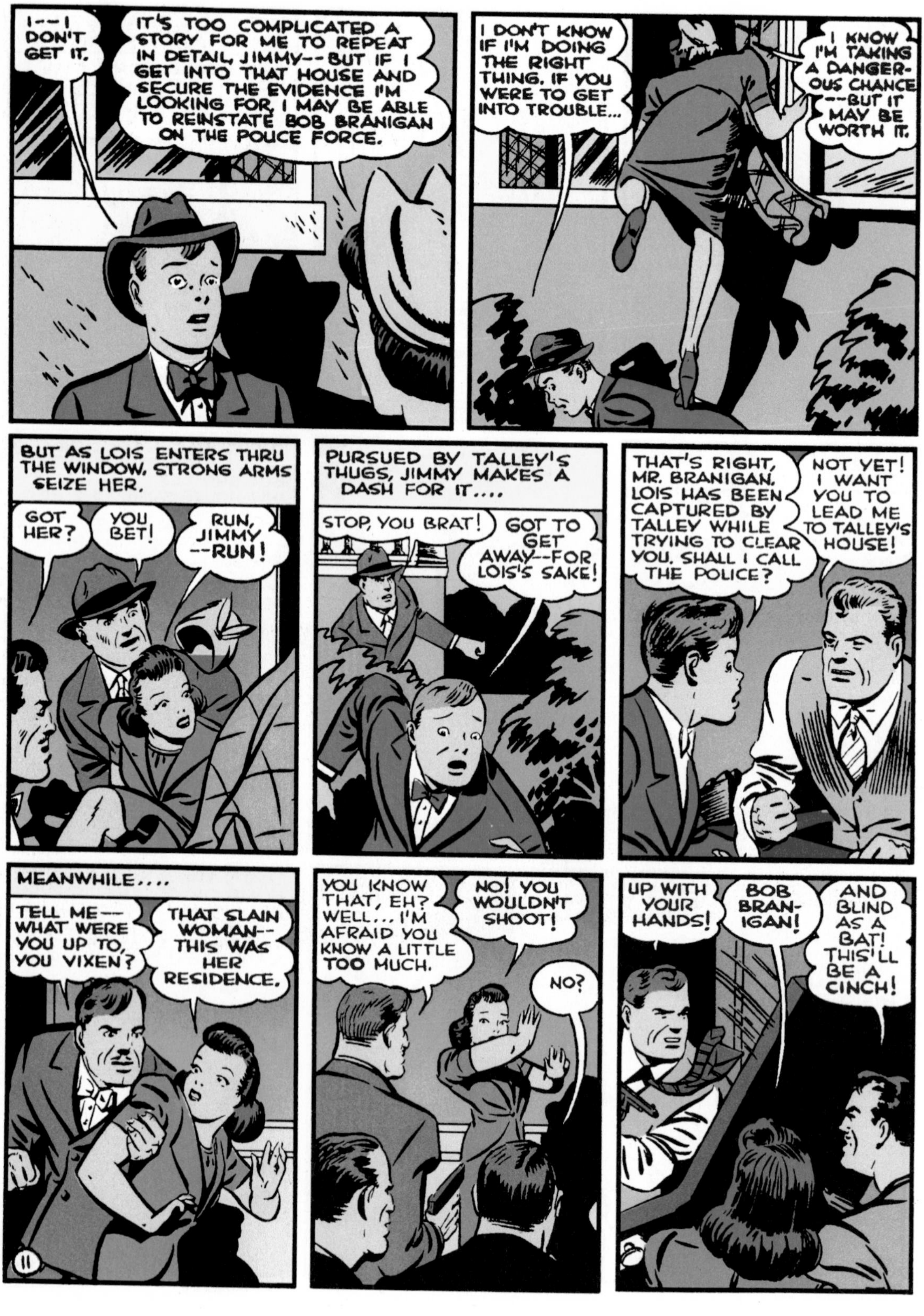

I--I DON'T GET IT.
IT'S TOO COMPLICATED A STORY FOR ME TO REPEAT IN DETAIL, JIMMY--BUT IF I GET INTO THAT HOUSE AND SECURE THE EVIDENCE I'M LOOKING FOR, I MAY BE ABLE TO REINSTATE BOB BRANIGAN ON THE POLICE FORCE.
I DON'T KNOW IF I'M DOING THE RIGHT THING. IF YOU WERE TO GET INTO TROUBLE...
I KNOW I'M TAKING A DANGEROUS CHANCE--BUT IT MAY BE WORTH IT.
BUT AS LOIS ENTERS THRU THE WINDOW, STRONG ARMS SEIZE HER.
GOT HER?
YOU BET!
RUN, JIMMY --RUN!
PURSUED BY TALLEY'S THUGS, JIMMY MAKES A DASH FOR IT....
STOP, YOU BRAT!
GOT TO GET AWAY--FOR LOIS'S SAKE!
THAT'S RIGHT, MR. BRANIGAN. LOIS HAS BEEN CAPTURED BY TALLEY WHILE TRYING TO CLEAR YOU. SHALL I CALL THE POLICE?
NOT YET! I WANT YOU TO LEAD ME TO TALLEY'S HOUSE!
MEANWHILE....
TELL ME--WHAT WERE YOU UP TO, YOU VIXEN?
THAT SLAIN WOMAN--THIS WAS HER RESIDENCE.
11
YOU KNOW THAT, EH? WELL... I'M AFRAID YOU KNOW A LITTLE TOO MUCH.
NO! YOU WOULDN'T SHOOT!
NO?
UP WITH YOUR HANDS!
BOB BRANIGAN!
AND BLIND AS A BAT! THIS'LL BE A CINCH!

I'LL VISIT BRANIGAN AND SEE HOW HE'S DOING!

THAT'S ODD --HE'S NOT THERE! I'D BETTER DROP IN ON TALLEY AND SEE HOW HE'S BEHAVING HIMSELF!

JIMMY--WHAT ARE YOU DOING HERE?

LOIS CAPTIVE IN THERE-- AND BOB BRANIGAN TRYING TO SAVE HER!

STEALING UP ON THE BLIND EX-POLICEMAN, ONE OF THE THUGS SLAMS HIM WITH AN IRON BAR....

UH-HH!

HO! HO! THAT WAS EASY!

EASY, EH? THEN TRY IT ON ME!

YII-IIPE! SUPER-MAN!

THIS FOR THE IRON BAR...!

...AND THAT FOR YOU!

AND NOW, BOYS--IF YOU'LL JUST PUT YOUR CHINS OVER HERE--

BACK--GET OUT-- OR THIS BOTTLE OF NITROGLYCERINE BLOWS ALL OF US SKY HIGH...!

12

BEHIND TALLEY, BOB BRANIGAN REVIVES....

I—I CAN *SEE!* THAT BLOW BROUGHT MY VISION BACK!

YOU'RE LYING! IT'S A TRICK!

BUT AN INSTANT LATER, AS BRANIGAN LEAPS UPON HIM, TALLEY KNOWS IT'S THE TRUTH....

NOW TO GIVE YOU THE BEATING YOU DESERVE!

FLASHING LOW AT SUPER-SPEED, THE *MAN OF TOMORROW* SNAGS THE DANGEROUS LITTLE BOTTLE...

GO TO IT, BOB!

BOB MERCILESSLY SUBJECTS THE CRAVEN CRIMINAL TO THE BEATING OF HIS LIFE....

WHAT A THRILL TO HAVE MY SIGHT BACK... IF ONLY TO SEE YOU GETTING WHAT'S COMING TO YOU!

STOP HIM!

STAY WHERE YOU ARE!

A BEAUTY!

DON'T GO!

LET US THANK YOU!

SEEING YOUR VISION RESTORED IS ALL I ASK.

⑬

SLAIN MYSTERY WOMAN IS GANGSTER'S EX-WIFE

MORNING ST
CRIMINAL SLAYS EX-MATE TO AVOID ALIMONY PAYMENT—

Evening Bugle
BRANIGAN BACK ON FORCE

THE *DAILY PLANET*....

YOU SHOULD HAVE SEEN SUPERMAN GO INTO ACTION! BOB AND I OWE A LOT TO HIM!

FROM WHAT I HEAR, YOU WERE OKAY, YOURSELF!

THE END

SUPERMAN

by JERRY SIEGEL and JOE SHUSTER

AT THIS TENSE PERIOD WHEN THE UNITED STATES IS STRIVING TO REARM ITSELF IN AN ALL-OUT DEFENSE EFFORT, SABOTAGE OF DEFENSE PRODUCTION AND MILITARY OBJECTIVES IS OF STUNNING EFFECT. THEREFORE, WHEN THE MIGHTY *MAN OF TOMORROW* DISCOVERS THREATS ENDANGERING THE WELL-BEING OF OUR GREAT NATION, HE LAUNCHES A BATTLE AGAINST THE SABOTEURS THAT WILL LONG BE REMEMBERED!

GET DOWN TO THE NAVY YARD AT ONCE. THEY'RE LAUNCHING A NEW BATTLESHIP, THE Y-92.

RIGHT AWAY, WHITE!

WAIT FOR ME, CLARK. I WOULDN'T MISS THIS FOR ANYTHING!

LATER... AS THEY WITNESS THE IMPRESSIVE CEREMONY...

DOESN'T IT JUST THRILL YOU, CLARK, TO THINK THAT OUR DEFENSE PROGRAM IS PROCEEDING SO WELL?

IT CERTAINLY DOES! ("-UNLESS MY TELESCOPIC X-RAY VISION DECEIVES ME, THERE'S SOMETHING RADICALLY WRONG HERE!-")

WHAT CLARK SEES... A LOOSE PLATE AT THE BATTLESHIP'S BOTTOM...

SWIFTLY, NOISELESSLY, CLARK SLIPS AWAY FROM LOIS' SIDE...

("-I'VE GOT TO GET AWAY!-")

AWAY FROM ANY CHANCE OF OBSERVATION, THE *DAILY PLANET* REPORTER REMOVES HIS OUTER GARMENTS, TRANSFORMING HIMSELF TO DYNAMIC SUPERMAN!

UNLESS I ACT SWIFTLY, SEVERAL MILLION DOLLARS WORTH OF BATTLESHIP WILL GO TO WASTE!

RACING SO QUICKLY HE CANNOT BE SEEN, THE *MAN OF TOMORROW* SPEEDS DIRECTLY THROUGH THE CROWD'S CENTER AS THE CHRISTENING CEREMONY DRAWS TO A CLOSE...!

INTO THE OCEAN HE DIVES...

SECONDS TO ACT!

...AS THE Y-92 SLIDES DOWN THE WAYS AND INTO THE WATER!

②

BUT BENEATH THE SEA, SUPERMAN POUNDS THE PLATE BACK INTO PLACE WITH HIS BARE FISTS...

THERE! IT'S ALL RIGHT NOW!

MY GOOD DEED FOR THE DAY!

RACING BACK TO THE ALLEY, THE MAN OF TO-MORROW RESUMES HIS IDENTITY AS CLARK KENT...

NOW TO HURRY BACK TO LOIS!

WHERE WERE YOU? I'VE BEEN LOOKING ALL OVER FOR YOU.

AND I'VE BEEN DOING THE SAME. I GUESS WE GOT SEPA-RATED IN THE CROWD.

LATER...IN THE PRIVACY OF HIS APARTMENT, CLARK CHANGES TO SUPERMAN ONCE AGAIN...

TIME TO GO CALLING!

OVER THE CITY OF METROPOLIS STREAKS THE MAN OF STEEL AT BREATHTAKING SPEED...

THE SECRETARY OF THE NAVY OUGHT TO KNOW ABOUT THIS!

SHORTLY AFTER...THE MAN OF TOMORROW PLUMMETS DOWN OUT OF THE CLOUDS TOWARD SECRETARY HANK FOX'S HOME...

HE'S IN HIS STUDY, GOOD!

③

SUPERMAN!

SORRY I COULDN'T HAVE WAITED FOR AN INVITATION, MR. FOX-- BUT I'M CALLING ON AN URGENT MATTER!

MEETING YOU IS A DISTINCT PLEASURE... I'VE READ SO MUCH ABOUT YOUR BATTLE AGAINST INJUSTICES, BUT WHY HAVE I THE HONOR OF A PERSONAL CALL?

THE Y-92, JUST LAUNCHED TODAY, WAS OBVIOUSLY A VICTIM OF SABOTAGE. I FOUND A PLATE HAD BEEN LOOSENED IN ITS BOTTOM, AND REPAIRED IT IN TIME.

YOU'VE DONE YOUR COUNTRY A SPLENDID SERVICE. —SABOTAGE. OUR DEFENSE EFFORT IS BEING CONSTANTLY PLAGUED BY IT, AND THE WORST PART OF IT IS WE STRONGLY SUSPECT WHO IS REALLY RESPONSIBLE, BUT CAN DO LITTLE ABOUT IT.

WHOM DO YOU SUSPECT?

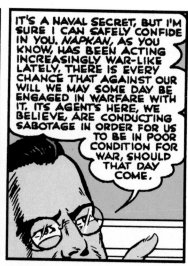

IT'S A NAVAL SECRET, BUT I'M SURE I CAN SAFELY CONFIDE IN YOU. NAPKAN, AS YOU KNOW, HAS BEEN ACTING INCREASINGLY WAR-LIKE LATELY. THERE IS EVERY CHANCE THAT AGAINST OUR WILL WE MAY SOME DAY BE ENGAGED IN WARFARE WITH IT. ITS AGENTS HERE, WE BELIEVE, ARE CONDUCTING SABOTAGE IN ORDER FOR US TO BE IN POOR CONDITION FOR WAR, SHOULD THAT DAY COME.

THANKS FOR THE INFORMATION. YOU CAN BE SURE I'LL PUT IT TO GOOD USE!

GOOD LUCK!

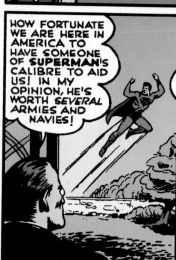

HOW FORTUNATE WE ARE HERE IN AMERICA TO HAVE SOMEONE OF SUPERMAN'S CALIBRE TO AID US! IN MY OPINION, HE'S WORTH SEVERAL ARMIES AND NAVIES!

SHORTLY AFTER... DOWN TOWARD THE NAPKAN EMBASSY DROPS THE MAN OF STEEL...

AGGRESSOR NATIONS MAKE A POLICY OF HAVING THEIR AMBASSADORS DEAL IN ESPIONAGE. IF NAPKAN REALLY IS BEHIND THIS WAVE OF SABOTAGE, I'LL KNOW SOON ENOUGH!

HOKOPOKO, NAPKAN AMBASSADOR IN METROPOLIS, IS INTERVIEWING A VISITOR AT THAT MOMENT...

I COME ALL THE WAY FROM EQUARU IN SOUTH AMERICA WITH NEWS OF IMPENDING VICTORY IN OUR CAMPAIGN THERE.

LET ME HAVE THE DETAILS, UTSUM!

IT APPEARS I'VE COME JUST IN TIME! MY SUPER-SENSITIVE HEARING SHOULD SERVE ME WELL, NOW!

④

I SUCCEEDED IN FORMING A PRO-*NAPKAN* PARTY THERE WHICH WILL ATTEMPT TO OVERTHROW THE *EQUARUIAN* GOVERNMENT TODAY! IF THEY SUCCEED, IT WILL BE BUT THE BEGINNING. WE WILL PERFORM SIMILAR COUPS IN THE OTHER LATIN AMERICAN NATIONS, UNTIL SOUTH AMERICA IS ALL ANTI-AMERICAN. AFTER THAT, ATTACKING THE UNITED STATES WILL BE A SIMPLE MATTER.

YOU HAVE DONE WELL. YOU MAY EVEN GET A MEDAL FOR THIS!

AND WHAT PROGRESS ARE YOU MAKING HERE IN THE U.S. IN YOUR WORK?

OUR SABOTAGE EFFORTS ARE INCREASING WITH MOST SATISFACTORY EFFECT. BUT SOON WE WILL STRIKE A GREAT BLOW THAT WILL MAKE ALL THE OTHERS LOOK PUNY BY COMPARISON!—AND NOW, GOOD DAY!

AT THAT MOMENT--SIGHTING THE *MAN* OF *STEEL* EAVESDROPPING, A GUARD RUSHES HIM...

GOING TO TRY TO GIVE ME THE OFFICIAL BOUNCE, EH?

YOU WILL GET A DEMONSTRATION OF JIU JITSU YOU WILL NEVER FORGET!

BUT AS THE GUARD SEIZES **SUPERMAN**...

I--I CAN'T EVEN BUDGE YOU!

IN THAT EVENT, I'LL SHOW **YOU** A LITTLE TRICK!

THIS ISN'T AS FANCY AS JIU JITSU... BUT EVEN **MORE** EFFECTIVE!

YII-II! HELP! HELP!

AS OTHER GUARDS DASH UP...

PLEASE DON'T THINK I'M RUNNING AWAY FROM A FIGHT. I'LL BE BACK...BUT FIRST THERE'S ANOTHER ERRAND I'VE GOT TO ATTEND TO!

⑤

ACROSS THE CONTINENT SPEEDS THE *MAN OF STEEL* AT INCREDIBLE SPEED...

SOUTH AMERICA... HERE I COME!

AND SHORTLY AFTER, HE IS STREAKING DOWN TOWARD THE CAPITAL OF *EQUARU*...

THE *NAPKAN* EMBASSY IN *EQUARU*... BELOW!

ATOP THE EMBASSY BUILDING, **SUPERMAN** LISTENS INTENTLY....

UTSUM WASN'T LYING!

WITHIN THE EMBASSY...

THE PRO-*NAPKAN* BLACK CIRCLE SOCIETY WILL TAKE OVER THE GOVERNMENT BUILDING AT THE APPOINTED TIME.

IN OTHER WORDS— TWO MINUTES!

THAT DOESN'T GIVE ME VERY LONG TO ACT!

AT THAT MOMENT, THE REVOLUTIONISTS ADVANCE ON THE GOVERNMENT BUILDING....

DOWN WITH THE GOVERNMENT!

HOORAY FOR *NAPKAN*!

THE BLACK CIRCLE MUST RULE!

TAKEN OFF GUARD, THE SMALL NUMBER OF DEFENDERS STAND THUNDERSTRUCK AT SIGHT OF THE CHARGING REVOLUTIONISTS...

⑥

WE'RE OUTNUMBERED! WE HAVEN'T A CHANCE!

WE MAY AS WELL SURRENDER!

NOT IF *I* CAN HELP IT!!

314

DOWN BEFORE THE CHARGING REVOLUTIONISTS DROPS THE *MAN OF TOMORROW*...

GOING TO AID *NAPKAN* IN ENCROACHING ON THE WESTERN HEMISPHERE, EH?

STREAKING IN AND OUT AMONG THE ARMED RIOTERS WITH SUPER-SPEED, *SUPERMAN* SNATCHES AWAY THEIR WEAPONS...

I'M AFRAID I CAN'T PERMIT *THAT*!

...SO THAT A MOMENT LATER THE REVOLUTIONISTS' GUNS ARE NEATLY PILED BEHIND THE GOVERNMENT BUILDING'S DEFENDERS!

YOU WON'T FIND THEM SO BELLIGERENT WITHOUT THEIR WEAPONS!

A MIRACLE!

ARREST THOSE TRAITORS!

MINUTES LATER...THE REVOLUTION HAS BEEN SQUELCHED...

WAIT! LET US THANK YOU!

MY JOB ISN'T FINISHED --YET!

THE ATTEMPT FAILED!

THAT MEANS WE'D BETTER HURRY OFF BEFORE SOME OF THE *BLACK CIRCLE* MEMBERS TALK!

BUT AS THE TWO CONSPIRATORS ARE ABOUT TO DRIVE OFF, *SUPERMAN* STREAKS DOWN AND RAISES THEIR CAR OVERHEAD...

GOING SOMEPLACE?

⑦

YOU'RE GOING WHERE YOU BELONG!

JOIN YOUR FRIENDS!

THE HEAD OF THE *BLACK CIRCLE* SOCIETY AND THE *NAPKAN* COUNSEL!

WHAT A CATCH THIS IS!

BACK TO THE *UNITED STATES* RACES THE AMAZING *MAN OF TOMORROW*...

TO THINK THAT IN A FEW MINUTES I CHANGED THE FATE OF SOUTH AMERICA!

AND LATER...AT THE DAILY PLANET...

NICE STORY YOU HANDED IN, CLARK, BUT HOW DID YOU CHECK THE FACTS?

I HAVE RELIABLE SOURCES OF INFORMATION.

AND AT THE *NAPKAN* EMBASSY...THE AMBASSADOR HAS SIMILAR THOUGHTS...

THIS REPORTER, CLARK KENT-- HIS FACTS HERE ARE SO ACCURATE, IT'S UNBELIEVABLE, HE'S A DEFINITE MENACE TO *NAPKAN'S* ASPIRATIONS FOR WORLD EXPANSION!

MAY I SUGGEST, THEREFORE, THAT THIS PRESUMPTUOUS MR. KENT BE--ER-- ATTENDED TO?

THAT EVENING...AS CLARK RETIRES...

I HAVEN'T DONE BADLY AT ALL...BUT THERE'S STILL THE GREAT WAVE OF SABOTAGE IN THE U.S. TO BE ATTENDED TO!

LATER...SHADOWY INVADERS ENTER THE DARKENED ROOM...

AND STILL LATER...

HE HAS CEASED STRUGGLING!

THE CHLOROFORM HAS TAKEN EFFECT!

8

OFF INTO THE NIGHT SPEEDS THE AUTO WITH THE APPARENTLY UNCONSCIOUS REPORTER...

("-WHAT A BREAK! SINCE THEY'VE COME TO *ME*, THAT SAVES ME THE TROUBLE OF GOING TO *THEM*!-")

SWIFTER SPEEDS THE AUTO. 80-90-100 MILES PER HOUR... CLARK IS HURLED OUT BODILY...

GUNFIRE FROM THE HURTLING AUTO SPRAYS THE FALLING FIGURE WITH BULLETS...

DOWN A STEEP SLOPE IT ROLLS... OVER AND OVER...

BUT AS THE AUTO SPEEDS OUT OF SIGHT, THE REPORTER'S FIGURE SOMERSAULTS AND SNAPS ERECT!

ALL CLEAR!

SWIFTLY HE REMOVES HIS PAJAMAS, TRANSFORMING HIMSELF TO **SUPERMAN**!

THEY MAY HAVE RID THEMSELVES OF CLARK KENT, BUT THERE'S STILL **SUPERMAN** TO BE RECKONED WITH!

UP THE PERPENDICULAR SIDE OF THE CLIFF RACES THE *MAN OF STEEL*...

I'M ON MY WAY!

IT TAKES HIM BUT SECONDS TO CATCH SIGHT OF THE FLEEING AUTO...

THERE THEY GO!

LATER... THEY'RE ENTERING THE *NAPKAN* EMBASSY-- AS I EXPECTED THEY WOULD!

HAVE YOU ATTENDED TO THE REPORTER?

HE WILL TROUBLE US NO LONGER!

GOOD, SPLENDID!

IT IS A FINE OMEN. IT BODES WELL FOR THE SUCCESS OF OUR MASTER STROKE OF SABOTAGE.

CAN YOU TELL US NOW WHAT THAT STROKE IS TO BE?

A FEW MINUTES FROM NOW, THE *NAPKAN* LINER, *SUNYAT*, WILL ENTER THE PANAMA CANAL WITH A SUICIDE CREW ON BOARD. AT THE PROPER MOMENT THERE WILL BE A DEVASTATING EXPLOSION... THOSE ON BOARD WILL BE KILLED IN THE "UNFORTUNATE ACCIDENT"...BUT AT THE SAME TIME WE WILL HAVE ACCOMPLISHED OUR PURPOSE...

THE DESTRUCTION OF THE PANAMA CANAL! WHAT A BLOW TO THE DEFENSE OF THE *UNITED STATES*! SUPERB!

GOT IT ALL FIGURED OUT, EH?

SUPERMAN!

STOP HIM!! HE OVERHEARD OUR PLANS!

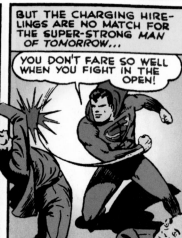

BUT THE CHARGING HIRELINGS ARE NO MATCH FOR THE SUPER-STRONG *MAN OF TOMORROW*...

YOU DON'T FARE SO WELL WHEN YOU FIGHT IN THE OPEN!

GET THIS! UNLESS YOU AND YOUR BLOODTHIRSTY CREW CLEAR OUT OF HERE IN RECORD TIME YOU'LL BE ANCIENT HISTORY WHEN I FINISH WITH YOU!

I--I'LL GET OUT!

W-WITH ALACRITY!

OFF RACES THE *MAN OF TOMORROW* ON HIS TREMENDOUSLY IMPORTANT MISSION...

THE FATE OF THE PANAMA CANAL IN THE BALANCE!

ACROSS THE OCEAN SWIMS THE MIGHTY *MAN OF TOMORROW* AT SO GREAT A SPEED THE OCEAN APPEARS SPLIT IN TWAIN....

SPEED... SPEED... AND **MORE** SPEED...!!!

MEANWHILE--THE *SUNYAT* BEGINS TO ENTER THE *PANAMA CANAL*....

THE SUICIDE CREW STANDS AT ITS POSTS, FACES SET IN EXPRESSIONLESS MASKS-- HIDING THE TERROR IN THEIR HEARTS...

FOR EACH ONE OF THE DOOMED SAILORS KNOWS THAT IN THE HOLD OF THE VESSEL A TIME-BOMB HAS BEEN SET INTO OPER- ATION THAT WILL DESTROY THEM ALL...

FOR THE GLORY OF *NAPKAN!*

...AND THE DESTRUCTION OF THE *UNITED STATES!*

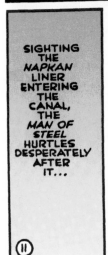

SIGHTING THE *NAPKAN* LINER ENTERING THE CANAL, THE *MAN OF STEEL* HURTLES DESPERATELY AFTER IT...

⑪

PERHAPS I'M STILL NOT TOO LATE!

A TERRIFIC BURST OF STRENGTH AND HE LIFTS THE MIGHTY LINER UP-- UP OUT OF THE WATER....!

UP YOU GO!!

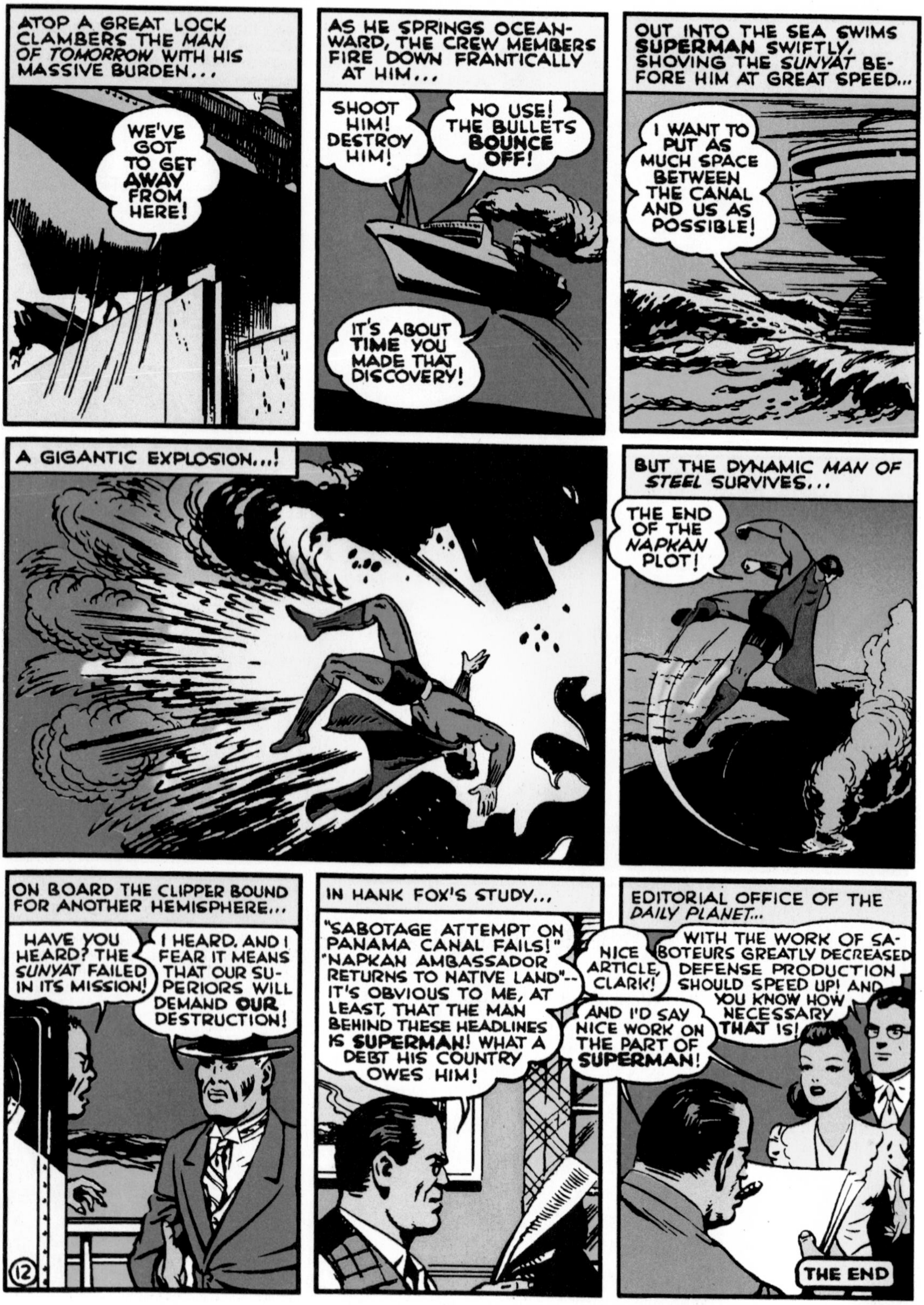

ATOP A GREAT LOCK CLAMBERS THE *MAN OF TOMORROW* WITH HIS MASSIVE BURDEN...
WE'VE GOT TO GET **AWAY** FROM HERE!
AS HE SPRINGS OCEAN-WARD, THE CREW MEMBERS FIRE DOWN FRANTICALLY AT HIM...
SHOOT HIM! DESTROY HIM!
NO USE! THE BULLETS **BOUNCE OFF!**
IT'S ABOUT **TIME** YOU MADE THAT DISCOVERY!
OUT INTO THE SEA SWIMS **SUPERMAN** SWIFTLY, SHOVING THE *SUNYAT* BEFORE HIM AT GREAT SPEED...
I WANT TO PUT AS MUCH SPACE BETWEEN THE CANAL AND US AS POSSIBLE!
A GIGANTIC EXPLOSION...!
BUT THE DYNAMIC *MAN OF STEEL* SURVIVES...
THE END OF THE *NAPKAN* PLOT!
ON BOARD THE CLIPPER BOUND FOR ANOTHER HEMISPHERE...
HAVE YOU HEARD? THE *SUNYAT* FAILED IN ITS MISSION!
I HEARD. AND I FEAR IT MEANS THAT OUR SUPERIORS WILL DEMAND **OUR** DESTRUCTION!
12
IN HANK FOX'S STUDY...
"SABOTAGE ATTEMPT ON PANAMA CANAL FAILS!" "NAPKAN AMBASSADOR RETURNS TO NATIVE LAND"-- IT'S OBVIOUS TO ME, AT LEAST, THAT THE MAN BEHIND THESE HEADLINES IS **SUPERMAN**! WHAT A DEBT HIS COUNTRY OWES HIM!
EDITORIAL OFFICE OF THE *DAILY PLANET*...
NICE ARTICLE, CLARK!
WITH THE WORK OF SABOTEURS GREATLY DECREASED DEFENSE PRODUCTION SHOULD SPEED UP! AND YOU KNOW HOW NECESSARY **THAT** IS!
AND I'D SAY NICE WORK ON THE PART OF **SUPERMAN**!
THE END

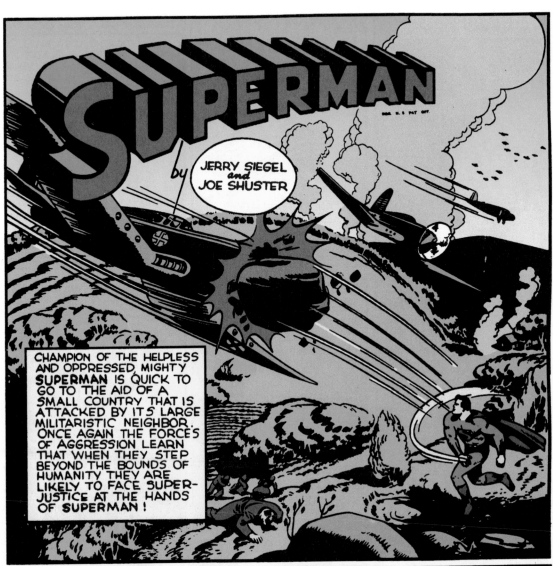

SUPERMAN

REG. U.S. PAT. OFF.

by JERRY SIEGEL and JOE SHUSTER

CHAMPION OF THE HELPLESS AND OPPRESSED, MIGHTY SUPERMAN IS QUICK TO GO TO THE AID OF A SMALL COUNTRY THAT IS ATTACKED BY ITS LARGE MILITARISTIC NEIGHBOR. ONCE AGAIN THE FORCES OF AGGRESSION LEARN THAT WHEN THEY STEP BEYOND THE BOUNDS OF HUMANITY THEY ARE LIKELY TO FACE SUPER-JUSTICE AT THE HANDS OF SUPERMAN!

OXNALIA INVADES NUMARK, ITS PEACE-FUL DEMOCRATIC NEIGHBOR...

OF ALL THE COWARDLY CRIMES!

GOSH! IF I COULD ONLY BE SUPERMAN FOR A FEW MINUTES, I'D CERTAINLY TEACH OXNALIA A LESSON!

BUT CLARK KENT, MEEK DAILY PLANET REPORTER, ACTUALLY IS SUPERMAN!

SO OXNALIA WANTS TO PLAY BULLY, EH?

A TREMENDOUS LEAP LAUNCHES *SUPERMAN* INTO THE SKY..

UP- UP- AND AWAY!

OVER THE VAST CONTINENT HE SPEEDS, PASSING CITIES, TOWNS, STATES IN MOMENTS.

EUROPE, HERE I COME!

THEN OUT OVER THE OCEAN..

SOLONG, U.S.A.! I'LL BE MIGHTY GLAD TO GET BACK TO YOU!

MID-WAY TO HIS GOAL, THE *MAN OF TOMORROW* IS SIGHTED AT SEA BY AN OXNALIAN VESSEL..

IT'S *SUPERMAN!*

WE MUST SEND A WARNING TO OUR NATION!

IN *OXNALIA*

URGENT! RUSH IT TO OUR BELOVED DICTATOR!

IN THE ORNATE THRONE ROOM OF RAZKAL, DICTATOR OF ALL *OXNALIA...*

SUPERMAN HEADED HERE! QUICK! I MUST HIDE IN MY AIR-RAID SHELTER!

A PROCLAMATION FROM OUR BRAVE DICTATOR! EVERY MAN MUST BE ON GUARD AND READY TO REPULSE THE INVADING *SUPERMAN!*

G-G-GULP!

S-SUPERMAN!

②

EUROPE! NOW THE FUN BEGINS! AND SO DOES THE *ACTION!*

FIRST TO PAY POOR *NUMARK* A VISIT!

SUPERMAN'S SUPER-HEARING PICKS UP A CONVERSATION...

WHAT'S THIS?

WHAT THE *MAN OF STEEL* OVERHEARS---

OUR DARING MOVE TO SLAY KING BORIS SHOULD END THE WAR SWIFTLY!

BORIS HAS UNDERESTIMATED THE FIFTH COLUMN MOVEMENT IN THIS COUNTRY.

EVEN NOW, OUR MEN STRIKE!

THE KING IN DANGER! THEREFORE IT'S THE PALACE FOR ME!

MEANWHILE--- FIFTH COLUMNISTS HAVE OVERWHELMED THE KING'S GUARDS...

THAT ATTENDS TO *THEM!*

NOW TO TAKE CARE OF KING BORIS HIMSELF!

WHAT DOES THIS INTRUSION MEAN?

IT MEANS THAT YOU ARE *GOING* TO DIE!

③

YOU'VE GOT TO LET ME THRU! THE KING'S LIFE IS IN DANGER!

YOU CAN'T PASS!

IT'S A TRICK OF SOME SORT.

A TERRIFIC LEAP LAUNCHES THE MAN OF TOMORROW HIGH OVER THEIR HEADS.

NO TIME TO EXCHANGE IDLE TALK WHILE YOUR KING'S LIFE IS THREATENED!

STOP HIM!

THERE IS NO STOPPING HIM!

KING BORIS FACES THE ASSASSINS CALMLY...

I'LL SHOW YOU COWARDS HOW A KING CAN DIE!

VERY NOBLE. BUT YOU'LL DIE ALL RIGHT!

MIND IF I BALANCE THE ODDS?

AN INTRUDER!

GET HIM!

WHIRLING, THE ASSASSINS FIRE AT THE MAN OF TOMORROW, BUT TO THEIR ASTONISHMENT...

THE BULLETS-BOUNCING OFF HIS SKIN!

TOUGH, EH?

HOPE YOU ENJOY THE RIDE--THERE IS NO EXTRA CHARGE!

AS GUARDS BURST INTO THE ROOM---

THERE'S THE MADMAN!

DO NOT HARM THE COSTUMED MAN. HE CAME TO MY AID!

BUT IMPRISON THE OTHERS!

THANKS, KING BORIS!

YOUR FAME HAS PENETRATED EVEN TO OUR LITTLE KINGDOM. YOU'RE SUPERMAN AREN'T YOU?

YES. AND I'VE COME TO ASSIST YOU IN YOUR STRUGGLE AGAINST OVERWHELMING ODDS!

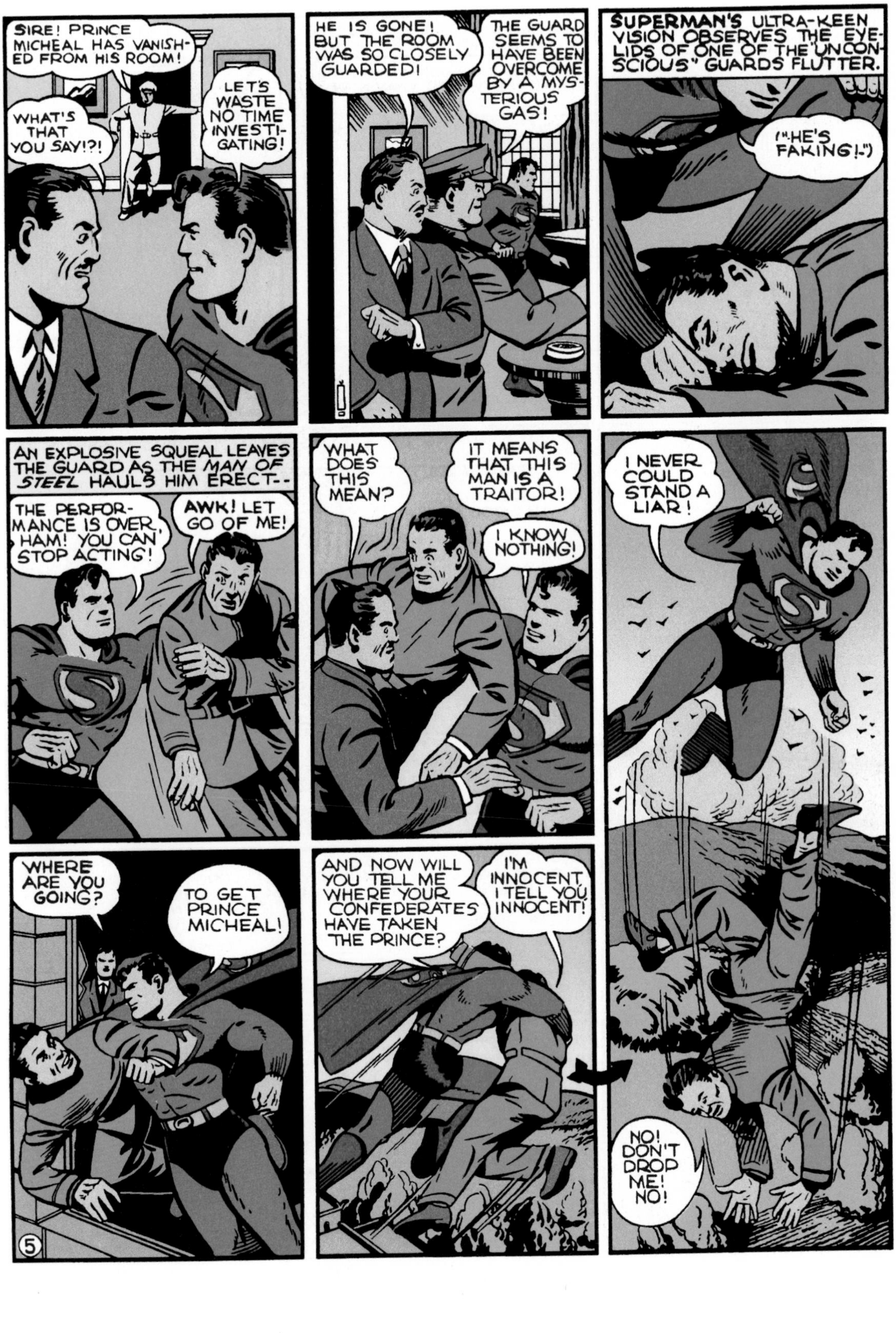
SIRE! PRINCE MICHEAL HAS VANISHED FROM HIS ROOM!
WHAT'S THAT YOU SAY!?!
LET'S WASTE NO TIME INVESTIGATING!
HE IS GONE! BUT THE ROOM WAS SO CLOSELY GUARDED!
THE GUARD SEEMS TO HAVE BEEN OVERCOME BY A MYSTERIOUS GAS!
SUPERMAN'S ULTRA-KEEN VISION OBSERVES THE EYELIDS OF ONE OF THE "UNCONSCIOUS" GUARDS FLUTTER.
("HE'S FAKING!")
AN EXPLOSIVE SQUEAL LEAVES THE GUARD AS THE MAN OF STEEL HAULS HIM ERECT--
THE PERFORMANCE IS OVER, HAM! YOU CAN STOP ACTING!
AWK! LET GO OF ME!
WHAT DOES THIS MEAN?
IT MEANS THAT THIS MAN IS A TRAITOR!
I KNOW NOTHING!
I NEVER COULD STAND A LIAR!
WHERE ARE YOU GOING?
TO GET PRINCE MICHEAL!
5
AND NOW WILL YOU TELL ME WHERE YOUR CONFEDERATES HAVE TAKEN THE PRINCE?
I'M INNOCENT, I TELL YOU, INNOCENT!
NO! DON'T DROP ME! NO!

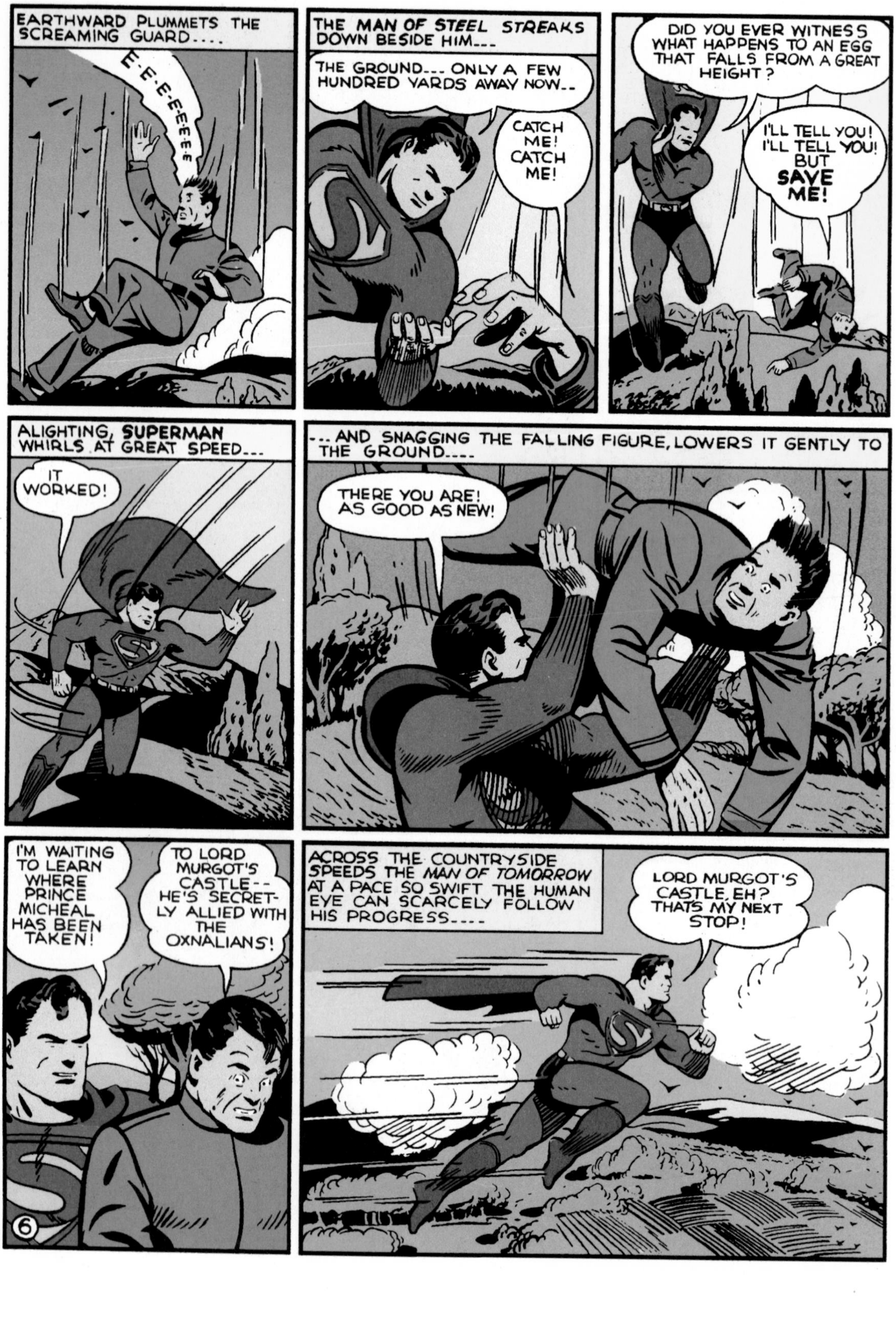
EARTHWARD PLUMMETS THE SCREAMING GUARD....
E-E-E-E-E-E-E-E
THE MAN OF STEEL STREAKS DOWN BESIDE HIM...
THE GROUND... ONLY A FEW HUNDRED YARDS AWAY NOW..
CATCH ME! CATCH ME!
DID YOU EVER WITNESS WHAT HAPPENS TO AN EGG THAT FALLS FROM A GREAT HEIGHT?
I'LL TELL YOU! I'LL TELL YOU! BUT SAVE ME!
ALIGHTING, SUPERMAN WHIRLS AT GREAT SPEED...
IT WORKED!
...AND SNAGGING THE FALLING FIGURE, LOWERS IT GENTLY TO THE GROUND....
THERE YOU ARE! AS GOOD AS NEW!
I'M WAITING TO LEARN WHERE PRINCE MICHEAL HAS BEEN TAKEN!
TO LORD MURGOT'S CASTLE-- HE'S SECRETLY ALLIED WITH THE OXNALIANS!
6
ACROSS THE COUNTRYSIDE SPEEDS THE MAN OF TOMORROW AT A PACE SO SWIFT THE HUMAN EYE CAN SCARCELY FOLLOW HIS PROGRESS....
LORD MURGOT'S CASTLE, EH? THATS MY NEXT STOP!

WITHIN THE CASTLE...

ORDER THEM TO LET ME GO, LORD MURGOT! MY FATHER WILL MAKE YOU PAY FOR THIS!

CALM DOWN, MY HOT-HEADED PRINCE! YOU'RE GOING FOR A LONG JOURNEY

THERE IT IS-- DIRECTLY BELOW!

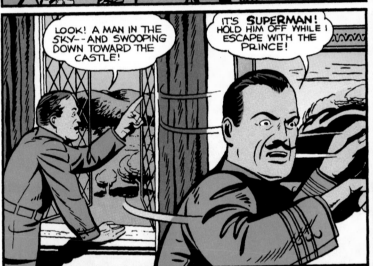

LOOK! A MAN IN THE SKY--AND SWOOPING DOWN TOWARD THE CASTLE!

IT'S SUPERMAN! HOLD HIM OFF WHILE I ESCAPE WITH THE PRINCE!

ALIGHTING ON THE CASTLE'S TURRET, SUPERMAN WADES INTO MURGOT'S HIRELINGS...

BET YOU WEREN'T EXPECTING THIS!

MEANWHILE--FORCING HIS YOUNG CAPTIVE INTO A FLEET PLANE, LORD MURGOT TAKES OFF---

NO ONE CAN OUTWIT LORD MURGOT!

YOU'LL PAY FOR YOUR TRAITOROUS ACTS!

⑦

YOU SAID IT, PRINCE! LORD MURGOT IS GO-ING TO LEARN THAT CRIME DOESN'T PAY-- AND LEARN IT THE HARD WAY!

STREAKING THRU THE FLEECY CLOUDS LIKE A HURTLING ROCKET, **SUPERMAN** QUICKLY CLOSES THE SPACE BETWEEN THE PLANE AND HIMSELF...

ALMOST THERE!

I'M COMING IN!

SUPERMAN!

THE BULLETS— CAREENING OFF YOUR CHEST!

CORRECT!

AS THE MAN OF *TOMORROW* LEAPS OUT INTO SPACE WITH THE PRINCE THE DAMAGED PLANE HURTLES EARTHWARD

YOU--YOU CAN **FLY!**

AND I'LL BET THAT LORD MURGOT WISHES AT THE MOMENT THAT **HE** COULD!

THE END OF A TRAITOR!

SMALL LOSS TO HIS COUNTRY!

AND SHORTLY AFTER...

FATHER!

MICHEAL! YOU'RE SAFE! *SAFE!*

⑧

YOU'VE SAVED MY SON FROM DEATH! ANYTHING IN MY KINGDOM IS YOURS FOR THE ASKING!

HEAR THAT? AIR-RAID SIRENS! UNLESS I ACT QUICKLY THERE MAY BE NOTHING LEFT OF YOUR KINGDOM TO GIVE!

A MONSTROUS FLEET OF DESTRUCTIVE OXNALIAN BOMBERS WINGS THEIR WAY OVER *NUMARK* ON A DEADLY MISSION... BOMBRACKS RELEASE THEIR DEADLY CARGO---

BUT AS THE BOMBS HURTLE EARTHWARD A STREAKING COSTUMED FIGURE WHIZZES INTO VIEW-- SCOOPS UP THE FALLING BOMBS---

I'LL TAKE THESE IF YOU DON'T MIND!

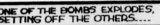

ONE OF THE BOMBS EXPLODES, SETTING OFF THE OTHERS....

IN MOMENTS, THE SKY IS CLEAR OF THE DEADLY MENACE---

HOW FORTUNATE WE ARE TO HAVE THAT INCREDIBLY STRONG MAN TO AID US!

WITHOUT HIM WE WOULD BE DOOMED!

NOW TO CARRY THE BATTLE TO OXNALIA ITSELF!

BUT AS THE MAN OF *TOMORROW* HURTLES OVER OXNALIA, HE IS SIGHTED BY RAZKAL'S VIGILANT WARRIORS---

FIRE!

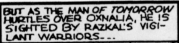

SUPERMAN IS STRUCK SQUARELY BY THE TREMENDOUSLY POWERFUL SHELL----

BUT THE MAN OF TOMORROW ESCAPES INJURY...

THE BOMB HASN'T BEEN INVENTED YET THAT CAN MAKE THE SLIGHTEST IMPRESSION ON ME!

BUT HERE'S WHERE I IMPRESS THE MEN WHO MAN THAT CANNON --- WITH MY FIST!!

FIRST YOU!

AND NOW YOU!

BUT HE IS!

EEK! HE CAN'T DO THIS TO OUR SUPERIOR RACE!

IN ANSWER TO THEIR OFFICER'S URGING, THE ENTIRE OXNALIAN ARMY CLOSES IN ON THE MAN OF STEEL ----

OH-BOY! THIS IS GOING TO BE A FIGHT THAT IS A FIGHT!

INTO THE GREAT ARMY STREAKS THE MAN OF STEEL, ARMED WITH NOTHING MORE LETHAL THAN HIS BARE FISTS-

JUST ONE ARMY TO CLEAN UP ON? GOSH!!! AND I WAS HOPING FOR OPPOSITION!

10

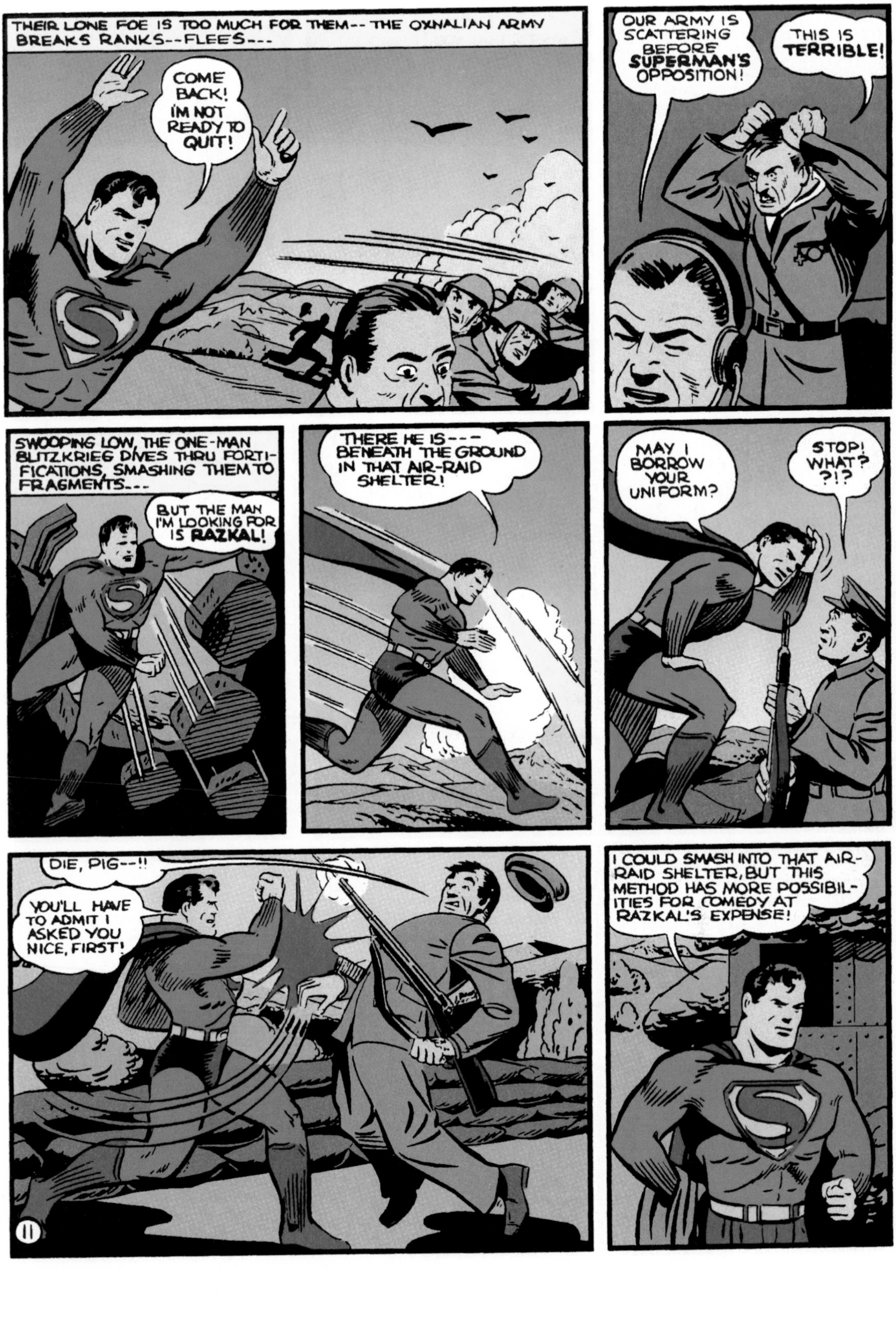
THEIR LONE FOE IS TOO MUCH FOR THEM-- THE OXNALIAN ARMY BREAKS RANKS--FLEES---
COME BACK! I'M NOT READY TO QUIT!
OUR ARMY IS SCATTERING BEFORE SUPERMAN'S OPPOSITION!
THIS IS TERRIBLE!
SWOOPING LOW, THE ONE-MAN BLITZKRIEG DIVES THRU FORTIFICATIONS, SMASHING THEM TO FRAGMENTS---
BUT THE MAN I'M LOOKING FOR IS RAZKAL!
THERE HE IS--- BENEATH THE GROUND IN THAT AIR-RAID SHELTER!
MAY I BORROW YOUR UNIFORM?
STOP! WHAT? ?!?
DIE, PIG--!!
YOU'LL HAVE TO ADMIT I ASKED YOU NICE, FIRST!
11
I COULD SMASH INTO THAT AIR-RAID SHELTER, BUT THIS METHOD HAS MORE POSSIBILITIES FOR COMEDY AT RAZKAL'S EXPENSE!

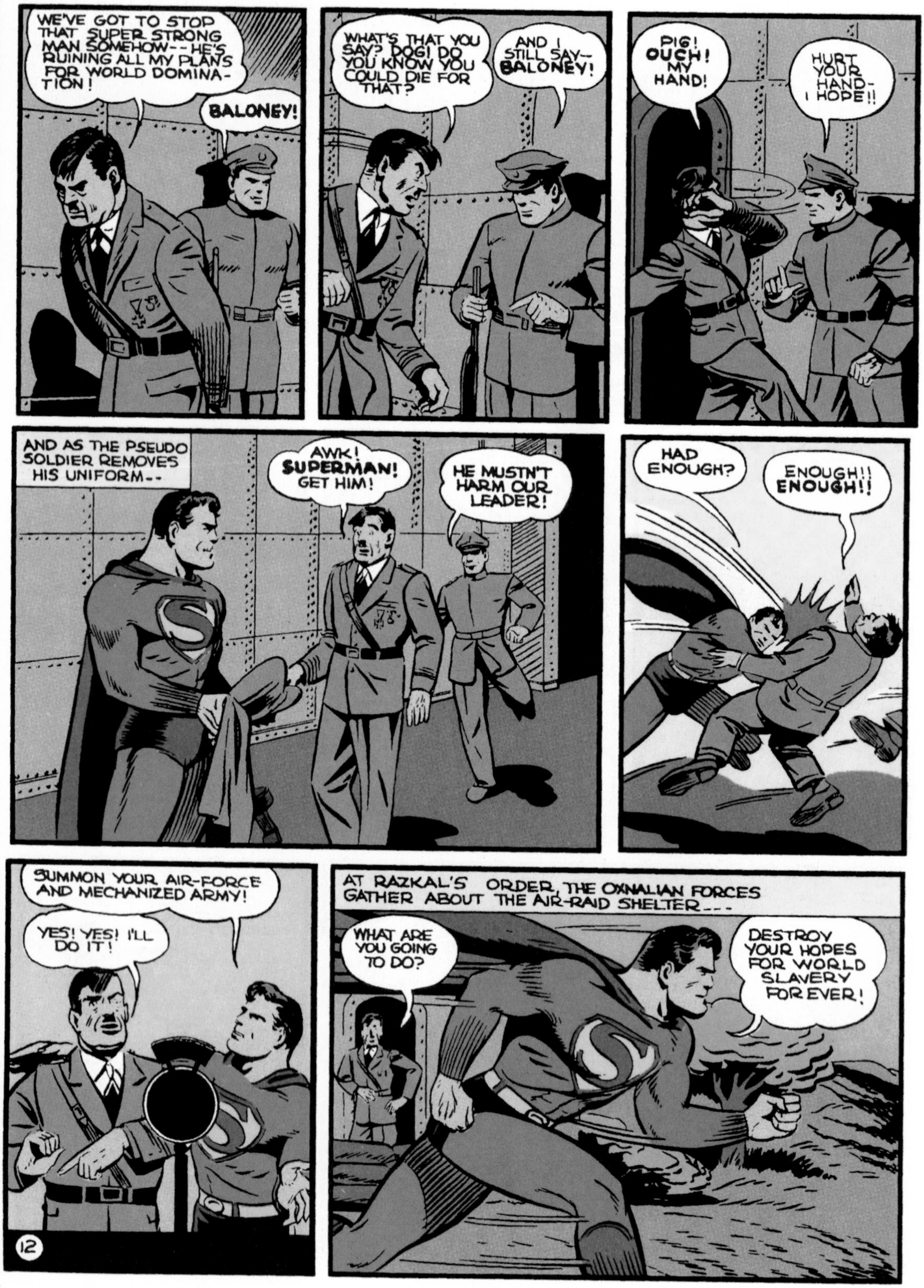
WE'VE GOT TO STOP THAT SUPER STRONG MAN SOMEHOW-- HE'S RUINING ALL MY PLANS FOR WORLD DOMINATION!
BALONEY!
WHAT'S THAT YOU SAY? DOG! DO YOU KNOW YOU COULD DIE FOR THAT?
AND I STILL SAY-- BALONEY!
PIG! OUCH! MY HAND!
HURT YOUR HAND- I HOPE!!
AND AS THE PSEUDO SOLDIER REMOVES HIS UNIFORM--
AWK! SUPERMAN! GET HIM!
HE MUSTN'T HARM OUR LEADER!
HAD ENOUGH?
ENOUGH!! ENOUGH!!
SUMMON YOUR AIR-FORCE AND MECHANIZED ARMY!
YES! YES! I'LL DO IT!
12
AT RAZKAL'S ORDER, THE OXNALIAN FORCES GATHER ABOUT THE AIR-RAID SHELTER---
WHAT ARE YOU GOING TO DO?
DESTROY YOUR HOPES FOR WORLD SLAVERY FOREVER!

WADING INTO THE MASSED TANKS, **SUPERMAN** DESTROYS THEM--

NO LONGER A THREAT TO YOUR PEACEFUL NEIGHBORS!

DITTO TO THE MIGHTY OXNALIAN AIRFORCE...

THE SCRAP HEAP FOR YOU!

RAZKAL FLEES...

GOT TO GET AWAY-- SAVE MY NECK!!

BUT HE IS BROUGHT DOWN BY ONE OF HIS OWN COUNTRYMEN-

YOU LED YOUR COUNTRYMEN ON THE PATH OF WAR.. AND NOW YOU SEEK TO ESCAPE THE CONSE- QUENCES.. BUT YOU **WON'T**!

SOLDIERS OF OXNALIA---- THROW DOWN YOUR ARMS SEEK PEACE WITH NUMARK

PEACE!

PEACE! WE WANT- - PEACE!

MY MISSION DONE--IT'S BACK TO THE UNITED STATES FOR ME!!

⑬

YOUR STORY ON HOW **SUPERMAN** ENDED THAT WAR IS A HUMDINGER! HOW LUCKY WE ARE TO HAVE SUCH A POWERFUL FORCE FOR GOOD IN THIS WORLD!

AND HOW UNFOR- UNATE THAT THE WORLD HAS TO BE CURSED BY THE EXISTENCE OF MON- STERS LIKE RAZKAL!

THE END

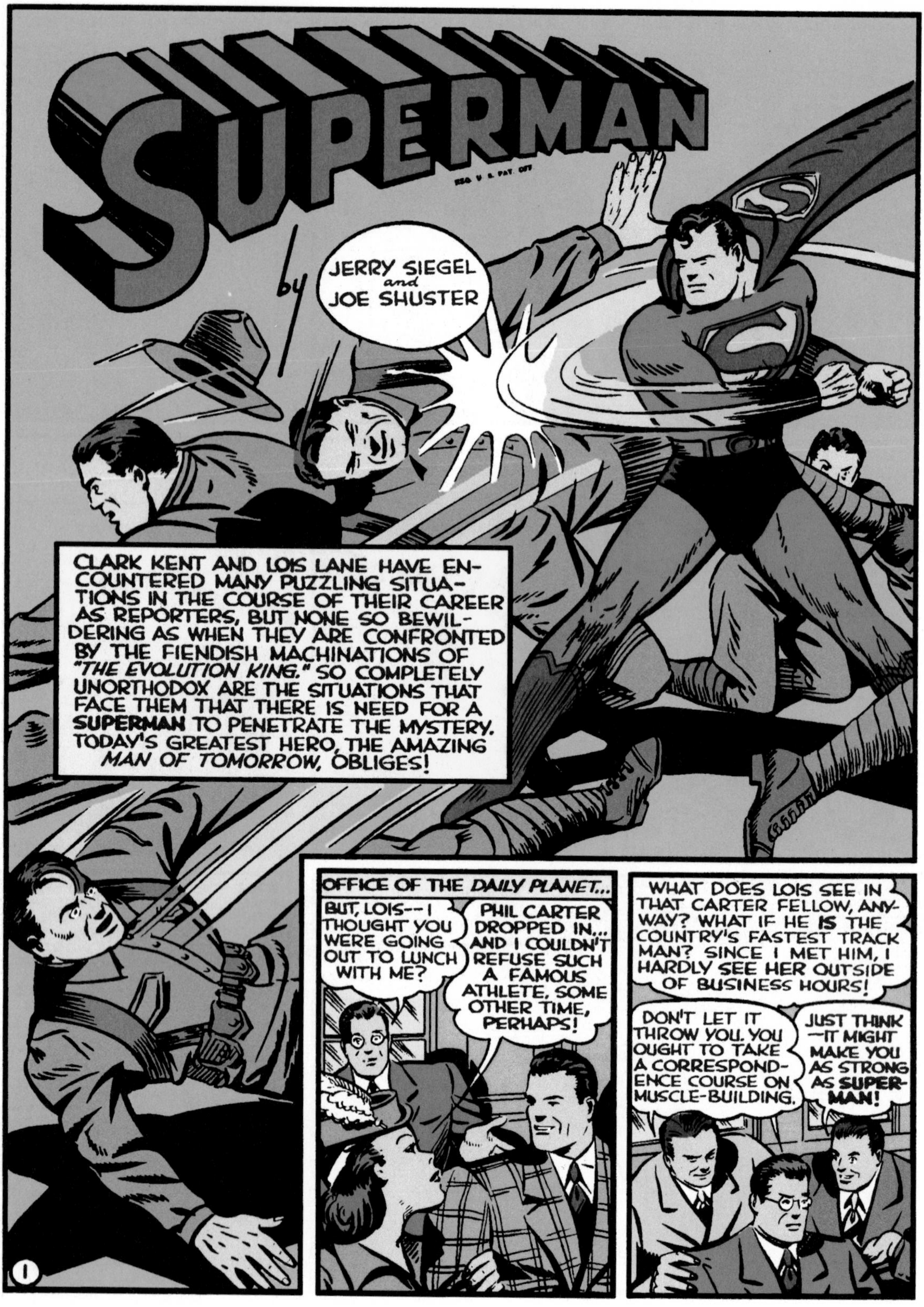
SUPERMAN
REG. U. S. PAT. OFF.
by JERRY SIEGEL and JOE SHUSTER
CLARK KENT AND LOIS LANE HAVE ENCOUNTERED MANY PUZZLING SITUATIONS IN THE COURSE OF THEIR CAREER AS REPORTERS, BUT NONE SO BEWILDERING AS WHEN THEY ARE CONFRONTED BY THE FIENDISH MACHINATIONS OF *"THE EVOLUTION KING."* SO COMPLETELY UNORTHODOX ARE THE SITUATIONS THAT FACE THEM THAT THERE IS NEED FOR A **SUPERMAN** TO PENETRATE THE MYSTERY. TODAY'S GREATEST HERO, THE AMAZING *MAN OF TOMORROW*, OBLIGES!
1
OFFICE OF THE *DAILY PLANET*...
BUT, LOIS--I THOUGHT YOU WERE GOING OUT TO LUNCH WITH ME?
PHIL CARTER DROPPED IN... AND I COULDN'T REFUSE SUCH A FAMOUS ATHLETE. SOME OTHER TIME, PERHAPS!
WHAT DOES LOIS SEE IN THAT CARTER FELLOW, ANYWAY? WHAT IF HE **IS** THE COUNTRY'S FASTEST TRACK MAN? SINCE I MET HIM, I HARDLY SEE HER OUTSIDE OF BUSINESS HOURS!
DON'T LET IT THROW YOU. YOU OUGHT TO TAKE A CORRESPONDENCE COURSE ON MUSCLE-BUILDING.
JUST THINK --IT MIGHT MAKE YOU AS STRONG AS **SUPERMAN!**

WEEKS LATER...

STRANGE...BUT I HAVEN'T SEEN PHIL CARTER FOR SOME TIME. I WONDER IF I COULD HAVE SAID ANYTHING THAT OFFENDED HIM?

YOU WON'T FIND ME UNHAPPY ABOUT IT! MAYBE YOU'LL PAY A LITTLE ATTENTION TO ME, NOW.

DAILY

CARTER VANISHES

SERGEANT CASEY TO SEE YOU, MR. KENT.

CASEY--TO SEE ME?

DON'T TELL ME YOUR PAST IS CATCHING UP WITH YOU, CLARK!

I'M NOT INSINUATING ANYTHING, CLARK-- BUT I'VE HEARD IT SAID THAT YOU WERE VERY JEALOUS ABOUT THE INTEREST LOIS SHOWED IN CARTER.

YOU'RE ON THE WRONG TRACK, CASEY. IF I KNOW CLARK KENT--AND I DO--HE'S INCAPABLE OF HARMING ANYONE-- LEAST OF ALL A ROBUST FELLOW LIKE PHIL CARTER!

NEXT MORNING...AS LOIS WALKS TO WORK...

I CAN'T FORGET PHIL'S STRANGE DISAPPEARANCE. I HOPE HE'S COME TO NO HARM!

LOIS! LOIS LANE!

YOU CALLED ME?

YES.--I--I MUST SPEAK TO YOU...

BUT--I DON'T KNOW YOU!

DON'T KNOW ME? DON'T KNOW WHO I AM? BUT YOU MUST! YOU MUST!

BECAUSE-- I AM PHIL CARTER!

YOU'RE OBVIOUSLY OUT OF YOUR MIND. IF YOU PERSIST IN ANNOYING ME, I'LL CALL A POLICEMAN.

DON'T GO! LISTEN TO ME-- *BELIEVE ME!*

BUT LOIS WALKS SWIFTLY ON, DISREGARDING THE OLD MAN'S PLEAS....

HE'S FOLLOWING ME, IF I COULD ONLY LOSE HIM!

THE ELDERLY MAN MOVES DESPERATELY AFTER HER. SUDDENLY A SLEEK CAR SWERVES SWIFTLY TO THE CURB....

N-NO!

GET IN!

LATER--AT THE NEWSPAPER OFFICE....

LET ME TELL YOU OF A PERFECTLY RIDICULOUS EPISODE THAT JUST HAPPENED, I WAS WALKING ALONG THE STREET, MINDING MY OWN BUSINESS, WHEN A TOTTERING OLD MAN ACCOSTED ME. HE *INSISTED* HE WAS PHIL CARTER.

BUT CARTER IS AN ATHLETE-- BURSTING WITH YOUTH AND ENERGY..!

NATURALLY, I SNUBBED HIM AND HURRIED OFF. YOU CAN IMAGINE HOW EMBARRASSED I FELT!

THERE'S SOMETHING ALMOST WEIRD ABOUT YOUR STORY. THE FELLOW MUST HAVE DELUSIONS, BUT THERE'S ONE WAY WE CAN CHECK UP ON HIS STORY.

WHAT IS IT?

DID HE TOUCH YOU OR ANY ARTICLE OF YOURS?

YES, MY POCKET-BOOK.

③

GIVE ME THAT POCKET-BOOK.

COME BACK! WHAT'S THE IDEA??

CLARK RETURNS SOME-TIME LATER....

I'LL THANK YOU FOR RETURNING MY POCKET-BOOK. NOW TELL ME, CLARK --WHAT WERE YOU UP TO?

IT DOESN'T MAKE SENSE, LOIS, BUT-- MAYBE THAT OLD MAN *WASN'T* LYING!

NOW **YOU** MUST BE GOING OUT OF YOUR MIND, TOO! EXPLAIN!

I TOOK YOUR POCKET-BOOK TO THE POLICE STATION. THEY EXAMINED IT AND FOUND CARTER'S FINGERPRINTS ON IT. WHEN I TOLD THEM YOUR FANTASTIC YARN, THEY THREW ME OUT!

AND I DON'T BLAME THEM. OBVIOUSLY, PHIL MUST HAVE TOUCHED MY POCKETBOOK BEFORE HE DISAPPEARED.

MAYBE--AND MAYBE NOT...

I WANT TO ASK YOU JUST ONE MORE QUESTION, LOIS, THEN I'LL LEAVE YOU ALONE. WHERE DID THE OLD MAN ACCOST YOU?

ON THE CORNER OF 19TH AND CHESTNUT STREET. NOW I HOPE YOU'RE SATISFIED.

MINUTES LATER--CORNER OF 19TH AND CHESTNUT....

HELLO, MR. KENT! DO YOU STILL THINK THAT MAYBE SOME DAY I'LL BE A REAL REPORTER JUST LIKE YOU?

QUITE POSSIBLE, TIM. BUT ONE OF THE MOST IMPORTANT REQUIREMENTS OF A REPORTER IS KEEN-EYED VIGILANCE. I'D LIKE TO TEST YOUR POWERS OF OBSERVATION, TIM.

DO YOU REMEMBER LOIS ACCOSTED BY AN ELDERLY MAN EARLIER TODAY?

I SURE DO, SHE WALKED OFF AND WHEN HE STARTED TO FOLLOW, SOME TOUGH GUYS GRABBED HIM AND PULLED HIM INTO AN EXPENSIVE-LOOKING CAR! HOW AM I DOING?

GREAT, TIM! ("-WHY SHOULD ANYONE HAVE WANTED TO SEIZE THAT OLD MAN? THIS GROWS MORE MYSTERIOUS EVERY MOMENT!-")

④

NOTICE ANYTHING ELSE, TIM?

WELL, I SAW THAT ONE OF THE TOUGH GUYS WHO GRABBED HIM IS TONY RICO--A MEMBER OF THE JOE GLOWER GANG!

LATER...

A REPORTER, EH? COME IN! JOE LIKES PUBLICITY!

IS GLOWER IN? I'M KENT OF THE *DAILY PLANET.*

CLARK KENT OF THE *DAILY PLANET*, EH? I LIKE YOUR ARTICLES, ESPECIALLY THE ONES ABOUT **SUPERMAN**. I SUPPOSE YOU'VE COME TO WRITE UP THE STORY OF MY LIFE?

SOMETHING LIKE THAT.

WELL, IT WAS NO CINCH WORKIN' MY WAY UP LIKE I HAVE. FIRST THERE WAS A COUPLE OF HARD MUGGS TO TAKE CARE OF, THEN...HEY, ARE YOU PAYING ATTENTION?

I--ER --GO ON...

I GET IT, NOW. YOU JUST CAME HERE TO SNOOP AROUND!

ER-- DON'T SHOVE...

--AND **DON'T** COME BACK!

THERE WAS NO NEED FOR VIOLENCE.

BUT BEFORE DEPARTING, CLARK FOCUSES HIS X-RAY VISION UPON JOE'S HOME...

IN THE CELLAR....!

I'VE FOUND THE MAN I'M AFTER! NOW IT'S UP TO **SUPERMAN** TO FREE HIM FROM JOE GLOWER'S CUSTODY!

ONE BLOW OF THE *MAN OF TOMORROW'S* FOOT SENDS THE CELLAR WINDOW FLYING INWARD OFF ITS HINGES....

OPEN SAYS-ME!

A NOISE IN THE BASE-MENT!

SOUNDS LIKE SOMEONE BREAKING IN!

GET DOWN THERE AND SEE WHAT'S TH' TROUBLE!

I'LL HAVE YOU FREE IN A JIFFY!

HEY, WOT--?

DON'T LET HIM GET AWAY WITH THE OLD GUY!

BUT IT'S SUPERMAN!

YOU MAY FIND THIS A TOUGHER ASSIGNMENT THAN YOU IMAGINE!

IT IS SUPERMAN! L-LET'S GET OUTA HERE!

WE HAVEN'T A CHANCE AGAINST HIM!

NONSENSE! THE STORIES WE READ ABOUT HIM ARE EXAGGERATED! WATCH!

6

SEE??

OUCH! OUCH! OHH-HH! MY HAND!

ANY MORE OF YOU LOOKING FOR TROUBLE?

NO!

WE AIN'T STARTIN' UP WITH YOU!

HE SEEMS DAZED!

HE DOESN'T SEEM TO UNDERSTAND MY TRANSFORMATION FROM **SUPERMAN** TO CLARK KENT.

LATER....

IS THIS THE ELDERLY MAN WHO ACCOSTED YOU?

YES! BUT WHERE DID YOU FIND HIM?

THAT DOESN'T MATTER. JUST ATTRIBUTE IT TO SOME ACTION ON **SUPERMAN'S** PART. THIS MAN CLAIMS HE'S PHIL CARTER. HERE'S WHERE WE FIND OUT!

WHAT DO YOU INTEND TO DO?

IN A NEARBY LABORATORY...

DAN, HERE, IS A FINGER-PRINT EXPERT. WE'LL SOON KNOW WHETHER THIS OLD FELLOW IS A LIAR OR A GREAT BIG MYSTERY.

WHAT'S THE VERDICT?

PHIL CARTER'S FINGERPRINTS, AND THE FINGER-PRINTS OF THIS OLD MAN ARE IDENTICAL!

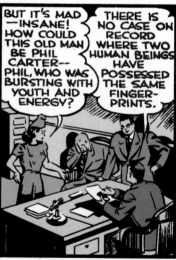

BUT IT'S MAD --INSANE! HOW COULD THIS OLD MAN BE PHIL CARTER-- PHIL, WHO WAS BURSTING WITH YOUTH AND ENERGY?

THERE IS NO CASE ON RECORD WHERE TWO HUMAN BEINGS HAVE POSSESSED THE SAME FINGER-PRINTS.

MEANWHILE -- JOE MAKES A TELEPHONE CALL....

BUT THERE'S NOTHING WE COULD DO ABOUT IT, BOSS! YOU CAN'T ARGUE WITH **SUPERMAN**--OKAY! OKAY!

⑦

SPREAD OUT...COVER THE TOWN THOROUGHLY! KEEP YOUR EYES PEELED FOR THE OLD GENT AND GRAB 'IM!

OKAY, JOE!

IF HE'S IN THE CITY, WE'LL FIND HIM!

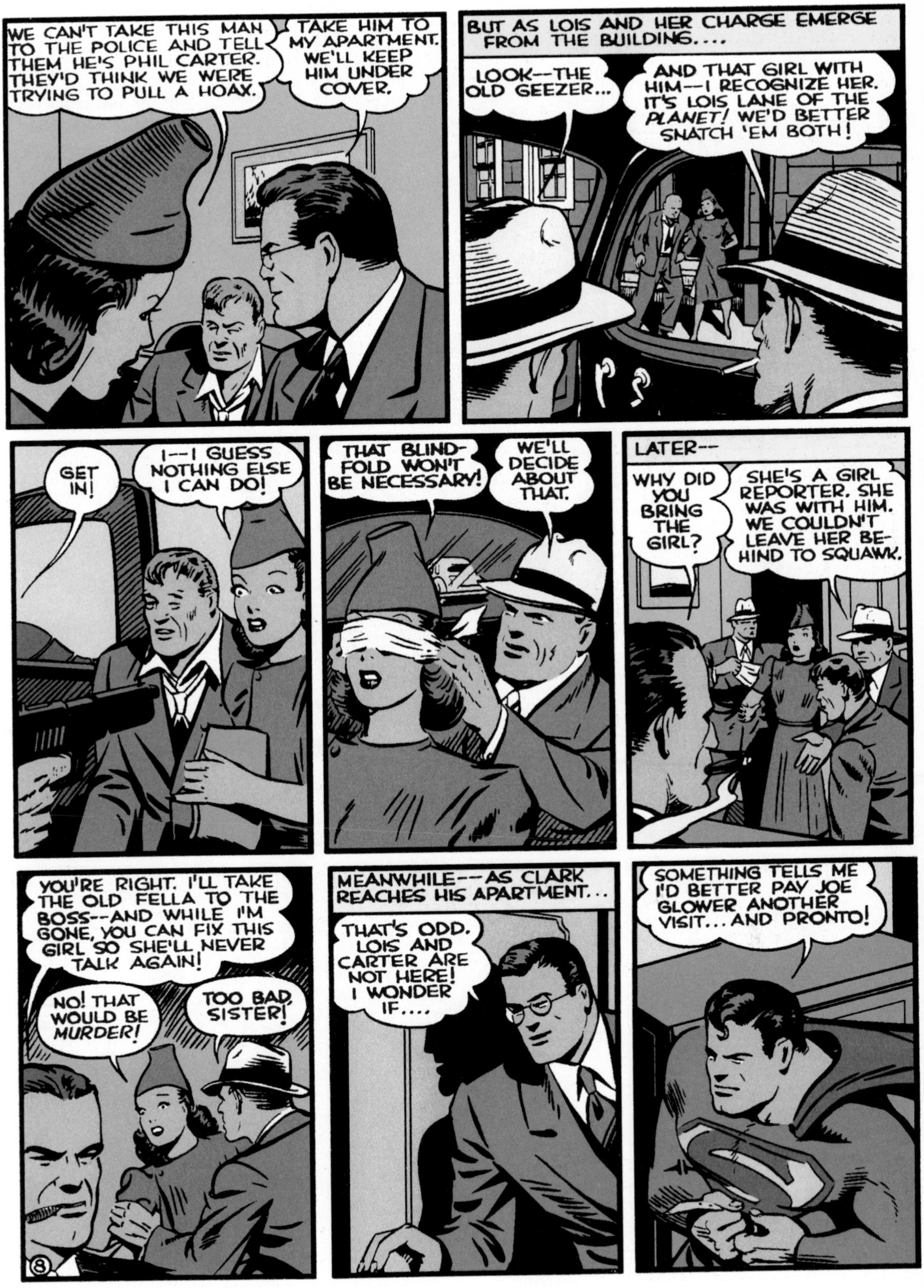
WE CAN'T TAKE THIS MAN TO THE POLICE AND TELL THEM HE'S PHIL CARTER. THEY'D THINK WE WERE TRYING TO PULL A HOAX.
TAKE HIM TO MY APARTMENT. WE'LL KEEP HIM UNDER COVER.
BUT AS LOIS AND HER CHARGE EMERGE FROM THE BUILDING....
LOOK--THE OLD GEEZER...
AND THAT GIRL WITH HIM--I RECOGNIZE HER. IT'S LOIS LANE OF THE *PLANET*! WE'D BETTER SNATCH 'EM BOTH!
GET IN!
I--I GUESS NOTHING ELSE I CAN DO!
THAT BLINDFOLD WON'T BE NECESSARY!
WE'LL DECIDE ABOUT THAT.
LATER--
WHY DID YOU BRING THE GIRL?
SHE'S A GIRL REPORTER. SHE WAS WITH HIM. WE COULDN'T LEAVE HER BEHIND TO SQUAWK.
YOU'RE RIGHT. I'LL TAKE THE OLD FELLA TO THE BOSS--AND WHILE I'M GONE, YOU CAN FIX THIS GIRL SO SHE'LL NEVER TALK AGAIN!
NO! THAT WOULD BE *MURDER*!
TOO BAD, SISTER!
8
MEANWHILE--AS CLARK REACHES HIS APARTMENT...
THAT'S ODD. LOIS AND CARTER ARE NOT HERE! I WONDER IF....
SOMETHING TELLS ME I'D BETTER PAY JOE GLOWER ANOTHER VISIT...AND PRONTO!

AS JOE DEPARTS WITH HIS ELDERLY CAPTIVE....

LET'S GET THIS OVER QUICK!

LET ME GO! LET ME GO!

LOIS —AT PISTOL-POINT!

DON'T PULL THAT TRIGGER!

AWK! WHA—?

SUPERMAN!

RACING THE BULLET, SUPERMAN BEATS IT TO ITS TARGET...

WANT IT AS A SOUVENIR, LOIS?

I WON'T MIND IF I NEVER SEE IT AGAIN.

PAPA SPANK!

WHERE'S CARTER?

I DON'T KNOW! THE GANGSTER CHIEF TOOK HIM AWAY WITH HIM.

AT THAT MOMENT—THE TELEPHONE RINGS....

PERHAPS I'LL SOON KNOW!

HERE'S WISHING YOU LUCK!

⑨

WHY HAVEN'T YOU COME, GLOWER? I INSIST ON PROMPTNESS--OR DO YOU WANT A TASTE OF THE FATE SUFFERED BY CARTER AND THE OTHERS?

("--THE MAN AT THE TOP-- JOE'S BOSS!")

THE MAN OF STEEL EXPERTLY DISGUISES HIS VOICE SO THAT IT SOUNDS EXACTLY LIKE THE GANG-LEADER'S....

SORRY, BOSS, BUT I...I MISPLACED THE ADDRESS.

218 FERNALD ROAD... AND HURRY...

BETTER LEAVE HERE IMMEDIATELY!

A GOOD IDEA!

SHORTLY AFTER --- HE DEPOSITS LOIS ATOP THE NEWSPAPER BUILDING....

I'M GOING AFTER CARTER--AND THE CRIMINAL RESPONSIBLE FOR HIS CONDITION.

GOOD LUCK!

MEANWHILE.....JOE GLOWER REACHES HIS DESTINATION...

HOW COULD YOU HAVE ARRIVED SO QUICKLY.... WHEN I SPOKE TO YOU ON THE TELEPHONE ONLY MOMENTS AGO?

BUT YOU DIDN'T SPEAK TO ME.

EVIDENTLY SOMEONE IS TRYING TO PUT ONE OVER ON US. IN THAT EVENT I'D BETTER TAKE PRECAUTIONS --JUST IN CASE WE HAVE AN UNEXPECTED VISITOR....

HERE IT IS-- 218 FERNALD ROAD...!

10

BUT AS SUPERMAN CRASHES IN, HE IS MET BY A DEADLY, PARALYZING RAY...!

WHAT --??

LOOKS AS THO I'VE BAGGED WORTHWHILE PREY THIS TIME!

S-SUPERMAN!

AS **SUPERMAN** STANDS POWERLESS BEFORE THE FORCE OF THE RAY....

A TOAST---TO THE DE-STRUCTION OF **SUPERMAN!**

BUT FIGHTING THE INSID-IOUS POWER OF THE RAY, **SUPERMAN** BATTLES FORWARD

GOT TO-- REACH THAT-- RAY...

HE'S MOVING!

ONE WELL-DIRECTED BLOW DESTROYS THE RAY-MACHINE!

AH-HHHH! THAT'S MORE LIKE IT!

STOP HIM!

JOE ATTEMPTS TO PREVENT **SUPERMAN'S** RUSH...BUT THE *MAN OF STEEL* HANDLES HIM AS EASILY AS THO HE WERE AN INFANT...

ONE SIDE... OR YOU MAY GET HURT!

SUDDENLY **SUPERMAN** PAUSES AS HE WITNESSES AN AMAZING TRANSFORMATION. JOE'S SKIN TIGHTENS...WRINKLES...HIS FIGURE STOOPS...AND....

MY HANDS... MY HANDS...

GOOD HEAVENS! YOUR FACE...

NEXT MOMENT...WHERE THE YOUTHFUL GANG-LEADER HAD STOOD IS AN OLD MAN...

--WHAT HAPPENED?

"THE EVOLUTION KING" DID IT TO GET ME OUT OF THE WAY.

⑪

DO YOU REALIZE THAT I'M THE ONLY ONE NOW WHO CAN GET HIM TO CHANGE YOU BACK TO NORMAL AGE? QUICK! WHERE HAS HE GONE?

AT... AT... *MITHROW TAVERN.*

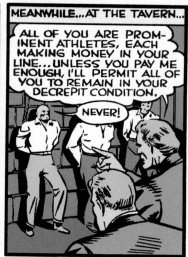

MEANWHILE...AT THE TAVERN...

ALL OF YOU ARE PROM-INENT ATHLETES, EACH MAKING MONEY IN YOUR LINE...UNLESS YOU PAY ME ENOUGH, I'LL PERMIT ALL OF YOU TO REMAIN IN YOUR DECREPIT CONDITION.

NEVER!

THE "EVOLUTION KING" SIGHTS IN A VISION-SCREEN...

SUPERMAN COMING!

MY CUE TO EXIT!

I SEE THAT THE EVIL SCIENTIST HAS FLOWN-- THAT MEANS YOU MEN ARE FREE TO RETURN TO YOUR HOMES. I'LL DO WHAT I CAN TO RETURN YOU TO NORMALCY.

THANK YOU...

FREED FROM THESE CHAINS AT LAST!

DAYS LATER...A NEW WAVE OF PUZZLING CIRCUMSTANCES STRIKES *METROPOLIS* AS NUMBERS OF INFANTS ARE FOUND.

I MUST BE CRAZY TO EVEN SUBMIT TO PERMITTING THESE TOTS TO BE FINGERPRINTED. YOU AND YOUR FANTASTIC THEORIES!

I'M SURE YOU'LL FIND THAT THEIR FINGERPRINTS CHECK WITH THOSE OF THE MISSING MEN.

AND SHORTLY AFTER....

BY GOSH --YOU'RE RIGHT! BUT WHAT'S THE EXPLANATION??

THIS IS THE WORK OF THE "EVOLUTION KING". ONE WAY OR ANOTHER HE HAS LEARNED HOW TO ADVANCE OR REVERT A HUMAN BEING'S AGE. AN INCREDIBLE FEAT --BUT HE'S ACCOMPLISHED IT.

12

LATER....LOIS AND CLARK ARE KIDNAPPED BY THUGS.

GET IN THERE!

BUT WHY?

"THE EVOLUTION KING" DOESN'T LIKE YOUR STORIES ABOUT HIM!

AND LATER.... IN THE "EVOLUTION KING'S" LAIR...

YES...I WAS DEFINITELY DISPLEASED BY YOUR ARTICLES, THEREFORE, YOU SHALL SUFFER THE FATE OF ALL THOSE WHO ANGER ME.

NO!

"-I'VE GOT TO THINK FAST!-"

SO **YOU'RE** THE ONE RESPONSIBLE FOR THE CHANGE IN AGE OF THOSE ELDERLY MEN AND THE INFANTS! BUT --HOW DID YOU DO IT?

I'LL SHOW YOU!

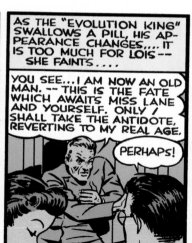

AS THE "EVOLUTION KING" SWALLOWS A PILL, HIS APPEARANCE CHANGES....IT IS TOO MUCH FOR LOIS-- SHE FAINTS....

YOU SEE...I AM NOW AN OLD MAN. -- THIS IS THE FATE WHICH AWAITS MISS LANE AND YOURSELF. ONLY I SHALL TAKE THE ANTIDOTE, REVERTING TO MY REAL AGE.

PERHAPS!

NOTING THAT LOIS IS UNCONSCIOUS, CLARK BURSTS FREE OF HIS BONDS

WHAT?

DIDN'T EXPECT THIS DEVELOPMENT, DID YOU?

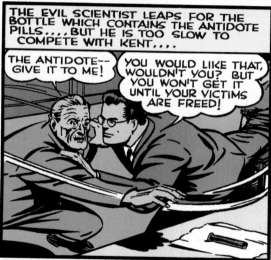

THE EVIL SCIENTIST LEAPS FOR THE BOTTLE WHICH CONTAINS THE ANTIDOTE PILLS....BUT HE IS TOO SLOW TO COMPETE WITH KENT....

THE ANTIDOTE-- GIVE IT TO ME!

YOU WOULD LIKE THAT, WOULDN'T YOU? BUT YOU WON'T GET IT UNTIL YOUR VICTIMS ARE FREED!

THE SCIENTIST LEAPS TO LOIS'S SIDE....

GIVE ME THE ANTIDOTE--OR I TRANSFORM THE LANE GIRL TO A HORRIBLE HAG!

YOU WIN! HERE IT IS!

HANDS SHAKING WITH EAGERNESS, THE "EVOLUTION KING" SWALLOWS THE PILLS HUNGRILY...BUT...INSTEAD OF GROWING YOUNGER, HIS AGE **INCREASES**...!

YOU FOOL! YOU GAVE ME THE AGE PILLS! I'LL DIE OF OLD AGE!

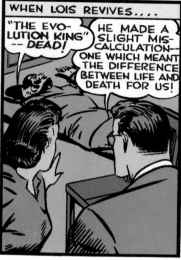

WHEN LOIS REVIVES....

"THE EVOLUTION KING" --DEAD!

HE MADE A SLIGHT MISCALCULATION-- ONE WHICH MEANT THE DIFFERENCE BETWEEN LIFE AND DEATH FOR US!

LATER--THE *PLANET* OFFICE

NOW THAT THE VICTIMS' AGES HAVE BEEN RESTORED, LOIS, HOW ABOUT STEPPING OUT WITH ME?

SORRY, CLARK, WHEN PHIL CARTER WAS RETURNED TO NORMAL, HIS FIRST REQUEST WAS FOR A DATE WITH ME. I ACCEPTED!

THE END

346

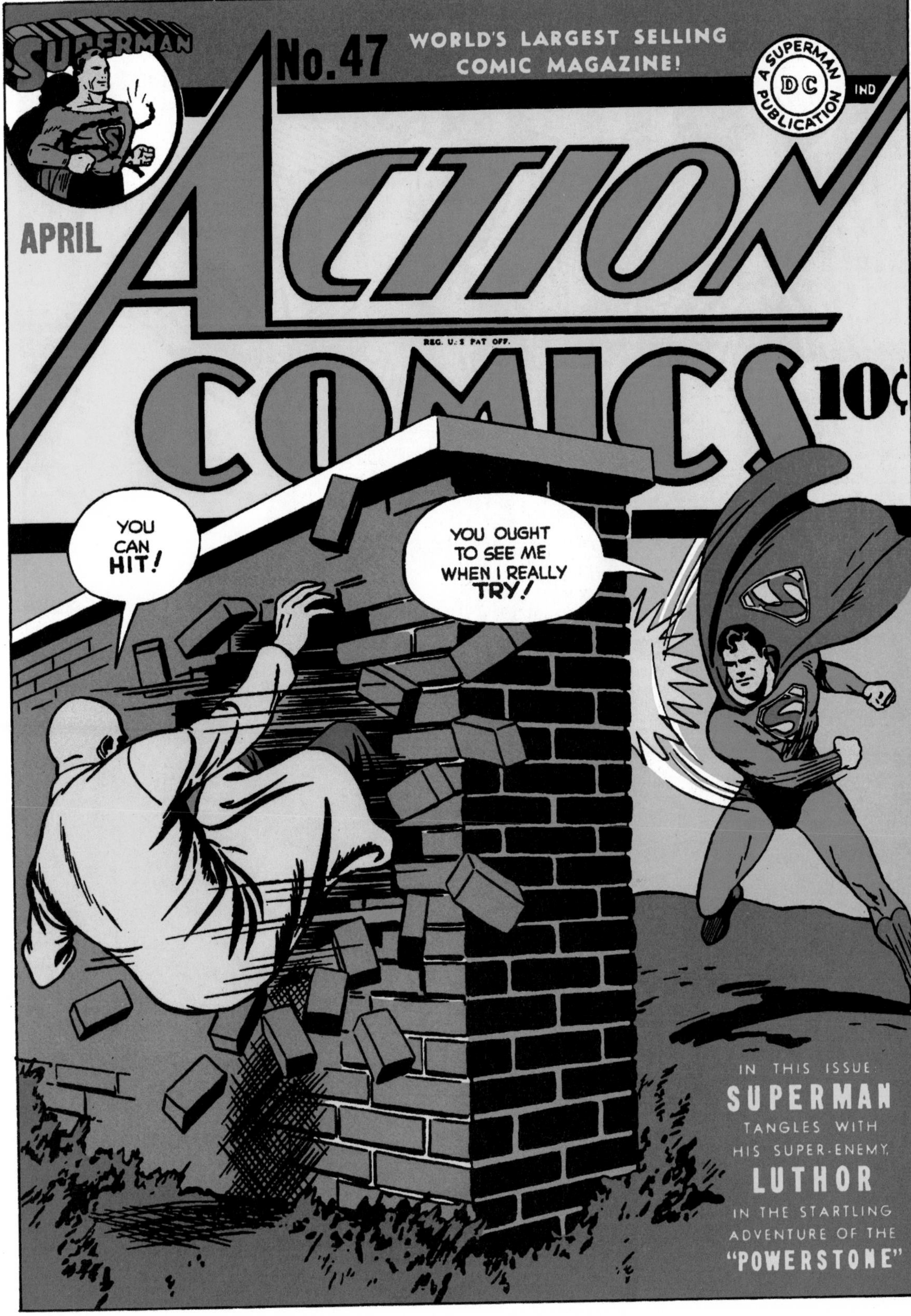

SUPERMAN
No. 47
WORLD'S LARGEST SELLING COMIC MAGAZINE!
A SUPERMAN DC PUBLICATION
IND
APRIL
ACTION
REG. U.S PAT OFF.
COMICS
10¢
YOU CAN HIT!
YOU OUGHT TO SEE ME WHEN I REALLY TRY!
IN THIS ISSUE: SUPERMAN TANGLES WITH HIS SUPER-ENEMY, LUTHOR IN THE STARTLING ADVENTURE OF THE "POWERSTONE"

SUPERMAN

A POWER-MAD, EVIL SCIENTIST, SUPERMAN'S MOST INVETERATE HATER, IS LUTHOR. HE COULD HAVE BEEN A MIGHTY FORCE FOR GOOD IN THE WORLD, YET HE CHOSE TO DIRECT HIS GREAT SCIENTIFIC BRAIN INTO CRIMINAL CHANNELS. BUT THOUGH LUTHOR HAS BEEN A DANGEROUS FOE IN THE PAST, A NEW DEVELOPMENT RENDERS HIM A HUNDREDFOLD MORE FORMIDABLE! SUPERMAN MEETS AN OPPONENT WORTHY OF HIM IN AS STARTLING A SUPERMAN ADVENTURE AS YOU HAVE READ IN A LONG TIME . . . . . "POWERSTONE"!

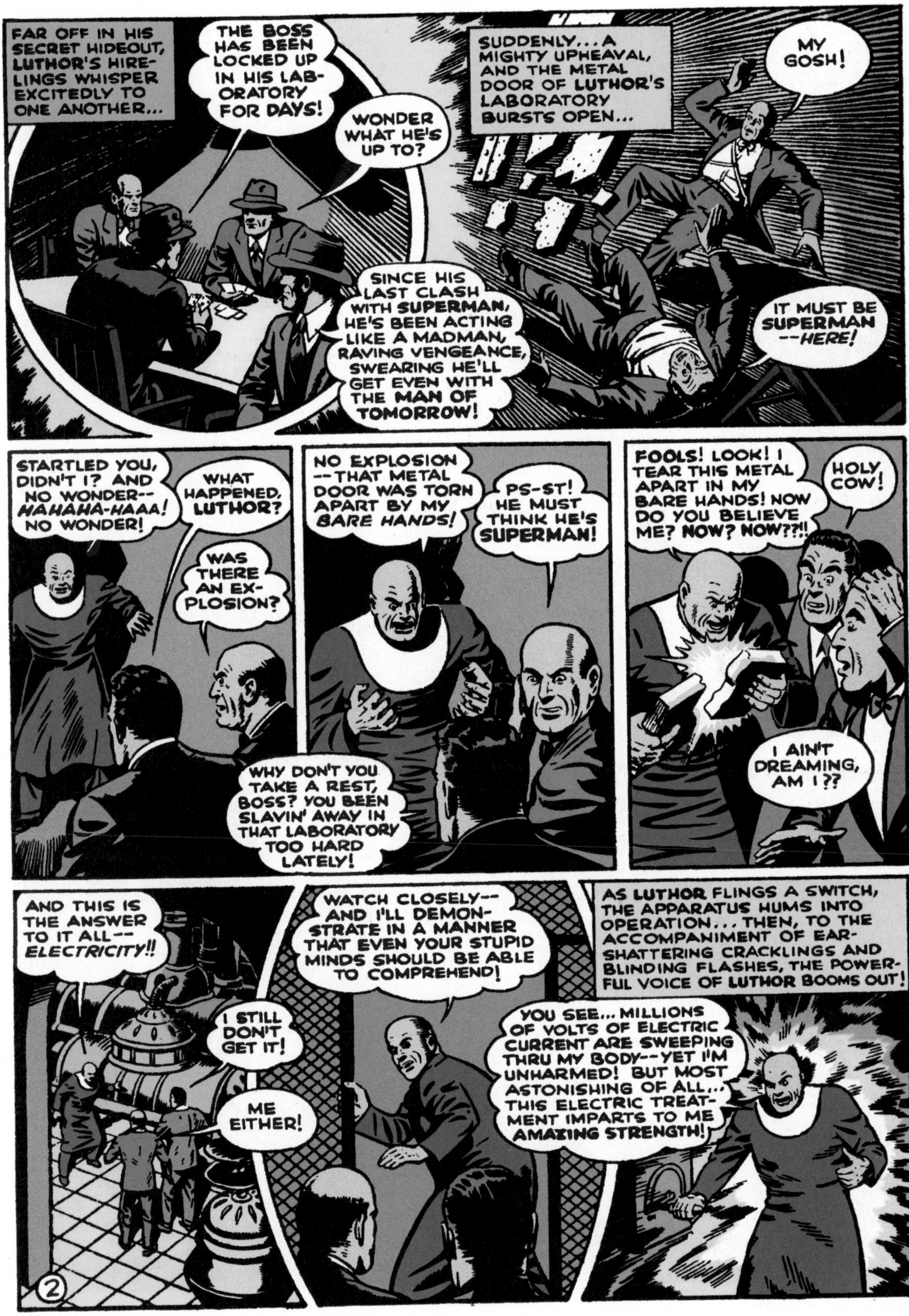
FAR OFF IN HIS SECRET HIDEOUT, LUTHOR'S HIRE-LINGS WHISPER EXCITEDLY TO ONE ANOTHER...
THE BOSS HAS BEEN LOCKED UP IN HIS LAB-ORATORY FOR DAYS!
WONDER WHAT HE'S UP TO?
SINCE HIS LAST CLASH WITH SUPERMAN, HE'S BEEN ACTING LIKE A MADMAN, RAVING VENGEANCE, SWEARING HE'LL GET EVEN WITH THE MAN OF TOMORROW!
SUDDENLY... A MIGHTY UPHEAVAL, AND THE METAL DOOR OF LUTHOR'S LABORATORY BURSTS OPEN...
MY GOSH!
IT MUST BE SUPERMAN --HERE!
STARTLED YOU, DIDN'T I? AND NO WONDER-- HAHAHA-HAAA! NO WONDER!
WHAT HAPPENED, LUTHOR?
WAS THERE AN EX-PLOSION?
NO EXPLOSION --THAT METAL DOOR WAS TORN APART BY MY BARE HANDS!
PS-ST! HE MUST THINK HE'S SUPERMAN!
WHY DON'T YOU TAKE A REST, BOSS? YOU BEEN SLAVIN' AWAY IN THAT LABORATORY TOO HARD LATELY!
FOOLS! LOOK! I TEAR THIS METAL APART IN MY BARE HANDS! NOW DO YOU BELIEVE ME? NOW? NOW??!!
HOLY COW!
I AIN'T DREAMING, AM I??
AND THIS IS THE ANSWER TO IT ALL-- ELECTRICITY!!
I STILL DON'T GET IT!
ME EITHER!
WATCH CLOSELY-- AND I'LL DEMON-STRATE IN A MANNER THAT EVEN YOUR STUPID MINDS SHOULD BE ABLE TO COMPREHEND!
AS LUTHOR FLINGS A SWITCH, THE APPARATUS HUMS INTO OPERATION... THEN, TO THE ACCOMPANIMENT OF EAR-SHATTERING CRACKLINGS AND BLINDING FLASHES, THE POWER-FUL VOICE OF LUTHOR BOOMS OUT!
YOU SEE... MILLIONS OF VOLTS OF ELECTRIC CURRENT ARE SWEEPING THRU MY BODY--YET I'M UNHARMED! BUT MOST ASTONISHING OF ALL... THIS ELECTRIC TREAT-MENT IMPARTS TO ME AMAZING STRENGTH!
2

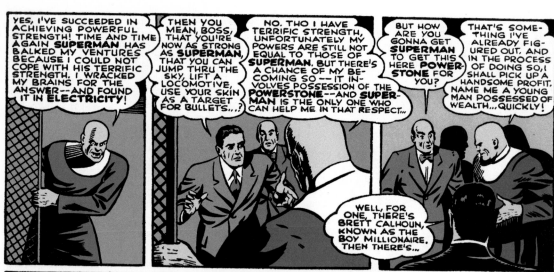

YES, I'VE SUCCEEDED IN ACHIEVING POWERFUL STRENGTH! TIME AND TIME AGAIN **SUPERMAN** HAS BALKED MY VENTURES BECAUSE I COULD NOT COPE WITH HIS TERRIFIC STRENGTH. I WRACKED MY BRAINS FOR THE ANSWER--AND FOUND IT IN **ELECTRICITY**!

THEN YOU MEAN, BOSS, THAT YOU'RE NOW AS STRONG AS **SUPERMAN**, THAT YOU CAN JUMP THRU THE SKY, LIFT A LOCOMOTIVE, USE YOUR SKIN AS A TARGET FOR BULLETS...?

NO. THO I HAVE TERRIFIC STRENGTH, UNFORTUNATELY MY POWERS ARE STILL NOT EQUAL TO THOSE OF **SUPERMAN**. BUT THERE'S A CHANCE OF MY BECOMING SO -- IT INVOLVES POSSESSION OF THE **POWERSTONE**--AND **SUPERMAN** IS THE ONLY ONE WHO CAN HELP ME IN THAT RESPECT...

BUT HOW ARE YOU GONNA GET **SUPERMAN** TO GET THIS HERE **POWERSTONE** FOR YOU?

THAT'S SOMETHING I'VE ALREADY FIGURED OUT, AND IN THE PROCESS OF DOING SO, I SHALL PICK UP A HANDSOME PROFIT. NAME ME A YOUNG MAN POSSESSED OF WEALTH...QUICKLY!

WELL, FOR ONE, THERE'S BRETT CALHOUN, KNOWN AS THE BOY MILLIONAIRE. THEN THERE'S...

BRETT CALHOUN WILL DO, AND NOW, MEN, I TAKE MY LEAVE. WHEN YOU NEXT SEE ME, I SHALL BE WELL ON THE ROAD TO BEING THE MASTER OF THE WORLD!

LATER --AS YOUNG BRETT CALHOUN SITS DROWSILY IN THE STUDY OF HIS MANSION, SLEEPILY REGARDING A BOOK, A HIGH-PITCHED SHRILL OF LAUGHTER FROM BEHIND CAUSES HIM TO WHIRL IN TERROR....

WHO-- WHO'S THAT ??

HAHAHA-HAAA! JUST LUTHOR, LAD!

WHAT ARE YOU DOING IN THIS HOUSE? GET OUT-- OR I'LL CALL THE POLICE!

YOU'LL DO NOTHING OF THE KIND!

IN FACT, YOU'LL DO EXACTLY AS I SAY, OR YOU'LL DIE! UNLESS YOU OBEY ME, I'LL SQUEEZE THAT WHITE THROAT OF YOURS AGAIN-- ONLY NEXT TIME I WON'T RELAX MY GRIP UNTIL YOU CEASE BREATHING!

WH-WHAT DO YOU WANT ME TO DO?

SOMETHING STRANGE--UNUSUAL-- THAT WILL STARTLE THE ENTIRE CITY OF METROPOLIS! PAY CLOSE HEED TO MY EVERY WORD...!

3

SHORTLY AFTERWARD... STRIDING INTO THE STREET, LUTHOR STEPS DIRECTLY INTO THE PATH OF A SPEEDING AUTO...

HALT!

A MAN SIGNAL-ING FOR THE CAR TO STOP—WHAT SHALL I DO, SIR?

HE MAY BE A HOLDUP MAN, WE CAN'T TAKE ANY CHANCES!

AS THE AUTO CONTINUES ON, LUTHOR CRASHES AGAINST IT... SLOWS IT DOWN. SIMULTANEOUSLY, A BLAST OF ELECTRICITY LEAVES HIS FIGURE AND BATHES THE ENTIRE CAR IN ITS FANTASTIC GLOW...

I WARNED YOU!

LEAPING TO THE RUNNING BOARD, LUTHOR SWIFTLY ANNEXES JEWELRY FROM THE SLUMPED FIGURES...

SHOCKED INTO INSENSI-BILITY-- BY THE TIME THE SHOCK WEARS OFF AND THEY RETURN TO NORMAL, I'LL BE FAR AWAY--AND SO WILL THEIR JEWELS! HAHAHA-HAAA!

AND STILL LATER--AVAILING HIMSELF OF THE IMMENSE ELECTRICAL POWER STORED WITHIN HIS FIGURE, LUTHOR BURNS HIS WAY THRU A BANK'S METAL DOOR...

NO OBSTACLE CAN PREVENT ME FROM REACHING MY GOAL!

④

ABOUT TO RETIRE FOR THE EVENING, CLARK KENT CHANGES HIS MIND WHEN HE HEARS A POLICE CALL....

CALLING CAR 85! BURGLAR ALARM RING-ING AT NATION-AL BANK! INVESTIGATE!

THAT'S JUST AROUND THE CORNER!

SWIFTLY, KENT WHIPS INTO HIS WORLD-FAMOUS BLUE COSTUME AND RED CAPE...

THIS IS ONE INVESTIGATION SUPERMAN IS GOING TO HORN IN ON!

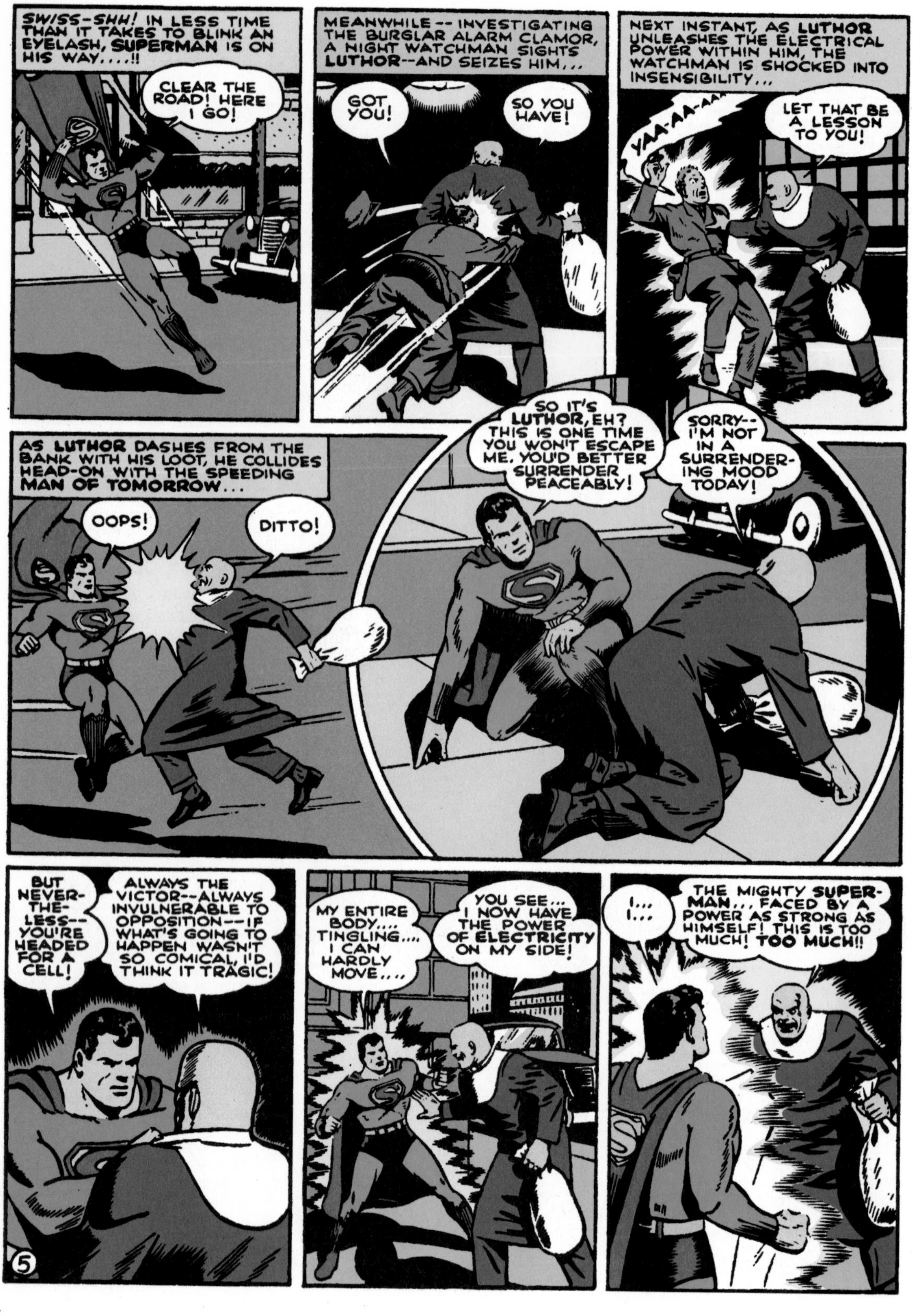
SWISS-SHH! IN LESS TIME THAN IT TAKES TO BLINK AN EYELASH, SUPERMAN IS ON HIS WAY....!!
CLEAR THE ROAD! HERE I GO!
MEANWHILE -- INVESTIGATING THE BURGLAR ALARM CLAMOR, A NIGHT WATCHMAN SIGHTS LUTHOR--AND SEIZES HIM,..
GOT YOU!
SO YOU HAVE!
NEXT INSTANT, AS LUTHOR UNLEASHES THE ELECTRICAL POWER WITHIN HIM, THE WATCHMAN IS SHOCKED INTO INSENSIBILITY...
YAA-AA-AA
LET THAT BE A LESSON TO YOU!
AS LUTHOR DASHES FROM THE BANK WITH HIS LOOT, HE COLLIDES HEAD-ON WITH THE SPEEDING MAN OF TOMORROW...
OOPS!
DITTO!
SO IT'S LUTHOR, EH? THIS IS ONE TIME YOU WON'T ESCAPE ME. YOU'D BETTER SURRENDER PEACEABLY!
SORRY-- I'M NOT IN A SURRENDERING MOOD TODAY!
BUT NEVER-THE-LESS-- YOU'RE HEADED FOR A CELL!
ALWAYS THE VICTOR--ALWAYS INVULNERABLE TO OPPOSITION--IF WHAT'S GOING TO HAPPEN WASN'T SO COMICAL, I'D THINK IT TRAGIC!
5
MY ENTIRE BODY.... TINGLING.... I CAN HARDLY MOVE....
YOU SEE... I NOW HAVE THE POWER OF ELECTRICITY ON MY SIDE!
I... I...
THE MIGHTY SUPER-MAN... FACED BY A POWER AS STRONG AS HIMSELF! THIS IS TOO MUCH! TOO MUCH!!

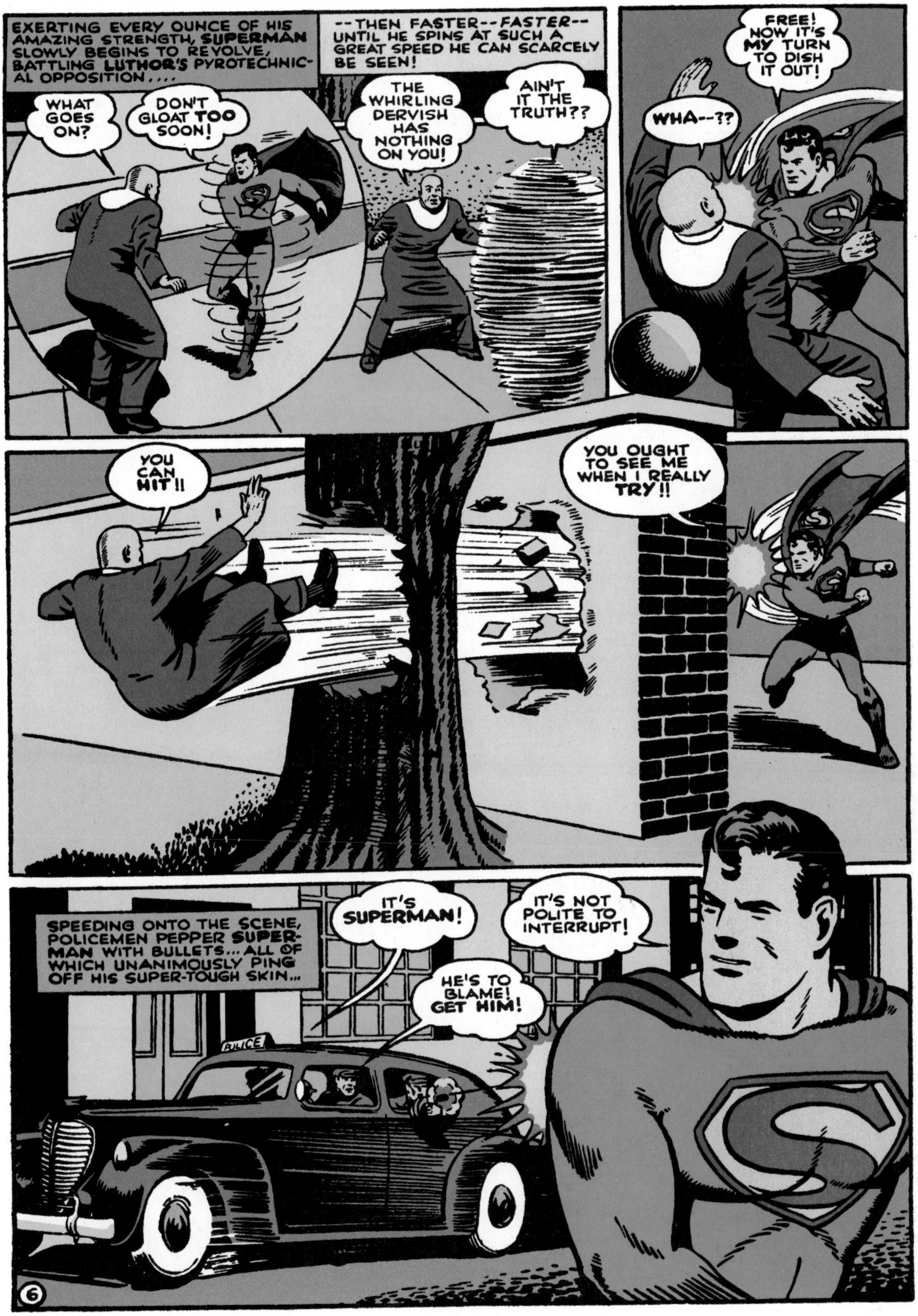
EXERTING EVERY OUNCE OF HIS AMAZING STRENGTH, SUPERMAN SLOWLY BEGINS TO REVOLVE, BATTLING LUTHOR'S PYROTECHNICAL OPPOSITION....
WHAT GOES ON?
DON'T GLOAT TOO SOON!
--THEN FASTER--FASTER--UNTIL HE SPINS AT SUCH A GREAT SPEED HE CAN SCARCELY BE SEEN!
THE WHIRLING DERVISH HAS NOTHING ON YOU!
AIN'T IT THE TRUTH??
FREE! NOW IT'S MY TURN TO DISH IT OUT!
WHA--??
YOU CAN HIT!!
YOU OUGHT TO SEE ME WHEN I REALLY TRY!!
SPEEDING ONTO THE SCENE, POLICEMEN PEPPER SUPERMAN WITH BULLETS... ALL OF WHICH UNANIMOUSLY PING OFF HIS SUPER-TOUGH SKIN...
IT'S SUPERMAN!
HE'S TO BLAME! GET HIM!
IT'S NOT POLITE TO INTERRUPT!
POLICE
6

SEIZING THE PATROLCAR'S FRONT BUMPER, SUPER-MAN GIVES IT A SHARP TWIST...

SWING IT!!

...SO THAT THE ENTIRE CAR WHIRLS ABOUT AND FACES THE OPPOSITE DIRECTION!

SAVE YOUR AMMUNITION... WE NEED IT FOR NATIONAL DEFENSE!

BUT WHEN THE MAN OF STEEL TURNS TO RESUME HIS BATTLE WITH LUTHOR...

HE'S GONE-- TOOK THE OPPORTUNITY TO FLEE! ELECTRICITY OR NO ELECTRICITY-- HE'S STILL A COWARD AT HEART!

BUT I'VE A HUNCH WE'RE GOING TO HAVE A RETURN MATCH! AND NEXT TIME THERE MAY BE NO CONVENIENT DISTRACTIONS!

NEXT MORNING...

WHAT'S COOKIN', CHIEF?

PLENTY! BRETT CALHOUN HAS INVITED REP-RESENTATIVES FROM ALL THE NEWSPAPERS TO HIS HOME. HE'S GOT AN IMPORT-ANT ANNOUNCE-MENT TO MAKE. GET GOING!

BRETT CALHOUN? TO THINK I'LL GET PAID FOR INTER-VIEWING HIM!

LATER-- AT THE CALHOUN MANSION...

I'M SURE YOU GENTLEMEN OF THE PRESS ARE BUSY, SO I'LL MAKE IT BRIEF. I'M GOING TO GIVE AWAY HALF OF MY FORTUNE--THREE MILLION DOLLARS--GOING TO GIVE IT AWAY TO A PERFECT STRANGER...

YOU'RE MR. CALHOUN'S LAWYER. IS THIS ON THE UP-AND-UP?

I'M AFRAID IT IS. HE MUST BE MAD.

ARE YOU SERIOUS?

WHO IS THIS STRANGER?

LEND AN EAR, YOU NEWS-HOUNDS! HERE COMES THE MOST INTERESTING PART OF MY ANNOUNCEMENT!

I WILL GIVE THE THREE MILLION DOLLARS TO WHOEVER CAN PROVE HE IS ALREADY THE RICHEST MAN IN METROPOLIS! ANYONE CAN COME HERE TONIGHT AND LAY CLAIM TO THE GIFT, BUT HE MUST DISPLAY AT LEAST $100,000 IN CASH TO THE MAN AT THE DOOR TO DEMONSTRATE HE IS QUALIFIED TO ENTER THE CONTEST. DETECTIVES WILL BE PRESENT TO PROTECT THE CONTESTANTS' FUNDS AND IDENTITY!

7

IS THIS ON THE LEVEL?

ABSOLUTELY! AND FOR THE LIFE OF ME I CAN'T MAKE ANY SENSE OUT OF IT! WHY SHOULD A MILLIONAIRE GIVE HALF OF HIS FORTUNE AWAY TO A PERFECT STRANGER?

AND WHY TO THE RICHEST MAN IN TOWN INSTEAD OF SOME DESERVING PERSON?

WOW! THIS IS THE KIND OF A STORY NEWS-PAPER EDITORS DREAM ABOUT! BE SURE TO GO TO THAT MEETING TONIGHT!

I WOULDN'T MISS IT FOR ANY-THING!

YOU COULDN'T KEEP ME AWAY FOR LOVE OR MONEY!

BUT THAT NIGHT, AS THEY ATTEMPT TO ENTER THE MANSION, THEY ARE RE-BUFFED BY DETECTIVES...

SORRY-- NO REPORT-ERS ALLOWED INSIDE!

ONLY HONEST-TO-GOODNESS MILLIONAIRES ADMITTED!

TELL CALHOUN I COULD USE A COUPLA MILLION BUCKS!

ME, TOO!

I'D BE SATISFIED WITH A TEN-DOLLAR BILL!

FLASH BULBS GLARE AS NEWSPAPER PHOTOGRAPHERS ATTEMPT TO SNAP THE PICTURES OF THE "LUCKY FEW" WHO GET BY THE DETECTIVES-- CLARK AND LOIS TAKE THE OPPORTUNITY TO SLIP AWAY FROM EACH OTHER...

AW, HAVE A HEART, MISTER! MY EDITOR DEMANDS PICTURES!

WHILE A TRUCK DRIVER ARGUES WITH A DETECTIVE, LOIS CLIMBS ON TO THE REAR OF THE DELIVERY TRUCK UNNOTICED....

NOW IF ONLY I'M NOT DISCOVERED, I'LL BE THE ONLY REPORTER IN THERE, GOSH-- A SCOOP-- AN EXCLUSIVE...!

AIN'T IT A SHAME? THEY'RE ALL COVERING THEIR FACES! HOW'S A GUY TO MAKE A LIVING?

MINUTES LATER, AS THE DELIVERY TRUCK DRIVES INTO THE ESTATE, LOIS SLIPS OUT OF THE REAR...

MADE IT!

STEPPING IN THRU AN OPEN WINDOW, LOIS HIDES BEHIND SOME DRAPES...

("- A GRANDSTAND SEAT! WHO COULD ASK FOR ANYTHING MORE? -")

AND AT THAT MOMENT-- A LITHE, COSTUMED FIGURE PLUMMETS DOWN TO THE ROOF OF THE MANSION...

POOR LOIS! WILL SHE FEEL BAD WHEN SHE LEARNS I'VE SCOOPED HER AGAIN!

8

GENTLEMEN, THE TIME HAS COME FOR YOU TO STATE WHICH OF YOU IS THE MOST PROSPEROUS, AND WHY HE WISHES THE ADDITIONAL FORTUNE I CAN GIVE HIM.

ME! LET ME SPEAK FIRST!

I OWN AIRLINES... RAILROADS... PUBLISHING FIRMS... MY COMBINED PROPERTIES ARE WORTH ONE HUNDRED MILLION DOLLARS. MY PERSONAL INCOME WAS AT LEAST FIVE MILLION A YEAR IN THE WORST DEPRESSION YEARS. WHY DO I WANT MORE--? BECAUSE I LOVE WEALTH, POWER... AND I CAN *NEVER* HAVE **TOO MUCH**!!

MY NAME IS DIGBY MASTERS-- BUT I AM CERTAIN THAT NOT ONE OF YOU HAS HEARD OF ME BEFORE. WHY? BECAUSE I AM A HIDDEN POWER IN THE COUNTRY-- I OWN THREE HUNDRED MILLION DOLLARS OF REAL ESTATE. WITH THE THREE MILLION DOLLARS, I'D BUY **MORE REAL** ESTATE. WHY? *I DON'T KNOW!* PURCHASING REAL ESTATE IS AN OBSESSION WITH ME.

GENTLEMEN... AS YOU ALL KNOW, MY FIRM IS WORTH THREE HUNDRED AND FIFTY MILLION DOLLARS. BUT WHAT YOU DON'T KNOW IS THAT I'VE SECRETLY INVESTED MOST OF THE STOCKHOLDERS' FUNDS WITHOUT THEIR KNOWLEDGE. TOMORROW, THE EXAMINERS CHECK THE BOOKS. I'VE REPLACED ALL BUT THREE MILLION DOLLARS. IF I DON'T GET CALHOUN'S MONEY, I'LL GO TO PRISON!

I AM VON SCHMERTZ. I PERSONALLY CONTROL FIVE HUNDRED MILLION DOLLARS IN A SAVINGS ACCOUNT. I WOULD LIKE TO HAVE THAT THREE MILLION DOLLARS BECAUSE I WOULD LIKE TO HAVE IT. THAT'S REASON ENOUGH FOR ME!

YOU KNOW ME AS KETTERING, THE RADIO ORATOR. BUT WHAT YOU DON'T KNOW IS THAT I'M HEAD OF THE *YELLOW SHIRTS,* A SECRET FASCIST ORGANIZATION. A LITTLE MORE MONEY-- A LITTLE MORE TIME-- A LITTLE MORE STUPIDITY ON THE PART OF THE PUBLIC, AND YOU'LL ALL BE GIVING ME EVERYTHING YOU OWN-- FOR I'LL BE DICTATOR OF AMERICA!!

I AM AN IMPOSTOR. I HAVEN'T A DIME IN THE BANK-- NOT EVEN A CENT IN MY POCKET. I TRICKED MY WAY IN HERE PAST THOSE STUPID DETECTIVES. WHAT WOULD I DO WITH THE THREE MILLION *IF* I HAD IT?-- I'D EXTERMINATE THE WHOLE FILTHY LOT OF YOU!!!

YAH-HH... THAT'S ME... SCARLETTI. SURE I MADE MILLIONS DURING PROHIBITION, BUT I GOT BIG IDEAS, SEE... ALL I NEED IS A LITTLE MORE COIN AND I'LL HAVE ENOUGH DOUGH TO SWING A SWEET LITTLE RACKET I GOT IN MIND. IF ANY OF YOU GENTS ARE INTERESTED IN BACKING ME, SEE ME AFTER TH' PERFORMANCE!

GENTLEMEN... MY INSPIRATIONAL BOOKS HAVE BROUGHT ME UNLIMITED WEALTH... BUT I HAVEN'T SPENT A CENT ON MYSELF... I STILL LIVE IN POVERTY... WHY..? BECAUSE SOME DAY I AM GOING TO FOUND A UTOPIA... AS SOON AS I COLLECT... ENOUGH... SHEKLES...!!!

⑨

AND NOW, GENTLEMEN, WHILE YOU WAIT FOR MY DECISION, LET ME INTRODUCE AN ACQUAINTANCE OF MINE TO YOU-- LUTHOR!

WHO'S HE?

HOW'D HE GET IN?

GOOD EVENING, GENTLEMEN. I TRUST ALL OF YOU HAVE MENTALLY DECIDED WHO WILL RECEIVE THE THREE MILLION... LET'S HEAR WHO THINKS HE'S ENTITLED TO IT.

ME! **ME!** **ME!** **ME!**

ME! **ME!!!** **ME!!**

WELL, YOU BLIND, IGNORANT FOOLS-- YOU WILL BE INTERESTED TO LEARN THAT THIS LITTLE PARTY WAS ARRANGED BY ME! I SHOULD BE ABLE TO SECURE A TERRIFIC RANSOM FOR THE WEALTHIEST MEN IN METROPOLIS--AND THE $100,000 EACH OF YOU BROUGHT SHOULD AMOUNT TO NO INSIGNIFICANT AMOUNT!

("-LUTHOR! I MIGHT HAVE GUESSED HE WAS BEHIND THIS FANTASTIC ENTERPRISE!-")

BUT BEFORE THE OTHERS HAVE A CHANCE TO MAKE AN OUTCRY, LUTHOR GIVES VENT TO A GIGANTIC ELECTRICAL DISPLAY THAT SHOCKS EVERYONE BUT HIMSELF INTO UNCONSCIOUSNESS....

HAHAHA-HAAA! THEY ALL THOUGHT THEY WERE SMART-- BUT THEY'RE FOOLS!

AS SUPERMAN CRASHES DOWN THRU THE CEILING...

RELEASE THEM!

I'VE BEEN EXPECTING YOU!

BACK-- OR I SEND ENOUGH CURRENT THRU LOIS TO ELECTROCUTE HER!

IF YOU HARM THAT GIRL.... OR THE OTHERS....

KEEP CALM, I'VE A PROPOSITION, IF YOU'LL LISTEN, CERTAINLY I WON'T HARM LOIS OR THE OTHERS...IF...YOU DO ME A SLIGHT FAVOR.

AND THAT FAVOR?

HIDDEN IN THE LOST MOUNTAIN OF KROWAK, IN SKULL VALLEY, IS THE POWERSTONE, AN ANCIENT GEM WHICH I COVET--FOR SENTIMENTAL REASONS. I'D GO MYSELF, BUT THE TRIP IS TOO, ER, DANGEROUS, BRING THE POWERSTONE TO ME AND I WILL RELEASE MY CAPTIVES UNHARMED.

IT'S A DEAL!

ACROSS STATES STREAKS THE MAN OF TOMORROW IN A MATTER OF MOMENTS....

SKULL VALLEY.... HM-MM.... MEN HAVE BEEN VANISHING INTO IT FOR YEARS...NONE EVER RETURNED ALIVE...! PERHAPS I'LL LEARN WHY!

10

MINUTES LATER... FLASHING DOWN, *SUPERMAN* SMASHES DIRECTLY INTO THE SIDE OF *KROWAK MOUNTAIN* ....

GANGWAY!!

MOLTEN METAL--THAT'S ODD-- THIS ISN'T A VOLCANO--CAN THIS HAVE DELIBERATELY BEEN PLACED HERE TO GUARD AGAINST INTRUDERS?

SUPERMAN SUDDENLY FINDS HIMSELF IN A CHAMBER FILLED WITH HYPNOTICALLY SWAYING SNAKES ....

THE SNAKES-- SWAYING-- SWAYING...

BREAKING FREE OF THE HYPNOTIC SUGGESTION, *SUPERMAN* SMASHES THE REPTILES ASIDE...

NO TIME FOR JITTER-BUGGING!

RACING THRU AN ADJOINING CHAMBER, *SUPERMAN* FINDS EERIE FLAMES LICKING AT HIS CONSCIOUSNESS, SAPPING HIS INTELLIGENCE ....

ON--I'VE GOT TO CONTINUE ON...!

HE EMERGES IN A GREAT ROOM TO MEET AN UNEXPECTED SIGHT. SLAVES LABORING AT A MILL...HIGH PRIESTS, SURVIVORS OF AN ANCIENT CIVILIZATION, DRIVING THEM SAVAGELY ON WITH CRUEL WHIPS... AND ABOVE THE ASSEMBLAGE REARS A GIANT MONSTER-STATUE ....

THESE SLAVES... THE MEN WHO VANISHED WITHIN *SKULL VALLEY*...! THERE--ON THE IDOL'S FORE-HEAD--THE *POWERSTONE!*

HOWLING, ANGERED HIGH PRIESTS SEEK TO HALT THE *MAN OF TOMORROW'S* RUSH, BUT ARE BOWLED ASIDE...

DON'T CROWD ME!

LEAPING TO THE MIGHTY IDOL'S SHOULDER, *SUPERMAN* RIPS THE *POWERSTONE* FROM ITS SETTING...AS HE DOES SO, THE IDOL SWAYS FORWARD...

A DEATH TRAP!

11

UP AVALANCHE FRAGMENTS OF THE BROKEN IDOL AS SUPERMAN ROCKETS INTO VIEW...

SPRING CLEAN-ING!

STRAINING, SUPERMAN SPLITS THE MOUNTAIN IN TWAIN--THEN...

GIVE ME ROOM!!

--PLACING THE ENSLAVED MEN ON A HUGE SLAB OF ROCK, HE RACES OFF WITH THEM...

DON'T BE FRIGHTENED! I'M FREEING YOU!

...DEPOSITING THEM ON THE OUTSKIRTS OF CIVILIZATION!

THANK YOU!

SO LONG, MEN!

YOU'VE SAVED US FROM A LIVING DEATH!

LATER...

THE POWERSTONE-- YOU'VE GOT IT! GIVE IT TO ME!

HERE YOU ARE. NOW RELEASE THOSE PEOPLE.

HAHAHA-HAAA! POOR, STUPID FOOL! DO YOU REALIZE WHAT YOU'VE DONE? YOU'VE GIVEN ME THE POWERSTONE--A STONE FROM ANOTHER PLANET WITH SCIENTIFIC PROPERTIES THAT WILL GIVE ME POWERS AS GREAT AS, EVEN GREATER THAN, YOURS! RELEASE THEM? NATURALLY NOT. NOW THAT I HAVE THE POWERSTONE, I'VE THE POWER TO DEFY YOU SUCCESSFULLY!

12

FUNNY, EH?

YES... NOW GO... BEFORE I BLAST YOU OUT OF EXISTENCE. I'D DO IT ANYWAY, BUT IT WILL BE MUCH MORE INTERESTING TO OBSERVE YOUR HELPLESSNESS WHILE I SECURE MASTERY OF THE WORLD!

SO YOU'RE MASTER OF THE SITUATION, EH? WELL, SUPPOSE I LET YOU IN ON A SECRET. THAT'S NOT THE *POWERSTONE* YOU'RE HOLDING, BUT AN IMITATION I FASHIONED MYSELF BEFORE COMING HERE, THE REAL *POWERSTONE* I'VE HIDDEN WHERE YOU'LL NEVER FIND IT!

BLAST YOU-- I'LL TEAR YOU TO SHREDS!!

TO THE AMAZEMENT OF THOSE OUTSIDE THE HOME, THE MANSION LITERALLY APPEARS TO FLY APART....

MY GOSH!

WHAT'S GOIN' ON IN THERE?

A HURRICANE??

A BATTLE OF COLOSSI....

WHAT--?? MY STRENGTH... DEPARTING!

THIS IS SOMETHING LIKE AN IRRESISTIBLE FORCE MEETING AN IMMOVABLE OBJECT!

THE FINAL TOUCH!--AND I DO MEAN FINAL!

OO-OUCH!

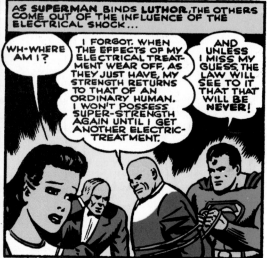

AS *SUPERMAN* BINDS *LUTHOR*, THE OTHERS COME OUT OF THE INFLUENCE OF THE ELECTRICAL SHOCK...

WH-WHERE AM I?

I FORGOT. WHEN THE EFFECTS OF MY ELECTRICAL TREATMENT WEAR OFF, AS THEY JUST HAVE, MY STRENGTH RETURNS TO THAT OF AN ORDINARY HUMAN. I WON'T POSSESS SUPER-STRENGTH AGAIN UNTIL I GET ANOTHER ELECTRIC-TREATMENT.

AND UNLESS I MISS MY GUESS, THE LAW WILL SEE TO IT THAT THAT WILL BE NEVER!

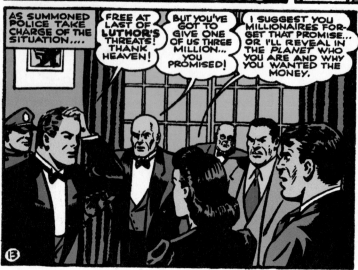

AS SUMMONED POLICE TAKE CHARGE OF THE SITUATION....

FREE AT LAST OF *LUTHOR'S* THREATS! THANK HEAVEN!

BUT YOU'VE GOT TO GIVE ONE OF US THREE MILLION... YOU PROMISED!

I SUGGEST YOU MILLIONAIRES FORGET THAT PROMISE... OR I'LL REVEAL IN THE *PLANET* WHO YOU ARE AND WHY YOU WANTED THE MONEY.

SO LONG, *SUPERMAN*, AND THANKS FOR A SWELL NEWS STORY!

DON'T THANK ME YET. I HAVE A HUNCH CLARK KENT WILL GET THE STORY INTO PRINT BEFORE YOU DO!

THE END